STRANGE WORLDS

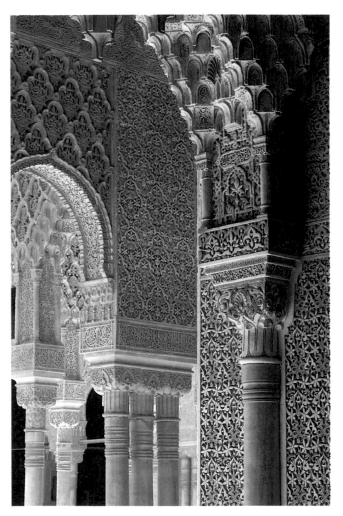

AMAZING PLACES

STRANGE WORLDS
AMAZING PLACES

A GRAND TOUR
OF THE MOST EXCITING
PLACES ON EARTH

Reader's
Digest

Published by The Reader's Digest Association Limited
LONDON · NEW YORK · SYDNEY · CAPE TOWN · MONTREAL

Strange Worlds Amazing Places

Published by
The Reader's Digest Association Limited
Berkeley Square House
Berkeley Square
London W1X 6AB

Strange Worlds Amazing Places
was conceived, edited and designed by
Marshall Editions
170 Piccadilly
London W1V 9DD

Editor	Mary Devine
Editorial Director	Ruth Binney
Assistant editors	Jane Garton
	Lindsay McTeague
	Gwen Rigby
	Janet Sacks
	Anne Yelland
DTP editor	Mary Pickles
Editorial assistant	Simon Beecroft
Writers	Duncan Brewer
	John Clark
	Casey Horton
Art Director	Dave Goodman
Design assistant	Helen James
Picture research	Richard Philpott
	Zilda Tandy
Research	Jazz Wilson
Production	Barry Baker,
	Nikki Ingram
	Kate Waghorn
Index	Hilary Bird

Text film output by Dorchester Typesetting Ltd UK
Originated by CLG, Verona, Italy
Printed in Italy by Arnoldo Mondadori Editore, Verona

The credits and acknowledgments that appear on page 432 are
hereby made a part of this copyright page

ISBN 0 276 42111 6

CONTENTS

INTRODUCTION 8

OUR INCREDIBLE EARTH
12

MONUMENTAL WONDERS
84

WATERY WORLDS
190

RIDDLES AND SYMBOLS
250

TIMELESS LANDSCAPES
310

LEGENDARY REALMS
366

ACKNOWLEDGMENTS 432

THE MYSTERIOUS POWER OF PLACE

S trange Worlds Amazing Places is all about the magic of the planet's most spectacular landscapes, natural features and man-made structures – those that exert a magnetic quality, captivating the traveller, real or armchair-bound, with spells that defy any easy or exact analysis. Some of these special places are the work of nature: mountains, volcanic islands, rivers and jungles. Others are sites of extraordinary human endeavour, where architecture and natural surroundings blend harmoniously in the form of temple complexes, royal palaces, monastic retreats and holy cities.

Landscape and imagination combine in the creation of legend, and some locations, such as the Minoan palace of Knossos on Crete, are directly associated with ancient myths. Others, like the Mayan city of Copán in Central America, tantalise us with half-discovered histories, enigmatic inscriptions and legends, passed down through the centuries, of prehistoric rituals that may still be practised in some form today.

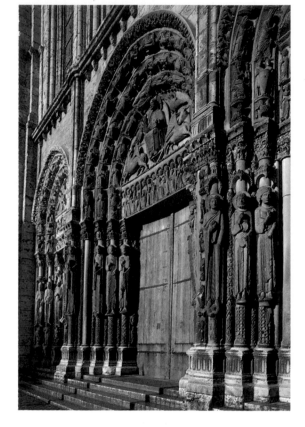

Chartres Cathedral

Many of the landscapes described and illustrated in Strange Worlds Amazing Places have attracted through the centuries knowledge-seekers – from holy men to poets – who were drawn by beauty, or remoteness, or both. Some of the locations within these pages exist entirely in the human imagination. Legendary utopias, they are the haunts of mythical heroes, such as King Arthur's Camelot, or they are elusive realms such as El Dorado and the drowned continent of Atlantis. Yet these places too weave a spell as profound as any that can be pin-pointed on a map.

The wondrous landscapes of the planet tell a story of ceaseless change. In the 4500 million years of its existence

Machu Picchu

the Earth has been tempered by fire, flood and ice. Millions of years of intense volcanic activity were succeeded by millions of years of rain. The Earth's crust cooled, hardened, cracked, melted again and recooled, as the earliest permanent rock-beds were laid down. Some of the planet's most ancient rocks are from this period of turmoil. Samples from Minnesota in the USA, Swaziland in Africa, and sites in Western Australia date back 3500 million years, and a volcanic pebble from Greenland is estimated to be 4000 million years old. Endless rains cloaked the planet with great seas in which, eventually, the first microscopic life forms would be nurtured. The slow, convective currents within the Earth's fluid mantle, powered by the heat of compaction and radioactive decay, still flow today, carrying the vast, rocky rafts known as tectonic plates, reshaping the continents and oceans that feature in these pages.

Many of the secret and wonderful areas of the planet have become accessible to all in the late 20th century. The combined skills of explorers, writers and photographers make you a world traveller within the pages of Strange Worlds Amazing Places. In it you will trek in the Himalayas and the High Andes, dive into the crystal waters of the Caribbean, and pilot the powerful currents of the Amazon River.

You will find the elusive enchantment of extraordinary landscapes and fabled sites present on every page – in an empty desert, an echoing forest, or even in an

Volcano, Hawaii

ancient temple still crowded with worshippers. You will encounter the wildlife of the African plains and the rocks of the Galápagos Islands. Most of all, you will share the experience of the other human inhabitants of the globe, often far removed in time as well as geographical distance. Who were the worshippers at Stonehenge, the builders of the Great Wall of China, the rock painters of Australia's Northern Territory? In discovering others we discover ourselves. A waterfall, a rocky arch, a mountain top fill us with the same awe as that experienced by men and women speaking other languages, worshipping other gods, and sometimes inhabiting other millennia. Perhaps the most captivating aspect of special places and landscapes is that, ultimately, they show us our common humanity.

KEY TO FEATURED PLACES

This map shows the 84 main locations featured in **Strange Worlds Amazing Places**. Sites are indicated by numbers, which correspond to the list of places below (page numbers are shown in italics).

OUR INCREDIBLE EARTH

H umans, with their relatively short lifespan, live with the illusion that the planet's surface is unchanging. The processes that shape the natural landscape are, in the main, slow to the point of invisibility. Riding the tectonic plates that float on the Earth's molten interior, continents slide inexorably apart or together, a few millimetres a year. The ceaseless cycle of the seasons sculpts massive rock formations a few grains at a time. The long, slow heave of subterranean pressures thrusts seabeds upwards to become mountains – which erosion will, in turn, reduce to rocky pinnacles and flat plains. The drip and flow of water, obeying gravity, excavates caves and carves canyons.

But sometimes nature startles us out of our illusion of changelessness. Volcanic eruptions may create islands, like Iceland's Surtsey, before our startled eyes. Or they may obliterate familiar landscapes, as when lava from Vesuvius overwhelmed Pompeii in AD 79. The natural landscape is never at rest. It dwarfs all human endeavours, and never ceases to amaze us with its beauty and power. The icy hauteur of the French Alps and the burning sands of the Namib Desert are a constant reminder that humans are ill-equipped to survive the extremes of natural conditions. And the menacing fracture of the San Andreas Fault makes us uneasily aware that all human works are temporary compared to the Earth's natural substance.

MONT BLANC: PINNACLE OF THE ALPS

The mighty Alps straddle the borders of six nations. At the heart of this formidable massif lies Mont Blanc, western Europe's highest mountain, thrust skywards at a time when the Earth's crust heaved and buckled under its own stupendous forces.

Snow-capped peaks glisten in the sun as eagles, soaring on thermals rising from the valleys below, scour the hillsides for prey. These are the Alps, a range of mountains that on a map of Europe looks like the spiny backbone of some sleeping prehistoric lizard.

The Alpine range extends for about 750 miles (1200km) and at its widest, between Verona in Italy and Garmisch-Partenkirchen in Germany, is more than 125 miles (200km) across. It rises near Nice on the Mediterranean coast of France and gently arcs to encompass parts of Switzerland, Italy, former Yugoslavia and Germany before sweeping into Austria and melting into the Danube plain.

The Alps were created around 40 million years ago when two tectonic plates – sections of the Earth's crust – one bearing Eurasia, the other Africa, collided, grinding against one another with unimaginable force. Under these immense pressures, the Earth's crust rippled and folded over. Rock that had been buried deep within buckled and rose up to form a chain of mountains.

These peaks appear very different today from when they were first created. Most Alpine rocks are sedimentary, and at the edges of the range erosion of this relatively soft sandstone and limestone has weathered them into a more rounded landscape. The backbone of the range, however, is of much harder igneous rock, and it is the erosion of softer rock covering the granite that has given Mont Blanc, the Matterhorn and other great peaks their spectacular, craggy appearance. The last ice age, which ended about 10 000 years ago, made its impression on the Alps too. Glaciers gouged deep valleys in many mountainsides, to create the unique environment left behind when the ice retreated.

Mont Blanc, the 'white mountain', in the western Alps on the border between France and Italy, reaches 15 771ft (4807m), the highest point in the whole Alpine system. The Mont Blanc massif is scarred by many glaciers and bristles with ten peaks more than 13 000ft (4000m) high.

This dramatic landscape is characterised by great extremes in climate. Warm Mediterranean air moves up from the south, while chill Arctic air flows down from the north. Moist air arrives from the Atlantic, and dry air – cold in winter, hot in summer – drifts in from the east. Whether there are blizzards or sunshine in the Alps depends entirely on the direction of the wind. Rainfall above 5000ft (1500m) is rare. At that level, snow falls

Tallest mountain *The Mont Blanc massif (*LEFT*) is the highest in the Alps, with ten peaks over 13 000ft (4000m) and many glaciers. The massif is scarred by slow, creeping glaciers, and aiguilles, sharp needles of rock created by the erosive powers of wind and snow.*

Climbers' paradise *Three mountaineers head along an icy ridge towards the summit of Mont Blanc. Many climbers are buried on the mountain and a crucifix on Mont Blanc (called 'the birthplace of mountaineering') commemorates the dead.*

THE ICE MAN

In September 1991, two German hikers on a remote pass high in the Tirolean Alps stumbled on the body of a man lying half-buried in the snow, with one hand shielding his head and eyes as if to protect himself from a snowstorm. The corpse was first thought to be that of one of the many climbers who have perished in the mountains over the last 200 years; later it was discovered by fascinated scientists to be the mummified remains of a Bronze Age man more than 5000 years old. The dead man was about 5ft 2in (1.57m) tall and weighed 121lb (55kg). He wore leather shoes and a leather tunic and leggings which had been padded with dry grass for insulation against the cold. The stone bead strung on a leather thong around his neck may have been worn as jewellery or was perhaps a badge of rank. He also carried hunting tools. The scientists who examined the body (now kept in a deep freeze at Innsbruck University in Austria) have given him the nickname Otze, after the Otztaler Alps where he met his death.

in prodigious quantities – depths of 30ft (9m) are not uncommon. Even on the valley floors, temperatures often sink to 23°F (–5°C) and they plummet further at higher altitudes. But of more significance is the wind-chill factor, the combination of low temperatures and wind, which can magnify tenfold the effects of cold. Scientists believe that the uncovering in 1991 of the mummified corpse of a prehistoric man that had been buried under snow and ice for more than 5000 years was caused by a combination of wind, sun, snow and glacial movement.

The volatile climate that claimed, and preserved, the ice man has forced intense adaptation in the flora and fauna of the mountains. As altitude increases, deciduous trees give way to species of hardy conifers until eventually even these cannot thrive. Between this point and the fringe of the year-round snow line are the *alpages,* the lush meadows after which the Alps are named. Sheep and cows graze here during the short summer months, but the *alpages* and surrounding slopes soon become the exclusive

terrain of creatures better adapted to harsh winter conditions. The grouse-like ptarmigan, for example, develops white plumage as soon as the first snow falls; its toes are feather-covered for warmth and to grip the ice, and it burrows deep into the insulating snow to sleep.

Weapons and tools discovered in the Alps indicate that people have been living here for some 50 000 years, although little is known of the early inhabitants, except that they were itinerant hunters. Even in the Middle Ages, the thin soil and savage climate meant that people lived here only on a seasonal basis, moving high into the mountains to take advantage of summer pasture, and coming down into the valleys to winter. This way of life continues in some remote areas, but in most places, with the influx over the past 100 years of tourists, walkers, climbers, and now skiers, it has undergone a major change.

The first visitor to publish his impressions of Mont Blanc, in 1744, was Peter Martel, son of a French refugee in Geneva. His description of the mountain established a

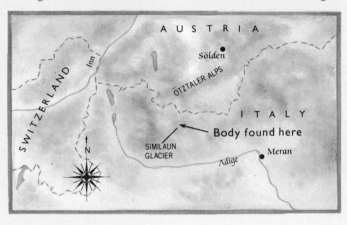

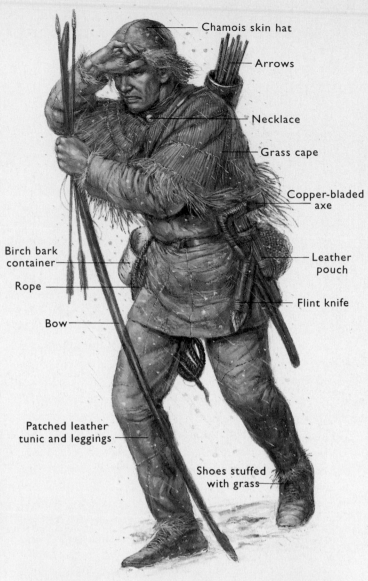

Chamois skin hat

Arrows

Necklace

Grass cape

Copper-bladed axe

Birch bark container

Rope

Leather pouch

Bow

Flint knife

Patched leather tunic and leggings

Shoes stuffed with grass

Prehistoric hunter? *A flint knife, a longbow and arrows in a wooden-framed quiver were among the items discovered* *with the remains of the ice man* (ABOVE). *He also possessed an axe, its copper head bound to the handle with leather thongs.*

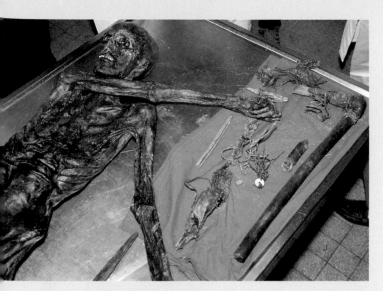

AUSTRIA

Sölden

ÖTZTALER ALPS

SWITZERLAND

Inn

ITALY

Body found here

SIMILAUN GLACIER

Adige

Meran

N

fashion for visiting the 'glaciers' and kindled the desire in some adventurers to climb the mountain. But it was not until August 1786 that the local doctor Michel-Gabriel Paccard and Jacques Balmat, a guide, displaying great fortitude in the face of terrible hardship, became the first to struggle across the icefields and reach the summit.

The intrinsic inhospitality of Mont Blanc meant that even as late as the 1940s it took 18 hours to travel the one treacherous route around it. In 1959, it was decided to bore a tunnel under the mountain to join France and Italy; six years later the 7 mile (11km) link, of immense economic and social importance, was completed and one barrier formed by the formidable mountain was overcome.

Surprise attack *In 218 BC, the Carthaginian soldier and statesman Hannibal led an army of 35 000 men and 37 elephants over the Alps to* *rout the Romans on their own territory. The trek took 15 days and cost the lives of thousands of men, although all the elephants survived.*

FRASASSI'S CAVERNOUS WONDERLAND

A network of twisting passages and glistening palatial chambers with awesome limestone formations has created an enchanted underground realm.

In 1971, a team of cave scientists exploring the area around the Frasassi Gorge in Ancona, Italy, made one of the most exciting cave discoveries this century. They came upon an extraordinary labyrinth of underground caverns and walkways that uncoiled for 8 miles (13km) beneath the Apennine Mountains.

With only dim torchlight to guide them along the passages of the intricate cave system, the team waded knee-deep through still, clear pools and banks of mud, gazing in awe at stalagmites rising like a forest of crystal columns around them. As they ventured deeper into the chilly, dank atmosphere of what proved to be a vast network of caves, a fantastic array of giant marble-like pillars and delicate curtains of frosted rock, the work of more than a million years of erosion, began to emerge.

Meandering for almost 2 miles (3.2km) between steep rock walls, the Frasassi Gorge was carved by the rapid currents of the River Sentino, a tributary of the Esino, which flows from the Apennines north-east to the Adriatic. The steep limestone walls of the gorge are riddled with cave openings, one of which – *Il Sanctuaria della Grotta*, the Sanctuary Cave – houses an 11th-century chapel dedicated to Santa Maria del Frasassi and an octagonal church built at the request of Pope Leo XII in 1828. With the discovery of the astonishing subterranean wonderland now known as the Frasassi Caves, this hitherto sleepy corner of Ancona became internationally renowned.

The hills that embrace the gorge are typical of karst landscape (karst is the term geologists use to describe

Wealth of wonder *The deeply fluted stalagmites and stalactites lend an eerie atmosphere to the Great Cave of the Wind* (RIGHT), *the largest cave in the Frasassi complex.*

Majestic marvels *Like a tireless conjuror, the dripping mineral travertine creates a fantastic array of decorative sculptures and large lacy 'flowers' of stone* (BELOW).

FRASASSI'S CAVERNOUS WONDERLAND

Water fantasy *Deep within the Great Cave of the Wind a shining sheet of stone replicates a torrential wall of water in the amazing natural feature known as the Niagara Falls* (LEFT). *Less spectacular examples of this formation are found in many other limestone caves around the world, including the vast system of passages and caverns beneath Cheddar Gorge in the west of England.*

limestone terrain modelled by the dissolving action of acidic rainwater). Interlinked caves, sinkholes, disappearing rivers and meandering underground streams are all typical of such landscapes.

The Frasassi complex consists of several cave systems, the largest of which is *La Grotta Grande del Vento*, the Great Cave of the Wind. Public access to this fantasy world follows a smooth path for about a mile directly into the limestone hills. A short tunnel bored through the rock provides a spectacular entrance to a cathedral-sized chamber. In the centre is the Ancona Abyss, its velvet darkness plunging to as yet unfathomed depths.

Close to this abyss stands *Il Gigante*, the Giant, an enormous limestone column with a deeply ribbed surface. Facing the Giant is *La Cascata del Niagara*, the Niagara Falls, a cascading sheet of limestone. Its appearance brings to mind the thunderous roar and ceaseless flow of the mighty falls after which it is named. Deeper still in this complex maze of caves lies *La Sala delle Candeline*, the spectacular Room of the Candles. Here, the floor is strewn with gleaming white stalagmites that emerge from the surface of a shallow pool like glowing candles, encircled at their bases by white 'cups', their beauty enhanced by imaginative lighting.

The caves are best known for their geological significance and ethereal beauty, but their specialised habitat also supports a variety of fauna. Environmental advantages, such as constant temperatures and high humidity, are counterbalanced by the disadvantages of darkness and scarcity of food, but flatworms and millipedes flourish in such conditions, as do blind cave salamanders and crayfish. Bats are the most prolific inhabitants, roosting by day in *La Grotta del Nottole*, the Cave of the Bats, and emerging into the night air to feed.

SCULPTED CAVES

Limestone caves and their formations, such as those of the Frasassi and the spectacular Guilin Caves in China, are created by the effects of water and time.

As rain falls, it absorbs a tiny amount of carbon dioxide from the air, turning it into dilute carbonic acid which dissolves calcium carbonate, the principal constituent of limestone. As rainwater seeps down through cracks in the rock, it wears away the limestone, slowly forming sinkholes and shafts. As water flows into horizontal rock fractures, it creates underground streams and rivers that carve out chambers in the rock. When the water table drops, these caves are left behind.

Fabulous dripstone formations are created by deposits of calcium carbonate, contained in the water, dripping from the cave's ceiling and gradually forming stalactites. Deposits also accumulate where drops splash on the cave's floor and grow into stalagmites.

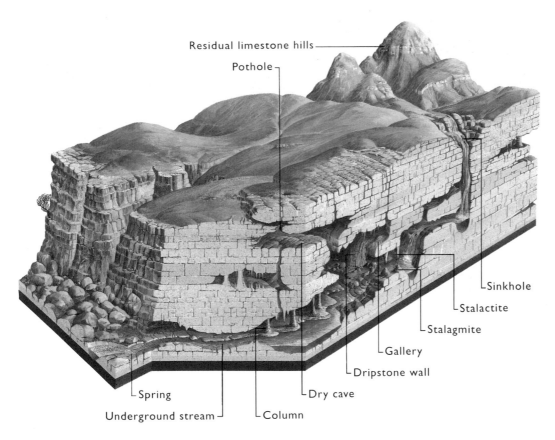

Residual limestone hills
Pothole
Sinkhole
Stalactite
Stalagmite
Gallery
Dripstone wall
Dry cave
Column
Underground stream
Spring

Candlelight cave *In the spectacular Room of the Candles (BELOW), most of the stalagmites make candle-like shapes on the floor; but some have joined with stalactites, linking ceiling and floor in pillars of stone.*

Infinite beauty *With its dazzling array of bright alabaster-like stalagmites, the Room of the Infinite (BELOW) is breathtaking. Dramatic artificial lighting makes the pillars sparkle and shimmer.*

SHIFTING SANDS OF THE WESTERN ERG

Under the scorching heat of the desert sun, giant crescent-shaped dunes inch their way imperceptibly across vast areas of the Sahara, like an ocean of golden sand stretching to the horizon.

The shifting, barren sands of the Great Western Erg were described as 'a land of useless and irreplaceable beauty' by the Algerian-born writer Albert Camus, for whom this bleak, haunting landscape was home. Here, the tireless wind whips the sand into fantastic shapes which it destroys again within a matter of days. The intensity of the desert sun makes this one of the hottest, driest regions on Earth, with temperatures than can soar to well above 38°C (100°F). And if the searing heat were not test enough of human endurance, the burning temperature of the sand causes a quivering of the air that blurs the edges of the landscape and confuses the eye. Moreover, the disorientating effect of a sea of identical, smooth-sided, sharply crested dunes ever-shifting towards the horizon can unnerve even the most lucid observer.

To most people, the word 'desert' conjures up images of

Water break *A group of palm trees provides a shady respite from the heat. Most oases are linked to underground springs or streams.*

Barren beauty *Like a sea of golden waves against an azure sky, the inhospitable terrain of the Great Western Erg covers an area of 30 000 sq miles (78 000 km²). Camel caravans, armies and entire villages are known to have been engulfed by the sands, and attempts to halt their advance have failed.*

SHIFTING SANDS OF THE WESTERN ERG

miles of gently rolling, golden sand dunes (in Arabic the word 'erg' means 'large area of sand'). But in fact less than a quarter of the Sahara, the world's largest desert, is made up of such a landscape: 80 per cent is characterised by monotonous gravel plains, sterile rocky plateaux, arid mountain peaks and mirage-inducing salt flats.

An erg's surface layer of sand is subject to the caprices of the wind. Where strong steady winds blow from a single direction, the sand is heaped up as high as 400ft (120m) to form the familiar, great crescent-shaped dunes. In confused air patterns, where swirls and eddies mean a constantly changing wind direction, the dunes are piled up into a complex assortment of shapes. In some areas they form large parallel ridges separated by broad troughs; elsewhere, converging air currents stack and sculpt the sand into huge mounds and towering pyramids.

This eeriest of regions is rich in local legend and folklore. Nomads tell of fearful cries piercing the night, and of scuttling figures seen trailing camel caravans in the darkness. But more frightening is the reality of the violent sandstorms that are experienced here, when winds rush across the erg with frantic fury, sweeping up huge clouds of sand in their wake. The 19th-century British traveller Sir Samuel White Baker described the onset of such a storm: 'I saw approaching from the south-west apparently, a solid range of immense brown mountains, high in the air. So rapid was the approach of this extraordinary phenomenon, that in a few minutes we were in actual pitchy darkness.... We tried to distinguish our hands placed close before our eyes, not even an outline could be seen.'

Witnesses have described walls of sand 300 miles (480km) wide travelling at speeds of 30mph (48km/h) and there are tales of entire caravans disappearing without trace during sandstorms. While the heaviest, densest sand does not rise much above ground level, finer grains and dust can be swept as high as 1 mile (1.6km), occasionally blocking out the sun in places far removed from the heart of the storm. Saharan dust can also be carried by the wind over great distances. After a particularly severe storm in Algeria in 1947, some of the snowy peaks of the Swiss Alps were tinged pink by red Saharan dust.

The sands of the Great Western Erg were not borne by the wind from some far-off place, as was once thought, nor are they the residue of an ancient, long-dried-up

DESERT CONVOY

In spite of increasing competition from motorised vehicles, camel trains gliding across the Sahara are still a familiar sight. The Arabian camel, known as 'the ship of the desert', has adapted well to prevailing conditions. Its broad, two-toed, thick-soled feet prevent it from sinking into the sand, and the fat stored in its hump can readily be converted to a source of water in times of drought. Bushy eyelashes and thick eyelids protect its eyes from sand and dust, and muscles in its face allow it to open and close its nostrils at will. Furthermore, the camel's shaggy coat protects it from the harmful effects of flying sand, and an insulating layer of air within the coat prevents the animal overheating.

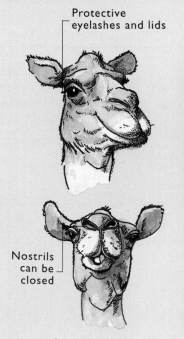

Protective eyelashes and lids

Nostrils can be closed

Saharan sea. Before the last great Ice Age loosened its grip on the northern continents some 10 000 years ago, the Sahara was a far cooler place, criss-crossed by an extensive river system. As the blanket of ice across Europe began to melt, the moist Atlantic air currents shifted away from Africa towards Europe. The rivers of the Sahara – now dominated by hot, dry winds – evaporated. With no moisture to bind the soil together, it broke down, in the process losing its fertility, until gradually the rich earth became a sterile sea of shifting sand. Today, only the nomadic Tuareg continue to roam the vast plains of the Sahara Desert, but they too may soon be compelled, both by the forces of nature and changes in the law, to abandon their once-proud, traditional way of life for ever.

Sons of the desert

Thousands of Tuareg nomads lost their animals and livelihoods after the drought of 1972. They were forced to trek southwards to towns and villages, and their migration generated conflict in the new regions. Having lost everything and become settled in towns, the Tuareg are unlikely ever to be able to return to their former nomadic existence.

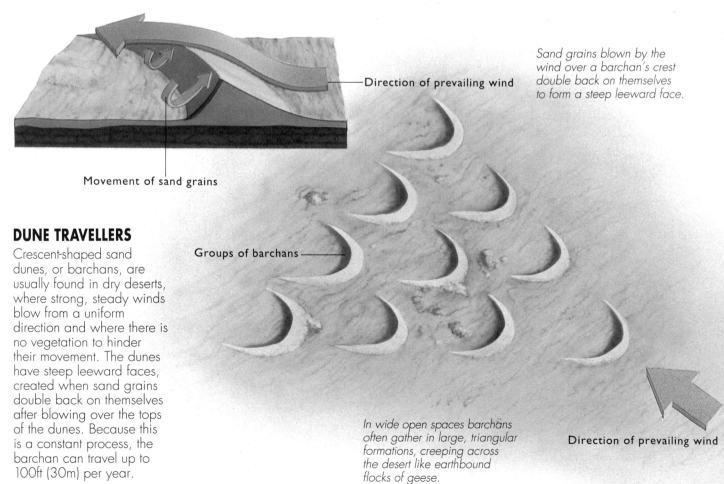

Direction of prevailing wind

Sand grains blown by the wind over a barchan's crest double back on themselves to form a steep leeward face.

Movement of sand grains

Groups of barchans

DUNE TRAVELLERS

Crescent-shaped sand dunes, or barchans, are usually found in dry deserts, where strong, steady winds blow from a uniform direction and where there is no vegetation to hinder their movement. The dunes have steep leeward faces, created when sand grains double back on themselves after blowing over the tops of the dunes. Because this is a constant process, the barchan can travel up to 100ft (30m) per year.

In wide open spaces barchans often gather in large, triangular formations, creeping across the desert like earthbound flocks of geese.

Direction of prevailing wind

NAMIBIA'S FOGBOUND DESERT

An inhospitable expanse of barren emptiness stretches like a pale ribbon along Africa's south-western coastline: the Namib. This is no ordinary desert, however, where relentless sun beats down on burning sands, for every ten days or so fog rolls in from the sea and swathes the area in impenetrable mist.

C hill sea winds gust across the eerie wastes of the great Namib Desert. On confronting this barren expanse of ghostly, mist-shrouded sand dunes in the 1850s, the Swedish explorer Charles Andersson wrote: 'A place fitter to represent the infernal regions could scarcely in searching the world around be found. A shudder, amounting almost to fear, came over me when its frightful desolation first broke upon my view. Death would be preferable to banishment in such a country.'

This curious, fogbound wilderness is one of the oldest and driest deserts on Earth. Stretching for some 1300 miles (2100km) along the Atlantic coast of Namibia from the Angolan border in the north to the Orange River in the south, it ranges in width from 100 miles (160km) at some points to less than 6 miles (10km) at others.

The Kuiseb River, which flows into the Atlantic at Walvis Bay, divides the Namib Desert in two. To the south lies an immense sea of sand, where rippling dunes and troughs, known graphically as streets, alternate in regular parallel lines. The ancient gravel terraces beneath the dunes conceal a spectacular trove of buried treasure – the largest single deposit of gem diamonds in the world.

Before the dunes were formed a million years ago, the rushing waters of the Orange River carried a rich mixture of jewels and muddy gravel from the area around Kimberley in South Africa to the sea. As the gravel settled on the seabed, the glistening gems were swept north by coastal currents and deposited along the Namib shore, where they were eventually swallowed by mud and silt from the Orange River valley.

North of the Kuiseb River the landscape is characterised by rocky gravel plains. These in turn are bounded to the west by treacherous coastal waters that have earned this seaward stretch of desert the macabre name Skeleton Coast, the place 'where ships and men come ashore to die'.

Although less than 1in (25mm) of rain falls along this desert coastline each year, the region's unique source of

Dune dwellers *Several creatures have adapted to conditions in the Namib. The darkling beetle* (TOP) *quenches its thirst on water droplets condensed from fog on grains of sand or small twigs. The sidewinding sand viper* (LEFT) *leaves a distinctive curved signature in the sand as it slithers in search of its lizard prey.*

Swirling sands The tireless westerly winds erode the Namib's reddish bedrock into crumbling sand, piling it in soft, towering dunes which the winds then etch with striking parallel ridges.

A gemsbok journeys towards the gravel plains and rugged mountains of the north. There, occasional thunderstorms offer respite from the searing heat and replenish the underground streams and small water courses. The result is a temporary abundance of plant life.

NAMIBIA'S FOGBOUND DESERT

Breeding grounds *Off the coast, the cool, northerly Benguela Current sustains a rich marine fauna. The shores of Cape Cross* (ABOVE) *are home to the only colony of breeding fur seals on the African continent.*

Nightmare waters *Rusting hulls of ancient vessels bear silent witness to the raging storms, howling gales and treacherous currents that for centuries have claimed the lives of countless mariners along* *the aptly named Skeleton Coast* (RIGHT). *The sands shift continually to bury and then reveal fragments of human bone and the wrecked remains of long-lost ships washed up along the shoreline.*

TATTERED DESERT SURVIVOR

The extraordinary welwitschia, a desert plant resembling a giant radish, grows on the gravel plains north of the Kuiseb River. Unique to the Namib, this bizarre species can survive for up to 2000 years. The plant has just two leathery strap-like leaves that curl and trail along the ground, but the leaves of individual specimens are frequently shredded to ribbons by the relentless desert winds.

  As the rolling fog condenses on the plant's surface, it takes in moisture through the pores in its leaves. It can also absorb any water that seeps into the ground through a network of small rootlets. The welwitschia's central root, which can measure up to 10ft (3m) long, serves as its larder, storing food and water to provide sustenance in times of drought.

moisture – its mists and fogs – supports a variety of small animals. Every ten days or so, as warm moist air from the Atlantic blows over the cold Benguela Current, a dense night fog is generated. This fog rolls inland, shrouding the coast and much of the desert in swirling damp cloud. Beetles, termites, wasps, spiders and lizards depend on the fog for water, and each creature displays remarkable evolutionary ingenuity in extracting the moisture it needs.

As the white mists approach, headstander beetles stagger up the windward side of coastal dunes and adopt the ungainly stance that has given them their name: they balance upside-down with their heads between their legs and their backs turned to the wind. The gusting fog that strikes their backs condenses, and the water that collects trickles down into their parched mouths. Button and darkling beetles, by contrast, dig minute parallel furrows in the sand at right angles to the direction of the wind. The descending mist condenses on the exposed individual grains of sand which the beetles then suck dry. Beetles also feed on organic debris trapped in the dunes.

Members of the lizard family derive their moisture from these small insects, with clown dune crickets and darkling beetles providing succulent feasts. The nocturnal gecko, in addition, has evolved an exceptionally long, flexible tongue with which it licks the dew from the surface of its own eyes to 'top up' its moisture supply. The lizard's greatest foe is the sidewinding sand viper, which skims across the dunes, leaving parallel tracks at a 45° angle to the direction of its own movement. When hunting, the snake buries its body in the sand; only its eyes protrude, scouring the surface for unsuspecting prey. Lizards that venture too close are injected with venom and devoured whole.

Larger animals have difficulty adapting to life in the desert. They require more water than is usually available, and the intense heat of the sun can warm their blood to a temperature so high that it destroys their brains. The gemsbok, however, has adapted to the heat by remarkable means: it simply stops sweating when deprived of water, and its hot blood is cooled through a capillary system in its nose before entering its brain.

RUWENZORI: MOUNTAINS OF THE MOON

A curtain of cloud enshrouds Africa's elusive Mountains of the Moon, making them invisible at ground level for some 300 days a year. When the cloud eventually lifts, an awe-inspiring skyline of snow-covered peaks is revealed, below which everyday plants grow to gigantic proportions.

On his final expedition to Africa in 1888, the Anglo-American journalist and explorer Henry Stanley was camped on the damp, misty south-western shore of Lake Albert when he beheld a rare sight. As the mist cleared to the south-east 'a peculiarly shaped cloud of a most beautiful silver colour, which assumed the proportions and appearance of a vast mountain covered with snow' began to emerge.

Stanley had heard about the Mountains of the Moon, which the Greek mathematician and geographer Ptolemy (AD 90–168) had claimed were the source of the River Nile. Rumour linked them with a remote mountain range known as the Ruwenzori. As Stanley watched the mist clear, he realised that this was no mirage of a mountain 'but the solid substance of a real one, with its summit covered in snow.... It now dawned upon me that this must be Ruwenzori.'

In 1906, an Italian expedition led by the Duke of Abruzzi plotted the first maps of the mountains. The Ruwenzori form a 75 mile (120km) ridge from north-east to south-west along the Zaire–Uganda border. Although the range lies only 30 miles (48km) north of the equator, its peaks are permanently capped in snow, because of its

A glimpse of mountain
The contours of Mount Baker (BELOW) emerge from the cloud that hangs over its heights near Bujuku Lake. Here, the groundsel – ordinarily about 1ft (30cm) high – has reached the size of a tree. Its leaves can grow to 2ft (60cm) long.

Lush valley slopes *The Portal Peaks tower 14 000ft (4270m) above the dense vegetation of the Mobuku Valley, where the coral tree is in bloom.*

Enchanted forest *Tree heathers – giant versions of the scrubby bushes found in gardens – draped with trailing beards of lichens create an eerie and improbable landscape in the Bujuku Valley at an altitude of 10 000–12 000ft (3050–3660m). Botanists believe that the success of these monster species is due to a combination of high rainfall, strong sunlight, acidic soil and lack of competition for space from trees.*

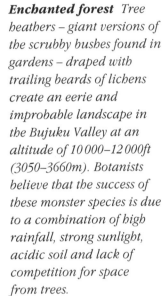

31

RUWENZORI

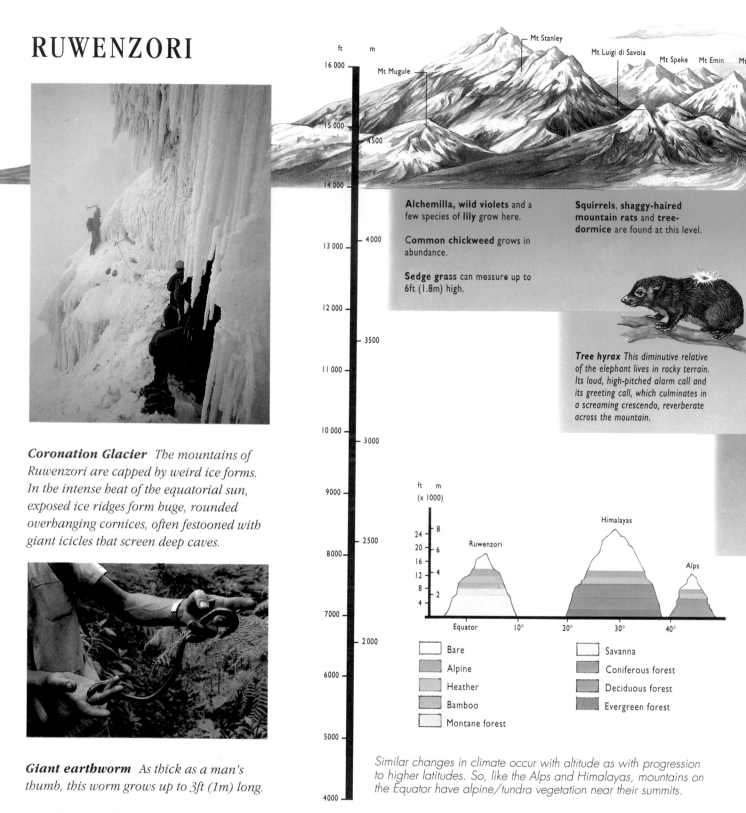

16 000 ft / 4500 m — Mt Mugule · Mt Stanley · Mt Luigi di Savoia · Mt Speke · Mt Emin · Mt Bak

Alchemilla, wild violets and a few species of **lily** grow here.

Common chickweed grows in abundance.

Sedge grass can measure up to 6ft (1.8m) high.

Squirrels, shaggy-haired mountain rats and **tree-dormice** are found at this level.

Tree hyrax This diminutive relative of the elephant lives in rocky terrain. Its loud, high-pitched alarm call and its greeting call, which culminates in a screaming crescendo, reverberate across the mountain.

Coronation Glacier *The mountains of Ruwenzori are capped by weird ice forms. In the intense heat of the equatorial sun, exposed ice ridges form huge, rounded overhanging cornices, often festooned with giant icicles that screen deep caves.*

Giant earthworm *As thick as a man's thumb, this worm grows up to 3ft (1m) long.*

Ruwenzori · Himalayas · Alps

Bare · Savanna · Alpine · Coniferous forest · Heather · Deciduous forest · Bamboo · Evergreen forest · Montane forest

Similar changes in climate occur with altitude as with progression to higher latitudes. So, like the Alps and Himalayas, mountains on the Equator have alpine/tundra vegetation near their summits.

altitude. Nine of its peaks are over 16 000ft (4877m) high, with the highest, Mount Margherita, reaching 16 763ft (5109m). Unlike other mountains in East Africa, such as Mount Kilimanjaro and Mount Kenya, the Ruwenzori are not volcanic. The granite rocks were thrust upwards around 2 million years ago when titanic earth movements caused major subsidence and faulting, resulting in the creation of the neighbouring Rift Valley.

In a local African dialect the word Ruwenzori means 'rainmaker' – an appropriate name since the mountains affect the weather over a vast area. Westerly air currents passing over the steamy rain forests of the Congo basin become laden with water vapour. They are forced upwards by the Ruwenzori range and condense at high altitude to form rain and ice crystals. This creates the almost permanent cloud cover that swathes the peaks.

Rain washes sediment and debris into the valleys and foothills of the Ruwenzori. In these marshy conditions,

VEGETATION ZONES OF RUWENZORI

Mt Gessi

Cagni

Kinyangoma

Mosses and dark lichens are the only types of vegetation that grow at this altitude.

Giant lobelia *The candle-shaped flower spike rises 6½ft (2m) from a rosette of leaves. Smaller maroon-ribbed leaves covered in fine silvery hair cloak the purplish-blue flowers.*

Alpine swifts are twice as large as the Eurasian variety.

Ruwenzori leopards have been hunted almost to extinction in the lower valley: they store the remains of their kill in tree branches.

Verreaux's eagles, also known as black eagles, can grow to 3ft (1m) in height. The male makes spectacular flights of display prior to mating.

Giant forest hogs are Africa's largest wild pigs. Black and hairy, these powerful creatures weigh about 350lb (160kg) and stand 3ft (1m) at the shoulder.

Clawless otters grow to about 4ft (1.2m) and live in swamps and mountain streams. Their fingers and toes are webbed only at the base.

Long-haired mole rats are both eyeless and earless.

Golden moles have iridescent golden or green fur. Blind and stout-bodied, these burrowers are virtually tail-less.

Golden cats grow to twice the size of domestic cats.

Mountain buzzards are the most common birds of prey in this region.

Triple-horned chameleon *Local tribesmen regard this scaly-skinned creature with heavy-lidded, swivelling eyes as a bad omen.*

Scale-tail flying squirrels use the bony projection under the tail to scale trees. Their fore and hindlegs are joined by a 'parachute' of skin.

Rousette fruit bats, also known as dog-faced bats, are cave-dwellers that use both eyesight and echolocation (animal 'sonar') to navigate.

Ruwenzori otter shrews are tiny creatures with webbed feet. Their powerful flat tails have a rudder-like action that helps them to swim.

Everlasting flowers bloom where little else can survive.

St John's wort is a tree noted for its tulip-sized orange-yellow flowers.

Giant groundsels have writhing stems crowned by a head of spiky leaves resembling a witch's broom.

Tree heathers, occasionally with pink flowers, grow abundantly.

Sedge grasses flourish in boggy valleys; some varieties grow in tussocks.

Sphagnum moss covers the ground between grassy tussocks; colours vary from green to yellow and russet-gold.

Mountain bamboo grows to a height of 30–40ft (9–12m) and flowers every 30 years.

Tree orchids with striped orange and crimson flowers grow in the forks of many of the larger trees.

Forest buffalos are smaller and redder than the lowland species.

Ruwenzori turacos are large birds, measuring 2ft (0.6m) long, with magnificent blue, black and crimson plumage and an emerald crest. Their distinctive call is a monkey-like chuckle.

Red stinkwood and **yellow-wood trees** dominate here, both frequently draped with creepers. True to its name, the stinkwood releases a cyanide-like odour when the bark is slit.

Elephant grass grows to a height of 10ft (3m) in the valleys.

Acacia trees yield true gum arabic.

Flame of the forest is named after the bright-red sepals of its flower.

Wild date palms grow on the wooded banks of streams.

Coral tree *Scarlet flowers adorn its leafless branches.*

African elephant *The tall grasses of the foothills are its natural habitat, but it can also be found roaming bamboo groves.*

reeds and grasses grazed by elephant and buffalo grow to over 6½ ft (2m) tall. From around 6560ft (2000m) the grasslands give way to lush forest, home to a variety of animals from serval cats to the three-horned chameleon. Many bird species frequent these altitudes – buzzards, kites, warblers and exquisite tiny sunbirds.

There is no birdsong to be heard above 11 000ft (3350m) and animals are scarce, but the plant life is spectacular. Several species, such as groundsel and lichens, which are low-growing in temperate climates, grow to enormous sizes at this altitude.

The science-fiction atmosphere created by these monstrous plants is in keeping with Ruwenzori's legendary name of 'Mountains of the Moon'. Ptolemy was near to the truth in proclaiming that the source of the Nile lay in these mysterious mountains. Meltwater from glaciers near the summit and abundant rainfall drain into the Semliki River, one of the headwaters of the White Nile.

CATACLYSM AT KRAKATOA

The obliteration of the island of Krakatoa by a volcano, thought by many to be extinct, may have been the result of the loudest explosion ever. Its aftermath, a giant tidal wave, wreaked further devastation and killed tens of thousands of people.

T he eruption of the island of Krakatoa on 27 August 1883 has been called the greatest explosion in history. It destroyed 300 villages and killed 36 000 people: houses were cracked open 100 miles (160km) away; the volcano's roar was heard over distances of 3000 miles (4800km); the shock wave in the air blasted around the globe seven times; and bodies and wreckage floated in the sea for days afterwards.

At the beginning of 1883 Krakatoa (or Krakatau) seemed an ordinary volcanic island lying in the Sunda Strait between Java and Sumatra in the Dutch East Indies (present-day Indonesia). Few islanders worried about the 2700ft (820m) peak that dominated the skyline: there had been no sign of activity since a recorded eruption in 1680 and some assumed that the volcano was extinct. But on 20 May 1883 the mountain's cone burst into life, hurling hot ash high into the sky. This initial explosion soon died down, and further eruptions as the summer advanced were also minor. Still few local people worried: such tremors were common in the islands. By August, however, loud groans were heard coming from deep underground.

At 1pm on 26 August a deafening explosion shook the island. One hour later, an enormous cloud of black ash 17 miles (27km) thick hung in the air. Many of the

islanders took to the sea. An Englishman who escaped the devastation in this way recorded: 'The poor natives, thinking that the end of the world had come, flocked together like sheep, and made the scene more dismal with their cries.'

The climax came the following morning when a violent upheaval ripped the island apart. Two-thirds of Krakatoa simply ceased to exist. More than 4 cu miles (19km³) of rock were pulverised into dust and hurled 35 miles (55km) into the air. Before long an area 180 miles (280km) wide was plunged into total darkness. The noise of the explosion temporarily deafened the citizens of northern Java, 100 miles (160km) away, and the inhabitants of the Indian

Volcanic cycle *After the 1883 eruption, all that remained of the island of Krakatoa were small, jagged islets. Renewed activity in 1952, however, thrust up a new island, appropriately called Anak Krakatau, 'Son of Krakatoa'* (LEFT). *After repeated spells of volcanic turbulence, by the mid 1980s the island stood 622ft (188m) above sea level and measured more than ½ mile (1km) across.*

Image of destruction *The early stages of the eruption were photographed, and engravings were made* (ABOVE) *showing Krakatoa as it once was – remote and covered with lush, tropical vegetation. When the volcano was again quiet, all life on the remains of the island was covered in a thick ash. Five years elapsed before Krakatoa's plants and animals began to re-establish themselves.*

CATACLYSM AT KRAKATOA

Ocean island of Rodriguez, some 3000 miles (4800km) to the west, imagined that a great naval battle was taking place just beyond the horizon.

A giant crater, 4 miles (6km) across and some 900ft (275m) underwater, was all that remained of the island. As the crater filled with seawater it set off a massive tidal wave, 120ft (40m) high, that surged out from the island at the rate of 700mph (1100km/h) – almost the speed of sound. The great wall of water destroyed neighbouring islands, flooded coastlines and was felt as far away as Hawaii and southern California. By 28 August all was quiet, although minor tremors continued until February 1884.

The explosion had dramatic consequences. In the seas around Java and Sumatra, rafts of pumice – ejected by the volcanic cone – hampered shipping for several days, and for months afterwards blocks of this material floated around the Indian Ocean. Volcanic dust remained in the atmosphere for more than a year, creating spectacular sunsets around the globe and haloes around the sun. The dust also made the sun and moon appear green or blue on occasions and, it seems, reduced temperatures below their normal levels.

Volcanic activity is always intense where tectonic plates collide. At least 100 volcanoes – including Krakatoa – are situated along the line where the Indo-Australian plate meets the Eurasian plate in Java and Sumatra. Fresh upheavals in December 1927 produced the beginnings of a new island beneath the surface of the sea. A massive explosion 25 years later thrust this underwater landmass upwards to form a small island, Anak Krakatau. At some time in the future it will face the same fate as its parent.

DEATH AND BIRTH OF AN ISLAND

The 1883 eruption of Krakatoa was just one phase in a continuing cycle of destruction and rebirth in the Sunda Strait. More than 1 million years ago, the volcano built up a cone-shaped mountain composed of alternating layers of volcanic rock, cinders and ash. The total height of this mountain was about 7000ft (2100m), some 1000ft (300m) of which was below sea level. Further activity (in AD 416, according to the Javanese *Book of Kings*) destroyed the top of the mountain, forming a caldera, or bowl-shaped depression. Portions of the caldera projected above sea level as the small islets of Rakata, Rakata-kecil and Sertung.

Over the years, three new cones were thrust into the air; these eventually merged into the single island that erupted in 1883. At the end of 1927, there was renewed activity on the sea floor on the line of the old cone which by January 1928 had created the small island of Anak Krakatau below sea level. Since then continued upheavals have pushed the island above sea level.

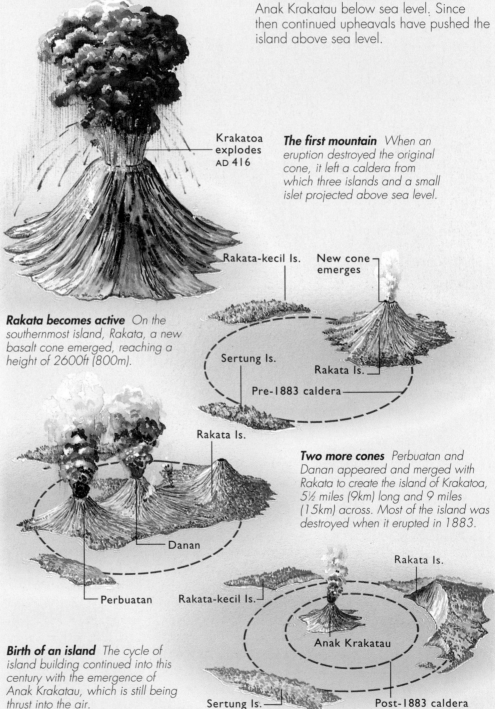

Wall of water *Against the backdrop of the new island, Anak Krakatoa, the shallow waters of the Sunda Strait rise to form a miniature tidal wave, or tsunami. The force of such waves is governed by their depth: those that occur in deep waters, such as filled the crater of Krakatoa, are infinitely more powerful than those in shallower waters.*

Krakatoa explodes AD 416

The first mountain *When an eruption destroyed the original cone, it left a caldera from which three islands and a small islet projected above sea level.*

Rakata becomes active *On the southernmost island, Rakata, a new basalt cone emerged, reaching a height of 2600ft (800m).*

Rakata-kecil Is.

New cone emerges

Sertung Is.

Rakata Is.

Pre-1883 caldera

Rakata Is.

Danan

Perbuatan

Two more cones *Perbuatan and Danan appeared and merged with Rakata to create the island of Krakatoa, 5½ miles (9km) long and 9 miles (15km) across. Most of the island was destroyed when it erupted in 1883.*

Rakata Is.

Rakata-kecil Is.

Anak Krakatau

Birth of an island *The cycle of island building continued into this century with the emergence of Anak Krakatau, which is still being thrust into the air.*

Sertung Is.

Post-1883 caldera

GALÁPAGOS ISLANDS: KEYS TO EVOLUTION

A five-week visit to this lonely group of Pacific islands by Charles Darwin changed human understanding by providing a solution to the most crucial question in biological science: how did species originate?

An isolated group of islands in the Pacific Ocean has become synonymous with the name Charles Darwin and the word 'evolution'. In fact, Darwin spent only five weeks on the islands, but those weeks were the culmination of a voyage around the coasts of South America, including periods ashore, during which he had become convinced of the truth of his theory of evolution. Over a period of 20 years, he returned time and again to the written notes of observations he had made in the islands before he fully appreciated that those weeks had given him the key to how evolution worked: by natural selection. In 1831, when Darwin boarded HMS *Beagle* as official naturalist, the accepted opinion in the Christian world was that God had created the planet and everything on it, more or less as it then existed. With the publication of *On the Origin of Species by Means of Natural Selection* in 1859, Darwin showed that view to be wrong.

The voyage of the *Beagle* gave Darwin an opportunity to study a wide variety of terrain and an incredible diversity of plants, animals and birds. And, unlike other scientists and observers, he had the chance to witness them at first hand, rather than from books and museum specimens. The first three years of the trip convinced him that species did not remain unchanged, but 'transmuted' over time. The first crucial pieces of evidence for this were fossils, which proved that some species had died out. Darwin could not accept the explanation that the Creator 'wiped out' those creatures that had served their purpose and replaced them with higher beings, of which humans were the ultimate example. For one thing, many of the fossils and bones he unearthed in the course of his trips ashore seemed to be of creatures that were very like those he saw around him, but larger.

The *Beagle* reached the Galápagos Islands in September

Hot rocks, cold blood
The cold-blooded marine iguana feeds in icy offshore waters, where its temperature may fall by as much as 10°C (18°F). To regain its body heat, back on land, it must spend long periods lying motionless absorbing the warmth of the sun.

1835. The 19 islands and their associated rocks and islets of volcanic lava are spread over an area of some 23 000 sq miles (59 500km²) of ocean, and are situated more than 600 miles (1000km) from the South American mainland. Darwin was initially puzzled that any wildlife had become established on such unpromising and isolated terrain. He also remarked that most of the creatures on the islands were unique to the Galápagos, although almost all bore some resemblance to those he had observed on the South American mainland, with local variations.

The range of creatures on the islands was also curious. At the time of Darwin's visit there were only two mammals in the Galápagos: mice, which he decided had evolved there, and rats, which probably came on a ship. (In fact seven species of rodent and two of bat are indigenous to the islands.) There were no amphibians, but reptiles existed in profusion.

The range of creatures and their similarity to South American species, Darwin eventually concluded, were due to the way all living things reached the islands. The first organisms to colonise the rocky islands of lava were plants, their seeds and spores carried by wind or water. (Darwin kept seeds in water for months, then tried – successfully – to germinate them.) Once a stable plant environment existed, animal settlers could gain a foothold. All animal life on the Galápagos Islands – except those species introduced by humans – has evolved from accidental 'pioneers'. Winged creatures, like the birds, bats and some of the insects, must have flown in from the South American mainland (or been blown off course by strong winds during their annual migrations), hence their similarity to those Darwin had already observed.

All other creatures evolved from individuals which were carried on logs, rafts of vegetation or flood debris initially washed out to sea through river estuaries, then carried on the currents to the islands. Soft-structured frog and toad spawn could not have survived a long saltwater crossing,

Father of evolution
Darwin returned to England in 1836 and spent 20 years refining his ideas. The first public presentation of his findings was to the Linnean Society of London in 1858.

Descended from apes?
The first edition of 1250 copies of On the Origin of Species *sold out in a day, but Darwin's conclusions were not universally popular and prompted savage cartoons.*

Ship to shore *During the Beagle's four-year voyage around South America, Charles Darwin had ample opportunity to explore. At Bahia (Brazil) he dug up bones of extinct giant species; and while the ship was being repaired in the Santa Cruz River (Argentina) he went upriver, finding the flightless rhea. High in the Andes he uncovered fossil seashells.*

Warbler finch

Medium insectivorous
tree finch

Small insectivorous
tree finch

Full advantage *One of
the few birds known to use
a tool in feeding, the cactus
finch snaps a spine off the
cactus and uses it to probe
for insects inside the flowers.*

Large insectivorous
tree finch

Vegetarian tree finch

Tool-using finch

Mangrove finch

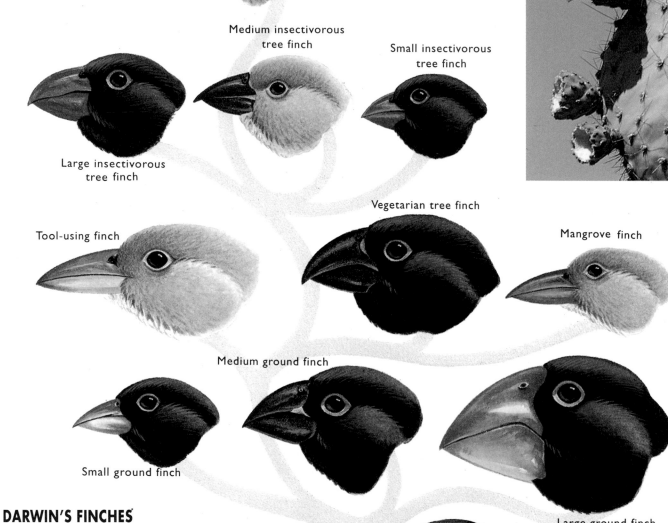

Medium ground finch

Small ground finch

Large ground finch

DARWIN'S FINCHES

Without competition from
other species, the finches of
the Galápagos evolved to
take advantage of every
habitat and foodstuff on
offer. The 13 species are all
4–8in (10–20cm) long and
brown or black in colour.
Birds differ, however, in the
shape of their beaks. Some
have a slender curved beak
for probing flowers, others
a parrot-like beak for
crushing nuts and seeds.
Two species have perfected
the ability to hold cactus
spines to search for grubs.

Cactus ground finch

Large cactus
ground finch

Sharp-beaked
ground finch

and even if they had travelled on a raft of seaweed or other vegetation, the arid islands could not have provided the fresh water they need. Reptile eggs, by contrast, are protected by tough shells that are less likely to be damaged as they drift with the currents.

Probably the most dramatic reptiles were the giant tortoises (after which the islands are named: *galápago* is Spanish for tortoise). In Darwin's day the islands sheltered hundreds of thousands of these creatures. In the absence of carnivorous predators, they can grow to more than 4ft (1.3m) in length, weigh up to 395lb (180kg), and live for well over 100 years. Not only did the tortoises reach the islands – probably as eggs or hatchlings – in sufficient numbers to establish a breeding colony, they also spread throughout the islands. The vice-governor of the Galápagos told Darwin that he could tell from which island a tortoise had come, simply by looking at it. Darwin noted this statement, but did not at that time appreciate its significance. The subtle differences between the tortoises seemed to be governed by local conditions. On those islands where water and vegetation were plentiful, tortoises cut grasses close to the ground, so the fronts of their shells formed a shallow curve over the neck. In other areas, where they had to reach high for food, their necks were long and their shells curved upwards at the front like a saddle.

The iguanas showed a similar diversity. There were two distinct species on the islands, which Darwin felt must have had the same ancestor, but which had developed along

Tame bird *The blue-footed booby was so named for its lack of guile: it was unafraid of the sailors who* *reached the Galápagos. A diving bird, it has evolved a long thin bill which it uses to spear fish and squid.*

Free from human habitation *Only four of the Galápagos islands are today inhabited by humans, some 12 000 in all. The rest, like Bartolomé, provide havens for wildlife. All the islands are volcanic in origin, consisting of peaks of lava thrust up from the ocean bed in the last two million years. The ruggedness of the landscape is accentuated by high rocks and volcanic craters, many of which are active and have erupted during this century.*

different lines, again presumably to take best advantage of available food stocks. Land iguanas eat cactus buds and pips; marine iguanas have evolved long muscular tails that help them to swim out to sea and dive as much as 35ft (11m) to feed off algae growing on underwater rocks.

The reptiles gave Darwin a series of observations which supported the conclusions he finally drew from his studies of the wealth of bird life, in particular the variety of finches. They provided the evolutionary key: natural selection or the survival of the fittest (the phrase, used by Darwin, was in fact proposed by his contemporary, the philosopher Herbert Spencer). Darwin conjectured (correctly) that '…from an original paucity of birds…one species had been taken and modified for different ends'. The finch is the only land bird in the Galápagos and, in the absence of competition and predators, evolved to fill every available environment. Each island had its own population of finches that had developed the characteristics that gave them their best chance of survival. Those characteristics were passed on to the next generation, and any creature that did not adapt was doomed to extinction.

The proliferation of species of finch, tortoise and iguana is repeated in the shellfish, seabirds and lizards: the population on each island is different and the differences are recognisable. This fact, Darwin wrote in his journal, 'strikes me with wonder'. His genius was to construct from this a viable hypothesis that would offer a plausible explanation of the workings of the natural world.

Spines of salt *The crest along an iguana's back is coated with salt, ingested as it feeds. This is removed from the blood by a gland that opens into the nostrils. When the iguana 'sneezes', a salty solution coats its spines.*

Sailors' bounty *The slow-moving giant tortoise once roamed all the continents, but proved easy prey for generations of seamen who valued its ability to survive for long periods without food or water. It was ideal to take on long sea voyages as a source of fresh meat and high-quality oil, to be slaughtered when the occasion arose. Tortoise numbers have also been reduced since the introduction by humans of dogs, cats and rats, which eat eggs and hatchlings. They are now extinct everywhere except in the Galápagos and the Seychelles in the Indian Ocean.*

43

SAN ANDREAS FAULT

*Some of the Western world's major conurbations
sit astride one of Earth's most dangerous fault lines.
Californians living along the San Andreas Fault are
poised for a potentially devastating earthquake.*

A t first sight, the streets of Taft in central California look much like those of any other North American town. The broad avenues are lined with houses and gardens, cars are parked outside and the street lamps are sited at regular intervals. But something is amiss. A closer look reveals that the street lamps are not quite in line, and occasionally a whole street is kinked, as if its ends were being pulled in opposite directions. These strange distortions have occurred because Taft, like many of California's major urban centres and a section of San Francisco's Bay Area Rapid Transit System, is built along the San Andreas Fault, a fracture in the Earth's crust that for 650 miles (1050km) of its length cuts through the United States mainland.

A swathe that stretches from the coastline north of San Francisco to the Gulf of California, and extends down into the Earth for some 10 miles (16km), marks the meeting point of two of the 12 tectonic plates on which the continents and oceans sit. These plates, with an average thickness of some 60 miles (100km), are constantly in motion, drifting about on the fluid layer of the Earth's inner mantle and jostling each other with enormous power as their positions shift and slide. When they collide directly, the impact throws up huge mountain ranges, such as the Alps and the Himalayas. The circumstances that govern the San Andreas Fault, however, are quite different.

Here, the edges of the North American plate (on which the greater part of the continent sits) and Pacific plate (which supports most of the California coastline) meet like badly aligned gears, neither colliding head on nor meshing smoothly. As the plates edge past one another, there is nowhere for the frictional energy that builds up along their margins to be released. Depending on the part of the fault in which this energy is generated, a small tremor or a major earthquake can result.

At so-called 'creeping zones', where the plates move past one another most easily, the energy that accumulates is dissipated in thousands of small tremors that cause little damage and can, in fact, only be detected by the most sensitive seismographic instruments. By contrast, some stretches of the fault seem completely immobile, fixed in 'lock zones', with the plates so tightly linked together that nothing moves in any direction for varying periods of time – sometimes hundreds of years. Under such pressure,

Tortured land *In desert
areas, such as the Carrizo
Plain, 100 miles (160km)
north of Los Angeles, the
line of the San Andreas
Fault is clearly visible.
Earth movements are wildly
unpredictable here, and
streams that have followed
one course for decades are
suddenly rerouted by
successive earthquakes.
Displacements of up to 400ft
(120m) have been recorded
in the paths of streams.*

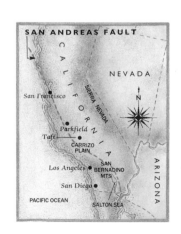

SAN ANDREAS FAULT

Seismic safety *The future of San Francisco may ultimately depend on buildings designed to withstand earthquake shock and land movement. Many modern skyscrapers, including the pyramidal Transamerica Building, are strongly braced to increase stability. And bridges are now built with strips of metal embedded in their concrete; in an earthquake, the metal should buckle rather than snap, thereby reducing the impact.*

SAN ANDREAS FAULT

great geological stresses build up until, eventually, the two plates force their way past each other in a violent release of pent-up energy. Earthquakes that measure at least 7 on the Richter scale, such as the 1906 devastation in San Francisco, are the usual outcome. (The Richter scale, named after the US geologist Charles Richter (1900–85), measures the intensity of earthquakes from 1 to 10: the smallest usually felt by human beings is 2, those assessed from 5 upwards are potentially damaging.)

Between these two zones are areas known as 'intermediate zones', where the activity, while not as devastating as that at lock zones, is still spectacular. The town of Parkfield, located between San Francisco and Los Angeles, sits above an intermediate zone, where earthquakes that may measure up to 6 on the Richter scale can be expected every 20 to 30 years; the last eruption to hit Parkfield took place in 1966. A cycle of earthquakes occurring regularly in a given area is unique to this region.

Geologists estimate that there have been 12 large earthquakes in California since AD 200, but it was the

THE EARTH AT FAULT

The San Andreas Fault is the meeting point of the Pacific and American plates, where the Pacific plate is sliding north and east, and the American plate south and west at the rate of around ½in (13mm) a year. Friction between the plates temporarily delays their movement in opposite directions. Stress energy builds up, which deforms material around the fault below the surface. In an earthquake, this stress energy is violently released and the plates move.

Pressure points Some of the most obvious signs that an area is sitting on top of the fault are cracks and fractures in the streets.

In the region of the San Gabriel mountains to the north of Los Angeles, streets buckle as the pressures that are built up along the fault compress the mountains. As a result, the western face of the mountains shatters and crumbles, depositing around 7 tons of debris every year. This material is gradually creeping closer to the city of Los Angeles itself, a pertinent reminder that, in this part of California at least, 'civilisation exists by geological consent'.

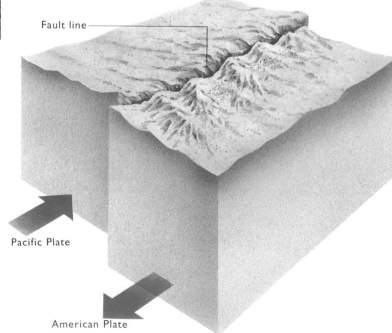

Fault line

Pacific Plate

American Plate

devastation of 1906 that drew the attention of the world to the San Andreas Fault. The earthquake was centred on the city of San Francisco itself and caused damage in an area that stretched for 400 miles (640km) north-south. Along the line of the fault, the ground shifted as much as 20ft (6m) in minutes – fences and trees were toppled and roads and pipelines broken (the resultant loss of water allowed the fire that followed the earthquake to rage unchecked through the city).

As geological knowledge becomes more advanced and techniques more sophisticated, measuring devices constantly monitor movements and water pressures beneath the Earth's surface. Scientists believe that seismic activity shows slight increases for a number of years before a major earthquake, so it may be possible to predict future upheavals, and give hours or even days of notice. At the same time, architects and structural engineers are taking future tremors into account in their plans, designing buildings and bridges that are capable of withstanding a certain amount of movement of the Earth's surface. As a result of this, the majority of the damage to buildings in the 1989 San Francisco earthquake occurred in old-style structures rather than modern skyscrapers.

The 1989 earthquake, which cost 63 lives, largely as a result of the collapse of a section of the double-decker Bay Bridge, was not the 'big one' that is expected to hit California at some time during the next 50 years. Estimates suggest that an earthquake measuring 7 on the Richter scale, and occurring in the Los Angeles region of southern California, could cause billions of dollars worth of damage and kill between 17 000 and 20 000 people, with fumes and fire affecting up to 11.5 million more. And, since the frictional energy that is built up along the fault line is cumulative, every year that passes before the earthquake occurs increases its likely magnitude.

Surface signs *Distortions in the rock formations that line Highway 14 at Palmdale to the north of Los Angeles indicate the powerful physical stresses in the fault-line area. Although most of the displacement along the San Andreas Fault is horizontal, the folded appearance of these layers of sediment is caused by vertical movement.*

Power of destruction *As the storm of dust and broken brick settled after the earthquake of 18 April 1906, fire swept through San Francisco. Recent estimates show that as many as 3000 people lost their lives. The earthquake was the most fierce in the continental United States this century, and measured 8.3 on the Richter scale.*

GRAND CANYON: AN ANCIENT CORRIDOR

Like a corridor through time, the staggeringly magnificent Grand Canyon slices into the surface of the Earth, revealing layer upon layer of ancient rock whose glowing colours shimmer with the play of light.

I t is difficult to comprehend the immensity of the yawning chasm that is the Grand Canyon; it merits all superlatives and exceeds all expectations. This sprawling gash in the surface of the Earth, in the middle of the Arizona Desert, is some 320 miles (515km) long and plunges at its deepest point – Granite Gorge – to a depth of 1 mile (1.6km). At its widest it is 18 miles (29km) across, and beneath Toroweap Overlook on the North Rim it measures just under ½ mile (0.8km).

Layer upon layer of stone make up the canyon's striated walls, whose deepest levels are formed of sombre schist (metamorphic rock that splits easily) and fossil-rich granite. Stark, sheer buttes, looking amazingly like ruined temples, break up the landscape into a complex labyrinth of gullies and crevices. It is small wonder that in the 19th century some scientists believed the canyon could only have been created by a gigantic earthquake.

Around 60 million years ago in this region, the wide expanse of the Kaibab Plateau separated two waterways, the Ancestral Colorado River to the east and a river system called the Hualapai to the west. Over the course of centuries the Hualapai cut back into the plateau in a process known as headward erosion. Moving gradually but steadily, it met the Ancestral Colorado and combined with it to create the awesome modern Colorado River, which – until it was tamed by the Glen Canyon Dam – surged through the plateau at an average of 20mph (32km/h), daily eroding millions of tons of rock and earth along its course.

The surface of the plateau, once the floor of an ancient ocean, was the uppermost of many layers of sandstone, shale and limestone rocks deposited between 600 million

History of the Earth laid bare *The bands of rock that are visible in the upper part of the canyon walls date from the Palaeozoic era, while those at the bottom of the deep granite gorge are ancient Precambrian schists. More recent rocks of the Mesozoic and Cenozoic eras have been completely worn away.*

GRAND CANYON: AN ANCIENT CORRIDOR

creating a large dome. Moving a fraction of a millimetre a year, the plateau rose 4000ft (1216m) in the next five million years. Meanwhile, abrasive particles of rock and sand in the rushing river carved out the gorge inch by inch.

While the river cut downwards, other erosive forces began to work on the rock faces it had exposed, splitting their surface. Extremes of heat and cold caused the cracks to widen; winter storms and spring snowmelts loosened a steady stream of sandy gravel and debris and bulldozed them through the stone channels. Gradually meeting less resistance, the river battered the earth with increasing force, tearing away the base of the valley as the rocks continued to bulge upwards, causing the walls through which it flowed to mount higher and higher.

Although apparently immutable, this awesome canyon is continuously changing and growing. The building of the Glen Canyon Dam upstream from the Grand Canyon National Park in 1964 has drastically reduced the mighty Colorado's power. But still the raging winter storms rip debris from the walls; plant roots find a foothold in crevices, and rocks still split and crash to the canyon floor.

Although the harsh landscape of the canyon appears dead and barren to the untrained eye, it is well endowed with plants and wildlife. The dry heat of the canyon floor supports a variety of desert creatures, including spotted skunks, yellow scorpions and whiptail lizards, and barrel cactus and mesquite flourish. The tassel-eared Kaibab squirrel is unique to the North Rim; the Albert squirrel prefers the warmer South Rim. The cooler sidewalls of the canyon provide homes for the Arizona grey fox and cliff chipmunks. Mountain lions also roam the rocks, but they are becoming increasingly rare. So, too, are the native

Mooney Falls *These sparkling waters, one of three major cataracts on* *Havasu Creek, cascade for 196ft (60m) into the clear turquoise pool below.*

and 250 million years ago in the Palaeozoic era. These rocks were laid down on top of even more ancient schist dating back 2000 million years to the Precambrian era.

As the newborn Colorado rushed along, slicing through everything it encountered, upheavals in the Earth's crust started to push up the rocks under its surging torrents,

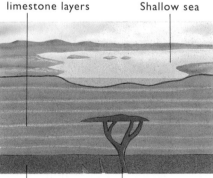

Sandstone, shale and limestone layers   Shallow sea

Vishnu schist   Granite intrusion

Shallow seas deposited layers of sandstone, shale and limestone, known as the Grand Canyon Series, on top of an ancient layer of igneous rock called the Vishnu schist. Later, molten rock forced its way through the schist, penetrating weaknesses in the

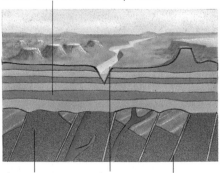

Further layers of sandstone, shale and limestone deposited

Fault blocks   River begins to form canyon   Fault line

layers, and cooled to form granite intrusions.
Upheavals in the Earth's crust created huge fault block mountains, which were eroded flat by weathering. Subsequent deposition resulted in further layers of sandstone, shale and limestone building

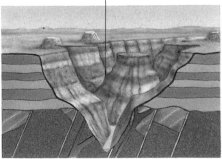

Canyon carved by river

up on top of the Grand Canyon Series and the embryonic Colorado River then began to slice its way into the strata.
After ten million years the Colorado has eroded into the Vishnu schist, forming the canyon as it is known today.

FROM ALGAE TO REPTILES

LATE TRIASSIC

220 million years ago

The dinosaurs of the Jurassic period evolved from early forms of reptile in the Triassic period. Animals such as **Rutiodon** marked the transition towards the larger ruling reptiles that took place 210–65 million years ago.

Kaibab limestone

Toroweap formation
(sandstone and limestone)

Coconino sandstone

Hermit shale

PERMIAN

290–245 million years ago

Despite the burning sun and droughts of this period, large reptile-like amphibians such as **Diadectes** emerged. A bulky land animal 10ft (3m) long, it is thought to have been one of the first amphibian herbivores.

Supai formation
(sandstone and sandy shale)

LATE DEVONIAN

365 million years ago

Between the Cambrian and Permian periods marine life developed dramatically, creating such giants as **Dunkleosteus**. A predatory fish 11½ft (3.5m) long, it had a heavily armoured head and a sinuous body.

Redwall
limestone

Muav
limestone

CAMBRIAN

570–500 million years ago

The advent of the Cambrian period saw the explosion of diverse life forms and the development of hard-shelled arthropods such as trilobites, some species of which measured up to 28in (70cm).

Bright
angel
shale

Tapeats
sandstone

PRE–CAMBRIAN

2000 million years ago

During this period, the shallow seas covering the area that is now the south-western United States would have been teeming with simple, multicellular cyanobacteria, including microscopic blue-green algae.

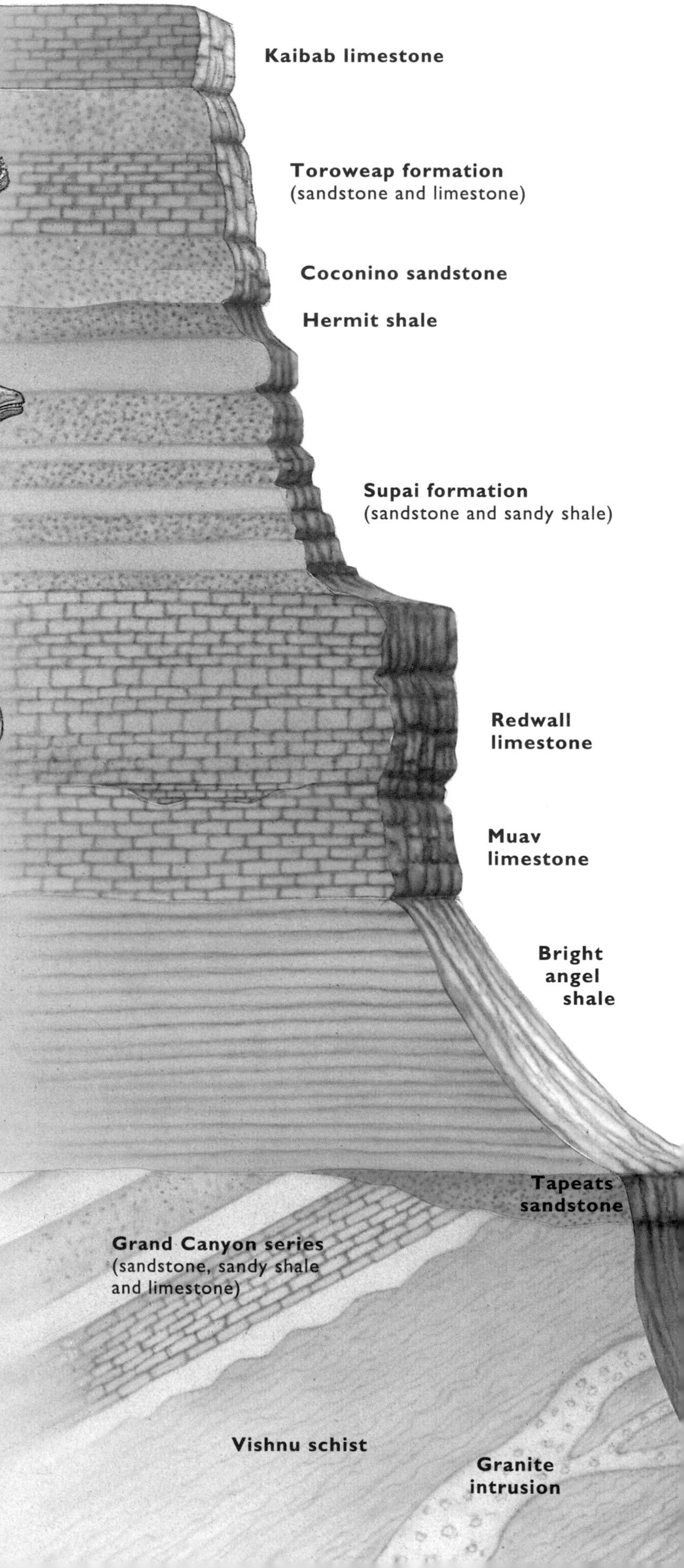

Grand Canyon series
(sandstone, sandy shale
and limestone)

Vishnu schist

Granite
intrusion

Colourscape *Chemical reactions of air and water on the minerals contained in the 20 or more different rock layers in the canyon walls give them their distinctive colours. Light playing upon the rocks brings a range of mysterious shapes out of the shadows, while revealing colours that range from black and olive to russet, orange, dusty pink and pale sandy cream.*

Peaceful sailing *The river flows some 240 miles (390km) through the canyon over a series of 200 rapids. Before the building of the Glen Canyon Dam, these rapids were some of the most dangerous in the world. The American explorer Major John Wesley Powell and nine companions were the first to travel down the Colorado by boat, in 1869. Today's adventurers use huge inflatable rafts.*

human inhabitants. Tourists, flying by helicopter into Havasu Canyon to view the remaining Havasupai Indians in one of the most remote reservations in the United States, are seeing the last of the region's indigenous people. At least 4000 years ago there were hunters in the canyon, and around AD 1000 Pueblo Indians lived there in cliff houses. They were succeeded about 150 years later by the ancestors of the present group.

Possibly the first Europeans to set eyes on this fantastic landscape were Francisco de Coronado, a Spanish caballero, and his band of 300 men, who in 1540 ventured into the territory in search of gold. He sent one of his captains to investigate the roaring river that could be heard to the west, but the patrol wandered along the canyon rim for three days without finding a path down to the river. They would have been astonished had they reached it, since from above they had gauged its width at only 6ft (1.8m).

More than 300 years later, in 1858, Lieutenant Joseph Christmas Ives, leader of an exploratory expedition in north-west Arizona, steamed up the Colorado River from its mouth on the Gulf of California for two hot months. Finally the waters became so treacherous that he decided to leave the ship and lead his soldiers overland. On the South Rim of what he called the 'Big Cañon of the Colorado', Ives rode a mule along a ledge that was 'within three inches of the brink of a sheer gulf 1000ft (300m) deep; while on the other side, nearly touching my knee, was an almost vertical wall rising to an enormous altitude'.

Although the grandeur and majestic dimensions of the Grand Canyon have since inspired every conceivable exclamation of wonder, Ives seemed somewhat unimpressed by what he saw and wrote: 'Ours has been the first, and will doubtless be the last party of whites to visit this profitless locality. It seems intended by Nature that the River Colorado, along the greater part of its lonely and majestic way, shall be forever unvisited and undisturbed.'

How wrong he was. Today the Grand Canyon is regarded as one of the most astounding vistas in North America and, like US President Theodore Roosevelt, many consider it 'the one great sight which every American should see'.

METEOR CRATER: A BLOW FROM HEAVEN

Thousands of years ago a cosmic missile hurtled to Earth, blasting a colossal crater in the arid landscape of the Arizona Desert.

S ome 30 000 to 50 000 years ago, many centuries before human beings arrived in North America, a giant chunk of rock struck the Earth near Canyon Diablo, between the towns of Flagstaff and Winslow in Arizona. It gouged out a huge saucer-shaped depression 4100ft (1250m) across and 570ft (174m) deep.

Viewed from the flat surrounding desert, the 150ft (45m) high rim of the crater appears as no more than a low ridge, and consequently the yawning hole it conceals was not reported by Europeans until 1871. Initially it was thought to be volcanic like similar craters, such as Sunset Crater nearby, which had already been explored. In 1890, iron fragments were discovered in the debris; although their significance was not immediately recognised, some scientists began to question the volcanic explanation and to lean towards the theory that this great scar must have been caused by an extraterrestrial body hitting the Earth.

After examining the site in 1902, Dr Daniel Barringer, a mining engineer from Philadelphia, became so convinced that a huge, iron-rich meteorite lay beneath the crater that he bought the land and in 1906 started to drill. At first he believed that because the crater was roughly round in shape, the body that had created it must lie under the centre. Later he discovered that a rifle bullet fired into soft mud, even from a low angle, would always make a round hole.

This fact, coupled with the knowledge that the rock strata on the south-eastern side of the crater were more than 100ft (30m) above the levels elsewhere, led him to conclude that the meteorite had come in from the north at a low angle and buried itself beneath the south-eastern rim. Drilling was started at this site. At 1000ft (305m) an increasing number of iron and nickel-iron fragments was found; at 1376ft (420m) the drill jammed completely – wedged, it seemed, in hard meteoric material. Money ran out and drilling stopped in 1929, but by now the scientific world was persuaded that the crater had indeed been caused by the impact of a meteorite.

The weight and size of the missile that hammered into the Arizona Desert has been a subject of speculation. In the 1930s, scientists estimated its weight at 14 million tons and its diameter at 400ft (122m). Later calculations scaled down the size of the meteorite to 2 million tons, with a diameter of 260ft (79m); current estimates suggest a weight of some 70 000 tons and a diameter of 80–100ft

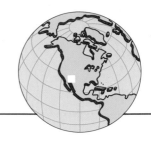

Clear definition *The low
sun and deep shadows in
this photograph, taken
in winter, emphasise the
clearly defined, almost
circular shape of Meteor
Crater. This indicates that
it is relatively young. Older
craters, such as that at
Sudbury in Canada, are
less clearly defined, since
erosion and movement of
the Earth's tectonic plates
have partly obscured, if not
destroyed, their original
outlines.*

*More than 120 impact
craters are known to exist
on Earth, and there are
millions on the moon. To
enable the Apollo moon-
landing astronauts to
recognise the signs and
products of meteorite
impact, all of them were
trained at Meteor Crater.*

Meteorite from Greenland
Agpalilik, the fifth-largest known meteorite, was discovered in 1963 by V. F. Buchwald, a Danish scientist, who estimated its weight at 18 tons. After its arrival in Copenhagen in September 1967, the meteorite was put on public display at the city's Mineralogical Museum.

'National Natural Landmark' *Meteor Crater, the most easily accessible large impact crater in the world, was accorded this protected status in 1967. Now it is used for scientific research, although (with permission) visitors can gain access to the crater floor via a steep trail which can take an hour to descend.*

(25–30m). Even if the size of the cosmic invader were no larger than the smallest estimate to date, its collision with our planet was nevertheless cataclysmic.

To make such an immense crater, it must have plunged through the atmosphere at a speed of around 43 000mph (69 000km/h). The earth-shattering impact generated a blast equivalent to 500 000 tons of high explosive (some 40 times greater than the force of the atomic bomb that obliterated the Japanese city of Hiroshima), throwing 100 million tons of pulverised rock into the atmosphere. It also banked up the material that now forms the crater's rim.

Drops of molten metal from the meteorite showered over an area of 100 sq miles (260km²), some landing as far as 7 miles (11km) from the point of impact. Many of these fragments were only the size of pebbles; the largest weighed as much as 1400lb (630kg). Both the rubble at the crater's rim and the material thrown outwards consisted of a mixture of sandstone and limestone – the remains of fossil-rich deposits from the prehistoric lake that had once flooded the region. A thick, lens-shaped layer of this same crushed mixture, called breccia, now covers the crater floor.

During the 1930s, considerable sums of money were spent on drilling bores through the breccia into the crater floor in attempts to locate deposits of iron that could be profitably mined. Traces of nickel-iron were found at depths up to 853ft (260m); below this level the rock was

undisturbed. Sophisticated modern techniques involving seismic, magnetic and gravitational surveying suggest that what remains of the meteorite does lie below the south rim, but that this is no more than ten per cent of the original mass. Most of the rest vaporised on impact, condensing to form nickel-iron fragments.

In 1960, traces of two rare forms of silica – coesite and stishovite – were discovered in the bowl, both of which can be generated artificially under extreme pressure and temperature. (Although stishovite can form under pressure deep within the Earth, it changes back into quartz before it reaches the surface.) Their natural presence on the site thus provided indisputable evidence of a colossal impact. Any doubts that might have existed about the crater's formation were erased, and Barringer's belief in the meteoritic origin of the crater that now bears his name was vindicated.

LIGHT FANTASTIC

The flash of a 'shooting star' is one of the most startling sights in the sky. The origin of such light does not, however, lie in a star but in a meteor, a fragment of stone or metal from outer space that has entered the Earth's atmosphere. As it hurtles down at immense speed, the air in front of the meteor, compressed by shock waves, becomes incandescent and heats its outer layers until they glow and finally melt. Burning gas and molten material are thrown out by the meteor during this process, causing the fireball, seen as a blazing streak across the sky.

Thousands of 'shooting stars' appear daily, but they are often so small they are not noticed or are burned up before reaching the Earth. But some, either because they were vast to begin with or because they are metallic, are not completely consumed by the heat of their flight, and the central core they retain – a meteorite – strikes the Earth with tremendous force. The massive fragment of nickel and iron that ploughed into the ground at Meteor Crater must have produced a stupendous fireball.

COLLISION COURSE

Impact craters form when meteorites collide with the Earth's surface at average speeds of around 9 miles (15km) per second (32 400mph/52 000km/h). A drop of water falling into a pool creates an identical phenomenon in miniature. Immediately after the drop has hit the surface, the pond water wells upward near the point of impact, and both ripples and water droplets form in the surrounding area. But unlike the pool, which quickly regains its smooth surface, the rocks 'melted' by the meteor's impact 'freeze' solid, and the new structure they adopt remains intact.

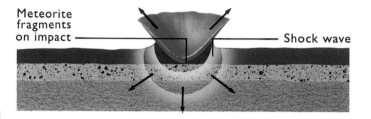

A meteorite less than 650ft (200m) across collides with the Earth creating shock waves which compress and melt the rock.

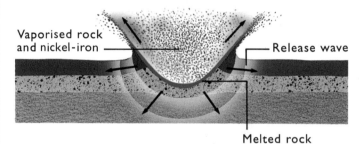

As the shock waves travel downwards and outwards, some of the rock directly below the point of impact rebounds upwards.

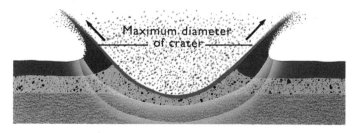

The force of the shock waves produces a wider cavity which now reaches its maximum depth. The rim is lined with broken rock.

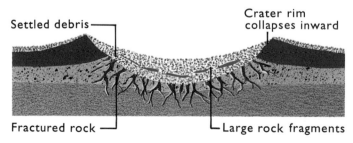

The cavity rim collapses, partly filling the crater with angular rock fragments embedded in finer rock and creating a breccia lens.

57

RAINBOW BRIDGE: SCULPTURE IN STONE

One of the world's greatest wonders, and the focus of Paiute and Navajo myth, a fabulous span of rosy sandstone curves over the rocky terrain of southern Utah like a rainbow turned to stone.

The Paiute and Navajo Indians of southern Utah told tales of a legendary 'rainbow of stone', but the precise location of this great stone arch that reputedly mimicked the shape and colour of a rainbow was known only to a few of their number. Intrigued by rumours of such a stunning spectacle not far from Navajo Mountain, in 1909 a three-man party set out on horseback through rocky wastelands and winding canyons in the hope of finding this remarkable phenomenon. Guided by two American Indians, they trekked through some of the most inhospitable country in the United States before finally discovering the great rainbow arch.

The horsemen were overawed by the sight that greeted them. Not only did the arch duplicate a rainbow in form but also in colour. Under a clear, bright sky, the naturally pink stone appeared dark lavender; in the late afternoon sun it was splashed with streaks of russet red and brown.

The largest and most perfect natural rock formation of its kind, the graceful 309ft (94m) long sandstone bridge spans a canyon 278ft (85m) wide, almost the length of four tennis courts placed end to end. Its height of 290ft (88m) from the base to the top of the arch exceeds that of Nelson's Column in London by 105ft (32m); the stone is 42ft (13m) thick and 33ft (10m) across, wide enough to accommodate two lanes of traffic. Its sheer size and magnificence prompted US president Theodore Roosevelt to declare it the greatest natural wonder in the world.

Jutting out from the cliff, of which it was once a solid buttress, the huge arch vaults the modest trickle of Bridge Creek. Over thousands of years the base of the stone buttress has been worn away by the creek's seasonal torrents

Mirror image *The smooth lines and remarkable symmetry of Rainbow Bridge, standing out against a crystalline desert sky, are replicated without a ripple or flaw by its reflection in Bridge Creek below. The Navajo Indians, who named the bridge* nonnezoshi, *'rainbow of stone', regard it as a sacred place.*

RAINBOW BRIDGE: SCULPTURE IN STONE

and abrasive silt, leaving the airy arch of the bridge suspended above it. The smooth lines of the stone sculpture were rounded and polished by the wind.

To the Navajo Indians, *nonnezoshi*, 'rainbow of stone', is a sacred place, and archaeological evidence found at the site indicates that it may once have been used as a place of worship. But access to the area, hidden away in a narrow canyon, is so difficult that when the first party of white men arrived there they understood why so few local Indians knew its exact whereabouts.

The bridge was declared a national monument in 1910, but only became generally accessible in 1963, following the completion of Glen Canyon Dam. The resulting lake, Lake Powell, raised the water level in the Colorado River, replacing 13 miles (20km) of fiendishly difficult overland trails with easily navigated water passages; visitors can now travel by boat to within shouting distance of the bridge.

Utah contains hundreds of similar sandstone arches, more than 200 of which are found in Arches National Park,

180 miles (300km) north of Rainbow Bridge. Landscape Arch is another record-breaker – its span of 290ft (89m) makes it the longest natural bridge in the world. As fragile as a collarbone – one stretch is just 6ft (1.8m) thick – its sandstone fin projects from the rugged outcrops of rock at an average height of some 30m (100ft) above the floor of the canyon.

Another of the park's majestic structures is Delicate Arch, known locally for its shape as Old Maid's Bloomers. Standing higher than a seven-storey building in proud isolation on the rim of a desolate rock bowl, it neatly frames the La Sal Mountains beyond.

Flying buttresses *Angel Arch, like the formation in the background, appears to be topped by a pair of spreading wings. Elsewhere in the geological wonderland of Arches National Park natural sculptures have inspired equally picturesque and apt titles, such as Dark Angel, Pine Tree, Partition and Skyline.*

Flowers of the valley The waters that once shaped this great natural arch now nourish the sweet-scented white datura flowers, which appear in July and August alongside sand lupins, yucca, daisies and mariposa lilies.

Fragile future A frail hoop, one of whose legs is only 6ft (1.8m) thick, Delicate Arch was formed in relatively soft rock known as Entrada sandstone. This graceful arch is, therefore, doomed to a short life in geological terms.

SCULPTURE IN PROGRESS

Although water is scarce in the Utah Desert, it is, paradoxically, the action of water that is responsible for many of the stone formations found there. Some arches were created by streams eroding the rock at the base of a cliff, while leaving the top intact. Others resulted from water seeping into fractures in the rock and slowly eroding them until only narrow fins of rock remained. Holes that were made through the fins were gradually enlarged by weathering and rock falls to form natural arches.

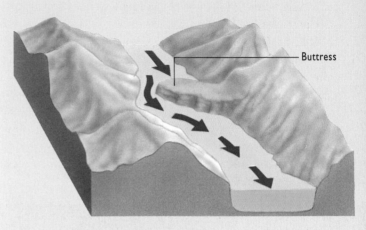

Buttress

Rainbow Bridge was formed by the action of the creek that still runs below it, Bridge Creek. Millions of years ago, a lone sandstone buttress jutted out from the side of the canyon. The water of Bridge Creek, carrying a heavy load of silt and other debris, would have continually crashed into the buttress in its headlong career downstream. During many centuries, this action, along with the weathering effects of wind and sand, gradually ate into the base of the buttress, wearing a small opening in the soft sandstone.

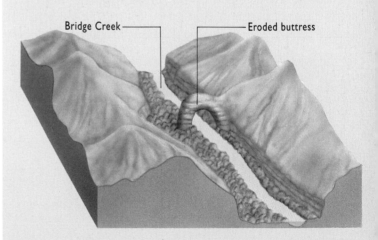

Bridge Creek — Eroded buttress

Constant bombardment with silt, and extreme shifts of temperature over thousands of years, would have caused the rock to expand and contract violently, slowly widening the hole in the sandstone buttress until it was eroded into the shape of a bow. At the same time, the water of the creek carved out a small canyon below what had become a huge arch, accentuating its height, while the wind sculpted and polished the stone of Rainbow Bridge into its present beautiful symmetry.

MONUMENT VALLEY: LAND OF ROCKY GIANTS

On a high, barren plain in Arizona, massive outcrops of red sandstone are etched against the sky like fragmented architectural relics.

The unique beauty of Monument Valley resides in its statuesque rocks, its dry clear air and the lengthening shadows of its monuments as thé desert sun sets. The valley, which straddles the Utah–Arizona border in the south-western USA, is named after the strange stone monoliths that loom over the sagebrush plain, for geologists use the term 'monument' to describe those remnants of erosion that are higher than they are broad. This factor means that they often resemble man-made buildings or artefacts, and the landscape of Monument Valley is dominated by visions of crumbling castles, ancient temples, skyscrapers, pillars and spires.

The extraordinary shapes of many of these towers have prompted fanciful popular names. Castle Rock is an impressive flat-topped plateau, or massif, 1000ft (300m) high, topped by crenellated 'battlements'. The Mittens are a pair of formations that stand close together; each consists of a narrow column of rock, the thumb, beside a broader butte (a flat-topped hill or column of rock), resembling the fingers. Nearby, Hen-in-a-Nest bears a similarity to a squatting chicken, while the sombre masses of Merrick Butte and Mitchell Butte might be natural replicas of giant tombstones. According to local folklore, their names commemorate two silver prospectors who were killed here by Indians in the 1880s. The Prioress, at

Desert flower *A symbol of the Wild West and the state flower of Arizona, the saguaro cactus is peculiar to the south-western USA and north-western Mexico. Its white bloom opens only at night, and its crimson fruit provides local people with a source of nourishment.*

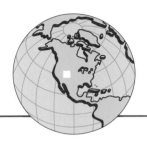

Stark silhouettes

Sandstone pillars, spires and buttes seared by the rays of the scorching desert sun dwarf the winding highway leading away from Monument Valley. The characteristic red-brown colour of the monuments is due to the large quantities of iron present in the sandstone.

MONUMENT VALLEY: LAND OF ROCKY GIANTS

Monumental formations
There are many unusually shaped rocks in Monument Valley, but the mesas and buttes above all are classic examples of the action of the forces of erosion on alternate layers of hard and soft rock. Millions of years of wind and weathering wore away much of the softer rock, resulting in mesas. Further erosion transformed mesas into buttes: these usually consist of a flat top of resistant rock underlain by steep cliffs of softer rock standing above gentle slopes that fall away to the surrounding plain. Daily rock falls scatter crumbling sandstone around the feet of both mesas and buttes.

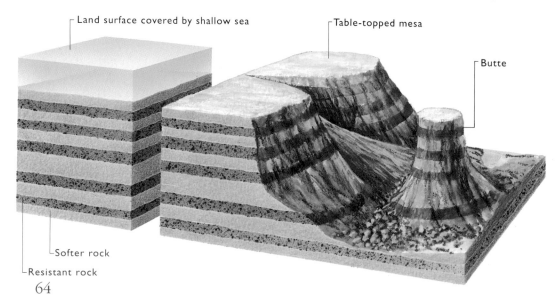

Land surface covered by shallow sea

Table-topped mesa

Butte

Softer rock

Resistant rock

TABLES AND COLUMNS

The forces of erosion created Monument Valley's buttes and mesas. Where the Earth's movements had opened fissures and faults, rainwater and wind cut into the underlying sandstone. Little by little, the broad sandstone terraces were chopped into rocky table-shaped plateaux, or mesas. Further erosion whittled many of these mesas into tall freestanding narrow columns, or buttes.

800ft (245m) high the tallest of a group of rocks known as the Three Sisters, bears a remarkable resemblance to a cowled figure, her hands clasped in prayer.

Monument Valley was not always such an impressive landscape of isolated buttes and massifs. About 250 million years ago, its red sands were covered by a shallow sea. Heavy mud deposits collected on the seabed as sediment, compressing the sand into porous sandstone, while the mud itself gradually turned into shale. Slowly, the sea receded and – some 70 million years ago – the Earth's crust thrust violently upwards, forming a wide, bulbous dome before cooling and solidifying again. What had once been the seabed was now an enormous plateau of sandstone with a covering of shale and conglomerate (a coarse sedimentary rock consisting largely of pebbles and gravel). Over millions of years, these exposed rock layers were transformed by wind and water, first into large plateaux crisscrossed by canyons and gullies, then into smaller mesas and finally into tall columns or buttes.

Like much of south-western USA, Monument Valley is spectacularly beautiful but deeply inhospitable to both humans and wildlife. Apart from the Navajo Indians, who still herd sheep and goats here, there is little sign of human habitation. The arid dunes and wasted scrubland support no game except rabbits and cold-blooded creatures that need little water, such as the collared lizard, the horned toad and the prairie rattlesnake. The yearly rainfall total rarely tops 8in (20cm), so the sparse vegetation is limited to a few hardy species – scrub juniper, sagebrush, pinyon pines and cacti – that can survive months without water. A sudden rainstorm often brings the buried seeds

Western epic *Merrick Butte provided the ideal backdrop for John Ford's US cavalry film,* She Wore a Yellow Ribbon. *Ford made more than 25 movies here, and many commercials have been filmed against the valley's other-worldly rock formations.*

of dozens of wildflowers to life, briefly spattering the landscape with brilliant colour, but the fragile blossoms never last more than a day or two.

Over a century, Monument Valley appears to have changed little, but the processes of erosion are constantly at work and rock falls are daily occurrences. It may well be that the final lofty remnants of the sandstone plateau will, over hundreds of thousands of years, be flattened to leave a monotonous, level plain.

Wearing times *Some layers of rock defy the erosive powers of wind and rain better than others. On this peculiarly shaped mushroom rock, a resistant top cap is supported by a more eroded sub-layer.*

NAVAJO INDIANS

With a population that numbers around 220 000, and the most extensive reservation lands, the Navajo are the largest group of North American native peoples.

Modern Navajo history dates from the Long Walk in 1864 when, after repeated outbreaks of fighting between the Navajo and their Spanish and Anglo-American neighbours, they were deported to Fort Sumner 300 miles (480km) from their traditional lands around Monument Valley. Four years later, they were allowed to return to a designated reservation within their ancestral homeland. The Navajo quickly re-established their former way of life as hunters and farmers, with sheep particularly important to their economy. Women weave rugs and blankets from the wool; many of the men are also silversmiths and produce fine-quality jewellery.

Doll maker The Navajo reservation surrounds an area allocated to the Hopi. Kachina dolls are traditional to Hopi culture and depict dancers in ceremonial costume. The dolls are given to friends as bearers of good fortune.

Men's work The first Navajo to make jewellery from silver and turquoise is reputed to have been Atsidi Chon in 1880. Hammer, hand-worked bellows and a steel anvil are the usual tools, while all the materials are from the region.

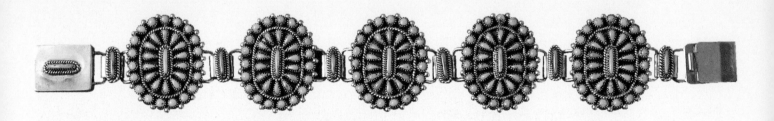

Market economy In the last 150 years, goods that were once made for home use, such as coiled baskets, have become integral to the Navajo economy.

At home Family life centres on the hogan, traditionally a cone of forked poles covered with earth; today it usually consists of soil-covered horizontal logs.

Rugs and blankets *Wool started to replace rabbit skin as the preferred material for blankets about 100 years ago. The designs of many blankets represent sand paintings, of which there are more than 800 different examples. They are produced on ceremonial occasions to restore balance and harmony in the world. In this blanket the central maize plant represents the tree of life; the two figures depict rain (LEFT) and thunder and lightning.*

Seeking pasture *Today the Navajo herd their flocks in Monument Valley, as they have since their ancestors first obtained sheep from the Spanish in the 17th century. Owning sheep is an indication of status within the tribe, and although herds had to be drastically reduced in the 1930s because the lands were becoming overgrazed, sheep farming is again a flourishing industry.*

THE GLITTERING PETRIFIED FOREST

Thousands of jewel-bright logs, made not of wood but of solid stone, lie strewn across the Arizona Desert. They are perfect replicas of tall trees, trapped halfway down hillsides or perched on crests, all of which were once alive.

Riding through the dusty sagebrush of Arizona's Painted Desert in 1851, US army officer Lt Lorenzo Sitgreaves stumbled by chance on the remains of a forest, the like of which he had never seen before. Although what surrounded him had the appearance of living wood, the forest was comprised not of trees with leaves or shoots, but of rigid logs of crystalline quartz. His discovery prompted two major questions: what were these iron-hard stumps and branches doing in the middle of an arid desert where no known tree could survive the scorching heat? And if they were once alive, how had their bark, sap and pulpy flesh been transformed into these extraordinary blocks of cold stone?

To the local Navajo Indians, the striped and gleaming logs were the bones of a legendary giant, Yietso, while the Paiute Indians believed them to be the arrow shafts of Shinauv, the thunder god. In fact, the trees of rock that form the largest petrified forest in the world are the result of a natural process that started around 200 million years ago when the Arizona Desert was a broad flood plain. Instead of today's coyote, bobcat and badger, dinosaurs roamed among the giant conifers that dotted the hills to the south and the lower slopes of the volcanic mountains that enclosed a swampy basin.

Most of these trees were some 100ft (30m) tall, with trunks that measured more than 6ft (1.8m) across; a few massive specimens grew to twice those dimensions. Some of the logs of the Petrified Forest also reach these proportions,

Hills of gold and blue
One of the most beautiful areas of the Petrified Forest is the Blue Mesa. Here, the many shades of banding in the flat-topped buttes and cones of rock show clearly the layers of the ancient marsh. The petrified log in the foreground, in common with most of the trees in the forest, is merely a fragment. The majority of 'whole' trunks are in the Long Legs area of the Jasper Forest.

Pictures on rock *Before the coming of the railway in the 19th century, the area of the Petrified Forest was home to Indian tribes, including the Navajo. Drawings chiselled into the sandstone walls are all that remain of the Puerco ruins, the largest of the forest's ancient sites, inhabited from AD 500 to 1400.*

THE GLITTERING PETRIFIED FOREST

Rings of quartz *Seen in cross-section, the logs of the Petrified Forest perfectly preserve the characteristics of the wood from which they derive. Every cell of the original tree was impregnated with silica, which crystallised. The annual growth rings, now made from quartz, chart the tree's life from a young sapling until the moment it toppled to the forest floor.*

Desirable crystals *At the end of the 19th century, many of the logs of the Crystal Forest – where the quartz exists in its purest form – were removed and smashed so that their gem-quality quartz crystals could be extracted. This was in part responsible for the decision to make Petrified Forest a national monument in 1906. In 1962, 146 sq miles (378km²) of the forest were designated a national park.*

but most were fragmented either before the process of petrification began, or as they surfaced.

The logs of the forest exist in a multitude of shades largely owing to the process of crystallisation. Where they exist in isolation, silica molecules crystallise into pure quartz, and many of the forest logs are formed from this substance. If other minerals are present during crystallisation, however, any one of a number of semi-precious gemstones, such as amethyst, agate, jasper, onyx and carnelian, may be produced. Regardless of their composition, in the case of the Petrified Forest the silica crystals took on the shape of their 'parent' tree cells, so that in time perfect stone copies of the structure of the logs were created, buried as deep as 1000ft (300m) underground.

They might have remained hidden forever, had it not been for the massive upheavals in the Earth's crust that took place around 65 million years ago. The turbulence that gave birth to the Rocky Mountains also raised the land in this part of Arizona, with two major consequences. The water drained away, and the crystallised remains of the coniferous forest were propelled upwards. Slowly, wind and rain eroded the sediment, shale and sandstone covering the logs, and the Petrified Forest was exposed.

There are five major concentrations of logs in the forest, named after their predominant colour or composition: Blue Mesa, Crystal Forest, Rainbow Forest, Black Forest and Jasper Forest, where the majority of trunks are opaque. Among the forest's other natural wonders is Agate Bridge, a timber log that has been transformed into a stone bridge. Agate is also integral to one of the few man-made features of the area, Agate House – a centuries-old 'hut' made from crystalline logs.

The processes that buried and then revealed the logs also created fossils of many of the plants and animals that populated this area 200 million years ago. Apart from the coniferous trees, the most common plants were cycads, which resembled palm trees but had fern-like leaves. Dinosaur fossils include the crocodile-snouted phytosaurs and their major prey, the fish-eating metoposaurs, and armadillo-like aetosaurs.

Although this area receives only 9in (23cm) of rain each year, most of that falls in brief violent thunderstorms that can wash away as much as 1in (25mm) of soil at a time. In this way, the logs and fossils of the Petrified Forest are constantly being augmented by evidence of life from the days when giant reptiles roamed the Earth.

A FOREST MADE OF STONE

Two hundred million years ago, tall conifers grew on a vast, swampy flood plain surrounded by a number of active volcanoes.

Floodwaters carried away many of the dead trees that littered the ground, but others became jammed at places such as riverbends or trapped in narrow gullies.

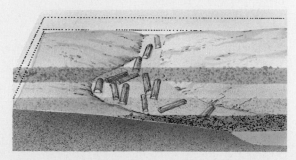

Thick layers of mud, sand and volcanic ash settled on top of the trees. Silica from the ash, dissolved in groundwater, seeped into the wood and crystallised.

Further sediment piled up on the buried logs. Over millennia, upheavals in the Earth's crust and erosion exposed the petrified wood.

WHITE SANDS: THE PORCELAIN DESERT

In the New Mexico desert, shifting dunes of brilliant white sand gleam in the sunshine like a pristine snowfield. White Sands is unique: a giant swathe of cool, crumbling sand that moves and changes, but is constantly replenished.

Under the scorching sun of the Tularosa Basin in the deserts of New Mexico, white sands gleam like freshly fallen snow. These powdery dunes are composed not of grains of quartz – the chief constituent of most desert sands – but of soft, chalky gypsum, or calcium sulphate. Unlike other desert sands, these dunes are cool to the touch, owing to the high rate of evaporation of surface moisture and the degree to which the grains reflect, rather than absorb, the sun's rays. White Sands covers an area of 275 sq miles (700km²) between the Sacramento Mountains in the east and the San Andreas Mountains in the west and is the world's largest surface deposit of gypsum, the mineral from which plaster of Paris is made.

Gypsum is one of the most common mineral compounds found on Earth but, since it dissolves readily in water, it is rarely seen on the surface. The origins of this extraordinary dune field in the arid south-western USA date back to a time, around 100 million years ago, when this area of the North American landmass was covered by a shallow sea. As its waters gradually retreated, saltwater lakes were left behind, which eventually evaporated in the

Survival tactics The hardy yucca (RIGHT) *is among the few plants that can withstand both the arid climate and shifting gypsum 'soil'. Yuccas belong to the lily family. They have tough leaves that restrict water loss and roots that grow constantly to stabilise the plants as they sway with the wind-blown sands.*

Border blossoms The hedgehog cactus (LEFT) *flourishes on the fringes of White Sands where water is more abundant. Its vivid red blooms provide a startling contrast to the white dunes.*

WHITE SANDS

sun. In addition to salt, gypsum was precipitated from the mineral-rich solution and laid down in thick deposits on the old seabed.

The Sacramento and San Andreas mountain ranges, with the Tularosa Basin in between, started to take shape around 65 million years ago. Giant upheavals in the Earth's crust folded and crumpled the land and the gypsum strata, thrusting them high into the air.

Seasonal rains and meltwater running off the mountains caused the gypsum to leach out and concentrated solutions were washed down the mountainsides. The gypsum-laden liquid accumulated in Lake Lucero, the lowest part of the Tularosa Basin. Water from the lake has no means of escape but evaporation, which leaves behind thin sheets of crystal-lised gypsum, or selenite. Weathering then reduces these crystals to fine, sandy grains which the prevailing south-westerly winds carry farther up the basin and pile in steep dunes that often tower as high as 50ft (15m) above the desert floor. Not only are the dunes formed by the winds, they are also carried along by them – by distances of up to 30ft (9m) a year. This endless process of change and regeneration gives the landscape the eerie appearance of having a life of its own.

This constant movement of the sands, combined with their alkaline nature and the lack of rainfall, makes it difficult for plants to thrive here. Those that do, such as the yucca, sumac and cottonwood, manage to secure a firm hold in the shifting gypsum by developing long, elaborate root systems. Cottonwood roots, for example, can reach as far as 100ft (30m) down into the dunes. Similarly, there are few permanent animal residents of White Sands. Among them, the bleached earless lizard and the apache pocket mouse, which is nocturnal and rarely seen, are found nowhere else on Earth. Both have developed pale protective colouring and their outlines merge into the desert's brilliant whiteness.

At the edges of White Sands, where the heat is less intense and water more readily available, plant and animal life is more abundant. About 500 species of wildlife live here, including many brilliantly coloured flowering plants. Gold buffalo gourds bloom alongside pink centauriums and purple sand verbenas. Coyote, skunks, kangaroo rats, gophers, badgers, snakes and porcupines all make their homes here during the day and by night occasionally venture into the dunes, leaving their distinctive tracks in the powdery porcelain sands.

The inherent beauty of White Sands lies in its ever-changing appearance yet essential permanence. For although the wind alters the contours of the land daily, the forces of nature constantly replenish the gypsum dune fields, as winter snowfalls perpetuate the Arctic tundra.

74

MUTUAL BENEFICIARIES

The yucca plant enjoys a special relationship with the yucca moth. Moth larvae feed only on the seeds of this plant, while the plant is pollinated only by the female yucca moth. After the female moth has mated, she enters a yucca flower to gather pollen, which she works into a ball with a pair of curved tentacles. She then flies to another flower, where she lays her eggs in the base of the flower's ovary. Next she removes some of the pollen from the ball she is still carrying and smears it on to the yucca's stigma, thereby fertilising the plant. The moth's eggs and the yucca's seeds develop together. On hatching, the moth larvae eat some of the ripened seeds, then drop to the ground, burrowing into the loose gypsum, where they continue to develop. The rest of the yucca seeds are dispersed by the wind.

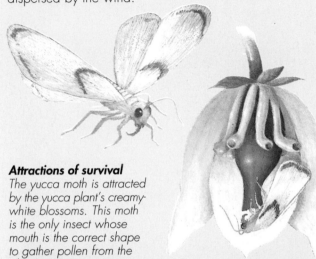

Attractions of survival
The yucca moth is attracted by the yucca plant's creamy-white blossoms. This moth is the only insect whose mouth is the correct shape to gather pollen from the plant's green stamens.

Sculpture show As the prevailing south-westerly winds sweep across the desert, they regularly fashion strange sculptures among the white dunes (ABOVE). Most are transitory, but occasionally a sculpture remains in place long enough for a mesquite tree or other plant to gain a brief foothold.

Protective measures White Sands dune dwellers have evolved different characteristics to enable them to survive. In other parts of the Tularosa Basin, earless lizards are brown; here, pale skin is a definite advantage, and the bleached variety (RIGHT), which is unique to this area, thrives. This lizard has also evolved the ability to shed its tail if seized by prey, then grow a new one.

BRUTAL BADLANDS

Desolate expanses of ravaged rock scar a grimly picturesque landscape. It was upturned millions of years ago by prehistoric turbulence, and the land is still slowly but relentlessly being torn apart today.

No place on Earth is more aptly named than the Badlands of South Dakota, in the United States. A forbidding vista of barren, jagged hills and saw-toothed ridges, slashed by shadowy gullies and crisscrossed with sharp ravines – a more inhospitable place is hard to imagine. Narrow, flat-topped hills loom menacingly like battlements on the horizon, capped in places by threatening masses of rocks and boulders.

The local Sioux Indians called this landscape *mako sica*, and to an intrepid band of 18th-century French-Canadian fur trappers it was *les mauvaises terres*. (Both names translate as 'bad lands'.) The trappers were travelling southwards down the Missouri River in search of pelts and trade. Just north of the White River they stopped suddenly in their tracks; they had entered the Badlands, a terrain more hostile than any they had ever encountered. The seemingly endless landscape, eerily empty and searingly hot, was also arduous to cross. Heavy summer cloudbursts had rendered the clay underfoot a morass of mud that made every step treacherous.

The plateau that is now the Badlands began to form about 80 million years ago. Extending over 6000 sq miles (15 500km²), between Mount Rushmore in the west and the Missouri River in the east, the area during that period was a shallow sea, its bed rich with a variety of sediments. Around 65 million years ago, the same upheaval in the Earth's crust that created the Rocky Mountains shattered the seabed and pushed it upwards to create an immense marshy plain. As the region gradually became drier, it evolved into a rolling prairie of lush green grassland dotted with conifers. But erosion started to take its toll, and the combined potent forces of wind, freezing temperatures and running water sculpted spires and ravines, transforming the rich pastureland into a gloomy wilderness with an atmosphere of decay.

The process of erosion is constant: the semi-arid Badlands are being worn away each year by the sudden, torrential June rains. About 15in (38cm) of rain falls every year, but most of it arrives in intermittent downpours so violent that a network of powerful rivers and gullies is created that covers the landscape and tears at the earth before vanishing. Water thunders from ridge to ridge, rushing through the narrow ravines with astonishing force. The ancient sedimentary layers, never compressed

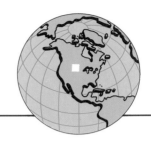

Subtle shades *The contrasting tints in the soft, multi-layered rock reflect its development from prehistoric times. Various strata contain silt from the overflow of long-vanished rivers and compacted ash from volcanic eruptions.*

Since agriculture was banned in the Badlands in 1978, the region's natural vegetation has grown without hindrance.

77

BRUTAL BADLANDS

by harder rock and with no vegetation to anchor them, offer no resistance to running water and are easily washed away. The enormous run-off of clay, stones and gravel pours into the great White River and from there flows into the Missouri. (Among the sediments are chalky grains which do not dissolve but remain churning constantly in the water – hence the name White River.) With each new summer storm, the ridges are further eroded and the gullies carved deeper. In this way, some pinnacles of rock, among them Vampire Peak, are shrinking by as much as 6in (15cm) every year.

As the elements relentlessly wear away the soft surface of the Badlands, a wealth of giant fossils is exposed, irrefutable evidence of the many species that have appeared and then disappeared as the area has undergone geological changes. The fossil species include fish and reptiles from the Cretaceous period, when the region was a vast sea, and land animals from the Oligocene period (which ended 23 million years ago). During this era, sabre-toothed tigers, three-toed horses and a type of camel no larger than a dog ranged the fertile grasslands.

For many years, the Badlands were stripped of their wealth of fossils by traders and trippers. Now that the area

Invisible monuments
Many of the blade-like ridges, or clastic dykes, that slice through the dusty floor of the ancient flood plain

lie in a natural depression. From the north, most are scarcely visible above the horizon, despite their awesome height.

Embolotherium

Dinohyus

TREASURE TROVE OF FOSSILS

Marine turtle shells are some of the most common fossils found in the Badlands – the largest was 12ft (3.7m) long. Equally prevalent here are the fossils of oreodonts, pig-like mammals with large teeth designed for ruminating. Knowledge of these animals comes entirely from their fossilised remains.

Some of the creatures that grazed and hunted here during the Oligocene period were massively built and grotesque, notably *Embolotherium*, whose skull swept up into a single horn on the nose, and the bull-like *Dinohyus*, 10ft (3m) long.

An oreodont jawbone perfectly preserved in stone.

78

is acknowledged as the richest Oligocene fossil bed in the world, constantly yielding up more fascinating finds, it is protected as a precious palaeontological resource.

Despite their virtually barren appearance, the Badlands support a variety of animal and plant life. Coyotes and jackrabbits make these forbidding plains their home, but reptiles such as rattlesnakes and bullsnakes, and rodents, including the Badlands chipmunk, are the principal inhabitants. Plants have great difficulty gaining a permanent foothold here, since a site that has provided them with a protected niche for more than a generation is apt to disappear overnight. Yet some sheltered pockets exist, especially on the fringes of the Badlands where the soil has gradually taken on many of the characteristics of the surrounding prairies. In this more stable environment plants are able to grow, thus binding the topsoil and

thereby preventing erosion. Here, buffalo grass and the prairie golden pea thrive, plants that once provided grazing for the vast herds of bison that roamed the prairies. On the outer fringes, too, prairie dogs – not dogs at all but burrowing squirrel-like rodents – establish their elaborate homes. Known as towns, these underground colonies include designated areas for sleeping, feeding and excretion. The region also supports a few tree species, including the juniper, red cedar and yellow willow, while rock wrens make their nests in sheltered crannies in the rock face.

The Badlands' story is not exclusively one of constant decay and struggle for survival. During the 1960s, small numbers of bison and bighorn sheep were successfully reintroduced into the area, together with the near extinct pronghorn antelope, which inhabits the outlying areas. In 1978, the Badlands were designated a national park.

Speedy survivor The *pronghorn, America's fastest-moving mammal, can cover up to 26ft (8m) in a single, extended stride. It can travel at a top speed of about 55mph (90km/h) in short bursts, and is capable of maintaining an even 43mph (70km/h) for some 4 miles (6.5km).*

Once nearly extinct, pronghorns now run freely through those outlying areas of the Badlands where prairie grasses are re-establishing themselves.

SURTSEY: AN ISLAND BORN OF FIRE

In the early 1960s, a series of volcanic explosions from deep within the Earth's core culminated in the creation of a barren crest of rock that jutted from the Atlantic Ocean, south of Iceland. Some 30 years later, the processes that govern life itself are at work on this new island.

Before dawn broke on 14 November 1963, the fishing vessel *Isleifur II* was gliding slowly through the icy waters of the North Atlantic to the south-west of Iceland. As the crew cast their nets into the calm waters to trawl for cod, a large wave suddenly hit the boat, pitching it steeply. When they recovered their balance, the fishermen saw a tall column of smoke rising from the water. The ship's captain assumed that another vessel was in distress and set out to offer assistance. But, as the *Isleifur II* neared the source of the smoke, the crew realised that this was no ship on fire: the 'smoke' was in fact steam and the 'fire' an underwater volcano erupting. These fishermen were witnessing the first stages in the birth of the island of Surtsey.

The vessel's crew started to fear for their own safety and, navigating a course through the clouds of billowing steam, headed for home. Periodic explosions hurled chunks of cooled lava into the air. Within three hours of the initial eruption the column of ash and debris was 12 000ft (3600m) high. In the course of the next two days, it reached as high as 50 000ft (15 000m) and was visible in Reykjavik, Iceland's capital city, some 75 miles (120km) to the north-west.

The underwater volcano ripped open 1 sq mile (2.5km²) of the seabed, lying just 420ft (130m) below the water's surface. Friction between dust particles generated enormous flashes of lightning across the blackened skies. Further explosions churned the seas, threatening passing vessels. The sudden conversion of so much water into steam set off another chain of undersea explosions that were so intense that they transformed orange-hot magma from the Earth's core into dust particles. The world's photographers, journalists and scientists flocked to witness the cataclysm at first hand, only to be showered with cinders, pumice and fine ash – a mixture known as tephra.

By 16 November, a huge ridge of rock had begun to form and harden in the heart of the dense, billowing cloud. Within a couple of weeks an island, around 130ft (40m) high and 1800ft (550m) long, was clearly visible. A month later, since the volcano appeared to have

The end of the world?
In Norse mythology, the arrival of the fire god Surtur, who was expected to ride across the Earth, striking it indiscriminately with his sword of fire, was just one of the cataclysmic events thought to herald Ragnarok – the twilight of the gods.

Skull island *When viewed from above, Surtsey has been likened to the skull of a giant rodent, with craters for eye sockets and a long snout pointing northwards to Iceland.*

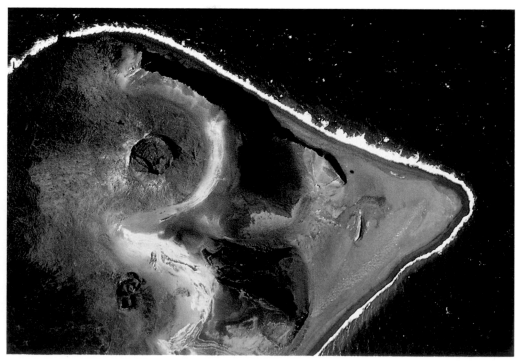

SURTSEY: AN ISLAND BORN OF FIRE

Rocky roosts *The first bird to colonise Surtsey was the fulmar, which started nesting on a ledge in the western cliffs in 1970. A year later there were ten nests, and by 1980 – thanks mainly to the absence of egg-stealing predators such as rats – a breeding colony was firmly established.*

The evolution of life
Surtsey's birth has given scientists a unique opportunity to study the colonisation of virgin land by plants and animals. Visitors were forbidden in case they carried seeds or spores in their clothing: only

scientists wearing sterile garments were permitted to explore. The first arrivals on the seashore were bacteria, seaweeds and other green algae, followed by mosses and lichens – an order that repeats the evolutionary process.

Volcanic greenery
Sufficient seeds have reached Surtsey, carried either on the breeze or by birds, to produce scattered wildflowers, grasses and sedges. The first flowering plant, a mayweed, took root in 1972.

quietened, a party of bold French journalists ventured on to the island, only to be pelted with more pumice and hot ash – evidence that the landmass was still growing.

By the end of January 1964 the island stood 500ft (150m) above sea level and covered an area of 1 sq mile (2.5km²), approximately half the size of New York's Central Park. The Icelandic government named it Surtsey, in honour of Surtur, the god of fire in Norse mythology. Scientists suspected, however, that the island's lifespan would be short, since the materials from which it had been formed, chiefly pumice and ash, were soft and unlikely to withstand the constant battering of waves and wind during a North Atlantic winter.

Surtsey would almost certainly have disappeared had a second volcano not erupted, depositing molten lava on top of the tephra. As the lava cooled and solidified, it formed a hard surface on the island's northern edge. Lava eventually flowed from the original volcano (Surtur I), too, increasing the size of the island and mingling with the tephra to strengthen the surface further and form a tough shield that could withstand the fiercest North Atlantic storms.

Since 1967, when eruptions ceased, Surtsey has become a laboratory where scientists have a unique opportunity to study exactly how life takes hold in a new environment. Volcanic activity constantly threatens, however, and one day Surtsey may be destroyed as it was born.

EXPLOSIVE FORCES

Surtsey lies along the Mid-Atlantic Ridge, a mountain chain that extends more than 10 000 miles (16 000km) from the Arctic to the Antarctic, mostly along the ocean floor. Iceland is the largest island of the ridge above sea level; others include the Azores, to the west of Portugal.

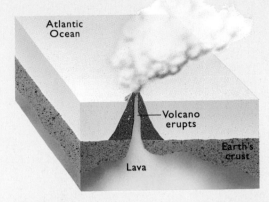

November 1963 *A fissure opens in the seabed and molten magma from the Earth's core is forced upwards. A series of explosions hurls dust skywards.*

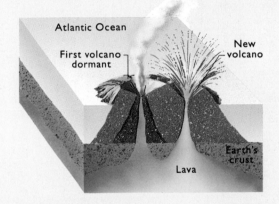

February 1964 *Near to the first cone, by this time dormant, a second volcanic peak, Surtur II, begins to deposit molten lava on the island.*

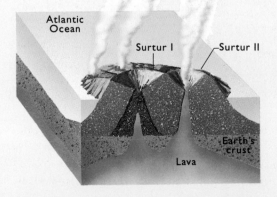

April 1964 *Continued eruptions pour more lava over the soft tephra base, increasing the island's chances of survival. Sporadic eruptions occurred until 1967; since then the island has been stable. Surtsey today stands 571ft (174m) above sea level at its highest point.*

Monumental Wonders

C ountless structures have been raised by human architects and builders from the time our remote ancestors first leaned two branches together to make a shelter, and of these many thousands have survived. Some are not mere aggregations of stone but are structures and sites imbued with a special sense of mystery or significance. Often these buildings have been constructed as places of worship. Always they have been built with an intense spiritual or emotional commitment, in which the genius of designer and artisan has entered into a happy coalition with a site of special natural beauty or character. On occasions, the combination of structure and location overrides the confines of a particular religion. The shrines of Jerusalem and Istanbul's Hagia Sophia have seen successive occupation by groups with differing beliefs; but all recognised the aura of sanctity and mystery that seem to have seeped into the fabric of these houses of God. Even the hurried tourist, impelled by curiosity rather than religious fervour, is often stunned into a reverent silence in sites combining natural beauty with human skills and devotion, such as the Temple of Apollo at Delphi in Greece. Sometimes the power of ancient legend lends significance to a site, as at Knossos in Crete; others, like the Taj Mahal, created by a grieving emperor for his dead wife, awe us with the emotions seeming to live on in their forms and silences.

ALHAMBRA: A MOORISH PARADISE

A palace-fortress concealing an interior of unsurpassed beauty, the Alhambra recalls Spain's Islamic past. It sits high above an ancient city, framed against the spectacular backdrop of the Sierra Nevada's shimmering snow-capped peaks.

The ancient palace of the Moorish rulers of Spain dominates the modern city of Granada just as its builders once dominated their extensive empire. A glowing red citadel, the Alhambra includes a maze of perfectly proportioned shady courtyards, filigreed galleries, sunlit patios and arcades.

The Moors were Muslims from North Africa who invaded Spain in the early eighth century AD. During the ninth century, they built a fortress on the remains of Alcazaba, an ancient stronghold. From the 12th to the 14th centuries, the Moorish kingdom was attacked again and again by Christian armies. The Christians took the city of Córdoba in the 13th century, and thousands of Moorish refugees fled to Granada.

Their shrinking kingdom now centred on Granada, the Moors at once strengthened the Alcazaba's fortifications with an enclosing wall, towers and ramparts, and built new aqueducts to improve the water supply. The restructured building was eventually called the Red Fort, or *Al-Qal'a al-Hambra* in Arabic – the origin of the modern Spanish name Alhambra. But the Alhambra's lasting fame derives less from its strength as a military fortress than from the beauty and originality of its interiors, created by King Yusuf I (1333–53) and King Mohammed V (1353–91). While the exterior of this bastion is somewhat austere, the courtyards and halls that lie within are uniquely imaginative in their conception, ranging in style from elegantly understated to overtly theatrical.

Descended from a desert race, the Moors had a deep fascination with water and incorporated it imaginatively into their architectural structures at every opportunity. They created restful pools to reflect the beautifully proportioned arches and galleries, and fountains with tinkling rivulets of water to provide visual refreshment in the scorching heat of the day.

Masters in the exploitation of space and light, the architects of the Alhambra designed marble-lined pools and floors that would reflect fragments of bright Andalusian sunlight, bathing the palace courts in an ever-shifting golden radiance. They built graceful arches and galleries to capture the cooling breezes and the echo of rustling leaves, and grand courtyards that led into shady, colonnaded arcades which opened out on to majestic terraces. The Alhambra's most dramatic architectural achievement is

Enchantment within
At various times in the Alhambra's history, its substantial walls have enclosed a harem and a residence for court officials. Hans Christian Andersen likened the exquisite carving (INSET) within this Moorish paradise to a 'petrified lace bazaar'.

ALHAMBRA: A MOORISH PARADISE

the stalactite ornamentation – an art form unique to Islam – in domes, niches and on arches, which creates the effect of a honeycomb composed of thousands of cells filled with natural light and shadow. This decorative device seems to soak up light reflected from adjacent surfaces and then, as in the ceiling of the Hall of the Two Sisters, explode with vibrant energy. The ceiling of the Hall of Abencerrajes is similar in conception. Reached by a doorway from the Court of Lions, the hall is named after a noble family of Granada who were supposedly massacred here in the late 15th century. The eye is drawn irresistibly to the detailed intricacies of the ceiling's profusion of stalactites.

Every court and corner of the Alhambra bears a distinctive feature, each more enchanting than the last. The Court of Myrtles is lined with two long myrtle hedges that border the gleaming marble paths on either side of the central pool. Its still water, like a sheet of glass, reflects the slim columns of the arcades, and goldfish weave flashes of gold through its crystal-clear waters. The Tower of Comares, which rises at one end of the pool, tops the Hall of Ambassadors, the largest room in the palace with a ceiling that rises to 60ft (18m). Here, foreign dignitaries came to pay their respects to the king, enthroned in a recess opposite the entrance.

The Court of Lions is named after the 12 marble lions that support the central fountain. From the mouth of each lion a stream of water pours forth into the circular channel surrounding the fountain. The channel is fed by four waterways, cut into the stone paving, which lead from the shallow basins of fountains situated in adjacent rooms. A total of 124 columns support the arcades around the court, while on its western and eastern sides two pavilions provide vantage points from which to view the water cascading from the lions' mouths.

The Alhambra was finally surrendered to the Christians in 1492. In 1526, as if to confirm Christian supremacy in Spain, King Charles V of Spain rebuilt parts of the Alhambra in the Renaissance style and began to build his own Italianate palace inside the fortress walls. But work on the new palace was never completed, and the Moorish achievement at Granada – the most splendid surviving example in Spain of their genius – remains unchallenged. An unsurpassed pure fairytale world of filigree, the Alhambra might have been built so that the Moors could possess their own Paradise on Earth.

THE ART OF SYMMETRY

The Moors' love of ornate embellishment coupled with mathematical symmetry is nowhere more evident than in the Alhambra, where the decoration is characterised by dizzying tangles of flowing curves and overlapping angles. The inspiration for the complex, abstract patterns worked into the mosaics, tiles and plaster reliefs was probably drawn largely from flowers and vines, since Islam expressly forbids the representation of human or animal forms in art.

The dramatic tiles, or *azulejos*, adorning the walls of halls, galleries and the Royal Baths, are coloured vivid shades of red, blue and green: the plaster and stone surfaces were also once painted in these bright hues. The plasterwork designs form a perfectly geometric web of lines, so ingeniously arranged that stars and flowers appear to be caught in their strands. Floral patterns are also common, and tiny motifs, endlessly repeated and extraordinarily delicate, add texture to the surfaces of pillars and softly rounded archways.

The *Sala de la Justicia* (Hall of Justice) contains the only surviving examples of medieval Muslim figure paintings, and even today they glitter with gold and bright colour. But everywhere, sayings from the Koran in the Islamic script – a parade of irregular curves and bold upright strokes – embellish the Alhambra's walls. One pertinent inscription reads: 'Nothing in life is more cruel than to be blind in Granada', attesting to the Moors' great love for this city.

Tranquil view *The austere battlements of the Tower of Comares* (RIGHT) *rise above the beautiful, oblong Court of Myrtles, also called the Court of the Pond. A long fishpond lined by myrtle hedges reflects the carved colonnades at either end of the court.*

Romantic inspiration *The American writer Washington Irving* (ABOVE) *visited the Alhambra in 1828 and lived in one of the palace's chambers for three months. His* Legends of the Alhambra, *published in 1832, celebrate the citadel, conjuring a world of oriental mystery and magic in a blend of fact and legend.*

Visual harmony *The Court of Lions* (BELOW) *is held to be the most splendid of the Alhambra's courts. The arcades are supported by elegant marble columns, and at the east and west ends are two ornately decorated pavilions. An Arab poem is engraved around the edge of the basin in the lion fountain.*

MONT ST-MICHEL

One of France's major tourist attractions is also one of its oldest spiritual sites. The rocky island of Mont St-Michel is an architectural wonder, crowned by an abbey church and a Gothic monastery.

P ilgrims and travellers have been drawn to Mont St-Michel, a small island in the south-western corner of Normandy, for more than 1000 years. Connected by a causeway to the mainland, Mont St-Michel rises dramatically from a flat expanse of sands washed smooth by the powerful tides that sweep into the bay. In fine weather the conical rock, encrusted with an abbey church, monastic buildings, houses, gardens, terraces and fortifications, can be seen for miles around; in the mist the dark outline of roofs and pinnacles seem to float like a ghostly palace on a cloud of vapour.

Centuries ago, the island formed part of the land, a rocky outcrop in the marshy woodlands of this part of Normandy. In Roman times it was known as Mont Tombe, probably preserving a folk memory that the rock had been used as a Celtic burial ground. The Druids worshipped the sun here, a practice that was continued under the Romans, who venerated the sun god Mithras at the rock. A legend from this period holds that Julius Caesar, wearing gold boots and sealed in a gold coffin, was buried under Mont Tombe. In the fifth century, the land in this area subsided, and 100 years later the rock had become an island, completely cut off at high tide and accessible at other times along a dangerous passage marked by tall stakes.

The island's peacefulness and isolation soon attracted a group of monks, who built a small oratory and remained the sole inhabitants until 708, when the Archangel Michael is said to have visited Aubert (later St Aubert), Bishop of Avranches, in a dream and commanded him to build an oratory on Mont Tombe. Aubert, doubting the dream, at first did nothing, which prompted the archangel to return with the same command. Only after a third visit, when St Michael rapped the bishop on the head with his finger, did Aubert begin to build on the rocky island. He was assisted by a series of miracles: the circumference of the proposed foundations was marked out by the morning dew; a stolen cow reappeared on the spot where the first granite stone should be laid; a babe in arms removed a boulder that was in the way with a touch of its foot; and St Michael appeared again to identify a source of fresh water.

The renamed Mont St-Michel rapidly became a place of pilgrimage, and in 966 a Benedictine abbey to house 50 monks was built on its summit. Work on the abbey

Rock of ages *Mont St-Michel is today joined to the French mainland by a causeway 1 mile (1.8km) long, built in 1879. At low tide, the island is surrounded by sandbanks, and is completely cut off two or three times a year when exceptionally high tides cover the causeway. The rocky outcrop, with a circumference of around 3000ft (900m) and almost 300ft (90m) high, is crowned by one of France's architectural wonders.*

MONT ST-MICHEL

church, which still crowns the summit of the rock, was begun in 1020. Because of the difficulties of building on such precipitous slopes, it took more than 100 years to complete the church. Partial collapses over the years have meant that large portions of the original church have had to be restored, but it is still largely a Romanesque structure with rounded arches, thick walls and massive vaulting, although the choir, added in the 15th century, is Gothic.

But the abbey church is only one of Mont St-Michel's wonders. The second was begun by King Philip II of France as compensation for having burned down part of the church in 1203, during an attempt to capture the island from the Dukes of Normandy, its traditional sovereigns. La Merveille, 'the Marvel', on the northern side of the island, is a Gothic monastery built between 1211 and 1228.

La Merveille comprises two main sections, each three storeys high. The ground floor of the eastern side houses the *aumonière,* where the monks dispensed charity and gave lodging to poor pilgrims. Above that is the *salle des hôtes,* the principal guest room where the abbot welcomed wealthy visitors. In one of the two enormous fireplaces in this room the monks' meals were cooked; the other provided warmth. The top floor is given over to the monks' refectory, a large room whose thick walls are cut by high, narrow windows that flood the interior with brilliant light. During meals, which were taken in silence, a monk would read from the Scriptures.

La Merveille's western section includes the *vellier,* a storeroom, above which was the scriptorium where monks once copied manuscripts slavishly. In 1469, after King Louis XI founded the Knights of St Michael, this hall, which is divided into four by rows of stone columns, became the assembly place for knights of the order. The cloister is situated on top of the western section where, suspended between Heaven and Earth, it provided a haven of tranquillity. Two rows of staggered, slender columns support arches decorated with sculpted foliage and human faces. The cloister was intended to lead to a chapter house, but this was never built.

Mont St-Michel has not always been a place of spiritual peace. Throughout the Middle Ages, the island was the scene of fighting as successive kings and dukes attempted to take control. It was fortified in the early 15th century during the Hundred Years' War, and survived repeated English assaults, and it withstood an onslaught by the Huguenots in 1591. The community of monks steadily declined, however, and when the monastery was dissolved at the time of the French Revolution, there were only seven monks still in residence. During Napoleon's reign, the island, then renamed Ile de la Liberté (Island of Liberty), was used as a prison and remained so until 1863, when it was classified as a national monument. Large portions of both the abbey church and the monastery were restored, and today Mont St-Michel is rivalled only by Paris and Versailles as France's major tourist attraction.

The tradition of Christian worship on Mont St-Michel resumed in 1922, and services have been held in the abbey church ever since. In addition, the spiritual tradition is maintained by the permanent presence of at least one monk, while for many others it offers a place of temporary retreat from the world.

THE ARCHANGEL MICHAEL

Twice a year, on the first Sunday in May and on 29 September, festivals of St Michael draw up to 60 000 pilgrims to Mont St-Michel, where a golden statue of the Archangel Michael, leader of Heaven's armies and protector of the Church on Earth, tops the church spire.

St Michael is often represented as a warrior, sword in hand. In a miniature from *Les Très Riches Heures du Duc de Berry,* an illuminated manuscript produced by the Limbourg brothers for Jean de France, duc de Berry, in the late 14th century, he attacks a winged dragon, symbol of evil, over Mont St-Michel.

MONUMENTAL WONDERS

Granite glory *Hotels, tourist shops (some of which date back to the 15th century) and houses line the winding – and in places stepped – main street of Mont St-Michel, leading to the abbey church and La Merveille. A major tourist attraction, the island also supports a permanent resident population of around 65 people, and at least one monk.*

PLAN OF MONT ST-MICHEL

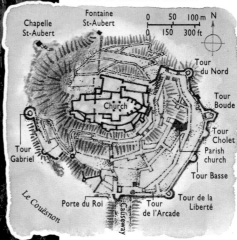

Saviour of pilgrims *The incoming tides around Mont St-Michel have trapped many would-be pilgrims over the centuries. The Virgin Mary came to the rescue of one victim, lifting her clear of the treacherous waters.*

ASSISI: TOWN OF SAINT FRANCIS

The hilltop town of Assisi in Umbria was the home of Saint Francis, 'the most saintly among saints'. Many of its narrow streets, churches and monasteries remain as they were when he lived there in the 12th century.

The Italian region of Umbria is characterised by tranquil countryside in which hilltop settlements are bounded by olive groves and orchards. But one town, Assisi, has a spirit all its own, for it was here that Saint Francis once lived and preached.

To visit the town today is to walk in the footsteps of *Il Poverello* 'little poor man'. Legend merges with reality in the narrow medieval streets of Assisi, where most of the notable buildings in the town and on the wooded slopes of nearby Mount Subasio are connected in some way with the saint's extraordinary life. The magnificent basilica that dominates the town; the Church of San Damiano, near Assisi; the Hermitage of the Carceri and the Church of Santa Maria degli Angeli all mark various stages in the spiritual development of the saint's life.

Giovanni Francesco was born in Assisi in 1182, the son of a rich wool merchant. Enthralled throughout his youth with the heroic idea of becoming a knight, he enlisted as a soldier when he was 20. He fought in the war between Assisi and Perugia but was captured and put in prison for a year. Soon after his release, he left Assisi once more – still in pursuit of his chivalrous dream – on an expedition to southern Italy that was to change his life for ever. No sooner had he arrived at Spoleto, some 25 miles (40km) from Assisi, than, according to legend, a voice in a dream

bade him return home at once. Near Assisi, he felt impelled to stop at the little Church of San Damiano to pray. While prostrate before the crucifix, the figure on the cross seemed to speak to him, urging him to 'Go, Francis, and repair my house, because it is falling into ruin'.

Taking these words literally, Francis sold his horse and some valuable cloth that belonged to his father, and tried to give the proceeds to the priest at the Church of San Damiano. But, reluctant to become involved in a situation that could cause a family quarrel, the priest refused the money. Francis, however, was determined to rid himself of material possessions and left the money in the chapel. Further such acts of generosity led to Francis being brought before a public tribunal instigated by his father, at which Francis renounced his inheritance and all worldly goods.

At the age of 24 Francis had become a beggar and, through his teachings in praise of poverty, joy and a reverence for nature, attracted many disciples. The first Franciscan order, the Friars Minor, was founded in 1209, followed in 1212 by the Order of Saint Clare, named after their first abbess, Clare of Assisi. As the number of 'Poor Clares' quickly grew, the Bishop of Assisi provided them with shelter in San Damiano, where Francis had received his call from God and where Clare spent the rest of her life.

Today, San Damiano is a small monastery where the

Splendid solitude *The Hermitage of the Carceri* (RIGHT), *built in the 15th century, stands in dense woodland on the mountain above Assisi. The small chapel that originally stood here and the many quiet grottoes nearby were favourite retreats of the young saint.*

Holy landscape *The Umbrian hills at dawn* (LEFT), *bathed in a dusky pink glow, may have inspired St Francis's*

Canticle of the Sun, *which praises the Lord 'for brother wind/And for the air and clouds and fair and every kind of weather'.*

ASSISI: TOWN OF SAINT FRANCIS

Franciscan message of simplicity and joy is powerfully present. A copy of the crucifix that allegedly spoke to Francis rests on the altar there; the original resides in the 13th-century Basilica of Saint Clare, where her 'mummified' body can still be seen. The Hermitage of the Carceri, hewn from the rock of nearby Mount Subasio, was used as a woodland retreat in the early days of the order led by Francis, and its sparse furnishings are a testament to the harsh and frugal existence he demanded of his followers.

On 3 October 1226, Francis died at the Portiuncula, a humble chapel in the woods on Mount Subasio. The Benedictines had granted the saint permission to worship there 16 years earlier, with lay preachers, or brethren, who, following his example, had renounced their wealth and dedicated their lives to serving God. When he realised that death was near, Francis begged to be carried to this peaceful retreat 'so that the life of the body should end where the life of the soul began'.

In the 16th century, the ornate Church of Santa Maria degli Angeli, was built around the tiny chapel. This grand edifice, which took 100 years to complete, would have shocked the gentle saint, who believed that 'even the Church should look poor'. The Basilica of Saint Francis erected in his honour would no doubt also have embarrassed him with its splendour. Here, Francis was canonised in 1228 and buried two years later.

Fiery wounds *Francis receives the stigmata* (RIGHT) *in this fresco by Giotto. While meditating on Mount La Verna in 1224, the saint had a vision of the crucified Christ as an angel, who emitted darts of flame, imprinting the five wounds of Christ on Francis' body.*

Tranquil retreat *In the centre of the richly decorated Church of Santa Maria degli Angeli stands the tiny Chapel of the Portiuncula* (ABOVE), *where St Francis prayed for guidance throughout his mission. Local folklore holds that at the moment of his death a flock of skylarks soared into the air from the chapel roof.*

Reverence for life *Saint Francis and his followers lived simply – Franciscan brothers still wear the Umbrian peasant tunic* (RIGHT). *The saint revered all of creation, preaching to animals and birds, while embracing flowers, trees, sun and water as his 'honoured brothers and sisters'. Legend has it that Francis once tamed a wolf, and he is said to have cautioned a friar whose coat was on fire against dousing it, since the water would harm the flames.*

NEUSCHWANSTEIN: A FANTASY FULFILLED

A tribute to the knights of Germanic legend, the castle of Neuschwanstein represents the fusion of the dreams and wealth of King Ludwig of Bavaria and the artistic vision of the composer Richard Wagner.

T he fairytale castle of Neuschwanstein, perched above the rugged gorge of the River Pollak in the Bavarian Alps, is the world's most magical castle. Against a backdrop of dark green fir trees, its ivory towers seem to hang in the air. Neuschwanstein, conceived and constructed by King Ludwig II (1845–86), looks more genuinely 'medieval' than anything built in the Middle Ages. One man's dream transformed into reality by limitless wealth, Neuschwanstein is the epitome of theatrical design.

The roots of Ludwig's dream lay in his childhood. From an early age he loved acting and dressing up and, according to his grandfather Ludwig I, by the age of six he was constructing 'astonishingly good buildings' with toy bricks. Family summers were spent at Hohenschwangau, the ancestral seat of the lords of Schwangau, which Ludwig's father, Maximilian II, had purchased in 1833. Something of a romantic, Maximilian had employed a stage designer rather than an architect to draw up the castle's 'restoration' plans. He had also indulged his taste for legend, and the walls were painted with scenes from various tales, in particular the story of Lohengrin, the Swan Knight, who was reputed to have lived at Hohenschwangau.

With this stimulation, it is small wonder that in 1861, when Ludwig, who was shy, sensitive and had a vivid imagination, heard his first opera, *Lohengrin*, he was overwhelmed. He asked his father to summon the composer, Richard Wagner (1803–83), to re-stage the production just for him. This was the start of a relationship that lasted for the rest of Ludwig's life. When Maximilian died and Ludwig ascended the Bavarian throne in 1864 at the age of 18, he wasted only five weeks before sending for Wagner and establishing him in a Munich villa. He saw their association not just as one of artist and patron but as one of joint creators. Although Ludwig was not musical, he offered money, advice, criticism and inspiration. Through his works Wagner, in return, gave a measure of reality to the dream-world in which Ludwig preferred to exist.

The impulse that attracted Ludwig to Wagner's music also lay behind his desire to construct fabulous palaces, where his dreams could be enacted. The first and finest of these was Neuschwanstein. In the spring of 1867 Ludwig visited the Gothic castle of Wartburg, near Eisenach in Thuringia. It appealed to his love of the theatrical and romantic, and he wanted one exactly like it. On a crag

Romantic fairytale
Inspired by King Ludwig's passionate involvement with operatic productions, Neuschwanstein has served in turn as the inspiration for hundreds of ballet and stage designs. And as the most magical castle in the world, it seems only fitting that it should have been the model for the princess's palace in Walt Disney's Sleeping Beauty.

Stuttgart • GERMANY N

Ulm •
Danube Augsburg •
Munich •

LAKE CONSTANCE

NEUSCHWANSTEIN ■
BAVARIAN ALPS

AUSTRIA

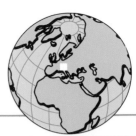

THE LEGEND OF THE SWAN

Lohengrin, which was premiered in Weimar on 28 August 1850, at a performance conducted by Franz Liszt, was Wagner's third major opera after *The Flying Dutchman* (1843) and *Tannhäuser* (1845). There are several versions of the tale on which Wagner (ABOVE RIGHT) based his opera, the earliest of which dates from a 13th-century collection of stories entitled *Parzival*.

According to Wagner's interpretation, Lohengrin, the Swan Knight, sails along the River Schelde to Antwerp in a boat drawn by a swan. There, he becomes the champion of a noble lady in distress, Else, the princess of Brabant. He eventually marries Else, on condition that she never asks

him his name or origin. But, on their wedding night, she breaks her promise and he answers her question, whereupon the swan reappears and Lohengrin departs as mysteriously as he had arrived.

A mural (ABOVE LEFT) depicting Lohengrin's arrival in Antwerp still hangs above a stove in the living room at Neuschwanstein. Ludwig's taste for the theatrical led him on one occasion to stage this scene on the Alpsee, a lake near the castle. His cousin, playing Lohengrin, was transported across the water in a boat drawn by an artificial swan, while an orchestra played the appropriate Wagnerian accompaniment.

1 mile (1.6km) from Hohenschwangau was a ruined watchtower. This, Ludwig decided, was to be the site of Neuschwanstein, his 'new home of the swan', and on 5 September 1869, the foundation stone of the main block, or *Palas*, was laid.

Following his father's practice, Ludwig commissioned Christian Jank, the scenic artist at the Court Theatre, to design the castle's exterior. Jank provided the king with fantastic sketches from which a host of painters and craftsmen built what amounted to a series of sets for Wagner's operas *Lohengrin, Tannhäuser* and *Parsifal*.

Neuschwanstein is essentially Lohengrin's castle. Plans for the *Palas*, which was originally conceived as a three-storey Gothic fortress, were gradually modified until it became the five-storey Romanesque structure Ludwig thought most appropriate to the legend. The inspiration for the courtyard came from the design of the Antwerp castle courtyard in Act II of an actual production of *Lohengrin*.

The inspiration for the Singers' Hall came from the opera *Tannhäuser*. Tannhäuser was a 13th-century German

poet who, according to legend, found his way into the Venusberg, a subterranean world of love and beauty that was presided over by the goddess Venus. One scene of Wagner's *Tannhäuser* was set in the Singers' Hall at Wartburg, so Ludwig commissioned Jank to reproduce it at Neuschwanstein. Ludwig also wanted to create a spectacular 'grotto of Venus' at Neuschwanstein, but a suitable site could not be found and he had to be content with a small, indoor version, albeit complete with a cascading waterfall and an artificial moon. (The outdoor grotto was built some 15 miles/24km to the east of Neuschwanstein at Linderhof, once a hunting lodge, but transformed by Ludwig into a miniature Versailles-style chateau.)

As the king grew older, the castle of Lohengrin and Tannhäuser became the Grail Castle of *Parsifal*. Lohengrin's father, Parsifal, was a knight of the Round Table who was given a sight of the Holy Grail. Ludwig's designs for a Hall of the Grail (conceived as early as the mid 1860s) became a reality in the Throne Room at Neuschwanstein. The room is dominated by a flight of white marble steps leading to

Musical madness *The ornate Singers' Hall, in which Wagner concerts are still held every September, gives some indication of the castle's exuberant interiors. The hall is decorated with painted scenes from the Parsifal story, and King Ludwig's obsession with the legend extends to the castle's Throne Room.*

King of dreams *Ludwig's obsession with Lohengrin dominated his life. He addressed letters to his future wife Sophie 'My dear Else', and on occasion dressed as the knight. After his death, the costume was found among his effects. However, a formal portrait, completed in 1887, shows him in more traditional attire.*

an empty platform – it never held a throne. In 1883–84, a year after Wagner's *Parsifal* – his last work – was premiered, painted episodes from the opera were also added to the walls of the Singers' Hall.

Ludwig spared no expense in creating his fantasies, and the finest craftsmen, painters, sculptors and woodcarvers were employed at Neuschwanstein and elsewhere. His building projects drained the state treasury and caused him to neglect his official duties. When news of his increasingly eccentric behaviour – he had begun to take regular midnight rides in a gilded sleigh and once invited his horse to dine with him – reached his ministers, they hatched a plot to have him declared insane. He was taken from Neuschwanstein and imprisoned in the castle of Berg on Lake Starnberg. Two days later his body and that of his doctor were found floating in the lake.

Ludwig wrote to Wagner: 'When we two are long dead, our work will still be a shining example to distant posterity.' The lasting allure of Neuschwanstein is the dramatic proof of the truth of his prediction.

SACRED SHRINE OF DELPHI

Beneath the dramatic cliffs of Mount Parnassus lies Delphi, the most famous sacred site of ancient Greece. Thousands of people journeyed here from faraway places to consult the oracle of Apollo, whose high priestess would foretell the future from a self-induced trance.

T he most powerful and respected oracle in the ancient world was to be found in central Greece in the Temple of Apollo at Delphi. To the ancient Greeks, Delphi was the centre of the world. According to legend, Zeus, father of the gods, released two eagles from opposite ends of the world and where they met – at Delphi – was judged the centre and marked by a stone called the *omphalos*, or navel. Around 1400 BC, Delphi was a sacred site dedicated to the earth goddess Gaia. Legend relates that the place was guarded by a large python which Apollo, son of Zeus, killed. Apollo then set up his oracle on the site, with a priestess, known as the Pythia, as the medium. In the seventh and sixth centuries BC, during the height of the oracle's popularity, thousands of pilgrims, rich and poor, made the journey to consult Apollo through the Pythia.

The journey to the site of Delphi, situated 1870ft (570m) above sea level on the southern slopes of Mount Parnassus, was arduous. Some pilgrims travelled on foot along the road from Athens. Others came by ship, disembarking at a port (now known as Itéa) on the north coast of the Gulf of Corinth, and making their way across a broad plain to Mount Parnassus. Once there, they would skirt the mountainside, and follow the Sacred Way to the Temple of Apollo.

In the inner sanctum of the temple, the Pythia sat on a sacred gold tripod placed over a deep crack in the earth. She was a local, middle-aged woman who would utter the oracle through a series of frenzied and incoherent sounds made while she was in a trance-like state, induced by chewing bay leaves or by inhaling the toxic volcanic vapours that rose from the chasm at her feet.

Questioners were first required to purify themselves in the waters of the Castalian spring nearby. Then followed a ritual in which a goat was sprinkled with cold water; if the animal trembled all over it could be sacrificed and the god petitioned. The pilgrim paid his fee and presented his question, written on a tablet, to the attendant male priest, who then submitted it to the Pythia. Her garbled reply, delivered in a voice not her own, was interpreted by a priest, who gave the answer in verse to the supplicant. At the height of the oracle's popularity, three priestesses were needed to cope with all the queries.

The Delphic oracle was consulted on political matters,

Dramatic view *The columns of the Temple of Apollo at Delphi* (ABOVE) *stand below a magnificent theatre cut into the mountainside.*

GREECE

Volos •

MT PARNASSUS ▲

DELPHI ■

GULF OF CORINTH

Athens •

PELOPONNESE

MEDITERRANEAN SEA

N

Circular shrine *Many Greek city-states built temples and treasuries at Delphi as an act of civic pride. This circular temple or tholos (*LEFT*), a short distance from the main site, was built by the Athenians in the fourth century* BC *as part of the sanctuary of Athena the Provident.*

Purifying waters *The Castalian spring at Delphi (*ABOVE*) was used for ritual purification by supplicants before they approached the oracle.*

SACRED SHRINE OF DELPHI

THE SANCTUARY AT DELPHI

The oracle was housed in the Temple of Apollo, which was reached via the Sacred Way. The small buildings below the temple were treasuries, built to hold the offerings made to Apollo.

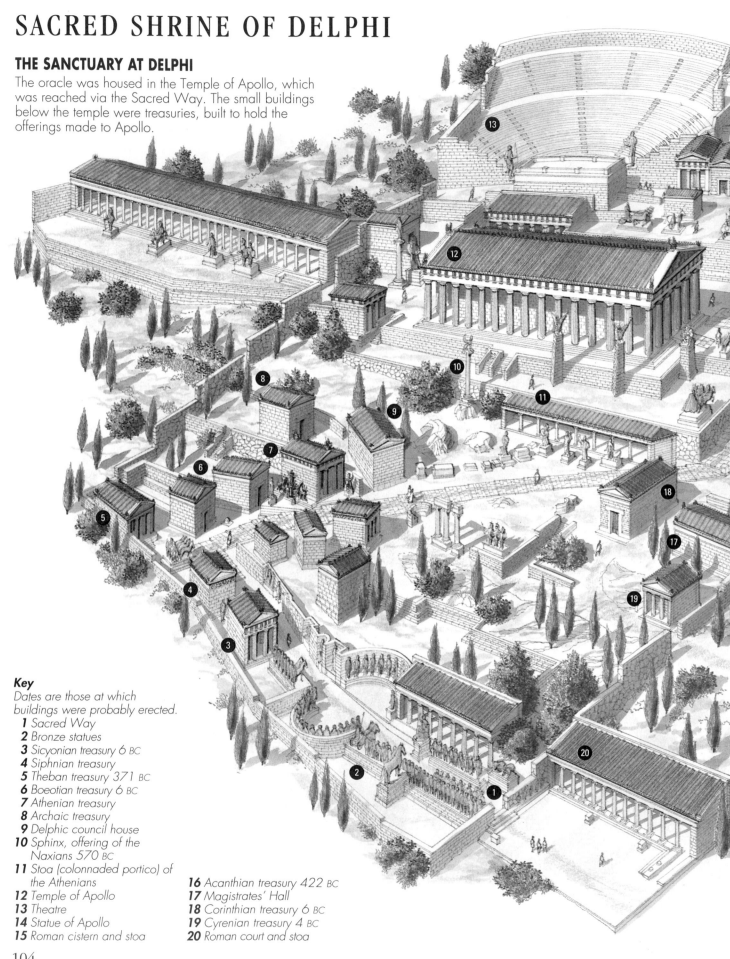

Key

Dates are those at which buildings were probably erected.

 1 *Sacred Way*
 2 *Bronze statues*
 3 *Sicyonian treasury 6 BC*
 4 *Siphnian treasury*
 5 *Theban treasury 371 BC*
 6 *Boeotian treasury 6 BC*
 7 *Athenian treasury*
 8 *Archaic treasury*
 9 *Delphic council house*
10 *Sphinx, offering of the Naxians 570 BC*
11 *Stoa (colonnaded portico) of the Athenians*
12 *Temple of Apollo*
13 *Theatre*
14 *Statue of Apollo*
15 *Roman cistern and stoa*
16 *Acanthian treasury 422 BC*
17 *Magistrates' Hall*
18 *Corinthian treasury 6 BC*
19 *Cyrenian treasury 4 BC*
20 *Roman court and stoa*

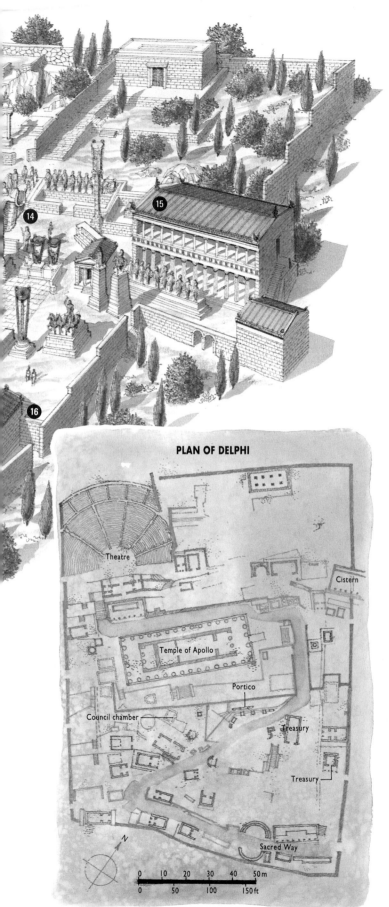

The navel stone *Apollo and his sister Artemis flank the navel stone on a vase in the British Museum* (ABOVE). *The fourth-century* BC *navel stone* (LEFT) *is in the Delphi Museum, and a Roman version is on site.*

PLAN OF DELPHI

Theatre

Cistern

Temple of Apollo

Portico

Council chamber

Treasury

Treasury

Sacred Way

N

0 10 20 30 40 50 m
0   50   100   150 ft

particularly the establishment of Greek colonies, as well as on everyday issues such as marriage, fertility or money problems. Sometimes the oracle's pronouncements were straightforward; for instance, Socrates was told that he was the wisest man in Greece. However, many of the oracle's replies were notoriously ambiguous. King Croesus of Lydia asked the oracle what would happen if he attacked Persia. The cryptic answer was that a great empire would fall. The king went ahead and attacked Persia, but it was his own empire that was destroyed.

Around the fifth century BC, the oracle's reputation for impartiality began to decline as its interpreters increasingly allied themselves with various city-states, such as Athens and Sparta. In the second century BC, Rome extended its rule as far as Delphi and the oracle's influence waned even more. When the Emperor Julian consulted the oracle in AD 360, it apparently replied: 'Say to the king that the beautiful temple has fallen into ruins; Apollo has no roof over his head; the bay leaves are silent and the prophetic springs and fountains are dead.'

The oracle at Delphi was officially closed by the Christian Emperor Theodosius in AD 385, the cult of Apollo ousted by a new religion. The site gradually became buried and a village was built on top of it. In 1892, however, the entire village had to be removed, and the villagers rehoused, so that the French archaeologist, Théophile Homolle, could begin the excavations that revealed the ruins that can be seen at the site today.

MAJESTIC MYCENAE

Perched on a hilltop in the Peloponnese are the remains of a site said to be the oldest city in Greece and the fortress–citadel of Agamemnon, the warrior king of Homeric legend.

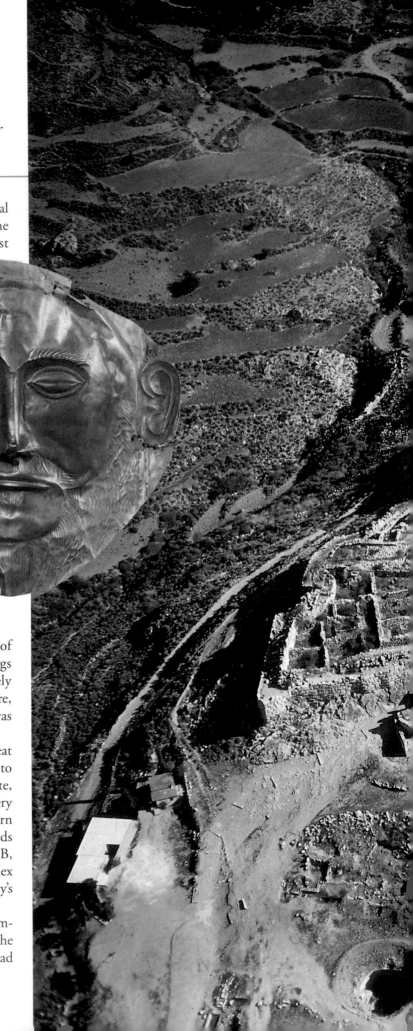

One of the most sensational events in archaeological history occurred on 6 December 1876 when the German adventurer and amateur archaeologist Heinrich Schliemann uncovered the first of five treasure-filled shaft tombs in the site now known as Grave Circle A at Mycenae. Excavation of the graves revealed 19 bodies, surrounded by gold jewellery, bronze weapons inlaid with gold and silver, gold breast plates, and gold and silver cups. Most splendid of all, in Shaft Grave V, Schliemann found a magnificent golden mask, which he was sure was the death mask of Agamemnon. According to the Greek epic poet Homer, writing in the eighth century BC, Agamemnon was king of Achaea (which has been identified as Mycenae) and leader of the Greek forces against Troy. Schliemann at once telegraphed the Greek king the thrilling message: 'I have gazed upon the face of Agamemnon.'

Schliemann's excavations uncovered a vast quantity of rich and extraordinarily ornate treasures. His findings showed that the Mycenaean aristocracy was immensely wealthy which, along with the city's advanced architecture, fuelled the widely held belief that the Mycenaean age was one of exceptional achievement.

The city of Mycenae itself was at the heart of a great civilisation that lasted for about 500 years from 1600 to 1100 BC and replaced the Minoan culture, based on Crete, as the dominant force in the Aegean and beyond. Pottery from Mycenae has been found as far afield as southern Italy, Cyprus, Egypt, Syria and Palestine, while hundreds of clay tablets, incised with a script known as Linear B, record the details of the rigid social hierarchy and complex economic system upon which the foundations of the city's wealth were laid.

Schliemann's assumption that he had located Agamemnon's burial site was probably based on the writings of the second-century AD Greek geographer Pausanias, who had

The first city *Mycenae is the oldest city on the Greek mainland: only Knossos, capital of the Minoan civilisation on Crete, is older. Mycenae was first excavated in the 1840s, but it was the work of Heinrich Schliemann, who went to the site in 1874, that yielded the most spectacular finds. Schliemann was convinced that the mask of beaten gold* (INSET) *he unearthed was the death mask of Agamemnon, the king who, according to Homer's* Iliad, *had sacked the city of Troy. Schliemann, obsessed with Homer's epic since childhood, had previously excavated Troy in 1871.*

107

MAJESTIC MYCENAE

stated that Agamemnon was buried inside the city and that his murderers, Clytemnestra and Aegisthus, were interred outside the walls in beehive tombs. The shaft graves of Grave Circle A are indeed situated inside the walls of Mycenae, under the market place, but modern methods have dated them to around 1600 BC. This date has also been attributed to the 'mask of Agamemnon', which proved to be only one of several similar gold masks later unearthed, most of which are too stylised to have been death masks in the generally accepted sense. More importantly, the Trojan War, if it happened in reality rather than in Homer's imagination, occurred around 1200 BC, some 400 years after the bodies and treasures in the shaft graves at Mycenae were buried.

The citadel of Mycenae occupied a powerful strategic position, commanding the plain of Argos and controlling the mountain passes as far north as Corinth. Its massive limestone walls, made of irregular blocks to a thickness of 16ft (5m), became known as Cyclopean, since later observers thought that only the mythical one-eyed giant Cyclops could have built them. At the main entrance to the city is the Lion Gate, constructed around 1260 BC. Here two large stone lions are carved above a lintel that measures 16ft (5m) long, 3ft (90cm) high and 8ft (2.4m) deep.

From the gate a road leads to the royal palace, two blocks of buildings linked by corridors of storerooms. Inside, painted plaster floors and elaborate frescoes on the walls, similar to those found in Cretan palaces, show that the Mycenaeans must have had some knowledge of Minoan architecture. Around the palace are clustered the houses of lesser-ranking citizens, including one, the so-called House of Columns, which was three storeys high.

Outside the citadel is Grave Circle B, a series of beehive tombs which are not as old as the shafts of Grave Circle A. These consist of up to 35 circular courses of huge stones, one on top of another, which became progressively smaller in the manner of an old-fashioned beehive. This type of grave was built over a period of about 200 years from 1400 to 1200 BC, usually into the side of a hill. A huge doorway at the end of a long passage gave entrance to the tomb; after each burial the doorway was walled up and the passage filled with soil. The most spectacular beehive tombs at Mycenae are the so-called Treasury of Atreus (Agamemnon's father) and the Tomb of Clytemnestra. But although they date from the 'right' period, there is no real evidence that these are their graves. These tombs may have contained treasures to rival those of the shaft graves, but centuries of looting have taken their toll and all that remains of the Treasury of Atreus is the basic structure.

The Mycenaean civilisation ended abruptly around 1150 BC when the city was either destroyed or abandoned: no one knows why. It was the last great early Greek culture and with its demise the country was plunged into the so-called Dark Ages: a period that only came to an end some 600 years later with the flowering of the Classical period.

THE WRITTEN WORD

The Mycenaeans used an early form of Greek script, known to modern scholars as Linear B. This remained unintelligible for more than 3000 years, until in 1952, after three years' work, the British architect Michael Ventris (LEFT) deciphered the ancient code. Employing methods used to crack enemy codes during World War II, he analysed the Linear B signs and symbols on some 400 clay tablets (BELOW) found at the Mycenaean site of Pylos in the Peloponnese.

By making notes of repeated signs, Ventris was able to construct a grid of consonants and vowels – but he still had no idea what language he was dealing with. He decided to work on the theory that Linear B was an archaic form of Greek, and the tablets made sense.

0		50		100		150		200
0			200		400			600 ft

THE GOLDEN CITY OF MYCENAE

The city of Mycenae, described by Homer as 'well-built', 'broad-streeted' and 'golden', combined the functions of royal palace, home for the king's subjects and graveyard. It was also a fortress, perched on a hill, surrounded by thick, impenetrable walls and commanding a large area of the Peloponnese. The royal palace itself was situated at the top of the hill to dominate surrounding, lesser buildings.

Key
1 Lion Gate
2 Market place (on top of the site of the shaft graves of Grave Circle A)
3 Royal palace
4 Houses for high-ranking soldiers and court officials

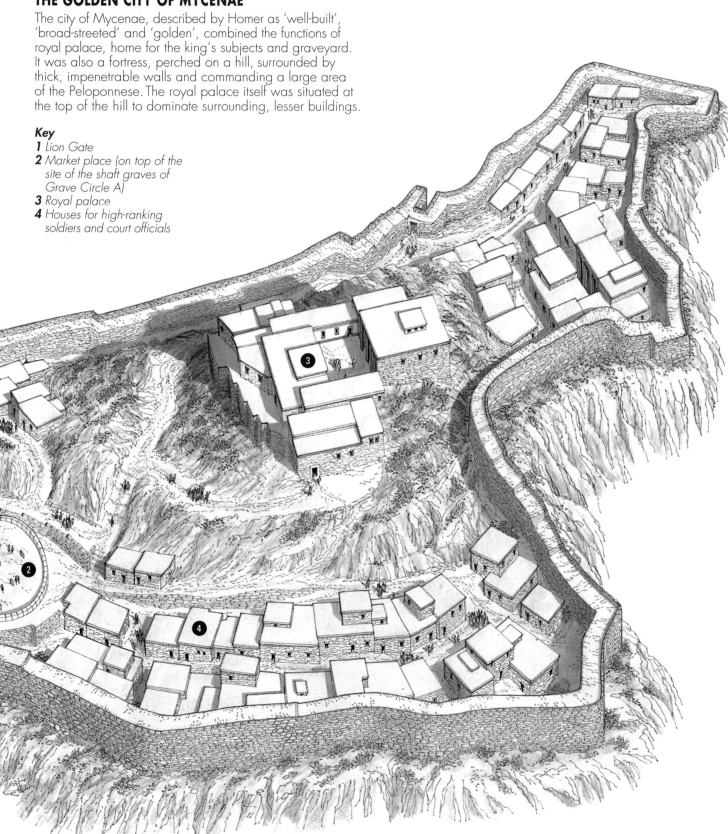

THE PALACE OF KNOSSOS

*The first major Aegean civilisation flourished on the Greek island of Crete
in 1500 BC. The zenith of its achievements is represented by the spectacular
palace complex at Knossos which was excavated and then reconstructed early
in the 20th century by a distinguished British archaeologist.*

The ancient city of Knossos, lying 2½ miles (4km) inland from the north shore of Crete, was the centre of one of the great civilisations of the prehistoric Aegean world. According to legend, the palace at Knossos was the home of King Minos and his daughter, Ariadne. When the British archaeologist Arthur Evans was seeking an identifying label for his discoveries, he settled on 'Minoan', a name that has been used ever since to describe the people who lived at Knossos.

The Minoans seem to have arrived on Crete in about 7000 BC, possibly from Asia Minor (now Turkey), but this is not certain. The splendour of the Minoan palaces (there was one at Phaistos in the south of the island, and another at Mallia on the north coast) indicates that these people were rich and probably powerful, and the absence of any obvious fortification suggests they were also peaceful. The number and size of the palace storerooms testify to the importance of commerce in Minoan life, as does the network of roadways. The paintings at Knossos, in particular a remarkable fresco of an athlete somersaulting over the back of a bull in a mysterious ceremony, are vivid illustrations of the perilous sports and rituals for which the city's inhabitants have become famous.

The Minoans built a series of magnificent palaces towards the end of the third millennium BC, each of which was destroyed by an earthquake and rebuilt on its own ruins. During the following millennium, the growth of Knossos and the spread of Minoan influence were spectacular, culminating in a pinnacle of achievement around

*Raging bull The north
entrance to the palace is a
steep open-air ramp with
bastions on either side,
each with a colonnaded
verandah on top* (RIGHT).
*The restored west bastion
is decorated with a replica
of a relief fresco showing
a bull rampaging through
an olive grove. Its theme is
derived from the Minoan
cult of the bull, which also
accounts for the bulls' horn
symbols* (BELOW) *that top
many of the exterior walls
at Knossos.*

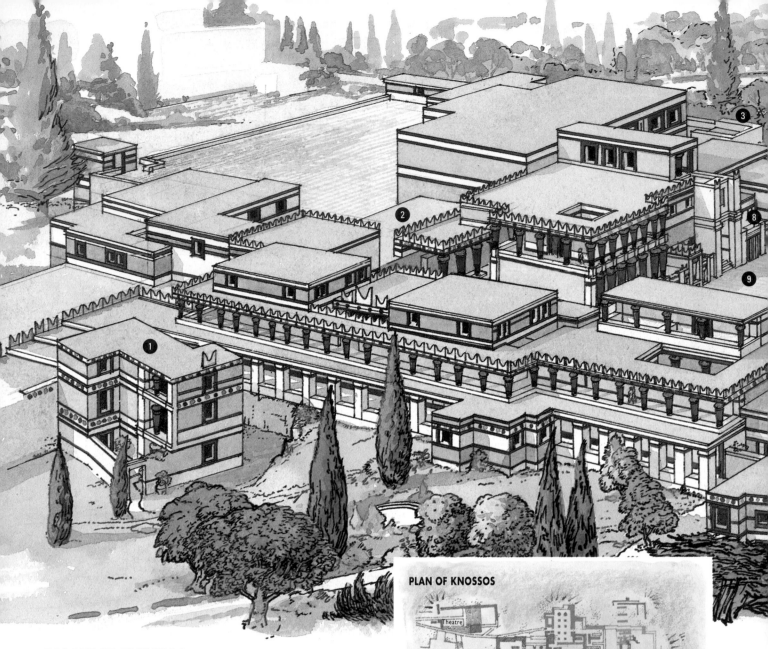

PALACE OF KNOSSOS

Key

1 & 11 *Entrance houses*
2 *Storerooms*
3 *Theatre*
4 *Custom house*
5 *Workshops*

6 *King's apartment*
7 *Grand staircase*
8 *Throne room*
9 *Central courtyard*
10 *Queen's apartment*

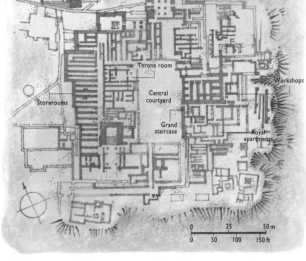

PLAN OF KNOSSOS

1500 BC. The ruins of the palace of King Minos at Knossos provide outstanding evidence of the artistic, architectural and engineering skills of this island people.

The flowering of Minoan culture was curtailed just over 100 years later when a devastating volcanic eruption on the neighbouring island of Santorini reduced Knossos to ruins, resulting in a swift decline in Minoan influence. Not until the beginning of the 20th century did comprehensive archaeological excavations reveal once again the splendour of the ancient palace of Knossos.

The palace is a vast construction of private apartments and public halls, storerooms and bathrooms, corridors and staircases chaotically grouped around a rectangular courtyard. Their arrangement makes it easy to understand how the legend of the Minotaur imprisoned in the labyrinth became attached to this rambling building. Unlike the ancient Greeks, the Minoans were not masters of

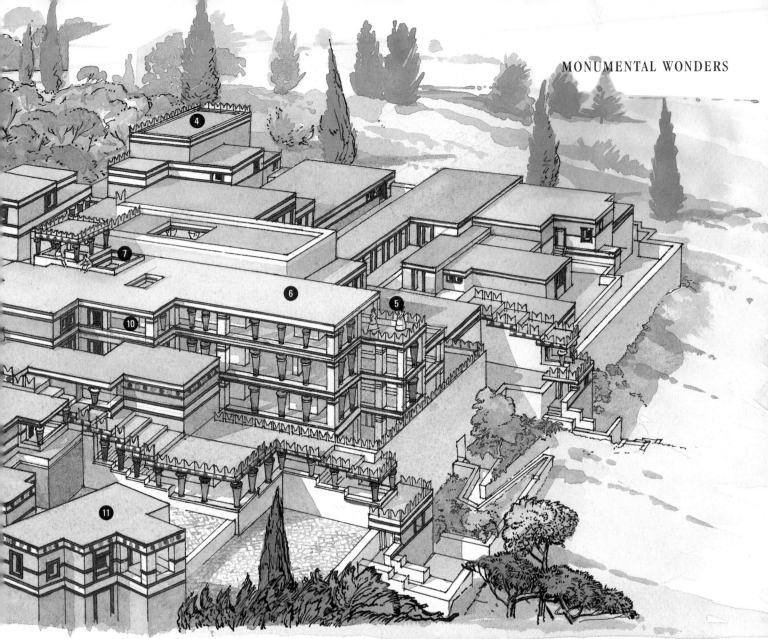

Regal comfort *The Queen's Hall, as envisaged by Arthur Evans, is probably the epitome of Minoan comfort, complete with a bath, running water, a sophisticated drainage system and a wooden-seated flushing lavatory. Vivid frescoes and spirals decorate the walls, as do lively dolphins – the Minoan symbol for joy.*

PROUD PIONEER

Sir Arthur John Evans, who excavated Knossos and helped bring to light a lost civilisation, was born into a prosperous family in 1851. He studied at Oxford University in England and returned there at the age of 31 to become the Keeper of the Ashmolean Museum. Evans had a passion for archaeology and, while travelling in Crete in 1894, visited the Hill of Kephala at Knossos, which was still virtually intact apart from a few trial trenches dug by the Cretan archaeologist Minos Kalokairinos in 1878. Fascinated by the area, Evans eventually bought the archaeological site in 1899.

Evans started work at Knossos in 1900. By the end of the year he had excavated the entire west wing of the palace of King Minos and was ready to start digging the east wing. Within two years the throne room, the central court, the grand staircase and the domestic quarters had all been uncovered. Work on the site continued until 1932. Nine years later Evans died, having dedicated 50 years to researching the Minoan civilisation. His discoveries inspired great interest on account of their antiquity because, as Evans wrote: 'The work of the spade has now brought out the essential and underlying truth of the old traditions that made Knossos the most ancient centre of civilised life in Greece and, with it, of our whole continent.'

Unearthed history *Sir Arthur Evans was the subject of a painting (detail shown* RIGHT*) by Sir William Richmond, presented to the Ashmolean Museum in 1907.*

Among Evans's many major discoveries at Knossos were dozens of huge earthenware jars, called pithoi, *many taller than a man, found in the cellars of the palace and used to store olive oil. The jars were tightly closed with an individual seal denoting its owner.*

symmetry: the wings, halls and porticoes of their palaces often look as if they were simply tacked on where they were needed, regardless of form or balanced design.

Each individual apartment, however, has an integral beauty, and many are decorated with highly sophisticated frescoes incorporating graceful figures that give an intriguing glimpse of life at the Minoan court. Slender-waisted young men dressed in kilts are shown enjoying sports such as boxing and bull-leaping. Vivacious ladies with elaborately curled hair are also depicted taking part in bull-leaping. These frescoes were influenced by other crafts in which the Minoans excelled, such as carving, metalwork, jewellery-making and pottery.

There are several entrances to the palace, and it seems that the rooms were arranged so that places devoted to cult practices were situated in the west wing and the living quarters in the east wing, which is cut into the hillside above the level of the courtyard. One end of the east wing houses the complex of rooms and corridors that made up the royal apartments, while at the other were the workshops belonging to the carpenters, potters, stonemasons and jewellers who provided the comforts and luxuries evident in the palace.

The royal apartments are reached via the grand staircase, a masterpiece of sophistication and artistry. The black and red pillars tapering inwards towards the base enclose a light-well that not only illuminates the apartments below, but also provides a bellows of sorts for the palace's natural air-conditioning. As the warm air rose up the stairwell, the doors of the King's Hall could be opened and closed to regulate the flow of cooler air – scented with wild thyme and lemon – from the colonnade outside. In winter, the doors could be closed, and portable hearths were brought in to provide heat.

The west wing was the ceremonial and administrative centre of the palace. Three walled pits at the western entrance were used in religious ceremonies, when the blood and bones of sacrificed animals, together with offerings of honey, wine, oil and milk, were returned to the earth from which they had sprung. The most splendid feature of the west wing was the throne room, still containing the high-backed gypsum throne guarded by painted griffins. The room could accommodate about 16 people for meetings with the king. Outside is a great porphyry basin, placed there by Arthur Evans, who believed that Minoans used it in purification rituals before entering the innermost chamber of the palace. The placing of the bowl is one small act in the extraordinary reconstruction of the palace of Knossos as it was in 1500 BC, visualised by a British archaeologist seeking to bring back to life the golden age of the Minoan Empire.

BULL WORSHIP

A young man somersaults over the back of a bull, while a young girl waits to catch him; at the same time, a second girl grasps the bull's horns and prepares to leap. Such scenes of bulls and bull-leapers are found in wall paintings and on numerous Minoan seal-stones, bronzes and ivories. The significance of this sport in Minoan culture is not understood, but it may have been part of a religious ritual, at the end of which the bull was sacrificed. There is no evidence of bull worship in Minoan culture, but to this race of people the bull was possibly a symbol of virility.

Bulls and bull-leaping may have been the source of the myth of the Minotaur. According to legend, King Minos kept the Minotaur, half man, half bull, in a labyrinth and required Athens, then subject to Minos, to send seven youths and seven maidens every year to be sacrificed to the monster. Theseus, prince of Athens, accompanied the victims to Crete and, helped by Minos' daughter Ariadne, succeeded in killing the Minotaur.

King's way The royal road linking the palace of King Minos with the Little Palace, a notable Minoan building a short distance away from the main palace, is almost certainly the oldest road in Europe. It was built between 3000 and 1100 BC.

HAGIA SOPHIA: A BYZANTINE MARVEL

This architectural masterpiece has had a profound influence on Christian and Islamic architecture.

For 1400 years, the dome of Hagia Sophia – the words mean holy wisdom in Greek – dominated the spiritual life of the city of Constantinople (present-day Istanbul). This massive construction of semi-domes, buttresses and outbuildings is offset by four elegant minarets, one at each corner, for Hagia Sophia was conceived and built as a Christian church, then converted by one of the world's most gifted architects to serve as an Islamic mosque.

Constantinople, capital of the Byzantine Empire, took up the mantle of guardianship of classical civilisation after the sacking of Rome by the Visigoths in AD 410. Successive emperors determined that the city – poised at the crossroads between Europe and Asia, on the Bosporus – should be the religious, artistic and commercial capital of the world. In AD 532 the Emperor Justinian, renowned for his many ambitious construction programmes, commissioned Hagia Sophia.

No one had attempted to build such a large church before. Justinian chose as his architects two Greek mathematicians, Anthemius of Talles and Isidorus of Miletus, in the belief that only men trained in mathematics would be able to calculate the curves and angles required in the domes, to assess the strains and stresses involved and to decide where to place buttresses and supports. He imported beautiful materials from all over the empire, from Greece and Rome, Turkey and North Africa. An army of 10 000 sculptors, masons, carpenters and mosaicists took five years to fashion red and green porphyry, yellow and white marble, gold and silver into the most magnificent church in Christendom.

Justinian is reputed to have exclaimed, upon entering Hagia Sophia, 'O Solomon, I have surpassed thee!' The interior is a masterpiece of light and space: a smooth marble floor; walls faced with glistening mosaics and panels of marble; deeply cut marble columns of so many hues that the contemporary historian Procopius likened them to a meadow full of flowers in bloom. Resplendent above these treasures is the dome, some 100ft (30m) in diameter, constructed using special bricks imported from the Greek island of Rhodes. Forty ribs extend from its centre to its base, which is cut by 40 windows like a crown studded by diamonds of light. Around the dome, to help spread and support its load in addition to overcoming the

Golden glory *Daylight pours through arched windows cut high in the balconies and dome of Hagia Sophia and is reflected by decorative precious metals, icons, hangings and mosaics. The interior is bathed in a mellow glow.*

External change *Sinan was unable to alter Hagia Sophia's exterior, save for the addition of four minarets from which muezzins called the faithful to prayer.*

117

Founding father *Under Justinian, the Byzantine Empire reached a zenith of artistic endeavour and military expansion. Perhaps his most lasting achievement, however, was to set in process the codification of Roman law, which influenced the entire course of legal history.*

A sixth-century mosaic from the church of San Vitale in Ravenna depicts the emperor with members of his court.

Hidden clue *It was rumoured that a number of Hagia Sophia's 107 columns were plundered from ancient ruins throughout the Byzantine Empire. Those in the gallery, 24 in all, were new, however, and incorporate among the carved acanthus leaves around their tops the monograms of Justinian and his wife Theodora.*

problem of how to sit a circular cupola on a square base, the architects devised smaller half-domes, beyond which are even smaller half-domes. The spaces between these were filled with elaborate plasterwork, then both dome and ceiling were covered in gold to reflect every polished surface of the interior.

Hagia Sophia was the centre of the eastern Christian world for almost 1000 years, but it was beset by problems from the start. Only 21 years after its completion it was damaged by an earth tremor and had to be partially rebuilt. Gradually its riches were plundered. In 1204 soldiers of the Fourth Crusade on their way to Jerusalem and hostile to the Eastern Orthodox Church (the formal split between the churches of Rome and Constantinople had been acknowledged in 1054) stripped the interior of the building. The last Christian service was held on the evening of 28 May 1453, when Emperor Constantine XI, tears in his eyes, took communion there. Although only a few hours later the Ottoman Turks stormed the city's walls, their commander Mehmet II expressly forbade his troops to desecrate the church.

Hagia Sophia was converted into a mosque in the 16th century under the direction of Sinan Pasha (1489–1588), one of the Islamic world's greatest architects, whose masterpieces include Topkapı palace and the mosques he built for the emperors Suleiman the Magnificent and Selim II. In accordance with Islamic tradition, Sinan painted over most of the representational frescoes and mosaics, replacing them with discs bearing texts from the Koran, and removed any remaining Christian statues.

In 1934 Hagia Sophia was stripped of any religious significance and is today a museum. To the many visitors drawn here each year, however, it remains a spiritual oasis in a bustling metropolis. And, although the interior is bare, its spatial magnificence is undiminished. In its cool marble floors, elegant columns and great dome rising towards the heavens, Hagia Sophia retains something of Justinian's vision.

Key
1 Aisle 2 Side gallery
3 Tympanum 4 Imperial pew
5 Apse 6 Prayer niche (mihrab)
facing Mecca 7 Pulpit
8 Side gallery 9 Aisle
10 Decorated floor where
Byzantine emperor's chair
formerly stood 11 Nave
12 Outer narthex
13 Narthex 14 Imperial
door 15 West gallery

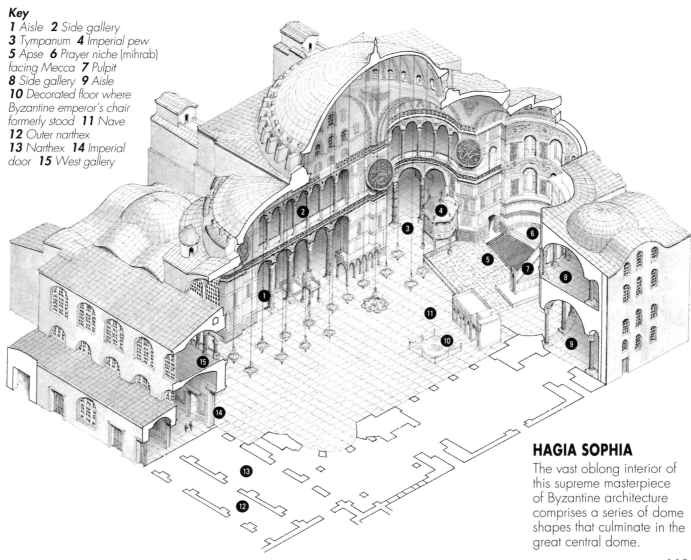

HAGIA SOPHIA
The vast oblong interior of this supreme masterpiece of Byzantine architecture comprises a series of dome shapes that culminate in the great central dome.

TROY: CITY OF MYTHS

The most evocative of legends, that of the siege and sack of Troy, had for many centuries compelled adventurers to go in search of the devastated city. But this fabled site eluded discovery until, in 1871, a German businessman and archaeologist discovered King Priam's treasures. Or did he?

T o identify the reality behind a myth is the spur that motivates both explorers and archaeologists. The legend of Troy – the city besieged during the Trojan Wars – was no exception, but its precise location and even its very existence had never been satisfactorily proved until the late 19th century.

Heinrich Schliemann, a German businessman, had as a child conceived a romantic passion for the story of Troy, and decided to devote the fortune he had made to locating the lost city. He knew that there had been an ancient settlement of some kind called Troy because it was mentioned in reliable historical sources, but it had not been recorded by name since AD 355.

After finding no trace of Troy at the site of his first dig in Turkey, Schliemann transferred his efforts to a man-made mound just outside the town of Hissarlik nearby. Local folklore supported this decision so, assisted by his young Greek wife and a team of about 100 local workmen, Schliemann began excavations there in 1871 and

Lost city *The ruins believed to be those of the Troy of Helen and Paris are surprisingly modest, measuring just 450ft by 600ft (137m by 183m), an area that would have provided barely enough space for 1000 inhabitants. This hardly tallies with the description in Homer's epic poem,* The Iliad, *which tells of a royal palace, wide streets, temples and massive walls studded with towers.*

Greeks bearing gifts *According to legend the Trojans were tricked by their Greek foes into accepting the gift of a huge wooden horse* (LEFT), *little suspecting that a band of Greek warriors was hidden inside. Once night had fallen and the Trojans were asleep, the Greeks climbed down from the horse and unbarred the city gates. The Greek army entered and massacred its enemy.*

PLAN OF TROY

N

Great Hall

Palace

Temple of Athena

Fortified gateway

Tower

Theatre

Sanctuary

Theatre

Pillar Hall

0   20   40   60m
0   50   100   150 ft

Early Bronze Age

Late Bronze Age

Classical Greek and Roman

121

TROY: CITY OF MYTHS

continued until his death almost 20 years later. (He did, however, leave the site of Troy during this period to excavate the Greek site of Mycenae.)

Schliemann was an enthusiastic but highly unsystematic amateur archaeologist. During his digging he unwittingly destroyed evidence that should have been carefully sifted through, and he also removed objects from site without documenting where they came from. He did, however, unearth some ancient fortifications and numerous weapons and utensils. Schliemann was convinced he had found Troy. Many ancient historians were sceptical, but his supporters included W. E. Gladstone, the British prime minister, who was himself an accomplished classicist.

With the help of Wilhelm Dörpfeld, a qualified archaeologist, the complicated history and structure of the city gradually began to emerge. Schliemann and Dörpfeld unearthed nine principal layers, each representing a new city of Troy built upon an older predecessor. They numbered them, starting with Troy I for the oldest, and ending with Troy IX for a city constructed in Roman times. Later archaeologists have refined this system, recognising many

__Ancient ruins__ A hundred Turkish workmen helped uncover the ruins of Troy at Hissarlik (ABOVE). *About 160 miles (250km) south of the site lies the town of Izmir (Smyrna), where the poet Homer, who told the story of Troy in* The Iliad, *was born 3000 years ago.*

__Caesar's legacy__ The best-preserved structure of the nine cities of Troy identified by Schliemann is the amphitheatre on the south side of the site (RIGHT). *The legacy of the rebuilding programme initiated by Julius Caesar in the first century BC, it forms part of the last and largest city of Troy – Troy IX.*

subsidiary layers that bring the total to 46 levels. Although Schliemann originally believed Troy II to be the city of his quest, Troy VIIa has since been identified as the Troy he sought. This layer was destroyed by fire, and the condition of human bones found there suggests that the citizens met a violent death around 1250 BC, the date generally accepted by scholars for the fall of the city.

The epic struggle between the Greeks and the Trojans had begun when Paris, the most handsome of mortal men, was asked to decide which of three goddesses – Hera, Athena and Aphrodite – was the most beautiful. Aphrodite won because she had bribed Paris with the reward of the love of any woman he chose in the world. He picked Helen, wife of King Menelaus of Sparta, one of the most powerful Greek states, and with Aphrodite's help, Paris escaped with his reward. The choice of Troy for his sanctuary, a city that lay approximately 300 miles (480km) away on the coast of what was then called Asia Minor, was not made rashly; although he had been raised as a shepherd, Paris was in fact a prince, one of the sons of King Priam, who was ruler of that doomed city.

King Menelaus vowed vengeance and his mighty fleet set sail to attack Troy. The walled city was besieged for ten years but would not surrender. Unable to win by force, the Greeks resorted to the cunning ploy that so enthralled Heinrich Schliemann 3000 years later. They built a huge wooden horse and hid a band of warriors inside. Then they left the horse outside the gates of Troy as a gift, so tempting the Trojans to take it inside the walls of their city. The Greeks then boarded their ships and ostensibly sailed away – but they went only just out of sight.

That night the Greek warriors crept from the horse, opened the gates of Troy for their army, which had returned under cover of darkness. Most of the male population, including Paris, was slaughtered and the women enslaved. Helen, whose beauty had launched the fleet of 1000 ships, was reunited with the victorious Menelaus. The city, which today lies 9½ miles (15km) inland, was burnt to ashes, the site providing a foundation for further settlements there. Eventually these too disappeared and were not to be seen again until Schliemann, in pursuit of a boyhood dream, blew away the dust of obscurity.

THE TREASURES OF TROY

While digging at Hissarlik, Heinrich Schliemann (1822–90) uncovered a shimmering hoard of gold jewellery, silver goblets and vases, and bronze weaponry that he wrongly took to be the treasures of King Priam.

Acting as his own 'curator', Schliemann dug out the treasures and passed them to his wife Sophia. She bundled them into her shawl and took them away from the site before Turkish officials could examine them. The public was happy to believe Schliemann's claims about the treasure, particularly when a photograph was published of Sophia wearing the spectacular diadem of 'Helen of Troy' (BELOW). Academics scorned Schliemann's account, however, and it was later established that the objects probably came from Troy II or III (c.2200 BC), 1000 years too early for King Priam's Troy.

The treasures were smuggled out of Turkey and, with the exception of a few small pieces, deposited in the Berlin Museum. After World War II, all but a few small objects disappeared from the museum. They were not heard of again until 1991, when it was confirmed that they were in the former Soviet Union, taken there by Russian soldiers.

Sophia Schliemann

Heinrich Schliemann

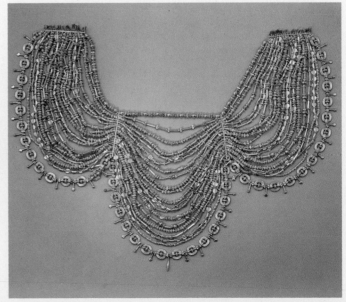

THE TOMB OF TUTANKHAMUN

Silent and secret for 33 centuries, the tomb of the young pharaoh Tutankhamun, buried underground in Egypt's Valley of the Kings, finally revealed a wealth of golden treasure that dazzled the world. The tomb was virtually untouched and guaranteed universal fame for its discoverer.

Dust and darkness surrounded Howard Carter, the British archaeologist, and his patron Lord Carnarvon as they stood facing a sealed doorway deep beneath the Valley of the Kings. Would this door reveal the treasures of the boy-king Tutankhamun, who ruled Egypt around 1361 BC? For eight exhausting years the pair had explored this valley – a burial ground for the pharaohs – on the west bank of the Nile near Luxor, in the hope of finding the elusive tomb, but without success. By the summer of 1922, Carnarvon was ready to give up the search and withdraw his patronage, but Carter had persuaded him to continue for another year.

Carter's team had already combed nearly every crevice in the valley, with the exception of one small area near the excavated tomb of Rameses VI. The Egyptian Antiquities Service had requested that he stay away from this particular area, since his excavations would block the path of tourists visiting the tomb. However, Carter was convinced that here was the place where he would find the prize he had sought for so long. Under Carter's directions, the Egyptian workmen started digging and, on 4 November 1922, a worker uncovered a shallow step clearly carved into the valley floor. Further digging revealed many more steps, until finally the top of a mud-plastered door, bearing the seals of the ancient necropolis guard, was uncovered.

The presence of the seals indicated that the tomb might contain the funerary objects of a high-ranking official, or even a king. When the entire stairway of 16 steps was excavated, Carter found to his delight that the door also bore seals engraved with the name Nebkheprure (Tutankhamun). The lower part of the door, however, had been rebuilt, which meant that the tomb could have been raided and might be empty.

The doorway was unblocked and the rubble and stone cleared away, exposing a long, sloping passage. At the end of it stood a second sealed door. A shiver of anticipation must have passed through the two Egyptologists as they stood before it, for this doorway would reveal either the fulfilment or the futility of their long-cherished dreams.

Three weeks later, on 26 November, Carter started his investigations. First he carefully chiselled a hole in the top left-hand corner of the door and poked through an iron rod to check for obstructions. Then he enlarged the hole, inserted a candle and peered inside.

At first he could discern nothing in the murky gloom. But as his eyes grew accustomed to the dim light, the glint

Pharaoh's rest *The Valley of the Kings had long been identified as the principal burial place for the pharaohs of the great 18th Dynasty (1567–1320 BC). The valley was meticulously examined by archaeologists in the early 1900s. In 1907, 15 years before Carter's discovery, the American millionaire and Egyptologist Theodore Davis believed he had found Tutankhamun's tomb in the foothills near the tomb of Seti I, and in 1914 he declared the valley 'exhausted' of antiquities.*

Golden boy *The sad, serene features of the youthful Tutankhamun were preserved for posterity in his death mask* (LEFT). *This exquisite mask of beaten gold is inlaid with lapis lazuli, semi-precious metals and blue glass strips. It bears the solid-gold heads of a vulture and a cobra, symbolising the king's rule over Upper and Lower Egypt respectively. The face of the young pharaoh's mummy was in a good state of preservation because it had been protected by the mask. The funerary unguents poured over the mummy had carbonised the rest of the body and its wrappings.*

125

of magnificent riches began to emerge from the shadows. 'Strange animals, statues, and gold – everywhere gold.... For the moment...I was struck dumb with amazement'. Waiting behind him in the darkness in almost unbearable suspense, Lord Carnarvon asked 'Can you see anything?' and Carter managed to gasp out 'Yes, wonderful things!'

The room before them was the tomb's antechamber filled with the pharaoh's funerary objects to be used in his afterlife. Thieves had broken in – Carter could even see their footprints in the dust – but they had evidently been disturbed by the necropolis guards, who had put back the objects any way they could. A gold-plated throne inlaid with jewels, gilt furniture including three couches, two golden chariots, statues of gold and alabaster and faience vases lay amid the chaos. But the one object Carter had most hoped to find, the pharaoh's mummy, was not there.

The priceless objects in the antechamber and annexe (a small room to the south-west of the antechamber) were recorded, photographed and prepared for the journey to Cairo Museum for safekeeping. This painstaking task, carried out inside the airless, cramped confines of the tomb, made great demands on Carter, and he was further hampered by the hordes of visitors and members of the press outside, constantly crowding around the entrance.

By February 1923 the antechamber had been cleared and Carter turned his attention to the third sealed door in the north wall. In front of an invited audience, Carter chipped away at the plaster to make a hole; he then inserted a light and peered inside. Less than 3ft (90cm) from the door, what appeared to be a solid wall of gold stretched as far as he could see. Carter quickly dismantled the door and discovered that the wall was not a wall but part of a huge rectangular shrine.

'It was, beyond any question, the sepulchral chamber in which we stood,' wrote Lord Carnarvon's brother Mervyn Herbert. 'For there, towering above us, was one of the great gilt shrines beneath which kings were laid. So enormous was this structure that it filled within a little the entire area of the chamber.' Fortunately Carnarvon lived to see this great find – he died later that year.

Beyond the burial chamber lay a fourth room which Carter subsequently dubbed 'the treasury' since it housed the most valuable objects in the tomb: caskets of precious jewels, vases, miniature boats, shrines, statuettes, a model granary and the gilded head of a cow representing the goddess Hathor. Carter had discovered the only tomb in the

Hidden entry *Directly below the entrance to the tomb of Rameses VI* (LEFT) *was a flight of steps leading down to Tutankhamun's tomb. The steps had been concealed since 1148 BC by the huts of the workmen who built the tomb of Rameses VI, so Carter knew that no one could have entered the boy-king's tomb between that date and 1922.*

Fit for a king *The body of Tutankhamun was enclosed in a nest of three coffins. The weight of the third, solid-gold coffin made them very heavy to lift, so the outer lid was raised by attaching ropes to its silver handles and using a hoist. Inside was the gold-inlaid face of the second coffin* (RIGHT), *which Carter dusted off before opening.*

Fierce guardian The entrance to the Treasury was guarded by the jackal-headed god Anubis, covered in a linen cloth and mounted on a shrine equipped with carrying poles. Anubis was revered by the ancient Egyptians as the patron of embalmers.

'KING'S RANSOM' WITHIN A TOMB

Although Tutankhamun – a young king who ruled for only nine years – was of minor importance, his tomb contained the most priceless and complete collection of funerary artefacts ever recovered. In building their pharaohs' tombs, the Egyptians took many precautions to prevent robbery. The tombs were constructed by as few workmen as possible, the entrances were hidden, the rooms sealed, and watch was kept by necropolis guards. Yet every grave, including Tutankhamun's, was entered by robbers, sometimes within hours of the burial.

Valley of the Kings to have been preserved almost intact.

Inside the shrine was a gilded wooden frame, covered with linen, which enclosed three more heavy wooden shrines, coated in gold and richly inscribed. And within the last of these lay a yellow quartzite sarcophagus with a pink granite lid painted to match the base. Once again an audience assembled, this time to watch the lifting of the lid. 'The contents were completely covered with linen shrouds,' Carter wrote. 'As the last shroud was removed, a gasp of wonderment escaped our lips, so gorgeous was the sight that met our eyes; a golden effigy of the young boy-king, of most magnificent workmanship, filled the whole interior of the sarcophagus.'

Carter had not yet uncovered the most precious of the tomb's ancient secrets. Within the sarcophagus nestled three coffins, each so tightly fitted inside the next that separating them posed more difficulties. When the lid of the second coffin was eventually lifted, it revealed a third coffin made of solid gold. And inside this was discovered the most dazzling treasure of all. Wrapped in linen, dusted with protective charms and draped with fabulous jewels, lay the mummy of the boy-king, his face enclosed in a priceless death mask of hammered gold.

Today, most of Tutankhamun's treasures are on display at the Cairo Museum, but the tomb itself still houses one of the golden coffins containing the king's body. But is it

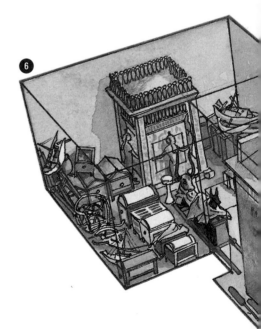

the king? To Carter's everlasting disappointment, no scroll, inscription or carving was ever found to confirm the identity of the body, although subsequent tests proved that the dead person was between 17 and 19 years old when he died. His rank and wealth was confirmed by the value of the fabulous objects surrounding him.

Carter spent ten years unearthing Tutankhamun's treasures, and his work provided later Egyptologists with a vast amount of new information about Egyptian life during the 18th Dynasty. His discovery also captured the imagination of people world-wide and immortalised both his own name and that of the mysterious boy-king.

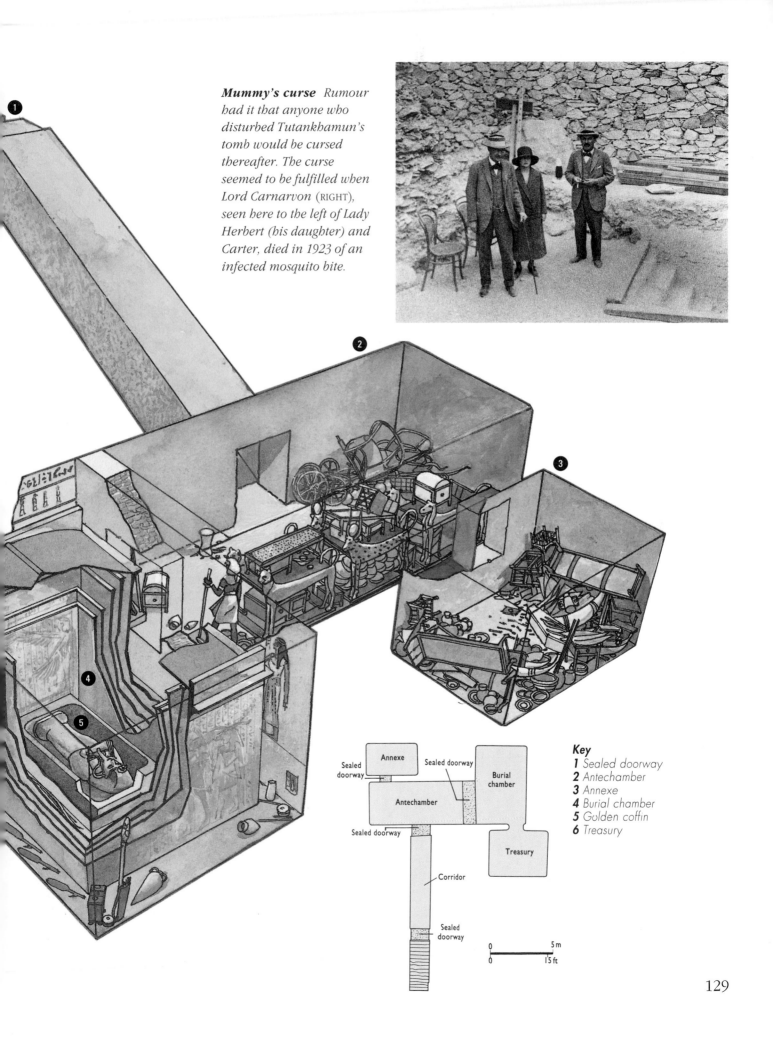

Mummy's curse *Rumour had it that anyone who disturbed Tutankhamun's tomb would be cursed thereafter. The curse seemed to be fulfilled when Lord Carnarvon (RIGHT), seen here to the left of Lady Herbert (his daughter) and Carter, died in 1923 of an infected mosquito bite.*

Annexe

Sealed doorway

Sealed doorway

Burial chamber

Antechamber

Sealed doorway

Corridor

Sealed doorway

Treasury

Key
1 *Sealed doorway*
2 *Antechamber*
3 *Annexe*
4 *Burial chamber*
5 *Golden coffin*
6 *Treasury*

0 5 m
0 15 ft

JERUSALEM: GOD'S HOLY PLACE

Jews, Christians and Muslims throng Jerusalem's ancient streets – a testimony to their common heritage. Yet today the holiest of cities is beset by violent quarrels.

Within the Old City walls of Jerusalem, rebuilt four centuries ago by the Ottoman sultan Suleiman the Magnificent, lie three pre-eminent shrines of the three great monotheistic religions: the Western Wall (more popularly known as the Wailing Wall), the Church of the Holy Sepulchre and the Dome of the Rock. The great religions of Judaism, Christianity and Islam come together in this ancient place.

Jerusalem was little more than a tiny hill town in the Judean desert when David captured it from the Jebusites in about 1005 BC and declared it the capital of his kingdom, Israel, which eventually stretched from the Red Sea in the south to the River Euphrates in the north. When David's son, Solomon, built the first temple inside the city walls to house the stone tablets inscribed with the Ten Commandments that were given to Moses, Jerusalem became sacred to the Jewish race.

In 587 BC, Nebuchadnezzar, ruler of the greatest empire in western Asia, besieged the city. He destroyed Solomon's Temple and took the Jews into captivity in his capital, Babylon. The Jewish exiles who later returned rebuilt the temple in about 520 BC, and this building stood for more than 500 years as a succession of foreign powers ruled over Israel. In 19 BC the temple was rebuilt yet again, this time by Herod the Great, whose name is for ever linked with the 'Massacre of Innocents'. According to the Bible, he ordered the slaughter of an entire generation of infant boys because he had heard of the birth of a child destined to become King of the Jews. This building stood until AD 70, when it was systematically destroyed by the Romans, following a Jewish rebellion.

Today, all that remains of Herod's Temple is the Western Wall, which to the Jewish people is the most sacred place on Earth. Its more popular name, the Wailing Wall, derives from the Jews' tradition of bewailing the fate of Jewish exiles and the destruction of the temple, while praying beside the wall's cherished stones. Many worshippers place written prayers inside crevices in the wall, and thereby inside the holy temple itself, in the belief that their words will rise directly to God.

The area of Mount Moriah where Solomon built the first temple is as holy and precious to the Muslims as it is to the Jews. The Prophet Muhammad (570–632) had been dead just six years when, in 638, the Muslim leader

Memorable sights *Mount Zion attracts both tourists and Christian pilgrims, particularly at Easter, Whitsun and the Feast of Tabernacles. The Dormition Abbey stands on the site where the Virgin Mary is said to have died. Its interior is adorned with dazzling mosaics, and a dark crypt commemorates her eternal rest. Nearby, a building houses three important Christian sites: the room known as the Coenaculum, in which the Last Supper was held; the room in which Jesus washed his disciples' feet following that sacred meal; and the tomb of David.*

131

JERUSALEM: GOD'S HOLY PLACE

Caliph Omar conquered the city and proclaimed the site a sacred precinct of Islam. At the summit of the mount is an outcrop of rock 12ft (4m) high, the place from which Muhammad, accompanied by the Archangel Gabriel, is said to have ascended to heaven on a stairway of light to receive instructions for his mission on Earth. Muslims believe that at the end of the world the call to judgment will sound from this very rock.

Enclosing the rock stands the Dome of the Rock, the oldest existing Islamic shrine and, after Mecca and Medina, the third most holy Muslim place of worship. A symmetrical octagonal building supporting a glittering cupola, it was built in AD 687–91 and designed both inside and out according to strict mathematical principles governing harmony and balance. The base of the supporting walls is decorated with marble, the upper part contains 45 000 glazed tiles. The dome, to many the most memorable symbol of the city, was originally built of wood and sheathed in sheets of pure gold. The present dome, which is made of aluminium alloyed with gold, and embellished with verses from the Koran, was completed in 1963.

The history of the Church of the Holy Sepulchre, which marks the spot where Joseph of Arimathea buried Jesus in a tomb carved out of the rock, dates from AD 135, when the Roman Emperor Hadrian razed Jerusalem to the ground, and built a temple to Venus over this sacred site. When Helena (later St Helena), mother of Constantine the Great, the first Christian emperor, made a historic pilgrimage to Jerusalem in AD 326, she located the tomb beneath the temple with the help of the Greek Bishop Makarios. Constantine had the temple demolished and built a basilica, a group of buildings enclosed within a rectangular framework, in its place. At the heart of this complex, which was consecrated in AD 335, was a circular shrine enclosing the tomb of Christ (the Tomb Rotunda). Other buildings included a cloistered open court – the site

Fiery ritual *The most spectacular moment of the Easter celebrations in Jerusalem's Church of the Holy Sepulchre is the appearance of the 'holy fire', which the Greek Orthodox patriarch brings from inside the holy tomb to present to the congregation. The believers, who wait with flaming torches and candles, greet the fire ecstatically.*

City at the crossroads *For centuries Jerusalem has been important to peoples of different cultures and creeds. A German engraving from the 16th century sets the city at the centre of the world, straddling the continents of Europe, Asia and Africa. The newly discovered continent of America, in this scheme, is positioned in the bottom left-hand corner.*

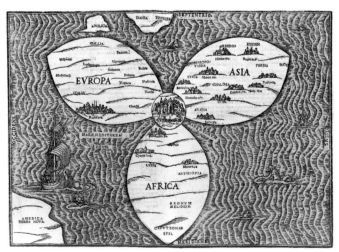

of Golgotha, or Calvary, where Jesus was crucified – and a church called the Martyrion where services were held.

The Madaba Map, a sixth-century mosaic found in 1884 in the church at Madaba, Jordan, includes the earliest known plan of Jerusalem, which shows the Basilica of Constantine. Beyond it is the Tomb Rotunda and close by an open space marked by a cross – Golgotha. These three major Christian landmarks were finally brought under the same roof in the 12th century when, after Constantine's basilica had been destroyed, rebuilt and destroyed again, the Crusaders constructed a magnificent Romanesque church which was consecrated in 1149.

The present Church of the Holy Sepulchre, built after an earthquake in 1927, is a faithful reproduction of the Crusaders' edifice. The religious significance of this collection of monasteries, chapels and tombs is such that six Christian communities – Roman Catholic, Greek Orthodox, Syrian, Ethiopian, Armenian and Coptic – share the maintenance of the premises and worship there side by side.

Today, history weighs heavily on Jerusalem, as the holy city is torn by religious and political strife. For many, it remains the city of God, but voices that could be raised in unison are often heard disagreeing over their inheritance. This sublime place is at once their glory and the subject of their quarrel.

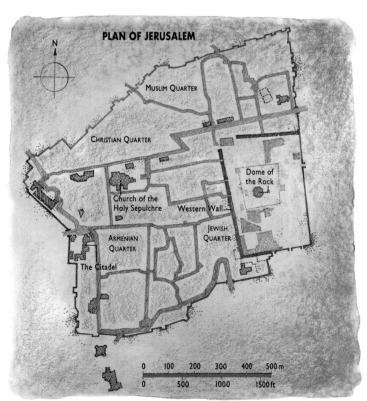

PLAN OF JERUSALEM

MUSLIM QUARTER
CHRISTIAN QUARTER
Dome of the Rock
Church of the Holy Sepulchre
Western Wall
ARMENIAN QUARTER
JEWISH QUARTER
The Citadel

0 100 200 300 400 500 m
0   500   1000   1500 ft

Golden magnificence
The juxtaposition of the Dome of the Rock and the Western Wall of Herod's Temple seems to symbolise the way in which the world's faiths come together in Jerusalem. The sacred wall evokes tears of joy in many Orthodox Jews, and so

revered are its stones that Jewish weddings and bar mitzvahs (coming-of-age ceremonies for boys aged 13) are held here.

The yellow-gold holy rock, Es-Sakhra, from which the Dome takes its name, lies beneath the cupola and is sacred to Jews and Muslims alike. It is said that the rock tried to follow Muhammad at his ascension, but was pushed back by the Archangel Gabriel and bears both the fingerprints of the archangel and the hoofmark of the prophet's horse.

Arched windows around the dome illuminate the interior, where light filtering through the pierced pottery tiles makes the intricate mosaics seem to swirl on a golden background. Islam, like Judaism, forbids the representation of human or animal forms, so plants are depicted on the mosaics.

PETRA: BEAUTY HEWN FROM ROCK

Unknown to the Western world for hundreds of years, the 'rose-red' city of Petra was once a thriving centre for travellers along the ancient trade routes. Ringed by high mountains and approached through a narrow gorge, its remarkable carved buildings have remained virtually untouched.

On a journey from Syria to Egypt in late August 1812, the young Swiss explorer Johann Ludwig Burckhardt came upon a group of Arab tribesmen just south of the Dead Sea who had an enthralling story to tell. They spoke of 'antiquities' in a nearby hidden valley called Wadi Mousa – the Valley of Moses.

Disguised as an Arab, Burckhardt followed his guide to a seemingly solid wall of rock which, as they approached, revealed a narrow, deep cleft. After walking for about 25 minutes through a winding, almost sunless gorge, known as the Siq, he was suddenly confronted by the reddish-pink facade of an elaborately carved building 90ft (30m) high. Stepping into the sunlight, Burckhardt found himself in the main street of ancient Petra – perhaps the most romantic of all 'lost' cities. It was a memorable moment, for he was the first European to set foot there since the Crusaders in the 12th century.

Petra's inaccessibility has been its salvation. Today, it can still only be approached by foot or on horseback, and the initial impact of the city is breathtaking: depending on the time of day it appears red, tangerine or apricot, deep crimson, grey or even chocolate brown. Archaeologists have now pieced together some of the city's past and dispelled the 19th-century belief that it was merely a necropolis – a city of the dead. Certainly there are some impressive tombs, such as the four Royal Tombs in the cliffs to the east of the city's central area, or the Deir to the north-west, but firm evidence suggests that Petra was

Royal tomb *The Deir boasts the largest facade in Petra (RIGHT). It is thought to have been the tomb of the Nabataean King Rabbel II, who died in AD 106, although it may have been a temple. The death of the king left the way clear for the Romans, who annexed Petra in the same year. During the early Christian era – the middle of the fifth century AD – hermits made their homes here and the Deir became known colloquially as the 'monastery tomb'.*

Romantic vision *A stream of western visitors followed Burckhardt through the Siq to witness Petra's wonders for themselves. Among them was Royal Academician David Roberts (1786–1864), who went there in 1839. Roberts was a fine draughtsman, and although he romanticised what he saw, his drawings are among the most accurate representations of Petra.*

PETRA: BEAUTY HEWN FROM ROCK

Pharaoh's Treasury *The dazzling rock-cut facade of the Khasneh (ABOVE), Burckhardt's first glimpse of ancient Petra, lies at the end of a narrow gorge and ranks as the city's masterpiece. The Khasneh's distinctly Greek-style statues, niches and columns are protected from wind, rain and sandstorms by the overhanging rock, and appear to be freshly cut. Burckhardt remarked 'Its state of preservation resembles that of a building recently finished.'*

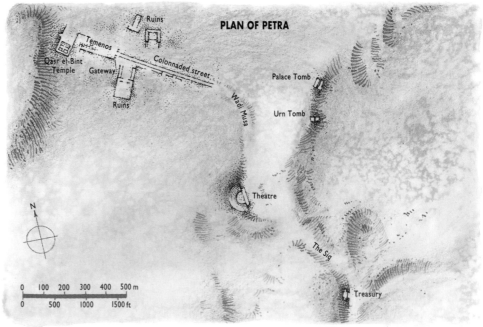

PLAN OF PETRA

Ruins

Temenos

Qasr el-Bint Temple

Gateway

Colonnaded street

Ruins

Palace Tomb

Urn Tomb

Wadi Musa

Theatre

The Siq

Treasury

| 0 | 100 | 200 | 300 | 400 | 500 m |

| 0 | 500 | 1000 | 1500 ft |

once a city of at least 20 000 people. The colonnaded main street – still visible today – ran parallel with the river bed of the Wadi Mousa, and was originally lined with shops; and the semicircular tiers of stone seats of the theatre, built by the Nabataeans but later refurbished by the Romans, could accommodate 4000 people.

The building most immediately associated with Petra is the Khasneh al Faroun, or Pharaoh's Treasury. Bathed in a dusky red glow, its impressive rock-cut facade is the first to greet the visitor stepping out of the Siq. Its name derives from the ancient belief that a pharaoh's treasure (probably that of Rameses III, who had owned mines at Petra) was hidden in the urn on top of the monument. It is said that local people used to fire bullets at the urn in an attempt to break it and release the treasure, but the container has remained intact.

Although the Khasneh probably dates from the second century AD, Petra's history stretches back far beyond that date. There are some unidentified prehistoric remains at Petra, but the first known people associated with the site are the Edomites, who lived there around 1000 BC. According to the Bible they were descendants of Esau, and references in the Book of Genesis to a place called Sela almost certainly refer to Petra (the name means 'rock' in Greek). The Edomites were defeated by King Amaziah of Judah, who cast 10 000 captives from the top of a rock

to their deaths. A tomb on a hill overlooking Petra is said to be that of Moses' brother, Aaron.

By the fourth century BC Petra was inhabited by the Nabataeans, an Arab tribe who cut many of the buildings out of the sandstone rock faces and lived in the numerous caves throughout the city. The site was a natural fortress; thanks to a series of channels and pipelines it had a constant supply of spring water, and it stood at the cross-roads of two major trade routes: east–west joining the Mediterranean and the Persian Gulf, and north–south connecting the Red Sea with Damascus. Originally shepherds, the Nabataeans, who became renowned for their honesty, readily adapted themselves to new roles as caravan guards and traders, and the levies they imposed on passing travellers helped them to prosper. Petra became a great commercial centre, and Greek travellers took home accounts of its wealth and luxury.

In AD 106 the city was annexed by the Romans, and continued to flourish until around AD 300, when the stability of the Roman Empire was beginning to crumble. Records show that during the fifth century AD Petra became the seat of a Christian bishopric, but was captured by Muslims in the seventh century and subsequently sank into decline and oblivion as more accessible towns, such as Palmyra to the north-east of Damascus, grew up along the trade routes.

MECCA: SACRED CITY OF ISLAM

Every devout Muslim is duty-bound to visit this sublime centre of worship at least once in their life. In ancient times Mecca, a tribal capital, was a tranquil oasis for the dusty caravans that once linked southern Arabia, east Africa and south Asia with the Mediterranean world.

The traditional words that echo throughout every Muslim's life are: 'If God decrees my death, it shall be on the road with my face towards Mecca.' Revered as the birthplace of the prophet Muhammad (born *c.* AD 570), Mecca is situated in Saudi Arabia, some 45 miles (72km) from Jeddah on the Red Sea. Muslims the world over yearn to visit Mecca before they die and this ancient city plays a fundamental part in their worship. Indeed, to make a pilgrimage, or *hajj*, to its Great Mosque is the solemn duty of every Muslim.

The city's religious significance predates the time of Muhammad. Within the Ka'aba, or 'square house' – a massive shrine that dominates the huge courtyard of the Great Mosque – lies the huge Black Stone of Mecca. Sacred to Muslims today, this stone was regarded by worshippers of more ancient gods as a source of miraculous power. Pilgrims then, as now, journeyed from all parts of Arabia to kiss and stroke the stone in the hope of absorbing some of its power. After purifying it in the name of Allah, Muhammad endorsed the custom of kissing the stone. In so doing he forged a bond of continuity, linking the new disciples of Islam with their pre-Islamic past.

The origins of the stone are obscure. Geologists maintain that it may be a meteorite; Muslims believe it fell from heaven into the Garden of Eden and was given to Adam to take away his sins after God had expelled him from Paradise. They believe also that it was then passed by the Archangel Gabriel to the Jewish patriarch Abraham to be used as the cornerstone of a temple, and that this temple is the Ka'aba. Islamic doctrine relates that the same archangel appeared to Muhammad in his sleep and revealed to him the word of God. When Muhammad awoke, the verses of the Koran were inscribed upon his heart. They decreed that the false gods worshipped by his people had to be destroyed, leaving Allah to reign supreme.

Only Muslims are permitted inside the city and the Great Mosque; in the past intruders were liable to be executed (today non-Muslims are fined). Nevertheless, over the past 200 years several adventurers disguised as Muslim pilgrims have violated this Islamic law. The first to record his visit to Mecca was Johan Ludwig Burckhardt, the Swiss explorer, in 1814, but perhaps the most famous was Sir Richard Burton, who entered the mosque in 1830 and later wrote in his book, *Pilgrimage to Al-Medinah and*

A goal fulfilled *Each year some two million pilgrims travel to Mecca in Dhu al-hijja, the last month of the Muslim year, to present themselves to God. As they sight the Ka'aba, the central sanctuary in the mosque's courtyard, they call out 'Labbaika! – Here I am!'*

138

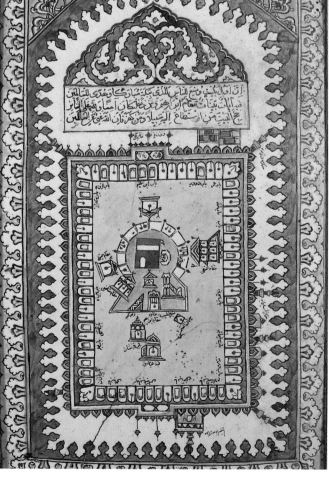

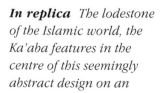
In replica *The lodestone of the Islamic world, the Ka'aba features in the centre of this seemingly abstract design on an* *18th-century Turkish tile. In fact, it is a stylised plan of Mecca's Great Mosque, depicting the courtyard enclosed by colonnades.*

Meccah, that 'of all the worshippers... who pressed their beating hearts to the stone none felt for the moment a deeper emotion than did the Haji from the far-north'.

Pilgrims to Mecca follow the traditional rites of the *hajj* ceremony. Before doing so, they don a white robe, the *ihram*; all worshippers dress alike to symbolise their equality before Allah. Muslims must wash their faces, heads, arms and feet before praying, so running water is essential at every mosque. At the Great Mosque, a few feet from the Ka'aba, stands the well of Zemzem, which in ancient times was the only water available in the city. The origin of the stream is said to date from Biblical times when, according to the Book of Genesis, Hagar, mother of Abraham's first-born son Ishmael, was driven into the wilderness by Abraham's barren wife, Sarah. To prevent the mother and child from dying of thirst, God directed them to a place where a freshwater spring bubbled from the sand. Muslims believe that Hagar's spring and the well of Zemzem are one and the same. Water from the well is still used to wash and clean the Ka'aba three times a year.

Daily duties *Even Muslim soldiers on active service pray five times a day – at dawn, noon, mid-afternoon, sunset and as night falls. In every mosque a* mihrab, *or niche, indicates the direction of Mecca, which Muslims should face when they pray.*

Sins of the world *This image of the sacred Black Stone is depicted in a history of the universe written nearly 700 years ago. According to legend the stone was initially pure white, but the combined sins of the many pilgrims who have touched and kissed its sacred surface have completely blackened it. The Ka'aba is now covered with black silk, with verses from the Koran ornately embroidered in gold and silver thread. Every year a new cloth is made to cover the shrine.*

Islam is a religion that governs by the sword rather than persuasion, and disagreements are often settled by violent action. Mecca has not been spared such conflict. In 1802, the sons of the puritan Muhammad Abdul Wahhab entered Mecca after perpetrating terrible slaughter outside its gates, smashing every shrine and image in the city, and accusing its inhabitants of idolatry. In 1979, there was a bloody battle within the precincts of the mosque. But in spite of its violent history, the city of Mecca remains steeped in mystery and intrigue. It has seen much bloodshed and yet appears to be a place of perfect peace.

Holy scripture *During his lifetime, Muhammad wrote in short verses the divine revelations he received from Allah; after his death they were collected into the Koran, the sacred book of the Muslims.*

THE PILGRIMS' WAY

The Five Pillars of Islam, the sacred duties of every Muslim, are laid down in the Koran. These are reciting the creed of Islam, prayer, almsgiving, fasting and, lastly, pilgrimage, or *hajj*, to the Great Mosque at Mecca and to its central shrine, the Ka'aba. The five-day pilgrimage takes place during the 12th month, Dhu al-hijja, of the Muslim year. All Muslims who are physically and financially able to perform the pilgrimage must do so at least once in their lives. But anyone whose family would suffer by his or her absence is not obliged to make the journey.

The pilgrimage begins on the first day at Mecca, when pilgrims walk seven times around the Ka'aba (1) and kiss it. They then run seven times between two small hills, al-Safa and al-Marwa (2), now enclosed and joined by a walkway. It was near these hills that Hagar and her son Ishmael ran back and forth searching for water, until she discovered the well of Zemzem. (The well is so called because Hagar is said to have shouted '*Zem! Zem!*', or 'Stop! Stop!', as its waters started to gush forth.)

The next two stages are the 5 mile (8km) walk to Mina (3), where the pilgrims stay overnight, followed by a 10 mile (16km) journey to the plain of Arafat (4), where Muhammad preached his last sermon. Here the day is spent in meditation and part of the evening in a search for 49 stones for the next stage on the following day, the procession to Muzdalifa (5) and the return to Mina (6). There, the pilgrims enact the ceremony of 'stoning the devils', throwing their stones at three pillars that mark the place where the devil was stoned by Ishmael as he tempted him to disobey Abraham.

The last stage (7) takes the pilgrim back to Mecca. The *hajj* ends with a festival at which an animal such as a sheep or goat is sacrificed in remembrance of Abraham's faith and obedience when he was told by God to sacrifice his son. Pilgrims' heads are then shaved and they again walk seven times around the Ka'aba to complete the pilgrimage.

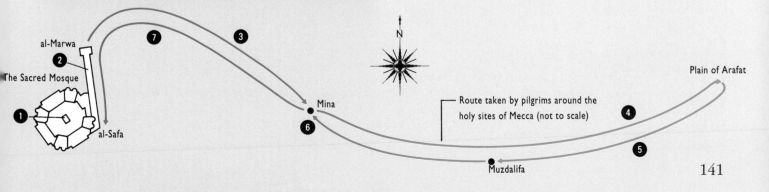

al-Marwa
2
The Sacred Mosque
1
al-Safa
7
3
6
Mina
N
Plain of Arafat
Route taken by pilgrims around the holy sites of Mecca (not to scale)
4
5
Muzdalifa

TAKHT-I SULAIMAN: SITE OF THE ROYAL FIRE

High in the mountains of northern Iran lie the time-ravaged ruins of an ancient city: it is the most holy site of a pre-Islamic religion, three of whose priests paid homage to the infant Jesus.

A great lake 330ft (100m) across lies at the heart of the ruined Sassanian city of Shiz, known to the Mongols as Saturiq and now known as Takht-i Sulaiman (Throne of Solomon). The waters of this pool, reputed to be bottomless, are rich in minerals and their ceaseless flow over millennia has caused a build-up of deposits. These have formed a stone basin around the lake with sheer sides of over 130ft (40m) deep, and stone channels that course down the hillsides.

Until the coming of Islam, this mysterious and beautiful lake and its surroundings were regarded as the principal religious site in Iran. And in 1959 excavations by the German Archaeological Institute proved that Takht-i Sulaiman was indeed the sacred centre of Zoroastrianism – an ancient religion based on the concept of the eternal struggle between the god of creation and the spirit of evil.

The Three Wise Men, or Magi, who were said to have travelled from Saveh in Iran to pay homage to the infant Jesus in Bethlehem, were likely to have been Zoroastrian priests (the Magi were originally members of a north-west Iranian tribe). From Magi comes the word 'magic', once used to describe the religious rites of Zoroastrianism.

The connection between Takht-i Sulaiman and Zoroastrianism provides an important physical link with the past for the remaining few thousand adherents of the religion alive today. The Zoroastrians left Persia in the eighth century to escape religious persecution by the Muslims, and contact with their Iranian counterparts was only

Fire cult *The fire altar on this third-century coin confirms the importance of Zoroastrianism in the Sassanian culture.*

Ancient history revealed
Takht-i Sulaiman was discovered in 1819, but it was not properly surveyed until 1937 and, again, in 1959.

142

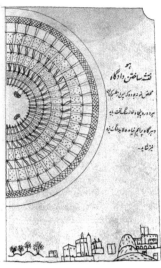

Burial plan *The holy book of the Zoroastrians, the* Avesta, *included plans for the way in which the dead should be placed on a* dakhme (ABOVE). *Men's bodies were laid out on one side, women's on the other. Once the bones had been picked clean, they were thrown down a central well in the* dakhme. *Because of the Zoroastrians' belief that fire must not be defiled, even contemporary devotees rarely resort to cremation.*

re-established in the 15th century. Today they are known as Parsees (Persians), and live mainly in Pakistan and India, but with followers scattered around the globe.

The history of Takht-i Sulaiman and the rise of Zoroastrianism are intertwined and begin with Iran's ancient founders, the Aryans (Iran means 'land of the Aryan'). The Aryans revered the natural elements, especially fire and water, as manifestations of their gods. Thus the area around Takht-i Sulaiman, which possessed two powerful earthly phenomena – volcanoes and thermal spring-fed lakes – was particularly important to them.

In about 600 BC, an Aryan priest named Zarathustra (known in Greek as Zoroaster), who saw himself as a prophet, attempted to redefine Aryan religious belief with its many gods. Breaking away from orthodoxy, Zarathustra established his own faith, which became known as Zoroastrianism. The new religion contained the beginnings of monotheism: Zarathustra considered Ahura Mazda, Lord of Wisdom, to be the supreme god who, helped in his task by lesser divinities, is destined eventually to win his struggle against the Evil One, Angra Mainyu. Zarathustra preached that Man's duty is to choose for himself where he stands in this struggle between good and evil and his soul will be judged in the hereafter.

Several important aspects of the old religion became part of the new. Fire, as the symbol of Ahura Mazda, remained sacred, tended on the family hearth as well as in the temples. Zoroastrians also went to great lengths to

Tower of death *The* dakhme (ABOVE) *provided a way of circumventing the Zoroastrian belief that bodies should not be buried or burned – instead they were left to the vultures.*

avoid defiling the elements and this was particularly illustrated in their attitude to death.

Bodies could not be buried for fear of contaminating the earth, nor could they be burned since to do so would sully the fire. Instead, large round stone-faced towers, called *dakhmes*, meaning towers of silence, were built, on top of which the dead were laid out naked. During this rite of exposure, the corpses were picked clean of their flesh by vultures, and the sun's rays 'drew the bodies' spirits heavenward'. This ritual is still practised by Parsees today.

With the accession of the Sassanian dynasty in the third century AD, under the rule of King Ardashir I, who was a member of the priest class, Zoroastrianism became Iran's state religion. Altars with perpetually burning fires were set up all over the country. Some, crowning rocky heights, burned in the open air. Others were enclosed in fire temples called *Chahar taq*, meaning 'four arches', after their basic plan – a square marked by four pillars joined by arches and crowned by a dome.

Nearly every town, village and province in Iran had its

144

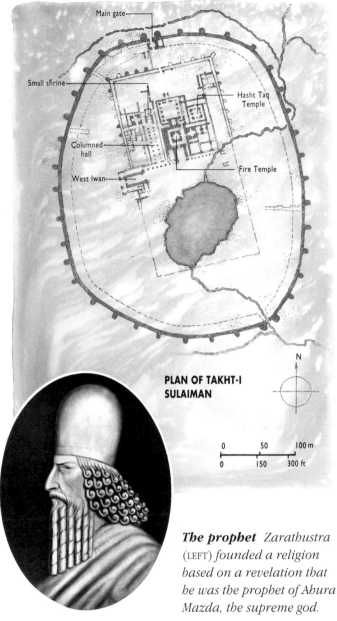

Main gate

Small shrine

Columned hall

West Iwan

Hasht Taq Temple

Fire Temple

PLAN OF TAKHT-I SULAIMAN

N

| 0 | 50 | 100 m |
| 0 | 150 | 300 ft |

Followers of Zarathustra
A Parsee priest covers his mouth to prevent his breath from contaminating the fire (ABOVE). *Every religious rite*

must be conducted by a priest. The priesthood is hereditary; no one born into a lay family can become a priest.

The prophet *Zarathustra* (LEFT) *founded a religion based on a revelation that he was the prophet of Ahura Mazda, the supreme god.*

own sacred fire. There were different categories of fire, too: Atur Gushnasp was the fire of warriors and kings; Atur Burzen-Mihr was the fire of farmers; and Atur Farnbag the fire of priests. Today, only the location of Atur Gushnasp, the Royal Fire, is precisely known – its divine flames burned in the fire temple at the site of Takht-i Sulaiman. The temple ruins are today reflected in the waters of the pool around which the ancient city stood.

The Sassanian king Khusrau I (AD 513–79) refurbished the fire temple and built a city on the already well-established religious site. He had previously built a palace at Ctesiphon, on the River Tigris, so fantastic that folklore held it to have been constructed by genies. Now he established Takht-i Sulaiman as Iran's foremost place of

pilgrimage and worship. Khusrau planned with precision and flair; he gave Takht-i Sulaiman a processional way which ran straight from a spectacular entrance at the north gate through to the fire temple and on to the lake. After their glorious coronation at Ctesiphon, the Sassanian kings made a pilgrimage to Takht-i Sulaiman to receive a divine investiture at the altar of the Royal Fire.

But Khusrau's vision was not everlasting. Takht-i Sulaiman was sacked in AD 624 and, although later rebuilt by the Mongols, it never regained its former glory. The Royal Fire had been extinguished; conquering Arabs imposed Islam as the state religion, and eventually this most spectacular of sacred sites was reduced to the desolate mass of ruins visible today.

145

SAMARKAND: THE SHIMMERING CITY

The fabled city of Samarkand, at the hub of the old trade routes of Central Asia, has attracted poets, pilgrims and plunderers across deserts and mountains for more than 2000 years. As the sunlight reflects off its richly decorated mosques and minarets, the city gleams like a great golden beacon that can be seen for miles over the surrounding plains.

In ancient and medieval times, Samarkand stood at the junction of the Silk Road leading from China to the Mediterranean and the trade route from India to the west. Its name still evokes dreams of distant lands, great riches and exotic goods and has inspired verse by Marlowe, Milton, Keats and Goethe.

One of the oldest cities in Central Asia, Samarkand is an oasis irrigated by canals from the Zarafshan River. In 329 BC, when it was known as Maracanda and was capital of Sogdiana, part of the Persian Achaemenid Empire, the city was captured by Alexander the Great, King of Macedonia, while he was en route to India. Later it came under the rule of the Turks, Arabs and Persians, but it was the repeated surges of nomadic armies in medieval times that had the most influence on the fortunes of Samarkand.

The first of these invasions was led by Genghis Khan (meaning 'Universal Ruler'), a minor Mongol chieftain who eventually brought all the nomadic tribes of Mongolia under his command. He then turned his attention to the settled peoples beyond the borders of his realm and started a campaign of plunder and conquest that led to the establishment of the great Mongol Empire, stretching from the Adriatic Sea to the Pacific Ocean.

The Mongols were superb horsemen, and under Genghis Khan's inspired leadership proved an unstoppable force. After laying waste to Beijing in 1215, Genghis Khan took control of the Silk Road and in 1221 besieged Samarkand. One hundred years later, when the Arab traveller Ibn Battuta arrived at the city, it still lay in ruins.

The second nomadic leader of importance to Samarkand, Timur Lenk, or 'Iron Limper' (a byname referring to a leg injury caused by an arrow), also known as Tamerlane, had a more positive influence on the city. He was born near Samarkand in 1336, and established himself as sovereign of the Chagatai line of khans – a dynasty started by Genghis Khan's second son. By 1367 the Mongol Empire was in decline and Timur was determined to become the leader who would restore it to its former glory. He proceeded to

Grand passion Timur Lenk's personal love of azure and turquoise is reflected in the intricately patterned tilework that decorates the exteriors of the city's minarets, mosques and madrasas.

Uzbek influence The city's Registan (marketplace) was dominated by Ulugh Beg's religious college until the 17th century, when the Uzbeks added two more such colleges to flank the square. One was the Shirdar madrasa (ABOVE).

SAMARKAND: THE SHIMMERING CITY

launch a succession of military campaigns from the Black Sea to the Indus Valley, ransacking towns and villages, massacring whole populations and building pyramids with their skulls. No mercy was afforded to those he captured; Timur spared only the lives of craftsmen from Azerbaijan, Isfahan, Shiraz, Delhi and Damascus, whom he dispatched to his capital.

These men transformed Samarkand into a city of graceful, glistening domes and lofty minarets, a capital worthy of a great emperor. Between military campaigns, Timur camped outside the city in luxurious silken tents to direct the building work. Every surface was covered with multicoloured glazed tiles in spectacular mosaic patterns that reflected the light, making Samarkand shimmer in the sunlight like a jewel.

On his triumphal return from India, Timur decided to proclaim his greatness by building the largest mosque in the Islamic world. The mosque, called Bibi Khanum, was started on the astrologically auspicious day of 11 May 1399, and was completed in five years using the skills and energy of 200 craftsmen, 500 labourers and 95 elephants. Its huge dome still dominates the city, and in the courtyard stands a lectern that once held a 6ft (2m) Koran.

Timur died in China in 1405 and was laid to rest in Samarkand, in the Gur-i-Amir (the Ruler's Tomb), originally built by him for one of his grandsons. The simple stone laid over him by his grandson Ulugh Beg is the world's largest piece of jade, from Chinese Turkestan. Under Ulugh Beg, Samarkand became a cultural and

The dome *Timur was a keen student of architecture and had been impressed by the dome atop the central mosque of Damacus. He had it copied for the Gur-i-Amir, his magnificent tomb in Samarkand. The style* continued *to be used by his successors, such as the Uzbeks, who built this dome on the Shirdar* madrasa. *Later, the idea of using domes to enhance buildings spread north to Russia and south to India.*

First star tables *Ulugh Beg's great passion was astronomy. He built a three-storey observatory on a hill outside the old city – its remains still stand today. It housed a double sextant – used for observing the Sun, Moon and planets – which had a radius of 133ft (40m) and was mounted on a bronze track calibrated in degrees* (LEFT).

The observatory made a fundamental contribution to the science of astronomy by producing the Zij-i-Gurkani, the first precise star tables, completed in 1437. The correct length of a year was also calculated there.

intellectual centre of the age. The ruler had built a fine two-storeyed *madrasa,* or theological college, decorated with a beautifully carved facade, that occupied the whole of the west side of the central square. Ulugh Beg lured some of the finest intellects to the city, not only to the college, but also to his large observatory, which contained the latest technological equipment for observing the heavens. There the first precise star tables, plotting the positions of the stars, were calculated.

In 1449, Ulugh Beg was assassinated at the instigation of his son. He was laid to rest alongside his grandfather in the Gur-i-Amir. Samarkand slowly declined as the importance of the Silk Road diminished and China closed its borders under the Ming Dynasty. The city became increasingly vulnerable to attacks by the Golden Horde (a group of Turko-Mongol tribesman), led by Khan Uzbek, and was finally conquered in 1500.

For all its brutality, the dynasty founded by Timur was responsible for the great artistic and intellectual renaissance in Samarkand in the 14th and 15th centuries, which made important contributions to Islamic architecture and to the science of astronomy. By the 18th century, the city's fortunes had so declined that it was actually uninhabited for 50 years from 1720. In the 19th century, the region came under Russian rule. As a provincial capital and with the coming of the railways in 1896, Samarkand began to recover economically and once again became an important centre, this time for the export of agricultural produce. Today it is part of an independent Uzbekistan.

Son of Timur *Shah Rokh, Timur's youngest son, is presented as a baby to his father* (ABOVE). *He became* *the founder of the Herat school of miniature painting in the 15th century.*

Medieval necropolis *The cemetery of Shah-i Zinde (Shrine of the Living King) was rebuilt in the 14th century by Timur Lenk as a complex of mosques and tombs for his family and friends. It began as a place of pilgrimage in the 11th century because it housed the shrine of Qasim ibn Abbas, the prophet Muhammad's cousin, who had converted the region to Islam. The mausoleums were decorated in the finest glazed tiles; mosaic patterns graced the most important tombs, such as that of Timur's favourite sister, Shirin Bika Aqa.*

149

TAJ MAHAL: SYMBOL OF LOVE

The love of a man for his wife is preserved in the gleaming white marble of the Taj Mahal. A vision of symmetry and delicacy, like a perfect pearl set against an azure sky, it is the world's best known mausoleum and one of the most exquisite buildings ever designed.

O n the southern bank of the River Yamuna (Jumna) at Agra is the Taj Mahal, arguably the most famous building in the world. Its silhouette is instantly recognisable and has become, for many, the unofficial symbol of India. The fame of the Taj Mahal rests not only on its architectural beauty – in which grandeur and delicacy are miraculously balanced – but also on its romantic associations. It was built by the 17th-century Mogul Emperor Shah Jahan as a memorial to his favourite wife, whose death plunged him into unshakeable grief. As a physical symbol of the devotion of a man to a woman, the Taj Mahal is unsurpassed. Tradition has it that when a couple goes there, the woman should ask her partner: 'If I were to die, do you love me so much that you would build me a memorial like this?'

Shah Jahan, 'king of the world' (1592–1666), ruled the Mogul Empire from 1628 to 1658. He was a noted patron of the arts, as well as a great builder, and during his reign the empire was at its peak both politically and culturally. When he was 15 years old, Shah Jahan (known in boyhood as Prince Khurram) met and fell in love with Arjumand Banu Begam, the 14-year-old daughter of his father's prime minister. She was beautiful, intelligent and high-born – seemingly a perfect match – but the prince

Perfect proportions *A massive gateway, which in Muslim tradition marks the transition between the realm of the senses and the realm of the spirit, allows entrance to the courtyard of the Taj Mahal. Visitors emerging from its shadows are greeted with the same compelling vision that met the eyes of Shah Jahan more than three centuries ago. The courtyard's tranquil watercourse mirrors the marble monument's perfect vertical symmetry.*

Timeless image *Equally impressive by day or by night – when it is bathed in moonlight and the breeze ripples the waters of the courtyard pool – the world's most famous mausoleum can arouse powerful emotions in those who gaze on its splendour. The British writer Rudyard Kipling (1865–1936) described the Taj Mahal as 'the embodiment of all things pure, all things holy, and all things unhappy. That was the mystery of the building'.*

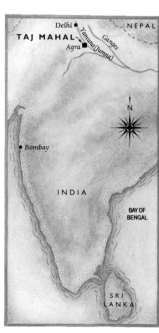

TAJ MAHAL: SYMBOL OF LOVE

was obliged to make a traditional 'political' marriage to a Persian princess. Muslim law, however, permits a man to take four wives so, in 1612, when the astrological signs were favourable, Shah Jahan married his beloved. The ceremony followed a five-year-long betrothal during which the pair did not once set eyes on each other. Her name was changed to Mumtaz Mahal ('Chosen One of the Palace') shortly afterwards.

Shah Jahan and Mumtaz Mahal were married for 19 years until 1631, when the queen died giving birth to their 14th child. The emperor's grief was as intense as his love. He locked himself away in his apartments without food or drink for eight days, and when he finally emerged, stooped and visibly aged, he ordered the whole kingdom into mourning: music, bright clothes, jewellery and even perfume and cosmetics were banned. To glorify Mumtaz Mahal, the emperor vowed to build her the most beautiful tomb the world had ever seen. (The name by which it is known – the Taj Mahal – is a variant of the queen's name.)

Work began at Agra, capital of the Mogul Empire, in 1632 and the central building of the Taj Mahal – the mausoleum – was completed in 1643. The mausoleum, however, is only one part of a large complex that includes a formal garden, two flanking mosques and a stately entrance gateway which is an important building in itself. An inscription records the official date of completion as 1648, but work evidently continued for a few more years.

To complete such a grand scheme in just over 20 years is a remarkable accomplishment, but it was achieved because Shah Jahan had used every resource available in his empire: some 20 000 workmen laboured on the construction, and more than 1000 elephants transported marble from quarries 200 miles (320km) away. Other materials – and the master craftsmen to work them – came from even farther afield, including malachite from Russia, carnelian from Baghdad and turquoise from Persia and Tibet. An English traveller, Peter Mundy, who visited the Taj soon after work had begun, was amazed at the lavishness of the materials: 'gold and silver were esteemed common, and marble but as ordinary stone'. Smiths set to work on the silver doors of the grand entrance gate – though these were later stolen by a local Hindu tribe. Masons, carpenters, calligraphers, inlay specialists and other craftsmen combined their skills to create an everlasting memorial to one woman.

The Taj Mahal and the two sandstone mosques that flank it stand in marble-paved gardens. The visitor's eye is led to the great horizontal plinth that supports the mausoleum along a straight, narrow watercourse, lined with dark green cypresses, in which the shimmering mirror-image of the Taj is perfectly reflected. The bud-shaped dome soars upwards in visual harmony with arches, cupolas and four minarets, built leaning slightly outwards so that if there were an earthquake they would topple away from the building. The splendour of the Taj

Ultimate love *Legend tells that Shah Jahan met Arjumand Banu Begam (later Mumtaz Mahal) while she was selling trinkets in a bazaar. It was no ordinary bazaar, but part of the traditional Muslim New Year festivities.*

Stolen glory *Within the tomb lies the cenotaph of Mumtaz, inlaid with delicate gemstone flowers, many of which have been stolen over the decades. It is said that the Moguls built with the might of giants and the skill of jewellers.*

is further enhanced by the play of light, particularly at dawn and at dusk when subtle shades of violet, rose pink and muted gold – in varying degrees of softness and intensity – are reflected in the contours of the monument. And in the early morning mist, the building seems to float ethereally in the sky.

While the outside of the Taj is unique in its perfect symmetry, the inside, with its elaborate mosaic work, is also unrivalled. The interior is organised around a central octagonal chamber containing the cenotaphs of the emperor and his wife, enclosed by a perforated marble screen studded with gemstones. Here, in contrast to the glare outside, soft light filters through the latticed windows and filigree mesh of the intricate marble screen and plays on every surface, illuminating and then gradually concealing in shadow the bejewelled inlay work all around.

It had been Shah Jahan's intention to build his own tomb in black marble on the opposite bank of the River Jumna, linking it with a bridge to symbolise a love that transcended death. But in 1657, before work could begin, the emperor fell ill and was deposed a year later by his power-hungry son, Aurangzeb.

History is unclear as to precisely where Shah Jahan was imprisoned. The most frequently cited legend claims that for the remainder of his life the emperor was held in the Red Fort at Agra. On his death in 1666, he was buried in his masterpiece alongside the adored queen who had been its inspiration.

Saving grace The Taj Mahal fell into disrepair after the decline of the Mogul Empire in the 18th century. In the 19th century, under the British Raj, it was a popular venue for open-air parties, and the music of regimental bands filled its terraces. The Taj Mahal was restored to its former glory as a result of building work instigated by Lord Curzon (ABOVE), a dedicated conservationist and Viceroy of India from 1898 to 1905.

Distant memory The white dome of the Taj, described by the American novelist Mark Twain (1835–1910) as a 'soaring bubble of marble', is clearly visible from the Red Fort at Agra. It is said that Shah Jahan spent his last days here, gazing across the River Jumna at the final resting place of his beloved Mumtaz.

POTALA: JEWEL OF TIBET

Once a palace, a fortress and a site of divine pilgrimage, the Potala, topped with shimmering gold roofs, rises through the Tibetan mist like a colossal castle that in a certain light appears to be crowned with flames.

L hasa, capital city of Tibet, 'the roof of the world', lies 12 000ft (3600m) above sea level in a spot so remote that even today few westerners know of its existence. Above the city's bustling bazaar and warren of winding streets, more remote still stands the massive Potala Palace crowning the summit of the sacred mountain, Putuo Hill. Around the city stretches a fertile plain with a river winding through it, villages surrounded by swampy meadows, willow groves, lines of poplars and fields of peas and barley; and encircling the plain is a great ring of mountains that can only be crossed over high passes. The difficulties involved in reaching the Potala, however, are also part of its enchantment.

Pale with ancient whitewash and glittering with gold, the Potala (its name is Sanskrit for Buddha's Mountain) is an extraordinary example of traditional Tibetan architecture. Hidden from the Western world for centuries, this majestic mountain of masonry, which was built by more than 7000 labourers, towers 330ft (110m) above the ground and measures roughly 1000ft (300m) from end to end. Accentuating the impression of great height, its huge walls slope inwards and its windows, rhythmically arranged in neat, parallel rows and narrower at the top than at the bottom, are lacquered black. The immense hole created by excavating stone for the building from the hillside behind the palace was filled with water and now forms a lake, known as the Dragon King Pool.

From 1391 until the Chinese occupation in 1951, Tibet was ruled, both politically and spiritually, by the Dalai Lamas, although from 1717 to 1911 they were themselves subject to Chinese overlords. Lhasa was the centre of

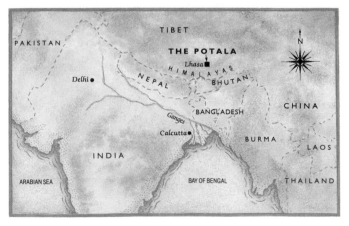

Grand illusion *Rising from the mist at dawn, the Potala Palace appears to grow straight from the hill that overlooks the city of Lhasa, whose very name means Ground of the Gods. The remote position of the palace, its imposing size and brilliantly gilded roofs* (ABOVE) *have all contributed to its mystique. According to legend, the fabulous golden turrets and pinnacles, ranged along the roof ridges of the pagodas and on the parapet, were put there to ward off devils.*

POTALA: JEWEL OF TIBET

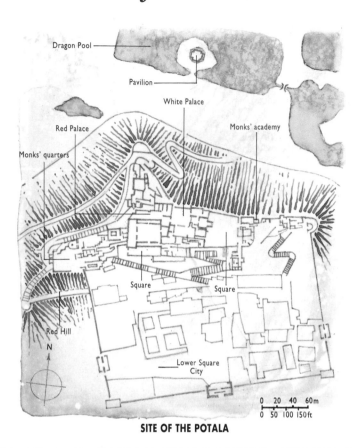

Dragon Pool
Pavilion
White Palace
Monks' academy
Red Palace
Monks' quarters
Square
Square
Red Hill
N
Lower Square City

0 20 40 60m
0 50 100 150ft

SITE OF THE POTALA

Lamaism, a blend of Tibetan Buddhism and a local religion called Bon. The fortress palace of the Dalai Lamas, the present Potala is a 17th-century structure on the site of a castle built 1000 years earlier by Songsten Gampo, Tibet's first warrior-king. The original palace was destroyed and rebuilt several times, before the fifth Dalai Lama (1617–82) ordered the present complex to be built as a palace within a palace. The outer White Palace, so-named for its white-washed walls, was completed in 1648; the inner Red Palace, whose name similarly derives from the deep red colour of its walls, was finished almost 50 years later in 1694. When the fifth Dalai Lama died unexpectedly, news of his death was withheld from the workers so that they would not be distracted from their task. At first they were told that he was ill, then that he had 'withdrawn from the world to devote every waking hour to meditation'.

The Potala is a maze of painted galleries, wooden and stone stairways and richly decorated prayer rooms housing almost 200 000 priceless statues. Today it can be visited as a museum and shrine, but originally it fulfilled every need of the resident monks. The White Palace contained their living quarters, administrative offices, seminary and a printing house, where the press used hand-carved wooden blocks. Paper was made from the bark of daphne or other

THE DALAI LAMA: DIVINITY INCARNATE

The two words in the title of this holy figure describe his position perfectly. *Dalai* is the Mongolian word for 'ocean', and *lama*, in the Tibetan language, means 'man of profound wisdom'. The Dalai Lama is, therefore, a mortal man whose wisdom is believed to be as deep as the ocean. He is also thought to be a divine being, an aspect in human form of the absolute Buddha.

Fourteen Dalai Lamas have occupied the position of the Tibetans' chosen leader since 1391. Each is said to be the reincarnation of his predecessor, and the search for a successor begins the moment the reigning Dalai Lama dies. Guided by omens, dreams and an official oracle, the Tibetan priests hunt for a boy, born at the precise moment of the Dalai Lama's death, who has specific physical traits and who can pick out the late incumbent's possessions from an assortment of objects.

The most recent Dalai Lama, Tenzin Gyatso, born in 1935, was recognised as the next ruler when he was two years old; he was enthroned at the age of five and governed from the Potala until the rising of 1959, when he sought refuge from the Chinese army in India. He established a government-in-exile in Dharmsala, Pakistan, where a Tibetan colony has formed. Deeply revered by the monks in the new Namgyal Monastery there, and by devout Tibetans who worship him from afar or travel to Dharmsala as pilgrims, the exiled Dalai Lama won the Nobel Peace Prize in 1989 for his tireless campaign for world peace and Tibetan freedom.

shrubs, soaked in water and pounded between stones. The pulp was then spread on wire gauze stretched over a wooden frame and left until it was dry; the resulting paper was cream-coloured, tough and coarse.

The Red Palace, which is still used for worship, was the spiritual centre of the complex and comprised the monks' assembly hall, chapels, 10 000 shrines and vast libraries containing Buddhist scriptures. The largest building in the Red Palace, the Hall of Sacrifice, became the final resting place of several Dalai Lamas, whose salt-dried and embalmed remains were enshrined there in elaborate funerary pagodas. Of the eight pagodas, or stupas, that remain intact, the sandalwood mausoleum of the fifth Dalai Lama is the most magnificent. Standing over 49ft (15m) high and coated with gold, this mausoleum weighs more than 4 tons, and its inlay of diamonds, sapphires, coral, lapis lazuli and pearls is supposedly worth ten times as much as the gold itself. The fabulous private treasury of the Dalai Lamas, a collection of ceremonial brocade robes, old Chinese porcelain, cloisonné, rare gems and exquisite jewellery, still rests in the Potala's strong rooms.

Heinrich Harrer, an Austrian mountaineer who lived in Lhasa for five years after World War II and eventually became the confidant and tutor of the 14th Dalai Lama, stayed at the Potala on several occasions. During one visit he reported an unusual presence at the palace. The Maharajah of Nepal had bestowed an elephant on the young Dalai Lama, the only such animal in the country, which was escorted to Lhasa over 700 miles (1125km) of road that had been carefully cleared of stones. The gigantic beast often joined the religious processions.

Until the Chinese occupation, Tibet was the world's last remaining theocracy – a society in which the ruler is also the religious leader – (today Iran occupies that position) and the Potala was both the home and winter palace of the ruler and the physical symbol of his spiritual and earthly powers. The 14th Dalai Lama was a youth of 15 when the Chinese invaded his country in 1950. He was allowed a limited form of rule until 1959, when, after a failed rebellion, he fled to India with 80 000 devoted followers. Tibet has since remained under Chinese control and in 1965 it became the Xizang Autonomous Region of China.

Although the god-king has departed, the Potala's magic lingers on. It seems to possess some transcendent quality that is quite unconnected with mere bricks and mortar: a mysterious land's central mystery.

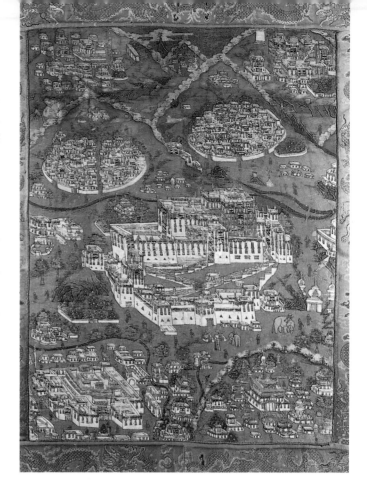

Miniature detail *A fine 18th-century Tibetan scroll, or* thang-ka, *accurately depicts the white-walled Potala. Lhasa's jumble of houses and narrow streets looked much the same until the Chinese occupation, but some modern buildings have now been erected.*

Holy image *Buddhists believe that Bodhisattva Avalokitshvara, the eight-armed Lord of Compassion depicted in this painting's central mandala, is reincarnated in each successive Dalai Lama.*

SHWE DAGON PAGODA

In shape and form the Shwe Dagon pagoda, one of the most sacred Buddhist shrines in the world and the dominating feature of the Rangoon skyline, is like any other pagoda. What makes it unique is that its domed-shaped stupa is covered with a skin of pure gold.

On a hilltop to the north of the Burmese capital, Rangoon, an edifice resembling a giant handbell gleams with pure gold, like sunlight that has been frozen and shaped. Burma has been called a 'land of pagodas', but Shwe Dagon, its central stupa emerging from a forest of spires of smaller pagodas and pavilions like a great ship, is the most magnificent of all. Covering an area of 14 acres (5.6ha), the pagoda is a complex of glittering pinnacles, and strange and familiar creatures – golden leogryphs (half lion, half griffin), sphinxes, dragons, lions, elephants. It is also a paradise for the senses.

The imposing structure at the summit of Singuttara Hill is the latest in a series of shrines built on this site, which has been considered sacred by Buddhists for some 2500 years. In the sixth century BC, soon after the fourth Buddha, Guatama, achieved the 'state of enlightenment', he encountered two Burmese merchants to whom he presented eight of his hairs as a memento. These, and relics of the three previous Buddhas – a staff, a water cup and a piece of clothing – were enshrined on Singuttara Hill and a gold slab was placed over the shrine. Finally, a series of pagodas in different materials, one on top of the other, was built over the sacred artefacts. The hill became a place of pilgrimage and the first notable visitor to pay homage to the relics was King Ashoka of India in 260 BC.

Over the centuries kings and princes undertook the care of the shrine, cutting back the encroaching jungle and rebuilding and restoring when necessary. The present shape and form date from the 15th century and the reign of Queen Shinsawbu, who was also responsible for gilding the stupa for the first time. In accordance with her wishes, it was plated in gold leaf whose weight equalled that of her own bodyweight of 90lb (40kg). Her son-in-law and successor, King Dhammazedi, was more generous still, donating four times his weight in gold to replate the stupa. Since the region's tropical seasonal rains constantly damage the fragile layers of gold, this process has had to be repeated many times. Today, the cost of regilding is borne by public subscription every 20 years. Pilgrims, too, paste sheets of gold leaf on the pagoda, or on one of the images of Buddha, as devotional offerings.

The base of Shwe Dagon, approached by covered stairways from each of the four compass points, consists of a series of rectangular and octagonal terraces, supporting

Golden glory *The Shwe Dagon pagoda towers above the tranquil waters of the Royal Lake, dwarfing the structures that surround it. The present edifice dates from 1768 and the reign of King Hsinbyushin, who authorised the 3538 bells, 10 million bricks and 100 000 brass screws that went into its construction.*

158

In the realm of the senses
As well as crowds of visitors, processions of saffron-robed pilgrims throng the pagoda's marble-floored terrace. With colourful silk sarongs glowing in the sunlight, the fragrance of jasmine, incense and sandalwood perfuming the air, and the tinkling of bells delighting the ear, the Shwe Dagon is a sensual paradise.

Objects of devotion *The ornate prayer pavilions, or* tazoungs, *which surround the main pagoda, abound with images of Buddha, many illuminated by* *flickering candlelight. Shops along the covered entrance walkways sell flowers, small flags and gold leaf for pilgrims to offer at the feet of the statues.*

the stupa, the shape of which is said to represent Buddha's inverted begging bowl. (The relics of the four Buddhas are now housed in the stupa.) From this a golden spire soars upwards and narrows to the *hui*, an elegant 'umbrella', from which gold and silver bells hang. From the *hui* rises a gem-encrusted vane, topped by a golden orb which is studded with more than 1100 diamonds, including one of 76 carats on the tip, and nearly 1400 other precious stones. From base to apex, the pagoda is 326ft (99m) high.

King Dhammazedi made two further important contributions to the Shwe Dagon. He had three stone tablets inscribed with the pagoda's history in Burmese, Pali and Mons, and he donated a massive bell, weighing some 20 tons. In 1608 a Portuguese mercenary stole this gift, intending to melt it down for weaponry, but his boat capsized under the weight of the bell, which was lost in the River Pegu. The present Maha Gandha bronze bell was donated by King Singu in 1779.

The Shwe Dagon is more than a sacred monument or a place for regular, organised worship. It is a focal point for Buddhist pilgrims and monks who wish to meditate and pray in the holiest of surroundings. Laypeople are also

drawn to the pagoda – to perform the ritual of pressing gold leaf on the stupa, or to leave an offering of flowers or to pay their respects to their planetary posts. In Burmese astrology there are eight days of the week (Wednesday is divided into two, at noon), each of which is associated with a planet and an animal. The eight planetary posts, one at each of the compass points, are situated around the base of the main pagoda, and, according to the day of the week on which a person is born, he or she leaves flowers and other offerings at the appropriate post. The same symbolism is repeated in the Eight Day pagoda situated within the complex, and likewise a special place of pilgrimage.

The clouds of incense, echoing prayers and, above all, the golden skin of Shwe Dagon have moved and inspired countless visitors over the centuries. Many, including author Rudyard Kipling, writing in the 1880s, contented themselves with descriptions of its physical splendour: 'A beautiful, winking wonder that blazed in the sun.' Others, among them many non-Buddhists such as Somerset Maugham, have touched on its spiritual significance. He recorded that the sight of the pagoda lifted the spirit 'like a sudden hope in the dark night of the soul'.

THE FLOATING CHIMES

One of the largest bells in the Far East is housed in a separate pavilion within the Shwe Dagon complex, to the north-west of the main pagoda platform. The Maha Gandha bell, which was cast between 1775 and 1779, weighs 23 tons, measures 14ft (4m) high and is 15in (38cm) thick.

In the course of the first Anglo-Burmese War, the British occupied Rangoon from 1824 to 1826 and ransacked Shwe Dagon, removing many of its treasures, including the Maha Gandha bell, which they intended to ship to Calcutta. But they lost their grip, and the prize plunged into the Rangoon River. After several attempts by the British to raise the bell had failed, the Burmese offered to retrieve it, on condition that it was returned to its rightful resting place. The British, thinking that Burmese attempts would also end in failure, agreed. Divers attached innumerable bamboo poles underneath the lost treasure, which then floated to the surface.

The last Buddha
According to legend, at the end of the previous world, five lotus buds sprang up on Singuttara Hill. From each bud rose a sacred bird carrying a sacred yellow robe. These birds symbolised the five Buddhas who would appear in the next (present) world. Four – Kakusandha, Konagamana, Kassapa and Gautama – have already lived; the fifth, Maitreya, is still awaited and with his birth the present cycle of the world will end. This special association between Shwe Dagon and Buddhism explains the profusion of effigies found in and around the pagoda.

161

ANGKOR: CITY OF TEMPLES AND MYSTERY

Hidden for centuries in the depths of the Cambodian jungle, the venerable crumbling stone temples of Angkor, capital of the medieval Khmer Empire, are among the world's greatest cultural treasures.

While hacking a pathway through the dense Cambodian jungle in 1850, the French missionary Father Charles-Emile Bouillevaux stumbled upon the sprawling ruins of an ancient city. Among them stood one of the world's greatest religious shrines, Angkor Wat. 'I discovered,' Bouillevaux wrote, 'some immense ruins which I was told were the site of a royal palace. On the walls, which were carved from top to toe, I saw combats between elephants, men fighting with clubs and spears, and others firing three arrows at a time from their bows.'

Ten years later the French naturalist Henri Mouhot, retracing Bouillevaux's footsteps, was equally astounded by what lay before him in the jungle clearing: more than 100 wats (or temples) dating from the ninth to the 13th centuries, with architecture that changed in religious focus from Hinduism to Buddhism. Statues, reliefs and carvings brought to life before his eyes scenes from Hindu mythology, exotic dancing girls, a king on elephant-back, an emperor leading his troops into battle, and row upon row of serene Buddhas. Mouhot's excited reports posed many questions: who had built this magnificent place and

Ageless beauty *Fashioned like lotus buds, the perfectly preserved central towers of Angkor Wat rise gracefully from the tangled vegetation of the jungle. The temple covers an area larger than the Vatican in Rome and was dedicated to the Hindu god Vishnu. Isolated from the surrounding buildings and countryside by a moat 650ft (200m) wide, it typifies the Khmer tradition of siting places of worship away from the bustle of daily life. Temples were designed as places for contemplation and veneration of the Khmer kings in whose honour they were built.*

History in stone *Khmer history, undocumented anywhere else, is recorded in the bas-reliefs adorning the outer terrace of the*

Bayon, a religious building at the centre of Angkor's main square. Here, foot soldiers fight alongside elephant-borne warriors

Silence of the centuries
*Monkey-headed guardians
gaze out from one of
Angkor's earliest Hindu
temples, Banteay Samre,
which lies at the eastern
edge of the Angkor complex.
In niches in the intricately
carved sandstone walls
stand statues of asperas, the
celestial dancers whose role
is to entertain the gods.*

163

ANGKOR: CITY OF TEMPLES AND MYSTERY

what was the story behind its rise and fall? The earliest Cambodian records dated only from the 15th century: now a previously unknown era of civilisation began to unfold.

The ruined city of Angkor lies about 150 miles (240km) north-west of Phnom Penh, the capital of Cambodia (formerly Kampuchea), near the great lake of Tonle Sap. At the height of its development in AD 1000, it covered an area of 75 sq miles (190km²), making it the largest city of the medieval world. Around 600 000 people lived and worked in its sprawl of streets, squares, terraces and temples, and the surrounding population numbered around one million.

The inhabitants of Angkor were the Khmer, whose religion, a form of Hinduism, was introduced to South-east Asia by Indian traders in the first century AD. Scholars today are still puzzled by the fact that, although this area was well populated and technologically advanced by 1000 BC, there is no evidence that any cities or towns existed until around the seventh century AD. After that date, civilisation blossomed, and Angkor is the supreme expression of the Khmer talent for creating stupendous works of art and monumental architectural structures.

Khmer documents, written on perishable materials such as palm leaves and animal skins, have disintegrated with time; therefore, to glean information about the city's past, archaeologists have referred to more than 1000 carved inscriptions, most of them written in Khmer and Sanskrit. These reveal that the key figure of the Khmer ascendancy was Jayavarman II, who freed his people from Javanese rule in the early ninth century. He worshipped Shiva, one of the main Hindu deities, and founded the cult of the

ARCHITECTURAL WONDER

The sprawling complex of Angkor extends for 15 miles (24km) west to east and 5 miles (8km) north to south. The plan shows the position of the temples (RIGHT), and the well-ordered layout of causeways, irrigation canals and the two reservoirs – the Eastern and Western Baray. Each could store 2000 million gallons (9000 million litres) of water, which was used during the six-month dry season to irrigate agricultural land. A wide, crocodile-infested moat surrounded the shrine of Angkor Wat, beyond which was the square of Angkor Thom, built by Jayavarman VII.

Ta Keo *(AD 1000) was the first major temple built of sandstone. Temples are the only buildings still standing at Angkor (hence the epithet 'the city of temples') because only the temples were built of durable materials such as brick or stone. All other edifices, including the kings' palaces, were made of perishable wood.*

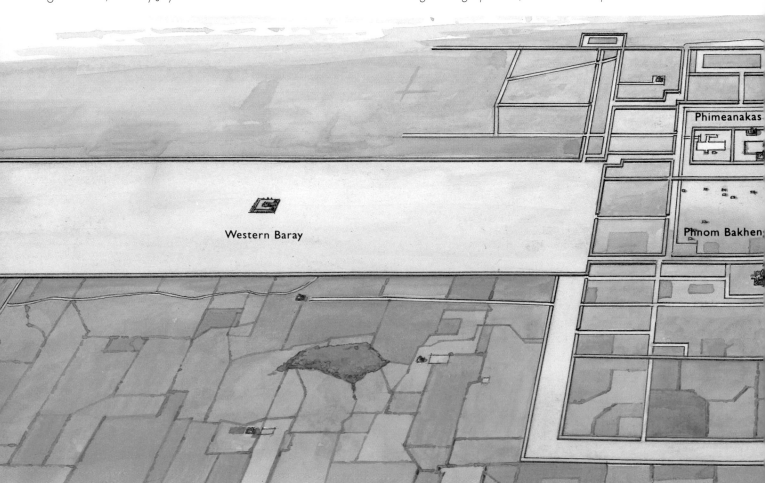

Western Baray

Phimeanakas

Phnom Bakhen

Phnom Bakheng (AD 900), the first temple at Angkor, was constructed on a natural hill. It was created by Yasovarman I, who was also responsible for diverting the Siem Reap River to fill the Eastern Baray – Angkor's first irrigation project.

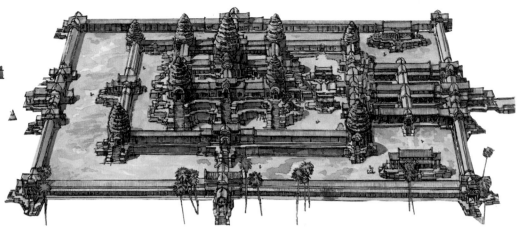

Angkor Wat (AD 1113–50), the finest and best preserved of all the temples at Angkor, is approached by a road exactly twice as long as the height of the tallest tower. Some 5000 craftsmen and 50 000 other workers were employed to complete the complex. Its labyrinth of corridors is lined with elaborate sculptures and carvings, including a 160ft (50m) long depiction of the Hindu creation myth known as Churning of the Sea of Milk.

Prasat Kravanh (AD 921), built by high court officials, is unusual for its interior brick bas-reliefs; brick and stone were generally used only for exteriors.

Phimeanakas (AD 910). According to legend, the Khmer king slept here each night with the serpent goddess to ensure her protection of his empire.

Bayon (begun AD 1200). In the 13th century Jayavarman VII's masterpiece was described as a golden tower flanked by 20 stone towers.

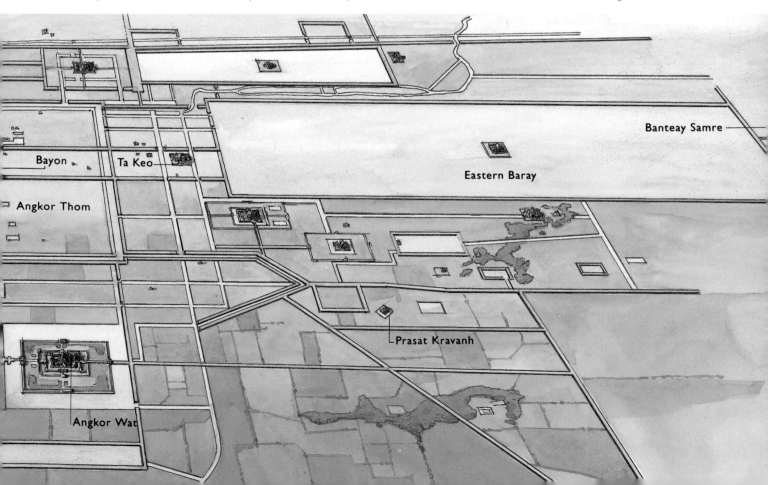

Banteay Samre

Bayon Ta Keo

Eastern Baray

Angkor Thom

Prasat Kravanh

Angkor Wat

ANGKOR: CITY OF TEMPLES AND MYSTERY

god-king, whereby his own mortal powers were enhanced by Shiva's creative energies. He, and each of his successors, built a temple to house his *lingam*, the phallic symbol of his spiritual and temporal powers. After the rulers' deaths, these temples became their tombs.

The city of Angkor (*angkor* means city in the Khmer language) became a huge metropolis, the size of present-day Manhattan. The finest building by far was Angkor Wat, built by Suryavarman II early in the 11th century as his own temple and tomb. Dedicated to the Hindu god Vishnu, Angkor Wat covers an area of nearly 1 sq mile (2.5km²) and is probably the largest religious complex ever built. This vast Hindu shrine is arranged as a series of rectangular and concentric enclosures, its tallest towers rising 200ft (60m) above the tangle of the jungle. At the mid-winter solstice, the nearby temple of Prasat Kuk Bangro forms an alignment with Angkor Wat, suggesting that it may also have had some astronomical function.

Angkor was a prosperous city: its rich soil yielded three crops of rice each year; fish were abundant in the lake of

Tonle Sap, and the dense forests supplied all the teak and other woods that were necessary for making temple floors and building galleries. The presence of such plentiful supplies of food and building materials makes it all the more difficult to explain Angkor's decline. Why did this once-magnificent city deteriorate into a deserted ruin?

Two theories have been put forward as to its collapse, both of which have a religious foundation. After the sacking of Angkor in 1171 by the Cham, the Khmer's warrior neighbours, Jayavarman VII lost his faith in the protective power of the Hindu gods; the Khmer adopted a form of Buddhism that renounced violence and espoused pacifism, and Jayavarman dedicated his temple, the Bayon, in Angkor Thom square, to Buddha. As a result of this religious conversion, the Thai army that attacked Angkor in 1431 met with little resistance and sacked the city after a seven-month siege. Angkor never regained its former glory.

The second, more fanciful, theory derives from Buddhist legend. A Khmer king was so offended by a priest's son that he ordered the boy to be drowned in the waters of Tonle Sap. In retaliation, an angry god caused the lake to overflow, thereby destroying Angkor. Since Tonle Sap is prone to flooding during the monsoon season, there may be at least a grain of truth in this story.

Today, the encroaching jungle vegetation is prising Angkor's remaining buildings apart, while mosses and lichens obscure the stones. Although chemicals have recently been used to remove this growth, the long-term effects of such treatment on the structures is not known. Even more destructive is the wholesale damage wrought over the past two decades by war and the ravishment of the temples by art thieves, who have removed carvings and statues to sell abroad. It appears that the future of this unique site is again in the balance.

Architectural treasure
The temple of Angkor Wat is contemporary with the great cathedrals of Chartres and Canterbury. While European architects prized interior space, which they achieved through high, vaulted ceilings, their Khmer counterparts never perfected the true arch on which these structures depend.

Safe route *Due to political unrest and civil war in Cambodia, from the 1960s until around the end of the 1980s the great square of Angkor Thom was closed to civilians. Now it is open again, and local people return from market through the square. But they still fear attack from Khmer Rouge guerrillas on jungle paths.*

THE FORBIDDEN CITY

At the heart of China's capital, Beijing, lies the Forbidden City, one of the finest palace complexes in the world and a symbol of China's dynastic past. Its name conjures images of mystery and intrigue, and the opulent way of life enjoyed by China's imperial rulers.

I t has been compared to a set of intricately carved Chinese work boxes: within each opened box sits another, similar but smaller. Even today, when the Forbidden City is open to Western eyes, it retains a sense of mystery. Just as it is impossible to know exactly what may be hidden within a given box, so many of the secrets of Beijing's stately palace complex may never be revealed.

The building of the Forbidden City was undertaken by the third Ming emperor, Yung Lo, who ruled between 1403 and 1423, after he had finally ousted the Mongols from Beijing. Whether he chose to build his city on the same site as the former Mongol palace that had so impressed Marco Polo on his visit in 1274, or merely took the palace of the Mongol emperor Khublai Khan as his model, is uncertain. But an estimated workforce of 100 000 craftsmen and a million labourers set to work, fashioning the city's 800 palaces, 75 halls, numerous temples, pavilions, libraries and studios, all linked by gardens, courtyards and pathways. In this city, which from its inception was forbidden to outsiders, 24 emperors of the Ming and Qing dynasties reigned, shielded behind a moat and a wall 35ft (11m) high – until the republican revolution began in 1911.

The Forbidden City is an architectural masterpiece whose beauty lies not so much in any one building as in the ordered layout of the whole and the exquisite combination of colours used in its decoration. Altogether, it reflects the Chinese view that the emperor, as the Son of Heaven, was the mediator responsible for order and harmony on Earth.

The formal entrance to the city is the Meridian Gate, where a drum and bell were sounded whenever an emperor passed by. The vast courtyard beyond the gate contains a section of the Golden River. Shaped like an archer's bow and spanned by five marble bridges, it leads to the Gate of Supreme Harmony, and from there into the courtyard of the Hall of Supreme Harmony – deemed the centre of the Chinese world. In this splendid chamber the emperor presided from the Dragon Throne and grand ceremonies were held on festive occasions. Behind it stands the Hall

Imposing entrance *Built around 1450, the* Wu Men, *or Meridian Gate, was reserved for the exclusive use of the emperor. From here, he reviewed his armies, sentenced prisoners, surveyed the flogging of miscreants, and announced the arrival of the new year.*

168

Palace guardians *Evil spirits were said to enter Chinese buildings through the roof. To ward them off, the roofs of the Imperial Palace* (BELOW) *were adorned with carved guardian figures, such as winged horses.*

of Complete Harmony, where the emperor prepared for audiences with envoys from abroad. No emperor ventured from the Forbidden City at all if he could avoid it. He entertained visitors in the most northerly of the three state imperial buildings, the Hall of Preserving Harmony.

North of these halls and repeating their layout is a group of three palaces which comprise the imperial residential quarters. Two of these, the Palace of Heavenly Purity and the Palace of Earthly Tranquillity, were the residences of the emperor and empress respectively. Between them lies the Hall of Union, symbolically uniting emperor and empress, Heaven and Earth, *yang* and *yin*, male and female. Beyond the palaces lie the imperial gardens, where pools, rockeries, temples, libraries, theatres, pavilions and pine and cypress trees complement the symmetry of the buildings.

There were also living quarters for the thousands of servants, eunuchs and concubines who spent their entire lives within the walls of the Forbidden City. For this splendid complex was not just a seat of power: the whole

Ferocious beasts *A pair of bronze lions flanks the Dragon Pavement. It alone allowed access to the Hall of Supreme Harmony, where* *the emperor reigned from a filigree-marble Dragon Throne. Bronze animals, including tortoises and storks, abound in the city.*

Imperial elegance *The Palace of Heavenly Purity was the emperor's own residence. He was the only* *adult male allowed inside the city's residential quarter: his wives and concubines were guarded by eunuchs.*

The last emperor *During the Japanese occupation (1934–45) Pu Yi ruled as puppet emperor of Manchuria and ended his days working at Beijing's botanic gardens.*

of the Forbidden City was also given over to the emperor's pleasure. Some 6000 cooks were employed to provide food for him and his 9000 concubines, who were guarded by 70 000 eunuchs. Nor was the emperor the sole beneficiary of this extravagant lifestyle. The dowager empress Tsu Hzi, who died in 1908, was reputed to dine on meals of 148 courses, and to dispatch eunuchs in search of young lovers who, once inside the city gates, were never heard of again.

The rule of the Dragon Throne ended with the outbreak of the Chinese Revolution in 1911. The following year, the leaders of the new republic forced the six-year-old emperor, Pu Yi (1906–67), to abdicate; he was permitted to live on in the Forbidden City as a virtual prisoner until 1924. Gradually, many of the buildings fell into disrepair.

Today most of the halls and palaces house exhibits that chart the Forbidden City's opulent past, and as more and more visitors gain access to this amazing labyrinth the secrecy that surrounded the emperor and his court as recently as 100 years ago becomes more difficult to comprehend. Yet echoes of the past reverberate through every wall and courtyard and can be discerned in the splendour and craftsmanship of the weapons, jewellery, imperial costumes, musical instruments and gifts on display, which were presented to the emperors by rulers from all over the world.

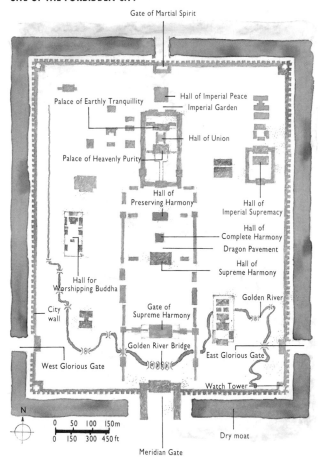

Imperial labyrinth Many of the wooden imperial buildings have been rebuilt since the 15th century. The overall plan of the Forbidden City is rectangular, aligned north–south like Beijing itself, and all the major buildings face south, the direction of the sun's beneficence and, therefore, holiness.

171

GREAT WALL OF CHINA

Both a barrier and a gateway to the wealth and enigma of the Chinese Empire, the Great Wall of China is a man-made work on such a gigantic scale that it has been called the Eighth Wonder of the World.

More superlatives have been heaped upon the Great Wall of China than on any other structure in the world. 'The greatest construction project ever undertaken by man', 'the longest bastion', and 'the world's biggest graveyard' are just three examples. The facts speak for themselves: the wall stretches for some 4000 miles (6400km) across China, following a twisting, curving path that has been likened to the body of a dragon. It was constructed over a period of 2100 years by millions of soldiers and labourers, and it cost the lives of untold thousands; in one ten-day period alone, in the seventh century AD, 500 000 men perished.

The origins of the wall date back to at least the fifth century BC. This period of Chinese history, referred to as that of the Warring States, followed the disintegration of the once unified kingdom of Zhou. To protect themselves against one another, the fractured states built defensive walls. In addition, the two most northerly states, Qin Zhao and Yan – both of which were largely agricultural – each constructed a series of dykes and earthworks to fortify their borders against incursions by the Xiongnu, the semi-nomadic cattle herders of the steppes to the north.

In 221 BC the Qin ruler, Shi Huangdi, subdued the Warring States and proclaimed himself first Qin emperor of China. In an 11-year reign, he established a ruthless and efficient empire, a system of justice, a standardised form of weights and measures, a network of roads, and a strict bureaucracy that controlled where people lived. He also ordered the consolidation and extension of all the existing walls to secure the empire's northern boundary. An army of 300 000 soldiers and up to a million pressganged labourers and prisoners set to work, tearing down and then rebuilding some of the old walls, and strengthening existing works.

In contrast to the earlier walls, which had consisted largely of defensive ditches with banks of earth made by pounding the soil into wooden 'forms', a variety of materials and construction methods was employed in the fabrication of Shi Huangdi's wall. As transport was difficult, local materials were used. In mountainous areas, blocks of stone were hewn from the rock face; oak, pine and fir logs infilled with tamped earth was the favourite combination in forested regions; and a mixture of earth, sand and pebbles was used in the Gobi Desert. Transportation was by human effort, by donkey, or by rope and pulley. Materials were carried on men's backs or passed along a 'human chain'.

The wall was never intended as a defensive fortification in its own right: it relied always on manned garrisons to

Between the towers *The watchtowers were probably constructed first, with the wall built to link them. Each tower could accommodate between 30 and 50 soldiers.*

172

Landscape architecture

The Great Wall stretches across deeply wooded forest, sandy desert and mountainous terrain (LEFT). It was once said to be the only man-made structure visible from the surface of the moon and, although this has proven not to be true, the wall holds a place in the record books as the largest building project ever undertaken.

Twist in the tail

The comparison of the wall to a dragon is not wholly fanciful. In many cases it was built to follow the contours of the terrain (BELOW), snaking along the tops of ridges, for example, to offer the soldiers stationed there maximum visibility over the surrounding area. Towers and forts were positioned where attack was most likely, such as in mountain passes, at road junctions or at the bends of rivers.

GREAT WALL OF CHINA

deter invaders. Line-of-sight communication between watchtowers meant that a message could travel from one end of the wall to the other in just 24 hours – a feat unequalled until the advent of the telephone. An incidental advantage of the garrison system to successive emperors was that the army was fragmented and – in some cases – miles away from the court in Beijing. Soldiers were therefore unlikely to be able to band together and mutiny.

After the death of Shi Huangdi, the emperors of the Han dynasty (206 BC–AD 220) continued to maintain and lengthen the wall. There were also later periods when rebuilding and consolidation meant that more time and manpower were invested in it. The final major phase of construction was undertaken by the emperors of the Ming dynasty (1368–1644), who, having repelled the Mongols first from Beijing and then from the rest of the country, sought to strengthen China's northern defences.

The sections of the Ming wall that have survived best are those constructed of masonry. These were made by levelling the ground, then laying foundations of courses of stone slabs. The wall has stone faces, infilled with a mixture of small stones, earth, rubble and lime. Once this structure was high enough – generally the Ming wall is 20ft (6m) high, 25ft (7.6m) wide at the base, and 20ft (6m) wide at the top – it was finished with bricks. If the angle of incline was less than 45°, the bricks were laid flat; if it was greater, they were fashioned into a staircase. Kilns were established at various points along the wall to manufacture vast quantities of bricks and tiles.

At the height of the Ming dynasty the wall stretched from Shanhaiguan on the Bohai Gulf east of Beijing to Jiayuguan in the central Asian province of Gansu: the westernmost limit was Yumenguan, 130 miles (200km) farther west, in the pre-Qin era. Today, those sections around the village of Badaling, some 40 miles (65km) from Beijing, are the best preserved. Elsewhere the condition of the wall varies from good to dilapidated – the latter particularly in the far west. Its current state of repair depends partly on the initial choice of materials, some of which have not endured, and partly on the extent to which the wall has been plundered by farmers for their own uses. Yet its power as a symbol is undiminished. To the Chinese it is a potent reminder of the nation's greatness, longevity (the political system laid down by Shi Huangdi was unaltered until 1911) and indestructibility. To the rest of the world it is a stunning monument that stands as a testimony to human strength, ingenuity and endurance.

Horsemen riding by The causeway that tops the wall allows six horses or ten *soldiers to stand abreast. A staircase every 600ft (180m) gives access to the wall.*

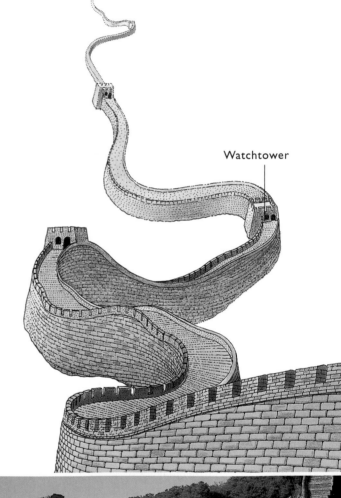

KEEPING WATCH

Some 25 000 watchtowers were spaced at 300–600ft (90–180m) intervals along the wall, each 40ft by 40ft (13m by 13m) at the base and standing an average of 40ft (13m) high. Garrison towers were never situated more than 11 miles (17.5km) apart. By day, a mixture of wolf dung, sulphur and nitrate produced smoke to signal to neighbouring towers the strength of an attack; at night, dry timber fires were used.

Watchtower

174

Reluctant warriors
Soldiers complained about conditions on the wall. After a march of anything up to eight weeks, many found themselves in a remote area with a harsh climate, among people whose language and culture were alien to them.

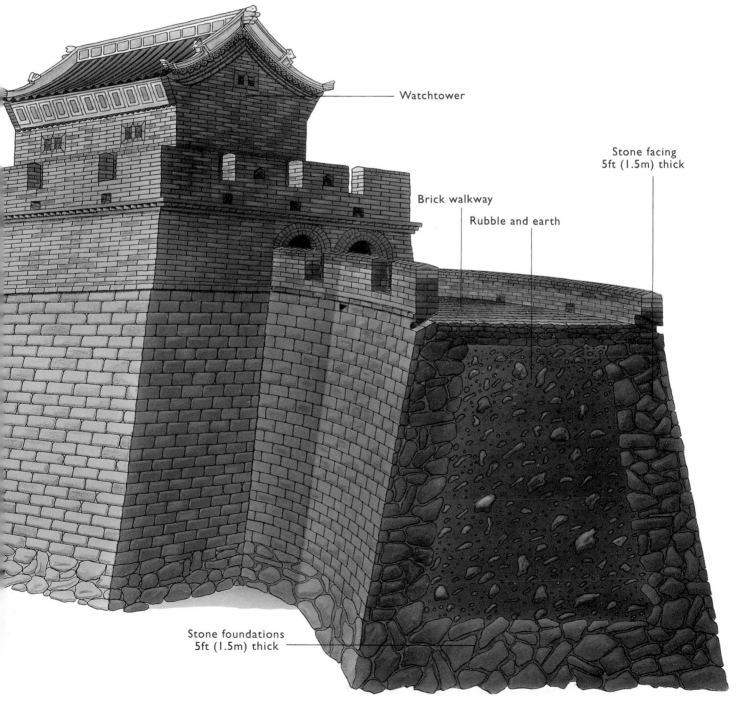

Watchtower

Stone facing 5ft (1.5m) thick

Brick walkway

Rubble and earth

Stone foundations 5ft (1.5m) thick

TEOTIHUACÁN: CITY OF THE GODS

An ancient religious capital of Mexico thrived a thousand years before the height of the Aztec Empire. In spite of more than a century of painstaking archaeological research, no one knows who built it, or when, or why – and even its demise is shrouded in mystery.

In translation its name means 'City of the Gods'; Teotihuacán more than lives up to that promise. It is the largest and most impressive of Mexico's pre-Columbian cities, situated some 7500ft (about 2285m) above sea level on the Mexican Plateau, almost exactly the same altitude as the other great New World metropolis, Machu Picchu in Peru. There the similarity ends. While the latter is squeezed into precipitous ravines, the spacious plain chosen as the site for Teotihuacán gave its builders free rein. The city covers about 9 sq miles (23km²), and its biggest building, the Pyramid of the Sun, is larger than the Colosseum in Rome which was erected at the same time.

Little is known about Teotihuacán. It was once thought to have been built by the Aztecs, but the city was abandoned 700 years before they discovered and named it in the 15th century. Even the identity of the original builders is unknown, but for convenience they are sometimes referred to as the 'Teotihuacanos'. Nor are there any historical records: what little is known about this ancient place has come solely from archaeological research.

There is evidence that the area was occupied as early as 400 BC, but Teotihuacán's most magnificent period was from the second to the seventh centuries AD. The present ruins are probably those of a city built around the time of the birth of Christ by a workforce drawn from a population estimated to have totalled 200 000 – making Teotihuacán the sixth largest city in the world at that time.

At its zenith Teotihuacán dominated the whole of Central America in cultural terms. Its potters produced vase-shaped and cylindrical vessels with three slab-shaped feet and stuccoed and painted decoration. Its most impressive sculptures are austere stone masks fashioned from greenstone, basalt and jade, and with eyes carved from obsidian or mussel-shell. Obsidian may have been the foundation

Dominating factor *The Pyramid of the Sun, built of sun-dried bricks called* adobe, *is estimated to have taken 3000 men, without the aid of pack animals, metal tools or the wheel, 30 years to construct. Today, as then, it dominates the site.*

Centre of the universe

No one knows the true significance of the Pyramid of the Sun, but since it is aligned on an east–west axis to follow the path of the sun across the sky, it has been seen as representing the centre of the universe: its four corners are the four principal points of the compass, and its apex (ABOVE) *is the heart of life.*

TEOTIHUACÁN: CITY OF THE GODS

Key 1 *Pyramid of the Sun*
2 *Pyramid of the Moon*
3 *Avenue of the Dead*

AVENUE OF THE DEAD

Teotihuacán's main artery extends south from the Pyramid of the Moon, past the Pyramid of the Sun, and on to the Ciudadela and the Temple of Quetzalcoatl. It has been interpreted as a symbol of the union of heaven and earth, linking the celestial areas of the city where the pyramids stand with the earthly section around the Ciudadela.

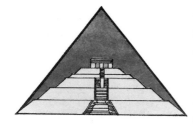

At 738ft (225m), the sides of the Pyramid of the Sun are about the same length as those of the Great Pyramid of Khufu (Cheops) in Egypt, but at 230ft (70m) it is only half the height.

of the city's wealth. This dark, glassy mineral, which came from nearby volcanoes, was highly prized, for it could be easily sharpened into blades for tools and weapons.

The people of Teotihuacán traded throughout Mexico's central highlands, and possibly in the rest of Central America too. Vases from the city have been found in graves all over Mexico. It is uncertain, however, whether the city established a political empire outside its own boundaries. Murals excavated from the site depict few military scenes, which suggests that the Teotihuacanos were not aggressive.

The skill of Teotihuacán's craftsmen was exceeded only by the unparalleled architectural genius of its creators. The city is organised on a giant grid, whose baseline is the 2 mile (3.2km) long principal thoroughfare, the Avenue of the Dead (named by the Aztecs, who mistook the platforms

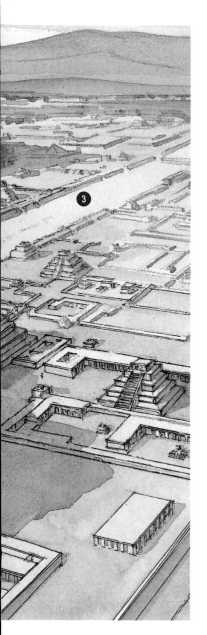

Smaller than the Sun
The Pyramid of the Moon is about two-thirds the size of the Pyramid of the Sun. Such discrepancies between solar and lunar symbols occur elsewhere: the spire crowned with the sun at Chartres Cathedral is higher than that crowned with the moon.

Feathered serpent The head of the god Quetzalcoatl, who represents the union of water and air, heaven and earth, alternates with that of the rain god Tlaloc along each row of panels on the facades of the six-tiered Temple of Quetzalcoatl.

that line the route for tombs). At its northern extremity is the Ciudadela, the 'citadel', an enormous enclosure which houses the Temple of Quetzalcoatl, the serpent god.

The Pyramid of the Sun, which dominates the site, was built on the ruins of an earlier structure. Some 20ft (6m) below its base, and extending for 330ft (100m), is a natural cavern that was a sacred place both before and after the 2.5 million tons of dried mud bricks were hoisted into place. The Pyramid of the Moon is architecturally more complex, with the lower tier of its main face consisting of several interlocking sloping stages rather than one continuous incline. Unlike the pyramids of Egypt, those at Teotihuacán were not used as tombs, but as temple platforms.

The religious buildings were not the only architectural wonders of Teotihuacán. Modern excavations of some of its palaces have revealed that each was constructed on the same geometric principles, with their many rooms arranged around a central courtyard. Although the roofs are missing, the walls are decorated with boldly designed frescoes whose reds, browns, blues and yellows are still vibrant.

No one knows what brought about the downfall of this great city and civilisation. The remains of charred roof beams support the theory that the city was sacked around AD 740, possibly by the Toltecs, who ruled the region from the 10th to the 12th centuries. A few survivors lived in Teotihuacán after the devastation, but its days as a thriving metropolis were over. Today, a visitor who stands in the ruins, with nothing on the horizon but mountains and sky, might find it difficult to believe that Mexico City lies just 30 miles (48km) to the south-west.

COPÁN: ROYAL CITY IN THE JUNGLE

After it was abandoned in the tenth century, Copán lay forgotten for 500 years, claimed only by the advancing jungle. Yet even in ruins this once-magnificent city is acknowledged as the pinnacle of Mayan achievement and possesses some of the greatest examples of Mayan architecture and stone carvings.

Bold carving *The Mayan civilisation was renowned for its magnificent carvings. This impressive stone skull dates back to the eighth century. It may depict a member of a princely caste.*

During the rainy winter of 1839, the American explorer John Lloyd Stephens and the English artist Frederick Catherwood reached a clearing in dense tropical forest and beheld the ancient Mayan city of Copán. Overgrown jungle concealed many of the buildings and blurred the outlines of those that still stood. The whole site had been ravaged by extremes of weather, earthquake shocks and the slow strangulation of creepers and tree roots. It had also endured a thousand years of erosion by the Copán River.

The substantial remains of this royal city lie in the heart of the Copán River valley in Honduras, a few miles from the Guatemalan border. Here, throughout the Classic Maya era, from about AD 250 to 900, a succession of at least 16 kings, with a court of priests and nobles, ruled over a large population of artists, merchants, craftsmen and farmers.

Stephens and Catherwood were not the first visitors to be intrigued by Copán. In the 16th century, more than five centuries after the city's abandonment, Spanish colonists had made mention of it in their writings, and in 1834 the Guatemalan government had financed a study of the ruins. But it was the work of these two men that brought Copán to the attention of the Western world. They bought the site for 50 dollars from the farmer who owned the land and set about exploring it and recording their findings. Catherwood, frequently ankle-deep in mud and wearing gloves to ward off the ubiquitous mosquitoes, spent his days sketching the ruins. His exquisite, detailed drawings fired the imagination of Western academics, and archaeologists have since excavated and partially restored Copán's plazas, buildings and monuments.

In its heyday, Copán was a wealthy city, trading widely throughout Mayan territory. The pyramids, temples, courts and other structures of the main complex are grouped around a series of four wide plazas, which were originally floored with smooth white plaster. The buildings, fashioned from andesite – a greenish volcanic rock – were often decorated with painted stucco reliefs. Traces of paint on walls and carvings indicate that Copán's entire main group of buildings and plazas and its sculptures must once have been vividly coloured.

From the four major plazas rise stepped, pyramid-like palaces and temples. Long, steep staircases ascend to the

Ancient ball game
Copán's ball court is in the city's ceremonial centre. Here, using hips, knees and heads (but not hands or feet), teams vied to strike a large ball of solid rubber against one of the projecting macaws' heads. The game was more of a ritual than a sport.

Spectacular sculpture
The exteriors of temples
were decorated with
intricate sculptures, such as
this one (LEFT) that adorns
the framework of the door
in the Temple of Meditation.

Powerful monument An
impressive stone head (FAR
LEFT) surveys the timeworn
landscape of this ancient
city. It is thought to represent
one of the multitude of
Mayan gods.

181

COPÁN: ROYAL CITY IN THE JUNGLE

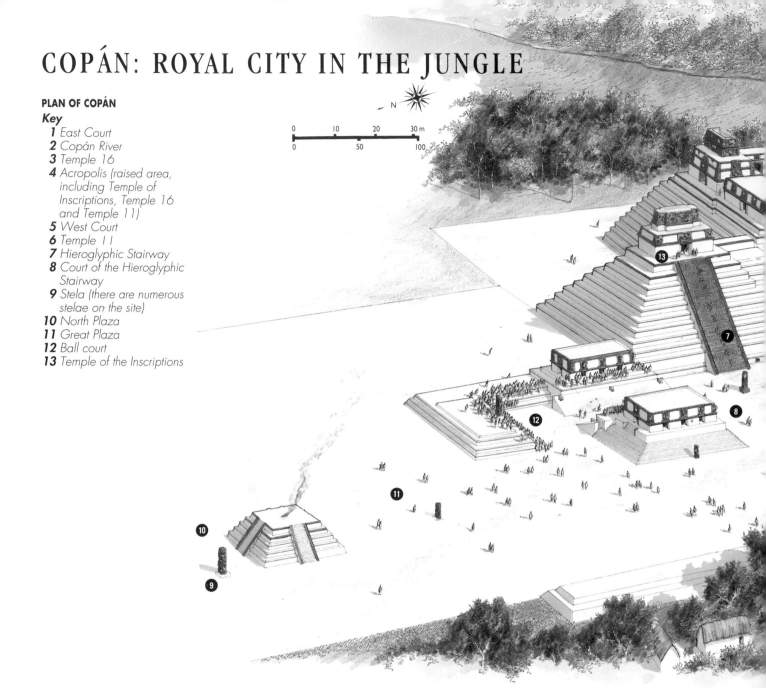

PLAN OF COPÁN
Key

1 East Court
2 Copán River
3 Temple 16
4 Acropolis (raised area,
   including Temple of
   Inscriptions, Temple 16
   and Temple 11)
5 West Court
6 Temple 11
7 Hieroglyphic Stairway
8 Court of the Hieroglyphic
   Stairway
9 Stela (there are numerous
   stelae on the site)
10 North Plaza
11 Great Plaza
12 Ball court
13 Temple of the Inscriptions

temples perched at the summit of the pyramids. The greatest of these, known as the Hieroglyphic Stairway, consisted originally of 72 steps, each 52ft (16m) wide and almost 18in (45cm) high. Detailed carvings on the riser of each step tell the stories of Copán's rulers, from the first warrior kings to the builder of the staircase, known as Smoke Shell, who came to the throne in AD 749. The continuous inscription of some 1250 stone pictograms or 'glyphs' is the longest found in any of the Mayan remains of Central America. The Hieroglyphic Stairway collapsed in the 19th century; today only 30 risers are in their original place, but the rest are being carefully restored.

Scholars have succeeded in deciphering the names and dates of Copán's rulers by closely examining carvings on the main stairway, walls and altars, and they have found further clues in the sculptured, staff-like stone pillars, or stelae, that the kings of Copán erected as monuments to

themselves. These portray larger than life-size royal figures clad in robes of state and adorned with symbols of power. Seven stelae, each about 11ft (3.4m) high, originally stood in the Great Plaza.

Altogether there are 38 stelae in and around the site, some of which are arranged in astronomical alignments – important for the Maya, since they used the positions of the stars and planets to guide them through life. The complex and sophisticated calendar systems the Maya used, based partly on the cycles of the planet Venus, allow the dates in their carvings to be read to the year, month and day with perfect accuracy. Numbers in these calendar systems are represented by horizontal bars, dots and shell symbols.

After about AD 900 the city was abandoned; from half-finished carvings that have been discovered it appears that this occurred quite suddenly. Although the royal city fell into decline, the Maya continued to live in the surrounding

valley in simple settlements, growing maize, squash and beans, as they do today. Historians are still trying to work out why the population of the city moved away. Copán's agricultural system may well have been too fragile and inadequate to support the demands of a large population, causing the disgruntled city dwellers to rise up against the kings and priests.

With the departure of its people, the once-magnificent city was left to the mercies of the encroaching jungle, the river and the elements. Today, descendants of the Maya live in the nearby town of Copán Ruinas, so the old and new worlds exist side by side.

Impressive idol *The earliest stelae at Copán are dated* AD *465 and 485. There are 38 stelae at Copán, all larger-than-life carvings of important persons with glyphs on the back giving biographical details.*

MACHU PICCHU: LOST CITY OF THE INCAS

High in the Peruvian Andes, the citadel of Machu Picchu appears suspended in mountain mists. Perched precariously on a rocky outcrop with huge drops either side, this city of a long-dead race eluded discovery until the 20th century, some 400 years after its downfall.

Today a traveller in Peru can make the 60 mile (96km) journey from the city of Cuzco to Machu Picchu in just a few hours by train and bus. In 1911 the American historian and archaeologist Hiram Bingham toiled for five days along the valley of the River Urubamba before reaching the now famous ruins. He believed he had discovered the Inca stronghold of Vilcabamba; a city that had been razed to the ground during the Spanish conquest of the Inca Empire in 1572. Bingham later made an attempt to communicate something of his astonishment at what he found in recollecting that 'it seemed like an unbelievable dream'.

Bingham persisted in the belief that he had discovered Vilcabamba, which had been his objective when organising the Yale Peruvian Expedition, but experts today maintain that the true site of this city is at Espiritu Pampa in northwestern Peru. The comparatively small fortified city that Bingham had stumbled upon was probably abandoned by the Incas before the destruction of Vilcabamba. The remains were in such an excellent state of preservation that it is unlikely that Machu Picchu was ever discovered by the Spaniards, who had a deserved reputation for plundering any settlements that they encountered. Furthermore, there is no mention of this site in their detailed chronicles.

Bingham's party chanced upon Machu Picchu largely by luck. They had made camp in a river canyon where they met a farmer who told them of the remains of an ancient city on a nearby mountain called Machu Picchu ('old peak'). Although sceptical, the next day Bingham and his party followed the farmer up the mountain through dense jungle. Near the top, 2000ft (610m) above the valley floor, they came across a stone-faced terrace hundreds of yards long and, beyond it, walls of pure white blocks of granite, covered in thick vegetation but remarkable nonetheless for their exquisite workmanship. Bingham wrote: 'Dimly, I began to realise that this wall with its adjoining semicircular temple over the cave were as fine as the finest stonework in the world.' In every respect, Machu Picchu was an extraordinary place, not least because the people who built it did not possess iron tools, draught animals or, indeed, the wheel.

Returning a year later to clear away the vegetation and excavate the site, Bingham uncovered a multilayered complex of squares, baths, courtyards, water channels, houses,

Fortress city Huayna Picchu towers over the ruins of Machu Picchu, perched high on an Andean mountain ridge above the River Urubamba. The sheer grandeur of the buildings suggests that the city may have been a mountain retreat for the aristocracy of the Inca capital, Cuzco, but the city probably had a permanent population of servants and farmers. Careful records kept by the Spanish conquistadors after the fall of the Inca Empire in 1533 make no mention of Machu Picchu, so the reasons for the city's decline can only be guessed at.

Interlocking stonework
The walls of the buildings are made of cleverly hewn blocks of granite that fit together neatly with no need for mortar (ABOVE). *Some of the largest blocks, which were shaped using only crude stone tools, weigh up to 100 tons and were probably hauled into position with ropes or levered into place.*

palaces and temples. The buildings were constructed of huge granite blocks, but no mortar had been used to hold them in place – the skilfully crafted blocks fitted together so precisely that a knife blade could not be inserted between them. Stonemasons had worked each block with several angled sides, so that when finished it fitted with the next like a piece in a giant jigsaw puzzle. This design greatly increased the stability of a wall, which was essential in areas as subject to frequent earthquakes as the Andes.

Sited on a ridge between the two mountains of Machu Picchu and Huayna Picchu, the city has magnificent natural defences. The steep cliffs allow for spectacular views of the narrow valley of the River Urubamba, along which enemies would have had to pass to reach the Inca capital, Cuzco, about 70 miles (110km) away. The strategic implications of the site were exploited to the full, as might be expected from a people who carved an empire comparable in size to that of the Romans.

Machu Picchu was founded some time during the 15th century and probably had about 1000 inhabitants, including priests, noblemen and workmen. Inca society was highly structured and hierarchical, each person having rigidly defined responsibilities, rights and privileges. The rough stone houses of the general populace stood on the lower terraces, while the homes and offices of the nobility were sited on the higher levels. To the west of the city is the sacred Intihuatana, meaning Hitching Post of the Sun, a low, irregular platform of perfect simplicity with a short stone pillar. In front of the Intihuatana are two temples, the Temple of the Three Windows and the Principal Temple. These too were simple buildings, and probably

American explorer
Hiram Bingham (ABOVE LEFT) *of Yale University remained convinced until the day he died that the mountain city he had discovered was*

Vilcabamba, the legendary last refuge of the defeated Inca Empire. One of his original photographs (ABOVE) *shows clouds descending over the mysterious citadel.*

roofless, thereby affording the priests ample opportunity to observe the heavens.

Both the sun and the moon were Inca deities. The sun, Inti, was the most venerated, as the ancestor of the ruling emperor and father of all Incas. Inti was the husband and brother of the moon, Mama Quilla, whose attendants were the stars and the planets (with the exception of Venus, who was a goddess in her own right). At the winter solstice ceremony, Inti was symbolically tied to the pillar of Intihuatana to ensure his return the following year, and the sacrifice of animals and children was common at festivals in honour of Inti.

The Incas probably abandoned Machu Picchu before the Spaniards arrival at the capital, Cuzco, in 1572, but the cause of the sudden evacuation is unknown. Wars among rival Inca tribes were common, and in some cases resulted in the annihilation of entire communities; this, or a devastating epidemic, may have been the reason for the city's desertion. Perhaps it was ravaged by a plague so terrible it was permanently quarantined by the authorities. The abandonment of Machu Picchu may forever remain a mystery, but the enigma continues to fuel an intense fascination with that ruined city, one of the most spectacular archaeological sites in the world.

Sun worship *The remarkable skill of the Inca stonemasons is nowhere better displayed than in the three trapezoidal windows in the Temple of the Three Windows* (LEFT). *The precise function of the temple is unknown, although the rectangular stone a short distance from the windows may have been used as a backsight for solar observations.*

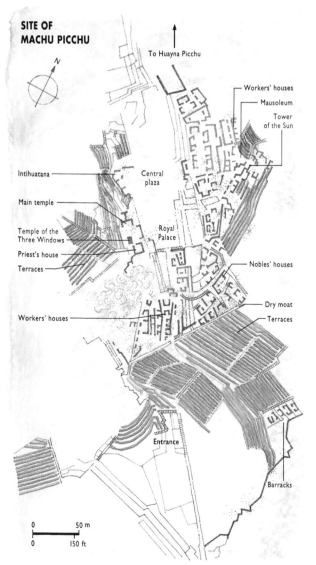

SITE OF MACHU PICCHU

N

To Huayna Picchu

Workers' houses

Mausoleum

Tower of the Sun

Intihuatana

Central plaza

Main temple

Temple of the Three Windows

Royal Palace

Priest's house

Terraces

Nobles' houses

Workers' houses

Dry moat

Terraces

Entrance

Barracks

0   50 m

0   150 ft

Inca timepiece *The Intihuatana* (ABOVE), *a sacred Inca stone dedicated to the sun god Inti and used in ceremonies, was carved from a single outcrop of rock. It bears testimony to* the Incas' interest in astronomy, for the high priests used it as a sundial and a scientific instrument able to indicate solstices, equinoxes and lunar movements.

SUN WORSHIPPERS

Festival of the Sun

Ceremonies honouring Inti, the sun god, are re-enacted today in Sacsayhuaman, near Cuzco, former capital of the Inca Empire. Traditionally, the celebrations were held at the midwinter and summer solstices and would last for eight days. They included prayers, animal sacrifices, offerings of cocoa leaves and the annual tethering of the sun to the sacred stone.

Sun god This pre-Columbian gold mask, fringed with flames representing rays of sunlight, was probably worn by an Inca priest as he played the part of Inti during the Festival of the Sun. Inca goldsmiths were expert at working this precious metal, and it was the hunt for their fabulous artefacts that inspired the Spanish conquistadors.

The Incas were a pre-Columbian people who, from the year 1200, established an empire based at Cuzco in Peru. By the time of the Spanish conquests led by Pizarro in 1532, Inca territory extended some 2000 miles (3200km) from Quito in Ecuador along the Pacific coast and down the mountain chain of the Andes to the River Maule in Chile, encompassing 12 million people. The last emperor, Atahuallpa, was tricked into going to Pizarro's camp, where he was captured and executed. The Spanish conquistadors then marched into Cuzco and eventually took control of the whole Inca Empire.

At the height of the empire, around the year 1500, the emperor was head of a royal family numbering 500. He was an absolute monarch who ruled firmly – sometimes harshly – over a society that was divided according to a strict hierarchy. Laws were applied uniformly throughout the empire, which was financed by a labour tax, collected by local governors in cash or in kind in the form of public duties such as farming or army service.

The Incas' supreme god Inti was represented as a man with a golden disc for a head, symbolising the sun; Mama Quilla – the moon – was represented by a silver disc with a human face. Other gods included the 'creator' Viracocha and the rain god Apu Illapu, as well as Mother Earth and the spirits of lakes and water. Belief in these gods was stamped out by the Spaniards, who abhorred idolatry.

The Incas were renowned for their gold and silver work, and many sites – such as Cuzco – yielded fabulous treasures made from these precious metals. Yet although the explorer Hiram Bingham found many objects wrought in such materials as bronze, obsidian and ceramics at Machu Picchu, there was no gold or silver.

The descendants of the Incas live on in the Andes, but as the peasants who today make up 45 per cent of Peru's population. They live largely by farming and herding cattle, and speak the Quechua language.

Ceremonial cup *The delicate art of the Inca craftsmen is displayed on this wooden drinking vessel called a ker'o. The design was incised in the wood, then overpainted to represent various gods in the* Inca pantheon. Key symbols include ears of maize, which is still the staple food of most of South America's indigenous Indians. Such a drinking vessel may well have been used for drinking maize beer.

Bear ancestry *An Indian woman wears the knitted mask of the Ukokos, a mythical creature believed to be descended from the union of a bear and a woman. It is worn during the Qoyllur Rit'i, an annual pilgrimage to the sacred glacier on Mount Sinakara in Peru. Like many South American religious practices, the original Inca festival has been adopted and adapted by the Roman Catholic Church.*

WATERY WORLDS

W ater stirs the human imagination like no other element. All life
stems from it, and without it all life would cease. Christians are
baptised into their faith with water, and Hindus are ritually
returned to the water after they die. Sages of many religions meditate
beside pools, waterfalls and rivers, and few of us remain unmoved by the
stately swing and flow of the oceans. All human civilisation is linked
inextricably with water, and in this lies our fascination with it in all its
forms. It is rarely still, and we associate its movements and rhythms with
our own lives and ultimate impermanence. The great rivers of the world
are alive with legend, and dominate the existence of those who live on
their banks. For millennia the Nile's annual flooding has enriched the
farmlands of its basin with silt that has regularly restored the soil's
fertility, and the Ganges remains the essence of Hindu religious life.
Water in violent motion drives home our own insignificance. The
thundering falls of Niagara and Iguaçu confuse the mind with their
deafening roar and massive volume; this is visible, audible power on
a scale that cows the human imagination. In different ways we are also
reduced to size by the scalding geysers of Iceland, the mighty iceberg-
spawning cliffs of the Ross Ice Shelf of Antarctica, and the icy depths of
Siberia's Lake Baikal, 25 million years old and containing one-fifth
of the planet's fresh water.

RIVER NILE: SOURCE OF LIFE

Snaking for thousands of miles across equatorial swamps, scrubland and parched desert terrain, the long ribbon of fertility that is the Nile gave birth to one of the world's great civilisations and still sustains its descendants.

For more than 60 centuries the River Nile has brought the gift of life to a country whose land-scape is dominated by barren desert. Symbol of rebirth and eternal existence to the ancient Egyptians, the river continues to grip the imagination of every generation that explores the wonders that line its banks.

Although the ancient Egyptians regarded the Nile as exclusively theirs, they were not the only people whose lives it touched, for this great ribbon of water flows over the immense distance of 4145 miles (6670 km) from central Africa to the Mediterranean Sea.

The Nile has several sources. The farthest headstream is the Kagera River, which rises in Burundi and flows into Lake Victoria. The Nile proper rises here, near Jinja, Uganda, and flows into Lake Kyoga, from where it continues as the Victoria Nile through swampy vegetation before descending over the Kabalega (Murchison) Falls. It

Movable feast *In 1966, during the building of the the Aswan High Dam, two temples at Abu Simbel were lifted more than 210ft (64m)* *above their original site to preserve them from flooding. A statue of Rameses II (ABOVE) adorns the smaller temple dedicated to his wife.*

Dawn of civilisation *For the last 700 miles (1130km) to Cairo, the tranquil river flows within a winding, flat-bottomed groove cut into a limestone plateau. At Naj Hammadi in Upper Egypt, scarps that reach a height of 1500ft (460m) above water level rise in the distance, while lush vegetation borders the banks, creating the same timeless landscape that the Egyptians once believed to have existed on the mythical Island of Creation.*

193

RIVER NILE: SOURCE OF LIFE

Buried treasure *A wooden model of a ploughman and his yoked cattle, dating from c.2000 BC, is among a wealth of archaeological treasures preserved by the dry desert sand that provide a valuable insight into the everyday life and customs of ancient Egypt.*

Primitive but effective *The shaduf, introduced as a means of irrigation during the New Kingdom (1567–1085 BC), is still in use. The device consists of a bucket on a long pole which is dipped into the water, then raised by a counterweight on the other end of the pole.*

then briefly enters the tip of Lake Albert (which is fed by the Semliki River from Lake Edward), and flows on as the Albert Nile to Nimule. There, the river enters the Sudan and eventually crosses the Sudd – an all but impenetrable floating mass of papyrus stems, water hyacinth and aquatic grasses some 200 miles (320km) wide and 250 miles (400km) long. At Khartoum, the swift-flowing Blue Nile sweeps in from its source in Lake Tana in the Ethiopian highlands, its grey-blue waters mingling visibly with the paler waters of the White Nile.

Some 200 miles (320km) farther north in the Sudan, the Atbara River, which also rises in Ethiopia, joins the flow. Now the Nile of legend, draining almost one-tenth of the African continent, starts on its course to Egypt and the sea, first traversing the Cataracts, an infamous series of rapids. These are so dangerous that from here to Lake Nasser – formed by the building of the Aswan High Dam – navigation is impossible. But once the river reaches Egypt, it becomes an unparalleled source of sustenance and means of transport for those who live on its banks.

In ancient Egypt, the floodwaters of the Nile drowned the land with predictable regularity in late summer and early autumn, leaving in their wake alluvial soil so fertile that agriculture flourished, creating great prosperity. The ancient Egyptians were possibly the first people to irrigate their land systematically. They threw up earthen banks along the floodplain, dividing it into a series of basins that would hold water for several weeks. Once the river receded, the water in the basins was allowed to drain away gradually, leaving behind rich silt in which crops were grown. Today the waters of the Nile are controlled by a series of dams and irrigation systems, notably the Aswan High Dam, which measures almost 2½ miles (4km) from bank to bank across the top and is 3215ft (980m) thick at the base and 360ft (110m) high. Irrigation is now possible all year round, but without the great annual flooding much of the fertile silt that once enriched the Nile valley collects at the bottom of Lake Nasser.

Within the network of religious observances and rituals that underpinned everyday life in ancient Egypt, the river became associated with a number of gods, but its own special deity was Hapi, Great Lord of Provisions and Lord of Fishes. Guarded by serpents, Hapi sat in a cavern below the mountains of Aswan and, from a bottomless jar, poured out the yearly floodwaters. Annual sacrifices were made to ensure that Hapi tilted the jar at the correct angle: a little too far could bring a deluge upon the land; not far enough, and drought and famine would result. A statue of Hapi which stands in the Vatican Museum at Rome shows him with his 16 children, each child measuring one cubit. The statue symbolises the ancient belief that if the annual floodwaters failed to reach the

DEATH OF THE DELTA

The fertile land of the Nile delta, which over the centuries has sustained and supported Egyptian agriculture, and thus its civilisation, is gradually disappearing: it is sinking by up to ⅕in (5mm) per year. Subsidence is an age-old problem, but the fertility of the delta remained undisturbed for some 7500 years because any soil that was carried away by changes in the sea level and erosion of the coastline by waves and currents was replaced by sediment carried down by the regular flooding of the Nile.

The completion of the gigantic Aswan High Dam in 1971 has made matters worse. The dam was built to control the flow of the river and to provide electricity and further irrigation, but it is now harming the region it was built to serve and indirectly threatening the lives and livelihoods of the one million people who occupy the most severely affected area. Enormous quantities of water are lost by evaporation from its 300 mile (480km) long reservoir, Lake Nasser, and the land below the dam is starved of fresh sediment, which remains trapped in the lake, so more fertilisers must be used to produce crops. And, because the river carries less silt, it is cutting a deeper channel, so irrigation systems are less efficient.

children's combined height of 16 cubits (about 25ft/7.5m) the harvest would fail and famine would ensue.

The vital annual cycle of planting and harvesting was mirrored in the legend of the life, death and rebirth of the god Osiris. He ruled Egypt, so the tale goes, until he was murdered by his evil brother Set, who cut up his body and distributed the pieces around the country. Isis, wife of Osiris, tracked down the pieces, reassembled them and revived her husband. After a son was born to them, Osiris left the earth to reign as king of the underworld.

In this symbolic tale, Osiris represented the Nile and Isis the earth – their union was the productive mating of soil and water. Set embodied the hot desert wind that consumed the waters of the river, which dried up when Osiris was killed; and when Isis found Osiris's body and brought him back to life, the river began to flood. As Osiris fertilised Isis, bringing forth new life and hope, so the river overflowed its banks to fertilise the fields.

The great prosperity created by the Nile enabled the Egyptians to build magnificent temples and memorials on its banks in honour of gods and kings. Rameses II, the great warrior pharaoh who ruled for 66 years in the 13th century BC and may have been the pharaoh in the biblical story of Exodus, was responsible for building almost half of the surviving temples. Many of these celebrate the recapture of Egypt's Asiatic empire from the Hittites, but perhaps his most outstanding architectural achievements are the temples hewn from the rock at Abu Simbel.

Rameses also left his mark downstream, with an amazing array of monuments surrounding the ancient capital of

Master of ceremonies
Hapi, deity of the Nile, represented both the Nile of Upper Egypt and of Lower Egypt. The cavern from where the god controlled the waters of the Nile was reputedly situated at the First Cataract on the Isle of Bigheh, just south of Aswan.

Thebes, including Karnak, one of the world's awe-inspiring temples. Dedicated to the ram-headed Amun, god of Thebes, the ruins are scattered over 5 acres (2ha) of land and include the remains of sphinx-lined avenues, huge gateways, shrines, temples and a sacred lake. Close to Karnak is Luxor, also dedicated to Amun; and across the Nile from Luxor lies the Valley of Kings, where many of the monarchs of the 18th dynasty (1570–1342 BC) were laid to rest. The most famous of Egypt's monuments, the great pyramids at Giza, stand near Cairo, close to the Nile delta.

Along the riverbank, farming, fishing and other daily activities reassert the ancient rhythm of existence; in places this seems scarcely to have changed since the time of the pharaohs. Bound by a cycle of fertility and famine, life and death, the Nile and Egypt continue to sustain one another and to fascinate the world with their intertwined histories.

South under sail Feluccas at Philae, near Aswan, move upriver powered by graceful triangular sails; they return north with the current. These shallow skimming vessels travel as easily across the flooded fields as on the river itself. In the first century AD the Roman statesman Seneca wrote: 'When the Nile overflows... there is no communication across the face of the earth except by boat, and the less land is visible, the greater joy is felt by the people.'

CLEOPATRA: QUEEN OF THE NILE

The last of Egypt's Ptolemaic rulers and arguably the most famous woman of antiquity, Cleopatra VII was a sophisticated, complex and charming woman. The daughter of Ptolemy XII, she was born in 69 BC and became queen in 51 BC, ruling jointly with her half-brother amid a tangle of intrigues in which she joined, skilfully manipulating those around her until she emerged as supreme ruler. Her life story, including the tale of her passionate romances with the Romans Julius Caesar and Mark Antony, was first chronicled by the Greek scribe Plutarch in the second century AD; the love of Cleopatra for Antony was later immortalised by Shakespeare, who based his tragedy on Plutarch's biography. The fascinating queen has been portrayed in numerous plays and films by several modern beauties, including Claudette Colbert (RIGHT), Vivien Leigh and Elizabeth Taylor.

RED SEA: EMBRYONIC OCEAN

It is a potential source of untold mineral wealth and one of the richest marine environments in the world. The Red Sea also offers geologists an opportunity to study the way the jigsaw of the planet's surface moves and changes, for it is an ocean in the making.

No one knows for sure how the Red Sea, dubbed 'the most extraordinary large body of water on Earth', got its name. It is often said to derive from the seasonal growth of algae that does, indeed, for short periods of the year, colour the usually bright blue waters red-brown. But as the desert sun sets, reflecting glowing pink hills in waters that are unruffled by wind, it is tempting to opt for a more poetic explanation.

In terms of geological time, the Red Sea is very young. It started to form around 40 million years ago, when the Earth's crust began to tear apart to create Africa's Great Rift Valley. As the African and Arabian continental plates separated, so the crust between them collapsed and gradually, over the millennia, sea water flooded part of the rift. Plate movement is constant, and the more or less straight sides of the Red Sea are pulling in opposite directions at the rate of ⅖in (10mm) a year. Although this rate of movement is a mere 39in (1m) per century, there are no indications that it will stop and it could even increase in speed. The sea's development so far almost exactly parallels that of the Atlantic Ocean; some 200 million years from now, it may well reach the same size as the Atlantic.

The movement of the crust below the Red Sea has several other effects. First, it causes the coastlines on either side of the growing sea to tilt away from each other, which means that any river water drains away from, rather than into, the Red Sea. Also, volcanic activity along the line of the separating plates results in water temperatures of up to 59°C (138°F) – the highest on the planet.

The Red Sea is also saltier than any ocean, with a salinity level of 4.1 per cent. (The oceans average some 3.5 per cent, the Mediterranean Sea is 3.8.) Before the passage to the Indian Ocean was fully opened some 25 million years ago, any water that flowed into the growing Red Sea evaporated, with the result that vast salt beds were laid down. More recent upheavals have disturbed these beds, distributing their salt throughout the sea. Rapid evaporation of the surface waters in the fierce tropical sun further concentrates the salt. With no inflowing rivers, and typical desert rainfall of around 1in (25mm) a year, the Red Sea loses the equivalent of a 6ft (1.8m) depth of water every year. Without the addition of waters from the Indian Ocean flowing in through the strait of Bab el-Mandeb, it would eventually evaporate completely. As it

Finger of water *At its widest just 190 miles (305km) across, the Red Sea extends south-eastwards from Suez for 1300 miles (2100km) to Bab el-Mandeb, which connects with the Gulf of Aden and thence the Indian Ocean. The sea separates the coasts of Egypt, Sudan and Ethiopia from those of Saudi Arabia and Yemen.*

At home in the reef

Squirrelfishes, of which there are some 70 species worldwide, abound among the rocks and coral of the Red Sea reefs. All are brightly coloured, the majority red, with patches of white, yellow and black, and they have large rough scales and sharp spiny fins.

Nocturnal creatures, they pass the day hiding in crannies and crevices in the rocks, emerging at night to scan the dark waters with their large eyes for small crustaceans to eat.

By vibrating their swimbladders with the aid of specialised muscles, squirrelfishes are able to make a variety of sounds; these noises are believed to play a significant part in the fishes' territorial behaviour and, especially, in their breeding rituals.

Growing pains

Few plants flourish on the fringe between tropical land and sea: oxygen is scarce and high salinity makes survival difficult. There are 26 species of mangrove, which use a variety of methods to remove salt. Some have developed salt filters in their roots, others glands in their leaves which secrete the salt so that it can be washed away, and salt can be stored in certain leaves which are then shed.

In addition, many species grow with their roots above ground to take oxygen directly from the air when the tide is out.

Flamenco skirts *The aptly named Spanish Dancer has a full red skirt fringed with white which it uses to propel itself away from danger. It is the largest sea slug in the Red Sea, some 20in (50cm) long and 15in (35cm) wide with its skirt fully extended.*

Swaying plantation *Garden eels are so called because they moor themselves to trenches in the seabed, where they drift like plants with the current. They do not move to feed, but filter water for fish eggs and small crustaceans.*

is, in midwinter, when water levels are at their lowest, the top layers of the coral reef that line its shores start to die.

Along the line of the rift, magma from the Earth's crust is constantly rising to fill the gaps created as the plates pull apart. In deep pockets where temperature and salinity are particularly intense, the minerals contained in the magma become highly concentrated. Scientists have found 15 such 'deeps' in which concentrations of heavy metals are thought to be up to 30 000 times those of ordinary sea water. The value of the iron, manganese, copper and zinc in the upper 30ft (9m) of sediments alone is estimated at 2000 million dollars. These minerals could prove to be the Red Sea's greatest riches.

Currently, however, the sea's finest treasure is its teeming marine life. Owing to the warmth of the water, the narrow fringes of the steeply plunging shores harbour some of the most abundant coral reefs in the world. They started to form only 6000 to 7000 years ago, so are also among the youngest. To date, 177 different species of coral have been identified, many of which usually thrive only in equatorial seas some 1550 miles (2500km) farther south. The dense reefs, where sometimes 20 or more species can be found in an area only 10ft (3m) across, in turn offer a home to more than 1000 species of fish, some 30 per cent of which exist only in these waters.

Multicoloured parrotfish use their well-developed teeth to grind up coral to extract nutritious algae; starfish and sea slugs crawl over the surface of the reef. The wrasse family is particularly prolific, with more than 50 different species, ranging in size from the diminutive six-stripe wrasse at just 1–1½in (2.5–4cm) to the giant humphead that measures more than 6ft (1.8m). Humpheads patrol the deeper coral cliffs, feeding off molluscs and sea urchins.

In common with reef fish in other parts of the world, some species have evolved the ability to change sex, so giving them the best possible chance of survival. If there is a shortage of males in a generation, some females, as they mature, become larger and more brightly coloured, transforming themselves into what scientists call supermales. At breeding time, a supermale attracts various females to spawn, and although he fights off other supermales, he often overlooks natural males, which are similar in appearance to females. In this way both sets of males reproduce, and the continuity of the species is assured.

The beauty and diversity of life under the sea provides a sharp contrast to the barrenness of the land that fringes it; this finger of water divides a desert that reaches from Mauritania in West Africa to the Gobi of central China. Some 200 million years ago the Red Sea was just a small depression in the huge Afro-Asian continent; today it is a deep tropical sea, and it may yet become a vast ocean.

The Exodus enigma *Although strong winds do sometimes part the waters of the Red Sea in the extreme north, the most likely explanation for the ease with which the Israelites crossed the 'Red Sea' is a mistranslation of the Hebrew yam suph, 'Reed Sea' – which possibly refers to the marshy region of the Bitter Lakes south of the Suez Canal.*

Fish a-plenty *Shoals of parrotfish are at their greatest around the Farasan Islands in the southern Red Sea in April, when a festival is held to celebrate their abundance.*

THE SACRED RIVER GANGES

Although the mighty River Ganges is heavy with pollution, to Hindus it is the most holy water on the Earth, with the power to cleanse the devout pilgrim's soul of its earthly sins and, at death, release it from the wearisome cycle of reincarnation.

To Hindus, the River Ganges is the personification of Ganga, the goddess of purification. Originally she flowed only in heaven but was brought down to earth by King Bhagiratha to purify the ashes of his ancestors. In order to break her fall, which would have swept away the people on Earth, she dropped first on the head of the god Shiva and trickled down through his tangled locks. Now, each year, in the hope that by drinking its water and bathing in it their sins will be washed away, pilgrims, some sick and dying, make long, arduous journeys to the Ganges. Their belief in the river's purifying properties stems from the cooling power of its waters. Many Hindu customs are based on the conviction that power is heat and, if the power is evil, cooling it with water

Eternal freedom *The sacred city of Varanasi exerts a magnetic pull on Hindus, for to die and be cremated here is to be granted* moksha, *or liberation, so ending the cycle of reincarnation.*

As dawn breaks, thousands of Hindus flock to the river bank (LEFT AND ABOVE) *to perform their ritual ablutions in the river's cleansing holy waters. Some pilgrims stand immersed to their* shoulders on the ghats (steps leading down to the river), others allow the water to lap only at their feet.

Hindu women, dressed in brightly coloured saris, make offerings of food and flowers, and throw marigolds and pink lotuses into the river. Cupping their hands, they have a ritual drink, then take water in containers to the temple, where they perform their puja, *or religious observances.*

will render it ineffective. Hindus also believe that if they are cremated on the banks of the river, and their ashes scattered across it, their souls will be released from the cycle of rebirth and may attain Paradise, or Nirvana.

The sparkling waters of the River Ganges first emerge into sunlight from the *Gomuhk*, or 'Cow's Mouth', a remote ice cave at the foot of the Himalayas. Here, India's holiest river is known as Bhagirathi. This energetic stream flows through a ravine in the Garhwal Hills, past stately pines, fragrant deodars and scarlet rhododendrons, on to the town of Devaprayag.

Below towering cliffs, the Bhagirathi's turbulent waters merge with those of the calm River Alaknanda to become the true Ganges, which flows more sedately on to the town of Hardwar, one of the river's holiest sites. Here, each spring, more than 100 000 Hindus celebrate the birth of Mother Ganges by launching tiny boats made of leaves filled with marigold petals dipped in ghee (clarified butter) which are set alight.

From Hardwar, the Ganges continues its journey east to Allahabad, where it is joined for a short distance by the River Yamuna. The Hindus also regard Sangumi, the point at which the rivers meet, as sacred, honouring it every

Pilgrims' progress
Hindus line the banks of the Ganges at Hardwar during the Maha Kumbh Mela *festival, held every 12* *years or so to celebrate the goddess Ganga's birthday. In 1986, some 4 million pilgrims congregated here to bathe in the river.*

THE SACRED RIVER GANGES

United forces *Below the grey cliffs of Devaprayag, the waters of the River Bhagirathi join with those of the Alaknanda to form the Ganges proper. Here, the ghats are lined with sturdy chains on to which worshippers can hold as they wash away their sins in the fast-moving waters.*

First steps *The Ganges rises in the craggy foothills of the Himalayas. But the remote tranquillity of its upper reaches sharply contrasts with the colourful scenes along its banks as it flows slowly through bustling towns on its long journey south and east to the Bay of Bengal.*

year with a colourful festival. Accompanied by pipers and buglers, *sadhus*, or wandering holy men, ride through the streets on camels and elephants lavishly adorned with feathers and ornate fabrics.

At Varanasi, formerly known as Benares, the holiest city on the Ganges and the oldest in India, the river sweeps past the famous ghats (waterside steps leading down to bathing places) that line the bank for some 2 miles (3km). Old and sick pilgrims hope to die at Varanasi, for it is here that Mother Ganges releases the Hindu soul from the weary wheel of life – the endless cycle of birth and rebirth. The bodies of the dead are burned at the famous Manikarnika burning ghat on pyres of *neem*, or sandalwood, which are watched over day and night by the *doms*, the hereditary attendants of the cremation ground. Throughout the night, Hindu holy men chant ancient epics on the river bank.

Just below Patna, the river turns southwards again, reverting to the name of Bhagirathi near the Farakka Barrage, at the apex of the delta. The eastern branch, still called the Ganges, flows on through Bangladesh, but the name of the western branch of the river changes again, to the Hooghly; this stretch is renowned for the difficulties it presents to mariners, and many sailors and boatmen have drowned in its waters. Stretching for about 50 miles (80km) on either side of the Hooghly, which is also regarded as holy, lie Calcutta, India's largest city, and its satellite towns. Finally, this great waterway reaches the Bay of Bengal, where it disperses into the many mouths of the delta and the swampy Sundarbarns.

At 1560 miles (2500km), the Ganges is not one of the world's longest rivers – both the Nile and the Amazon are more than twice as long – but no river has been more revered or proved more inspirational. It excited the imagination of the Roman poets Virgil and Ovid and of the medieval Florentine poet Dante, while the warrior and leader Alexander the Great believed the river to be the boundary of the universe. The Englishman Sir John Mandeville, who was regarded in medieval times as a great traveller (although many of his tales were about legendary places), said in his *Travels of Sir John Mandeville,* published in 1356, that the Ganges flowed out of Paradise and that there was gold in its gravel. Certainly, to Hindus, the waters of the river offer the chance to attain eternal bliss.

THE SACRED FIRE

At Varanasi, the business of cremation is governed by *doms*, a community of 400 officials who watch over the sacred fire with which the funeral pyres are lit. Relatives who wish the bodies of their loved ones to be cremated must pay the *doms* and buy the necessary firewood and incense. Many people cannot afford firewood, for as it becomes more and more scarce in India it becomes increasingly expensive.

In 1989, an electric crematorium was installed at one of the city's cremation ghats so that the poor could cremate their dead without using firewood. The *doms*, no doubt mindful that their lucrative monopoly was being eroded, and concerned that strict observance of Hindu scripture was threatened, fought this introduction.

In spite of the new technology, the bodies of the Hindu dead continue to be cremated on the banks of the Ganges in one of the world's most time-honoured and moving ceremonies. The bodies are dipped into the Ganges before being hoisted on to the pyre – at any one time there might be as many as half a dozen cremation pyres aflame.

GALÁPAGOS RIFT: A WORLD WITHOUT SUN

In some of the ocean bed's deepest, most inhospitable trenches, communities of creatures have evolved to live independently of energy from the Sun, overturning the theory that its light and warmth are essential to survival. Instead, they are nourished from deep within the Earth.

I n 1977 a team of scientists aboard the submersible *Alvin* were exploring the near-freezing depths of the Galápagos Rift, 240 miles (390km) north-west of the Galápagos Islands in the Pacific Ocean. They knew that in this area the tectonic plates that form the Earth's crust are moving steadily apart at a rate of up to 8in (20cm) a year. As hot liquid lava wells up through the gap between them and reaches the cold water, it solidifies, creating new pillow-shaped clusters of rocks on the sea floor. The *Alvin* team found the new rocks, but at depths of 8600ft (2600m) below the surface of the ocean they also discovered a wonderland of extraordinary new creatures living in complete blackness.

Sunlight never penetrates to such depths in the oceans, and water pressure is more than 100 times greater than that of the air in a car tyre. Temperatures hover between 2° and 4°C (36° and 40°F) all year round. Yet in this seemingly unpromising environment are oases of warmth, where marine life forms cluster. Springs of mineral-rich water at temperatures of up to 20°C (68°F) rise through crevices, or vents, in the solidified basalt of the seabed, and unique creatures that are not dependent on sunlight for their basic nourishment have developed there. Their very presence challenges the long-held view that all life on Earth is reliant on the sun's energy – in that green plants on land or in the sea use sunlight to convert carbon dioxide and water into food and, ultimately, all creatures depend on plants for food.

There are five distinct oasis sites in the Galápagos Rift. Four lie above fissures in the sea floor, through which spurts hot water from deep inside the Earth that has earlier filtered down through cracks in the rocky seabed. The fifth is a dead area, where temperatures are no higher than the surrounding ocean – close to freezing. The white shells of dead clams littering the gullies between the basalt pillows are the only indication that this, too, was once a hot-water oasis, but the warm water no longer flows.

Among the bizarre pillows of rock, the four warm oases house a multitude of creatures. Crowding the basalt are gleaming communities of giant clams, bigger than a man's hand, with white shells and flesh scarlet with haemoglobin (the substance that colours human blood red), and also densely packed reefs of mussels. Around them scavenge hordes of blind white crabs, working by feel and

Steam clouds gather
Surface clouds are the most dramatic sign that hot molten lava is pouring from the Earth's core into icy ocean waters.

Exploring the oceans
The submersible Sea Link *is just one of the new generation of underwater craft that have made in-depth exploration of the seabed possible.*

Stench of life *Hydro-thermal waters contain a high proportion of hydrogen sulphide and consequently smell of rotten eggs.*

WATERY WONDERLANDS

The vent world is crowded since, to survive, life forms must cluster around the heat source. As well as 'live' black smokers, there may be the clogged stump of a potential column or a white smoker exuding steam rather than sulphide-rich waters. Worms and shellfish are the most common inhabitants of the vents, but at least one species of fish, the grenadier, is also found.

Key

1 Black smoker chimney (a chimney is composed of solidified minerals)
2 Clogged chimney
3 White smoker chimney
4 Large red tube worms
5 Giant clams
6 Blind white crabs
7 Serpulid worms
8 Galatheid crabs
9 Grenadier, or rat-tail fish
10 Common black mussels
11 Water seeping through rocks on the seabed picks up dissolved minerals and is heated.
12 Molten lava and heated water are expelled as a cloudy black stream from a black smoker.

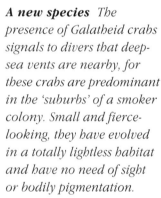

*A **new species** The presence of Galatheid crabs signals to divers that deep-sea vents are nearby, for these crabs are predominant in the 'suburbs' of a smoker colony. Small and fierce-looking, they have evolved in a totally lightless habitat and have no need of sight or bodily pigmentation.*

Since this crab is a relatively new discovery, scientific research has not yet concluded whether it is found elsewhere in the world.

smell, and small Galatheid crabs and serpulid worms filter food from the water, while limpets and tube anemones cling to the rocks. Some of the inhabitants of the depths look like no other creatures on Earth; they include animals that resemble dandelion seed heads and living spaghetti.

The most dramatic animals are giant tube worms which huddle close to the heat source. Their anatomy – white tubes that grow up to 10ft (3m) long, tipped with blood-red fronds – holds the clue to the most exciting aspect of life in the warm-water vents. They possess neither mouth nor gut, both of which are essential to conventional digestive systems. Instead, with the help of bacteria unique to their environment, they absorb the oxygen, carbon dioxide and hydrogen sulphide dissolved in the water that gushes from the vents through more than 300 000 tentacles on the tips of their tubes. Dense colonies of specialised bacteria inside the worms' body cavities convert the filtered elements (including the normally highly toxic hydrogen sulphide) into usable nutrients which are absorbed into the worms' capillaries.

This close relationship is repeated in every other organism of the vent communities. The gills of mussels, for example, and cobweb-like growths around the necks of clams both shelter the bacteria that perform the vital nutrient conversion. For this reason, scientists assume that these bacteria are the first creatures to congregate around new vents as they open up.

The teeming marine life is not the only wealth of the hot-water vents. Water seeping down through the cracks and fissures in the seabed picks up minerals and chemicals from the rocks under the ocean floor. As it is heated and forced back through the vents, the water brings these minerals with it (usually in suspension, which is why the water at vent sites tends to be cloudy). Eventually, many of the minerals solidify and spread out over the seabed. Since this process is constant, and happens in the same place time and time again, the minerals have nowhere to settle but outwards and upwards, so pillars of mineral-laden rocks up to 180ft (55m) high and 600ft (180m) across build up. These black smokers (so called because the water gushing up and out through their chimney is black with minerals) contain enormous concentrations of iron, barium, calcium, copper, zinc, lithium and manganese. Commercial mining of such sites may not be viable, but it is thought that they could help scientists locate similar riches on land that was once seabed.

As recently as the 1960s, the ocean floors were regarded as dark, cold, relatively lifeless deserts. The rich and varied fauna of the hydrothermal vent communities have proved that in one respect at least that assessment can no longer be considered accurate.

GREAT BARRIER REEF

The largest living structure on Earth, the Great Barrier Reef is a fascinating underwater kingdom, home to thousands of species of coral, fish and other marine creatures.

I n 1768, the English explorer Captain James Cook embarked on his first voyage to the Pacific in *HMS Endeavour*, a sturdy coal-hauling barque. He was taking a party of astronomers on a scientific expedition to Tahiti to observe the transit of Venus across the Sun.

Cook had also been directed to find the southern continent, or *Terra australis,* which scientists believed existed to balance the landmass of the Northern Hemisphere. Sailing south-west from Tahiti, Cook discovered New Zealand, which he spent six months charting. Continuing westwards, Cook came upon the south-east coast of Australia, landing in April 1770 at Botany Bay – which he and the naturalist Joseph Banks (who was also on board) named after the fascinating new flora they found on its shores. Turning north, he stayed close to the coast to map it accurately, but found himself in the shallow lagoon waters that separate all coral reefs from the shore – here between 10 and 100 miles (16 and 160km) wide. Despite his precautions, Cook's ship was soon stuck fast on the coral. He beached the *Endeavour*, and in the two months it took to repair it, Cook had ample time to study the marvels of the Great Barrier Reef.

Since Cook's day, generations of explorers, scientists and tourists have catalogued the reef and its wonders. It extends for more than 1250 miles (2000km) parallel to Australia's north-eastern coastline, meandering back and forth as it follows the contours of the continental shelf. Despite its name, the reef is composed of some 3000 individual interlocking coral rafts and islets, all at different stages of development and separated by narrow, winding

Stranded at sea *Many of the reef corals must have very shallow water in order to thrive, with the result that at low tide they are often left high and dry. It is even possible to walk over parts of the reef. Staghorn corals are supremely adapted to the environment: their network of branches enables them to trap waterborne food particles.*

Haven of life *Conditions on the reef are relatively stable all year round: the temperature rarely exceeds 38°C (100°F), nor does it fall below 21°C (70°F), and the concentrations of oxygen and salt in the waters that lap the reef are constant. These factors make the reef attractive to many species and contribute to the proliferation of life in and around it.*

Marine wonderland *In 1979 Australia designated a marine park now covering 134600 sq miles (348700km²) of the Great Barrier Reef, including One Tree Island* (LEFT), *and banned all development there. Although diving is permitted, there are strict rules to prevent souvenir hunting and disturbance of this unique environment.*

211

INHABITANTS OF THE GREAT BARRIER REEF

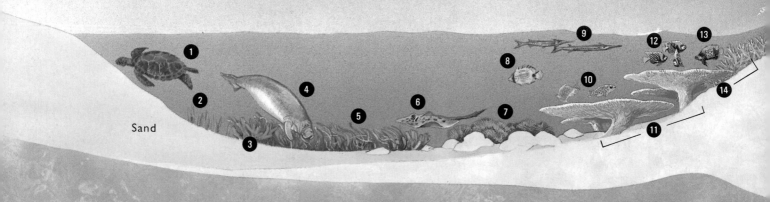

Sand

channels. In some places, as off Cape Melville in the north, the reef is a thin ribbon of coral, while near Cape Manifold in the south rafts can be 200 miles (320km) wide.

Corals were originally classified as plants. Their exquisite colours and patterns prompted the comparison of the reef to a garden, in which the corals were flowers. And, indeed, as the tentacles of coral drift back and forth in the warm clear waters, or open out like flowers as they prepare to take in prey, it is not difficult to visualise the whole reef as a vast plantation. But the analogy is false: coral polyps, whose chalky external skeletons comprise the solid substance of a coral reef, are invertebrate animals related to sea anemones. Unlike anemones, however, the soft, many-headed body of a coral polyp has a hard casing, which it creates in much the same way as a snail builds its shell. Each coral outcrop consists of a base of the accumulated skeletons of generations of dead corals and a surface coating of live coral polyps, which emerge through slits or holes in their shells to catch their food.

To build reefs, corals depend on single-celled algae that live attached to their bodies in a mutually beneficial relationship. The algae are protected by the coral and take nutrient from some of its body fluids; and because algae are plants, they are able to utilise sunlight to produce food, some of which the corals absorb. More important,

Key
1 *Green turtle*
2 *Yellow burrowing sponge*
3 *Tubular sponge*
4 *Dugong*
5 *Sea grass*
6 *Blue-spotted stingray*
7 *Turtle weed*
8 *Blue-patch butterfly fish*
9 *Half-beak fish*
10 *Blue barred parrotfish*
11 *Plate coral*
12 *Imperial angelfish*
13 *Blue-girdled angelfish*
14 *Staghorn coral*
15 *Shrublike corals on reef crest*
16 *Six-banded trevallies*
17 *Branching coral*
18 *Barracuda*
19 *Coral cod*
20 *Sea whip coral*
21 *Soft coral*
22 *Common dolphin*
23 *Hydroid coral*
24 *Gorgonian sea fans*
25 *White-tipped reef shark*

they enable corals to convert the calcium salts in sea water into calcium carbonate to form their skeletons. Without the algae, coral polyps would be simply sea anemones living in colonies, and coral reefs would not exist.

Reefs are formed only when conditions are exactly right. Shallow, clear water that allows penetration of sunlight is essential: there are no living reefs in waters deeper than 330ft (100m). The water must be clean, since any sediment prevents the coral's tentacles trapping the food it needs, and the temperature must be warm – not less than 21°C (70°F) all year round. Lastly, coral skeletons have to anchor themselves to something solid, so a rocky sea bottom is necessary. Corals colonise anywhere that these conditions are met, and as a result, many of the islands

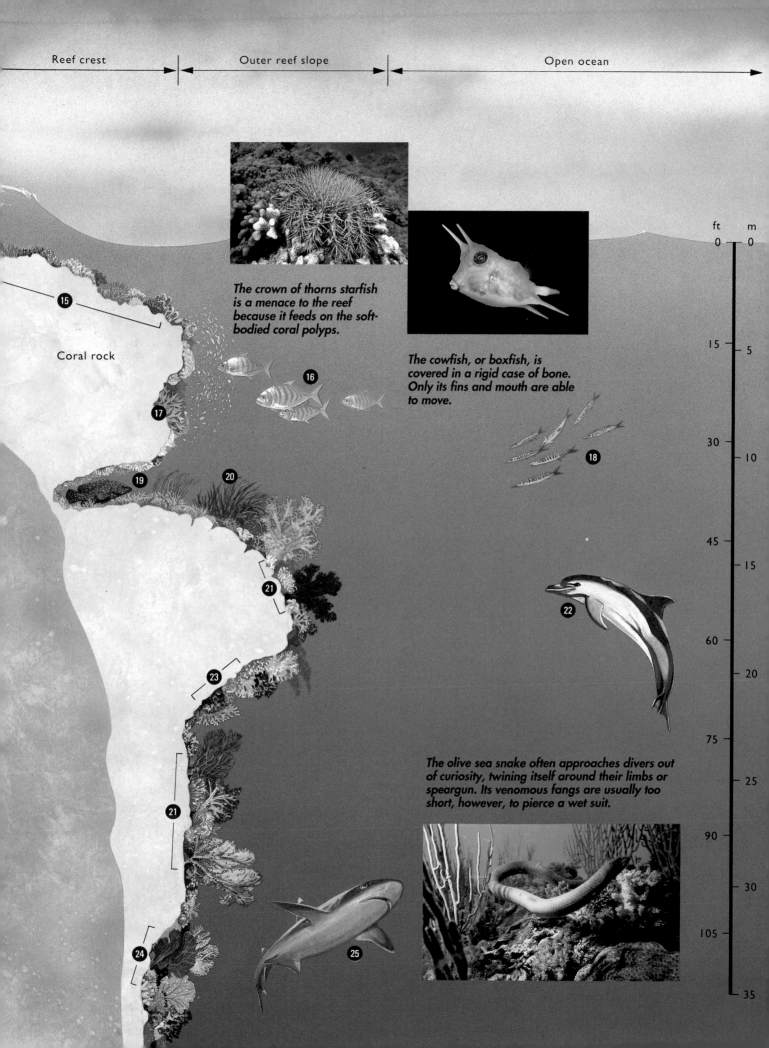

The crown of thorns starfish is a menace to the reef because it feeds on the soft-bodied coral polyps.

The cowfish, or boxfish, is covered in a rigid case of bone. Only its fins and mouth are able to move.

Coral rock

The olive sea snake often approaches divers out of curiosity, twining itself around their limbs or speargun. Its venomous fangs are usually too short, however, to pierce a wet suit.

ft m
0 — 0

15 — 5

30 — 10

45 — 15

60 — 20

75 — 25

90 — 30

105 — 35

Giants of the deep
Manta rays (ABOVE) can weigh up to 2 tons, yet frequently spring out of the water like flying fish.

Floating colony Porpita (BELOW) is a hydrozoan colony drifting on the sea's surface. The tentacles catch prey that is fed to the centre.

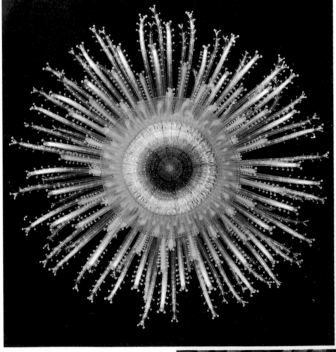

Hide and seek Many species depend on others for their survival. The clown fish (RIGHT) shelters from predators by swimming inside large sea anemones, where it also lays its eggs.

lining the Australian coast have their own fringes of coral.

There are at least 350 different coral species on the Great Barrier Reef and they vary enormously in shape, size and colour. Some are microscopic, others (such as the brain coral, whose rounded form and surface grooves bear a resemblance to a human brain) can grow as wide as 6½ft (2m). On the outer fringes of the reef there are rubbery species able to withstand the pounding of the surf, while delicate, lace-like varieties must shelter in the stillest waters. There are fan and dome-shaped corals, whips and antlers, miniature trees and flowers. Just as the waters that shelter them range from white, through azure, to indigo, so the corals themselves range from pale pink to deep rose, vibrant yellow, blue and brilliant green.

In the reef's fiercely competitive environment, a place in the sun is important, and different species have developed their own ways of ensuring they get the light they need. Some simply outgrow their competitors: many of the staghorn (*Acropora*) species, for example, can expand by up to 4 sq in (26cm²) a year. Others can change shape according to the depth of water in which they are anchored, growing flat in deep waters where light is scarce and into tall 'fingers' where the sun penetrates strongly.

The reef's varying depths, degrees of clarity and calm, temperatures and types of food mean that thousands of life forms can find the exact conditions they need. It is estimated that more than 1400 species of fish and shellfish, in addition to anemones, worms, sponges and birds, make their homes in and around the Great Barrier Reef; the coral itself constitutes only ten per cent of the reef's life. The invertebrate sea cucumber plays an essential role in protecting the reef's structure, for the microscopic fragments of shell and sand which it secretes sink to the

ocean bed, plastering any cracks in the coral foundations.

Many of the fish have had to become highly specialised in order to cope with the demands of life on the reef. The forceps butterfly fish, for example, has developed a long tube-like snout to enable it to probe fissures for food. The bright blue-striped cleaner wrasse keeps other species healthy by eating the parasites attached to them. The stricken fish puts aside any predatory instincts and remains trance-like, mouth and gills open, while the wrasse extracts the parasites, even from the inside of its mouth. The blenny, however, has adapted to look and behave just like a wrasse; but instead of removing parasites from another fish, the blenny takes a bite out of the fish itself.

Some fish on the reef draw attention to themselves with their gaudy colours, probably because the advantages of being seen by a potential mate outweigh the dangers posed by predators. Others possess an extraordinarily high degree of camouflage: scorpion fish are draped in long flaps of skin to resemble rocks covered in algae. Until they see their prey, they hang motionless, then move with astonishing speed. Groupers are able instantly to change colour and pattern to blend with their surroundings. They also have highly adapted mouths and jaws which open so wide they can suck prey straight into the gullet.

The coral reef habitat is finely balanced and easily upset by change. In the 1960s and 70s, the Great Barrier Reef was threatened when the population of crown of thorns starfish, which pour their digestive juices on to coral and kill it, expanded far beyond its normal limits. This was due to souvenir hunters stripping the reef of tritons – the predatory molluscs that usually keep starfish numbers down. Protection of the triton has reduced starfish levels again, but parts of the reef could take 40 years to recover.

The spectacular marine life and stunning surroundings make the Australian barrier reef one of the greatest natural wonders of the world. It is also one of the youngest: recent estimates based on analysis of samples drilled from its core suggest that parts are only 500 000 years old – very young in evolutionary terms – and even the more mature areas may be less than one million years old. The diversity of life that has evolved in so short a time testifies to the idyllic conditions existing for those creatures that have succeeded in adapting to conditions in the crystal-clear waters.

TWO TYPES OF CORAL

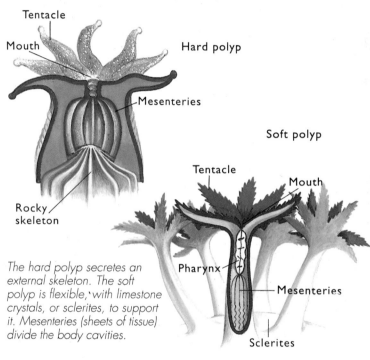

Tentacle
Mouth
Hard polyp
Mesenteries
Rocky skeleton
Soft polyp
Tentacle
Mouth
Pharynx
Mesenteries
Sclerites

The hard polyp secretes an external skeleton. The soft polyp is flexible, with limestone crystals, or sclerites, to support it. Mesenteries (sheets of tissue) divide the body cavities.

Attention seeker *The sea slug* (RIGHT), *with its horns and leaf-like skin, makes its way over the bright-red coral in search of seaweed to eat. This slug has no need of camouflage because, when attacked, it secretes noxious fluids from glands on its body.*

ROSS ICE SHELF

A towering ice cliff stretching as far as the eye could see confronted the early Antarctic explorers. They had come face to face with the world's biggest iceberg: it was almost the size of France.

On 5 January 1841 a British Admiralty team in the *Erebus* and the *Terror*, three-masted ships with specially strengthened wooden hulls, was picking its way through the pack ice of the Pacific approaches to Antarctica in an attempt to determine the position of the South Magnetic Pole. Four days later, they broke into open water and were hopeful that they might have a clear passage to their destination; but on 11 January the men were confronted by a gigantic wall of ice.

'Well, there's no more chance of sailing through that than through the cliffs of Dover,' exclaimed Sir James Clark Ross, the expedition's leader. Ross, who in 1831 had located the North Magnetic Pole, spent the next two years vainly searching for a sea passage to the South Pole; later his name was given to the ice shelf and the sea bordering it.

The Ross Ice Shelf virtually fills a huge bay that cuts into Antarctica, and its surface area is approximately the size of France. The shelf extends east to west for about 500 miles (800km) between Edward VII Peninsula and Ross Island and about 600 miles (970km) inland. The cliffs on the seaward side rise to a height of 200ft (60m) in places and the ice can be as thick as 2450ft (750m) in the shelf's gently undulating southern reaches, nearest to land.

The shelf, which is rather like a huge, loosely moored raft, is constantly pushing out into the sea at a rate of between 5ft (1.5m) and 10ft (3m) a day. The Beardmore and several other massive glaciers flowing down from the

Fearsome aspect The steep wall of the Ross Ice Shelf's seaward face dwarfs men, ships, whales and the icebergs that regularly sheer away from its mass. These monolithic cliffs thwarted early Antarctic explorers, but the flat surface of the shelf later provided an ideal starting point for expeditions making their way towards the South Pole.

ROSS ICE SHELF

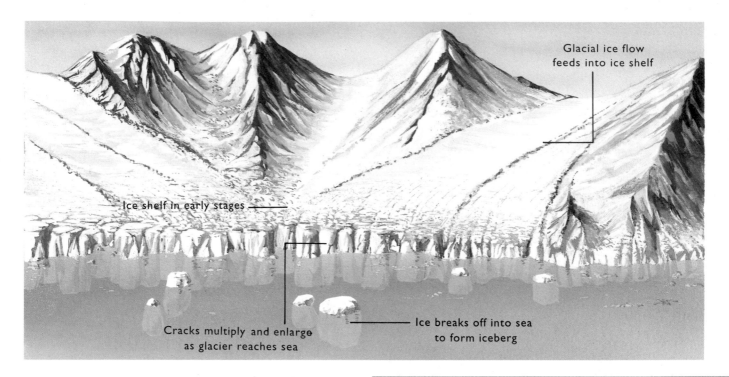

Glacial ice flow feeds into ice shelf

Ice shelf in early stages

Cracks multiply and enlarge as glacier reaches sea

Ice breaks off into sea to form iceberg

RELENTLESS FLOW

The Ross Ice Shelf is always in flux. Glacial ice thrusting from behind adds to its huge size; snow is compacted into ice by the weight of further falls; and freezing seawater adds to the shelf's thickness from beneath. Unable to resist these pressures, the shelf pushes seaward. Icebergs break off the cliff edge and drift with the ocean currents, enabling scientists to study the polar currents and the complex interaction between oceans and atmosphere.

Lonely endurance *The emperor penguin is the only animal to brave winter in Antarctica, breeding and raising its young here. The single egg is laid on the ice and is incubated by the male, which rests it on top of his feet, then settles a pouch of skin gently over it to keep it warm. Both parents feed the chick when it hatches.*

distant Transantarctic Mountains exert pressure on the rear of the shelf and add to its bulk. At the same time, freezing of the sea underneath the ice shelf increases the depth of the ice from below – by as much as 15–20in (38–51cm) some 200 miles (320km) from the coast. Crevasses and fractures that form at the inland edge of the shelf can run for many miles, often creating wide inlets of open water. When such an inlet encircles a mass of ice, gigantic bergs break free from the edge of the shelf; the largest known had an area of around 12 000 sq miles (31 000km²), slightly larger than Belgium.

For centuries the southern polar regions remained unseen and uncharted, although the ancient Greeks had

concluded that there must be a huge continent in the southern hemisphere to balance the northern landmass of Eurasia. This belief was reflected in all early European maps; even the great Dutch map maker Mercator (1512–95) showed an immense land around the South Pole which he called Terra Australis Incognita, despite the fact that, in 1578, Sir Francis Drake, driven far south by violent storms, saw no sign of the mythical continent.

Two hundred years later, Captain James Cook spent three years (1772–75) searching for Terra Australis; he found no trace of it, although he sailed beyond latitude 70° south. He was, nevertheless, convinced that there was 'a Tract of Land near the Pole, which is the Source of all

POLAR PIONEERS

Sir James Ross (1800–62) (RIGHT) and Sir Ernest Shackleton (1874–1922) (BELOW) have imprinted their names on Antarctica for ever by the bravery and determination with which they faced its perils. During his three years' sailing in Antarctic waters, Ross discovered Victoria Land, in addition to the ice shelf that bears his name, and began a survey of the coast of Graham Land. Shackleton landed at the western end of the shelf in 1908. His expedition reached the South Magnetic Pole and climbed Mount Erebus; Shackleton himself ascended the Beardmore Glacier to the polar ice cap and reached a point only 100 miles (160km) short of the South Pole. In 1911, Captain Robert Scott also set out from the Ross Ice Shelf on his ill-fated race to the pole against Roald Amundsen, who beat him by a month. Scott and his four companions headed back to base, only to die of exposure in the bitter cold.

Subsistence fare *Shackleton's hut at his base camp at Cape Royds is now preserved as a* museum. *The hut contains some of the meagre supplies with which the undernourished,* anaemic team of men faced the forbidding ice and bitter wind during the 1908 expedition.

the Ice spread over this vast Southern Ocean'. Early in the 19th century, the area came under increased scrutiny by British and American seal hunters. In 1820 a Royal Navy survey ship sighted the Antarctic Peninsula, and the first hunters landed the next year; later in the century, whalers superseded the sealers. Scientific curiosity as well as commercial interests prompted a flurry of exploration, but the ice-choked sea did not relax its guard on the land beyond.

Antarctica is packed with ice and snow to depths over 11 500ft (3500m). It is the world's highest continent, with half its area standing more than 6560ft (2000m) above sea level, and with many active volcanoes. One of the largest is Mount Erebus on Ross Island. Antarctica is

the driest place in the world – drier than the Sahara – and only some 2in (50mm) of snow falls inland, perhaps 20in (500mm) near the coast. It is also the Earth's coldest place; temperatures can drop so low that boiling water tossed into the air immediately forms crystals of ice.

Although the ice shelf presented an immense barrier to explorers, it eventually enabled them to reach the interior of this savage land, and more recently scientific research stations have been established on it. Scientists based here have discovered animal and plant fossils which reveal that Antarctica was once part of the ancient supercontinent of Gondwana, and they were the first to realise the existence of a hole in the ozone layer.

MILFORD SOUND: A WATERY WONDERLAND

Carved by a glacier 20 000 years ago, New Zealand's Milford Sound teems with unique varieties of wildlife. Here, fresh water and sea water meet uneasily to create an environment that is part lake, part ocean.

The majestic beauty of Milford Sound's soaring cliffs and deep blue glittering waters, edged by dense forests, prompted the English author Rudyard Kipling to declare it the 'eighth wonder of the world'. It is one of the wettest places on Earth: rain falls on two out of three days, giving an exceptionally high annual rainfall total of 246in (615cm). This precipitation swells cascades of water which tumble 1000ft (300m) or more into the inlet below. Looming above the entrance to the Sound is Mitre Peak, an awesome natural sentinel that rises to a height of 5560ft (1695m).

Situated 160 miles (260km) north-west of Dunedin, on New Zealand's South Island, Milford Sound is a typical fjord in many respects. It is a narrow inlet, 12 miles (20km) long, with steep sides and, like most fjords, is shallow at the mouth and deeper at the head. It was formed during the last ice age by a glacier, which gouged out a deep trench in the rock as it inched its way seaward. When the ice retreated some 10 000 years ago, the Tasman Sea flooded into the glacial valley.

The water in the sound lies in three layers. The surface layer has a low salt content because it is produced by fresh water flowing in from streams and waterfalls. It is less

Under cover *The crest of Mitre Peak, the highest point of the mountains surrounding the sound, is often shrouded in cloud and mist. Torrential rain pouring down the sides of the mountains replenishes the layer of fresh water on the surface of Milford Sound, sustaining a unique marine environment.*

Towering cliffs *Boats in Milford Sound are dwarfed by the world's tallest sea cliffs (*BELOW*), which rise sheer for about 5280ft (1584m) from the water and descend to a depth of 1300ft (400m) below it.*

NORTH
ISLAND

N

TASMAN SEA

NEW ZEALAND

Wellington

Nelson

SOUTH
ISLAND

MT COOK

Christchurch

MILFORD
SOUND

Queenstown

PACIFIC
OCEAN

LAKE TE ANAU

MITRE
PEAK

Dunedin

MILFORD SOUND: A WATERY WONDERLAND

Steaming torrent
*Spectacular cascades, such
as the Hanging Veil Falls
(ABOVE), plummet down the*

*mountainsides all round
Milford Sound, creating a
veil-like spray on impact
with the rocks below.*

dense than the sea water in the fjord and lies on top of it,
forming a layer 10ft (3m) deep or more. As the surface
layer drifts towards the sea, it carries with it some of the
salt water from below, creating a a transitional zone of
brackish water. This movement creates a counter current
that draws sea water into the fjord to a depth of 100ft
(30m); below this the water is salty but largely immobile.

The fresh water has a profound effect on the marine
life of Milford Sound, which presented the first divers to
explore it with something of a puzzle. For example, the
usual species of seaweed and shellfish that inhabit the tidal
waters along the rest of New Zealand's coastlines are not
found in the sound because they cannot survive in waters
of such low salinity. Instead, the upper layer is occupied by
species such as sea lettuce, blue mussels and barnacles that
can tolerate brackish water. Starfish cling to the underwater
cliffs in the uppermost salty layer, where they feed on
mussels. As the tide goes out and the water level falls, the
starfish move down the rock to avoid the top freshwater
layer, which they cannot tolerate; when the tide comes in
again, they climb back up to resume feeding.

The run-off from the mountains flows over beds of moss
and humus-rich soils, so when it reaches the fjord it is
stained the colour of tea. This brown water restricts the
penetration of sunlight, with the result that deep-water
marine species such as sea feathers, sea squirts, black coral
and lamp shells live high up among ledges and fissures of
the rocky walls at depths of between 20 and 130ft (6 and
40m) – much shallower than their usual habitat.

The rare black coral that usually lives in colonies at
depths below 150ft (45m) is found in Milford Sound at less
than 115ft (35m) and in some places survives at a mere
20ft (6m) deep – closer to the surface than anywhere else
in the world. Most of the coral colonies resemble miniature feathery bushes about 4in (10cm) or so high, but
some corals, estimated to be more than 150 years old, have
developed into huge treelike structures 13ft (4m) tall.

Milford Sound and its forested mountains, which are
protected as part of the Fjordlands National Park, shelter
a rare and strange bird known as the takahe. This flightless creature with vivid purple and blue plumage is about
the size of a domestic chicken, has a large bill, and feeds
solely on the leaves and seeds of snow grass. It was
thought to be extinct until, in 1947, a colony of about
100 birds was discovered on the muddy shores of Lake Te
Anau, some 34 miles (55km) south-east of Milford Sound.
Today the bird is protected and thrives in the park.
Almost as rare is the kakapo, a ground-dwelling, greenish
parrot that resembles an owl and lives in a burrow by day.
Although it can fly, it chooses not to. It, too, was nearing
extinction before being protected in the park.

MARINE MARVELS

A cutaway view of Milford Sound reveals its unique ecology. Freshwater species occupy the upper level, which is stained brown; beneath this, deep-sea animals inhabit the clear, warm, saltwater layer.

Key

1 Blue mussels
2 Girdled parrot fish
3 Sea urchins
4 Starfish
5 Red-banded perch
6 Black coral
7 Tube anemone
8 Fan scallop
9 Horse mussels
10 Blue cod
11 Brachiopods (lamp shells)
12 Gorgonian coral
13 Butterfly perch
14 Red coral
15 Brittlestars
16 Sea pens
17 Black coral
18 Sea perch
19 Saucer sponges
20 Hydroid coral
21 Feather star
22 Orange roughy
23 Black coral
24 Hake
25 Grenadier (rat-tail)

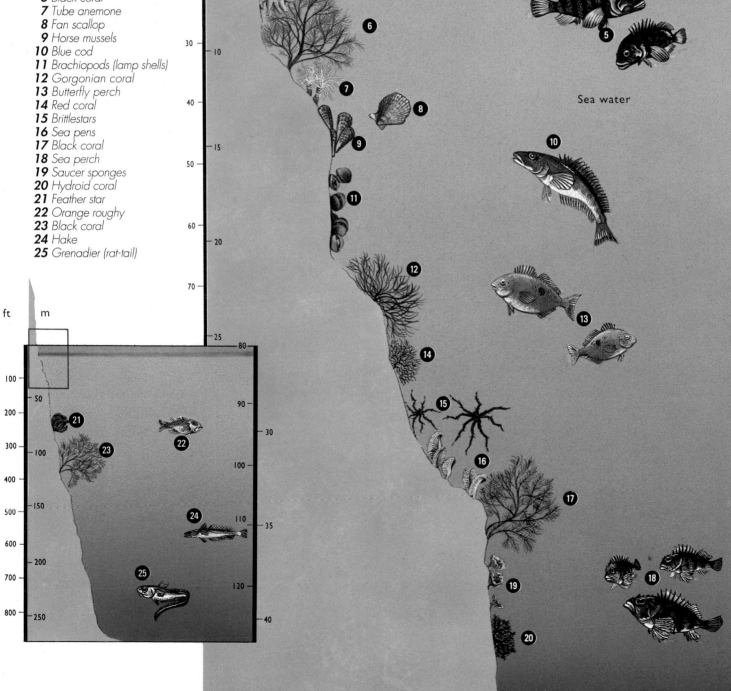

Low salinity layer

Transitional zone

Sea water

THE CASIQUIARE WATERWAY

After more than 150 years of heated debate, an exhausting, insect-plagued expedition in the first years of the 19th century finally proved conclusively the existence of the unique Casiquiare waterway, a natural canal linking two of South America's mighty rivers.

T hrow a twig into the murky headwaters of the Orinoco River, deep in the rainforests of southern Venezuela, and it may eventually reach the Atlantic Ocean at the river's delta, just south of the island of Trinidad. However, that same twig has a one in four chance of taking a very different route to the sea.

Some 200 miles (320km) from the Orinoco's source the river is funnelled through a narrow channel between two isolated cones of rock, one on each bank. Thus constricted, the river races between these obstacles and, once clear, turns sharply south-west and divides into two. Three-quarters of the water turns northwards again to continue as the Orinoco; the remainder enters a 150ft (46m) wide channel, gouged into the river's south bank by the pressure of floodwaters.

Here begins the Casiquiare waterway. A twig sucked into this unique conduit could float on for 220 miles (355km) until the waterway joins the Rio Negro, a tributary of the Amazon, before finally surging into the Atlantic at the Amazon delta, almost 1000 miles (1600km) south-east of the Orinoco delta. Geographers know of no other waterway like the Casiquiare. It is the world's only known natural canal linking two major river systems by crossing the watershed (land separating two river basins) between them.

After splitting away from the Orinoco, the Casiquiare snakes its way south-west in a series of loops, hemmed in on either side by rain forest. Gaining in volume as it is fed by tributaries, the waterway builds into a series of daunting rapids, and by the time it reaches the Rio Negro it has widened to 1500ft (450m). In many other parts of the

Dwindling population
The descendants of the Guaica Indians, whom the explorers Humboldt and Bonpland encountered near La Esmeralda, take advantage of an outboard motor but still pole their dugout canoes in shallow waters. In the 19th century, as many as 25 000 people lived along the banks of the Casiquiare; today there are fewer than 50.

Yellow ribbon *The Casiquiare meanders through dense, tropical rain forest. The water is yellowish-white from the vast quantities of mineral-laden silt carried into the waterway by its tributaries. This and other so-called white rivers are rich in the nutrients that support teeming populations of insect life.*

THE CASIQUIARE WATERWAY

Passages of time *Since Humboldt's historic expedition, numerous travellers have traced his journey in an attempt to explain how the Casiquiare was formed. Today's explorers cover the waterway by hovercraft in a matter of hours, yet it retains much of its fascination – not least because of its inaccessibility and the rigours of its climate. The rain forest, which crowds down to the very edge of the riverbanks, is inhabited by a few remaining Indian tribes.*

Green bell *Bees, ants, mosquitoes, sandflies and midges rule the Casiquiare, biting and stinging human flesh incessantly* (ABOVE). *The dense riverside vegetation is also home to many other predators. One night, the explorer Humboldt lost his mastiff to a jaguar* (BELOW).

world it would be considered a major river in its own right, but in South America the Casiquiare is dwarfed by the continent's other enormous water systems.

Missionaries and conquistadors, battling through the jungle to claim land and gold for Spain – and Indian souls for God – were the first Europeans to report the curious waterway that joined two great rivers. Driven by the search for gold, early explorers made various attempts to locate the mythical Lake Parima in the low country east of the Casiquiare, on whose shores legend placed the city of Manoa, home of El Dorado, the Golden Inca.

When, in 1641, a missionary priest called Padre Acuña first told of a waterway that linked the Orinoco in the north with the Negro in the south, no one believed him. One hundred years later Joseph Gumilla, a Jesuit priest, published *The Orinoco Illustrated*, a journal containing maps of a large and impenetrable mountain range that, according to Gumilla, lay between the Orinoco and Amazon river systems. In 1744, Portuguese slave traders guided another Jesuit explorer down the Casiquiare from the Orinoco to the Negro and he reported his journey to the French Academy of Sciences. Still Father Gumilla refused to accept that the waterway might exist and published an outraged rebuttal, *The Orinoco Illustrated – and Defended*. There were further expeditions over the next 20 years, but it was Alexander von Humboldt (1769–1859), described by Charles Darwin as 'the greatest scientific traveller who ever lived', who provided conclusive proof of the Casiquiare's existence.

With his botanist companion Aimé Bonpland, Humboldt carried out botanical, zoological and geological studies in South America between 1799 and 1804. They

'Living fossil' *The hoatzin can grip branches with the claws on its wings. This has led ornithologists to believe that it might be related to the first known bird,* Archaeopteryx.

Attentive observer *So faithful were Humboldt's recordings of the rain forest animals he encountered, that he is still regarded as the world authority on howler monkeys.*

ascended the Casiquiare from the Rio Negro in a large dugout canoe paddled by a team of Indians. Humboldt considered the ten days it took to reach the Orinoco the most miserable interlude of the entire expedition.

The Orinoco and Casiquiare are 'white' rivers, teeming with insect life; the dark, clear waters of 'black' rivers, by contrast, are acidic and relatively lifeless. For the Humboldt expedition, travelling from the dark, acidic Rio Negro into the whiter waters of the Casiquiare meant that the number of insects multiplied as they progressed north. The Europeans wrapped themselves in sheets and smeared themselves with rancid crocodile grease in a vain attempt to avoid the insect bites. Finally, after ten days of misery, the canoe reached the Orinoco. Humboldt had proved conclusively that there was no mountain range.

SARGASSO: SEA OF WEEDS

A sea within a sea, the Sargasso is like no other tract of water on Earth. Its still waters have long given rise to legends and fabulous tales, and it is bound not by continents but by the mighty currents of the Atlantic Ocean. What mysteries have made this marine wilderness so fertile a province for the imagination?

For generations, the Sargasso Sea has struck fear into seafarers. They believed legends of ships becoming ensnared in its floating vegetation and of sailors being dragged to their deaths. It remains an intriguing marine and biological oddity. European and American eels have spawned there since before their respective continents drifted apart. This slowly rotating tract of water situated between Bermuda and the Leeward Islands measures around 2 million sq miles (5.2 million km²), and has been likened to a gigantic raft of free-floating seaweed; it has also been called a biological desert. Yet neither description is accurate. While the seaweed is dense in some places, there are also many long stretches of clear water, and among the weeds and under the sea lives a bizarre population – the most grotesque of which is a species of angler fish, the sargassum fish, that clings to the branches of algae with grasping finger-like fins.

Tales of weeds, mists and mysterious becalmings originating from five centuries before the birth of Christ may mean that ancient mariners encountered the Sargasso Sea. It is more likely, however, that Christopher Columbus and his crew were the first to witness this marine phenomenon. On Columbus's voyage to the Americas in 1492, as his ships slowly traversed the tangled mass of vegetation, the sailors had ample time to study the olive and gold fronds that stretched from horizon to horizon, and to observe the berry-like, gas-filled bladders that keep the

Sea of myths *It is easy to understand why for centuries mystery has surrounded the Sargasso Sea. To the inexpert eye it is a stagnant expanse of weed-covered water that could spell doom for any sea captain rash enough to try to sail across it. In fact the Sargasso contains less weed than its reputation suggests and, far from being stagnant, the sea is constantly turning. It is propelled in a clockwise direction by the eastbound Gulf Stream to the north and by westbound currents flowing along the Tropic of Cancer to the south.*

'Actor fish' *The sargassum fish owes its nickname to its talent as a mimic. A skilled predator, it melts into the surroundings: its blotchy colouring blends with generations of weed growth; white bumps on its body resemble the scores of tiny life forms that live on the weed; and flaps of skin and arm-like pectoral fins mirror the movements of drifting fronds of foliage.*

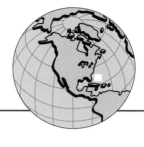

SARGASSO: SEA OF WEEDS

weed suspended near the water's surface. They named them *sargazo*, hence Sargasso, after the small grapes grown in their Mediterranean homelands.

The drifting raft of vegetation is largely made up of one particular species of weed, *Sargassum natans*. Also known as gulfweed or sea holly, it is unlike other seaweeds in two ways: it exists free of the coastal rocks on which it originated, and it reproduces by fragmentation. Every bud that forms on the parent plant has the potential to break off and thrive alone, perpetuating itself indefinitely.

It is the sargassum weed that fuels the Sargasso's food chain. Microscopic plankton – the tiny marine organisms that nourish the gigantic blue whale and herring alike – cannot thrive here, for the sea's waters are too warm. Nevertheless, a unique community of animals has grown to live on and around the seaweed.

Attached to the crevices of the weed fronds are small algae, such as floppy coral, and tube worms that sift the water for food. In places, the fronds appear to be covered in patches of mould. These are in fact moss animals or bryozoans – minute creatures found in waters from the tropics to the poles. Usually they develop from fertilised eggs, but here, like their weed host, new organisms break away from the parent fully formed. Using tiny hairs as 'arms', they sweep micro-organisms into their mouths. But if the added weight of ingested food proves too heavy for the weed clump, the moss animals sink to an icy death in the Atlantic depths. The tiny crabs, shrimps and prawns that live on the fronds fare better. As the clump starts to descend, they scramble on to a safer spot.

Little here is what it seems: camouflage is the only means of survival for many creatures. Shrimps develop white spots to resemble bryozoans, while long, slender pipefish look like branches of gulfweed. Probably the most impressive adaptation is that of the sargassum fish. With its weed-like coloration, it can surprise and devour prey up to 8in (20cm) long – nearly as large as itself. If threatened, it takes in gulps of water and inflates like a balloon to deter the attacker.

One of the Sargasso's strangest secrets, however, has also been one of it best kept. Until the early years of the 20th century the amazing life story of the European and American eels, spawned in the Sargasso, was a mystery and even today it is not fully understood.

The eel is not the only species to breed in the Sargasso. The sea's warm waters, and the absence of large predators due to the lack of plankton, attract dolphinfish, jacks and flying fish, which lay their eggs in long strings anchored to the gulfweed. As far as biologists can tell, the eel is the only creature that returns to this unique, ever-circling tract of water to die.

EEL MIGRATION

The mysterious breeding habits of these long-distance migrants of the Sargasso Sea have baffled scientists for centuries. Many of the forces that govern the remarkable life cycle of the eel are unknown, but the pioneering work of Danish oceanographer Johannes Schmidt (1877–1933) shed light on the basic facts.

Female eels lay their eggs in the warm waters of the Sargasso at depths of 1300–2500ft (400–750m). As the larvae hatch, they drift with the currents of the Gulf Stream. Larvae of American eels travel to North America, while those of European eels, after an 18-month journey, approach the continental shelf of Europe. By that time they are longer and thinner, and bear more resemblance to young eels. Known at this stage as glass eels, both types finally arrive close to fresh water.

For the next eight or nine years, males remain largely in estuary waters, while females make far longer journeys upriver. During this time both sexes feed and grow as if in preparation for the gruelling return journey. Then, one autumn, some impulse tells the eels it is time to spawn. The females start to descend the river systems, seeking salt water and the open sea. Six months later they are back in the Sargasso Sea, where they breed, then die.

Exactly what force guides the eels' journeys is unknown, but the Gulf Stream is thought to be sufficiently strong to carry the larvae along, whether or not they want to go. Thereafter a physiological change is possibly responsible for their developing a preference for fresh water. The return journey is more problematic than the outward journey. Do the eels navigate by the stars or by echolocation? Or are they influenced by the Earth's magnetic field? It seems likely that as the eels approach the Sargasso Sea some imprinted memory draws them back to the warm waters of their birth.

Safe hiding place
Through the evolutionary process, sea anemones (LEFT) have come to resemble the weed in which they take sanctuary. They lie in wait here for unsuspecting prey to pass by.

False belief The presence of the sargassum crab led Christopher Columbus to believe that land was near. In fact the crabs, just one species living in the weed, were 1000 miles (1600km) from shore.

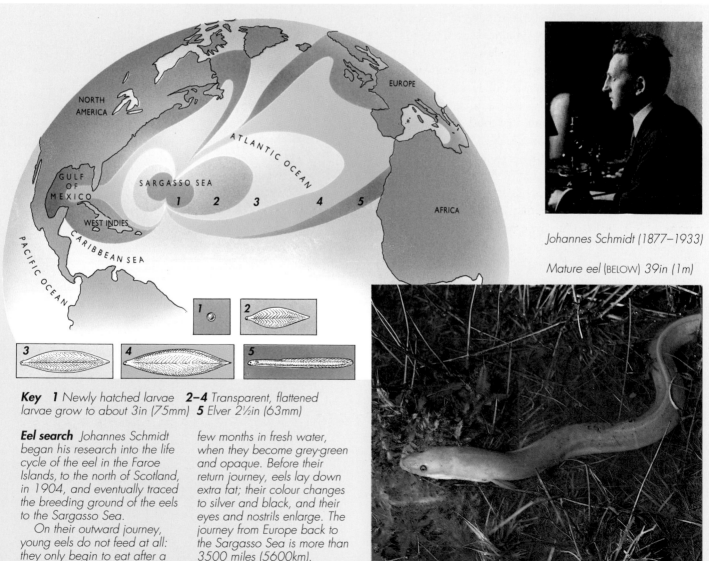

Johannes Schmidt (1877–1933)

Mature eel (BELOW) 39in (1m)

Key   1 Newly hatched larvae **2–4** Transparent, flattened larvae grow to about 3in (75mm) **5** Elver 2½in (63mm)

Eel search Johannes Schmidt began his research into the life cycle of the eel in the Faroe Islands, to the north of Scotland, in 1904, and eventually traced the breeding ground of the eels to the Sargasso Sea.

On their outward journey, young eels do not feed at all: they only begin to eat after a few months in fresh water, when they become grey-green and opaque. Before their return journey, eels lay down extra fat; their colour changes to silver and black, and their eyes and nostrils enlarge. The journey from Europe back to the Sargasso Sea is more than 3500 miles (5600km).

231

AMAZON: ROADWAY IN THE RAIN FOREST

This last great wilderness is a humid, tangled jungle that rings with the cries of cicadas, parrots and monkeys. The peoples who inhabit the riverbanks of the mightiest river in the world look upon the waterways that snake through their jungle as thoroughfare, playground and food source.

High in the Peruvian Andes, a trickle of meltwater is the starting point for the Amazon's 4000 mile (6400km) journey across the bulbous headland of South America. Along a course carpeted with the greatest rain forest on Earth the river is joined by thousands of tributaries, draining a vast land basin almost the size of Australia. Some of the tributaries – notably the Rivers Negro, Madeira and Tapajos – are giants in themselves and swell the main river to such a size that boats may take up to an hour to ferry passengers across.

The mouth of the Amazon River was discovered in 1500, when a Spanish expedition led by Vincente Pinzón sailed up it to a point 50 miles (80km) from the sea. Forty years later another Spanish expedition, of 50 men under the command of Francisco de Orellana, achieved an epic journey from the distant Andes by way of the Napo River and the Amazon mainstream to the Atlantic.

By the 19th century, naturalists had finally begun to probe the secrets of the rivers and the surrounding rain forest. Between 1848 and 1859, the British naturalist Henry Bates collected thousands of insect species entirely new to entomology, and the botanist Richard Spruce gathered some 7000 new plant specimens.

The water's edge offers a fine vantage point from which to observe the Amazon's exotic animal species. Colourful kingfishers, egrets and ibises haunt the riverbanks, while parrots and toucans feed on nuts and fruit in the tree tops

Thinly bedded *The earth below the shallow topsoil is poor in nutrients, so tree roots in the Amazon jungle rarely penetrate deeper than 3ft (1m). Buttress roots (ABOVE) aid stability. Flooding frequently washes away the topsoil, leaving the trees with little support other than that of vines.*

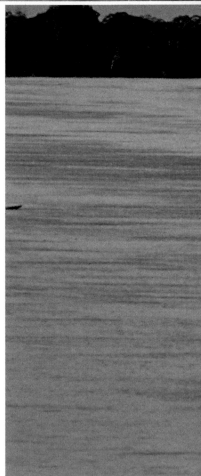

Impressive watercourse *One of the Amazon's sources, Lake Lauricocha lies high in the snow-capped Peruvian Andes just 120 miles (190km) from the Pacific Ocean. Together with more than 1000 mist-shrouded tributaries (RIGHT) the river drains a basin that extends over 2.5 million sq miles (6.5 million km²).*

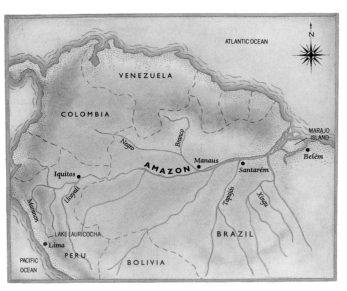

AMAZON: ROADWAY IN THE RAIN FOREST

until monkeys, hurtling through the branches, chase them away. A sudden splash might be an iguana plunging into the water, shaken from an overhanging branch by a plodding sloth or alarmed by a grazing capybara – at over 3ft (1m) long, it is the largest rodent in the world.

More than 2000 species of fish are known to thrive in the waters of the Amazon, ten times the number in all Europe's rivers combined and three times as many as in Africa's mighty Zaire river. They range from dainty, brightly coloured tetra and angelfish to deadly stingrays and electric eels. While some fish, such as the tambaqui, feed on fallen nuts, others are fierce carnivores. The largest of these, the pirarucu, grows to 10ft (3m) in length and weighs, on average, 440lb (200kg).

The most notorious fish of all is the red piranha. Although it grows to a maximum length of only 12in (30cm), it hunts in shoals, and the razor-sharp teeth of a group of red piranha can reduce a large, slow-moving mammal to a bare skeleton in seconds, particularly if it is old or wounded. Contrary to popular belief, this behaviour is exceptional in piranhas, for their staple diet is in fact fish, supplemented with seeds and fruit.

The largest predator in the Amazon basin is the black caiman, an alligator that can measure up to 15ft (4.6m) long and which has been known to attack humans. Its diet typically consists of aquatic mammals, such as the manatee, and forest dwellers such as capybaras and tapirs, which are plucked from the water's edge while drinking.

The enormous diversity of plant and animal species in the Amazon jungle makes it the greatest natural resource in the world. In 1 acre (0.4ha) of primary forest alone there are about 60 different tree species, 15 times the number found in temperate forests. Such is the density of plant life that, it is estimated, 900 tons of vegetation grow in just 2½ acres (1ha) of land. Yet the jungle is far from being an impenetrable mass. At ground level in the heart of the forest there is comparatively little undergrowth because the canopy of foliage blocks out growth-enhancing light. But, whenever a tree topples, the undergrowth bursts into bloom, so continuing the life-cycle of this ancient and enduring habitat.

River cruiser *Dolphins patrol the waters of the Amazon Basin, snatching fish between their long, toothed jaws. Visibility in the silt laden river is poor, so dolphins use echo-location – a 'sonar' system of high-frequency sounds – to track their prey.*

Blaze of glory *Pairs or groups of vividly coloured scarlet macaws can be seen at sunrise soaring over the tree tops to their feeding ground. At 3ft (1m) high, this is the largest South American parrot.*

Jaws of death At least 20 species of piranha dwell in the waters of the Amazon Basin, some measuring up to 2ft (60cm) long. The most feared variety is the 1ft (30cm) long red (or red-bellied) piranha, whose razor-sharp interlocking teeth can rip flesh to shreds in seconds. Its external nostrils are super-sensitive to the scent of blood. Within seconds, they can detect the presence of a wounded animal. Then a shoal of fish, sometimes numbering thousands, will quickly move in for the kill.

Fatal embrace At 550lb (250kg) or more, the anaconda is the undisputed heavyweight of snakes. This 33ft (10m) long giant will take deer, tapir and even jaguars as they drink at the water's edge. The anaconda usually waits in the water until its prey comes within reach, then seizes the prey between its jaws, winding itself more and more tightly around the victim until it is crushed to death or suffocated.

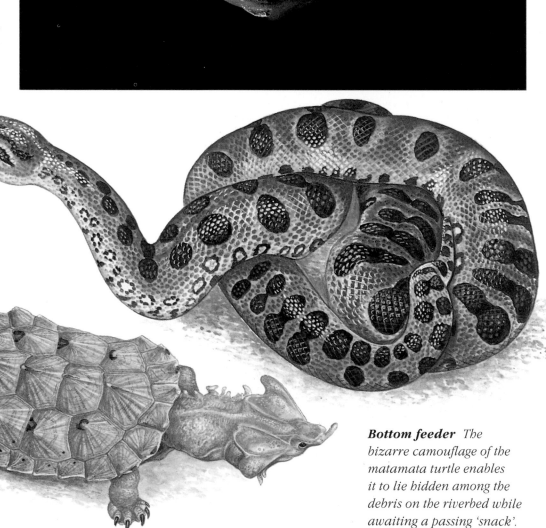

Bottom feeder The bizarre camouflage of the matamata turtle enables it to lie hidden among the debris on the riverbed while awaiting a passing 'snack'.

THE AMAZONIAN INDIANS

Five hundred years ago, many thriving Indian settlements were scattered along the Amazon and its major tributaries. Tribes such as the Tarumá and the Omagua reaped a rich harvest of maize, manioc and wild rice from land fertilised by nutrient-rich floodwaters, and abundant supplies of fish and turtles were readily available year after year. Gradually, however, almost all of these peoples have been wiped out by a combination of warfare, enslavement and disease introduced by slave traders and settlers.

Today, most of the surviving Indian groups of the Amazon are those that have traditionally lived deep within the forest, some distance from the principal rivers. Like their forebears, these scattered tribes are generally nomadic: they clear temporary plots in the poor soil for farming, but live mainly by hunting and fishing. Their knowledge of forest resources is extensive: the Tiriyo Indians, for example, recognise medicinal properties in more than 300 wild plants.

The population of Amazonian Indians has shrunk to around 100 000, but at least 150 linguistically distinct tribes remain, many of which, including the Krahó Indians of north-east

Living culture *Most Karajá favour Western clothing, but a few still dress in traditional style. The Karajá are noted for their face decoration – a dark circle tattooed on the cheek-bone – and head-dresses made from the plumage of colourful birds. This head-dress is made from macaw feathers.*

River life The basic dugout canoe (LEFT) doubles as a means of transport and fishing craft. Using simple paddles and employing navigational skills passed down through succesive generations, the Amazonian Indians manoeuvre their way through the often treacherous river currents.

Eagle-eyed hunter The skilful Karajá fisherman stands in his craft and surveys the surface of the water. When he sights a fish he takes aim and, with pinpoint accuracy, pierces his prey using bow and arrow.
· Once the Karajá decorated their whole bodies, but today the tribe's traditional artistry is demonstrated mainly in their headwear, such as this cap made of long feathers radiating from the centre.

Brazil (RIGHT), are protected by the National Indian Foundation. But they, too, are struggling to survive as the Amazon region undergoes rapid changes at an ever-accelerating pace. Towards the end of the 20th century the Amazon has become a serious environmental and political issue in quarters where, until fairly recently, it was a comfortably romantic symbol of tropical wilderness.

Conservationists are increasingly concerned about the relentless assault on the world's largest rain forest. Tree felling and logging are only the most obvious forms of depredation. Opencast mining requires forest clearance on an alarming scale, as do farming, oil exploration and the construction of hydroelectric dams. Huge swathes of forest are burned to allow crop growing and cattle ranching, and such clearances have had a devastating effect on the region's most accessible areas, the margins of the great rivers. But recently the rate of deforestation has begun to slow down. In 1989, 8100 sq miles (21 000km²) of virgin Amazonian forest was destroyed, but in 1990 the figure stood at 3860 sq miles (10 000km²).

Ancient craft The traditional skills of weaving, thatching and basketry are practised by both men and women of the Krahó tribe. They plait baskets that are used for carrying food. While working, the basketmaker sits on matting made from palm leaves. Strong and flexible, these leaves are also used for thatching the walls and roofs of village huts.

IGUAÇU FALLS: THE GREAT WATER

Cutting a swathe through dense, emerald rain forest, the Iguaçu River eventually cascades into a yawning chasm in Brazil's Paraná Plateau. Few sights in the world can match this overwhelming display of nature's raw power.

The corner of Brazil that borders Argentina is the setting for a spectacular series of waterfalls that together are almost four times as wide as Niagara Falls and 100ft (30m) higher. In a thunderous sweep almost 2½ miles (4km) wide, the Iguaçu Falls tumble over the rim of the Paraná Plateau and plummet into a gorge, aptly named *La Garganta del Diablo*, the Devil's Throat, 269ft (82m) below. A frothy white torrent of mist and spray rises from the rocky jaws of the gorge, rainbows arch over and through one another, and the perpetual sound of roaring water can be heard 15 miles (24km) away.

On visiting this spectacular site, Eleanor Roosevelt, wife of US President Franklin D. Roosevelt, remarked: 'It makes our Niagara Falls look like a kitchen faucet.' And the Swiss botanist Robert Chodat (1865–1934) described its imposing grandeur thus: 'When we stand at the foot of this world of cascades and, raising our eyes, see 269 feet above us the horizon filled with a line of waters, this awesome spectacle of an ocean pouring into an abyss is almost frightening.'

Around 275 individual waterfalls, divided by rocky, tree-covered islands, make up Iguaçu's mighty cascade. The plateau over which the waterfalls flow is formed of solidified lava and tough volcanic rocks such as basalt. These rocks are not easily eroded and resist the rushing water, forcing it to flow into narrow channels around them – hence the formation of numerous rocky islands. Some falls plunge from rim to gorge in one continuous spill, others splash from ledge to ledge before reaching the bottom. At the base of the gorge the falls merge with turbulent rapids, and flow on swifly to join the Paraná River about 14 miles (22.5km) farther south.

Only two South American rivers, the Amazon and the Orinoco, are mightier than the Iguaçu River, which feeds the falls and is 1500–3000ft (450–900m) wide for much of its length. The river's rise and fall – and thus the volume of water toppling over the falls – depends on the seasonal rainfall that collects in its drainage basin. At the height of the rainy season, from November to March, the swollen river hurls almost 3 million gallons (13.6 million litres) of water per second down the Devil's Throat – enough to fill six Olympic-sized swimming pools. In the dry season, from April to October, the flow reduces considerably, with only 500 000 gallons (2.3 million litres) of water spilling

The Devil's Throat *Into this deep, narrow canyon rushes the bulk of the water that thunders over the Iguaçu Falls, its terrifying force and fury throwing up a cloud of mist 100ft (30m) high. As the water spills over ledges and terraces dense with forest trees, palms, orchids, birds and myriad butterflies, it looks as if a mossy carpet has been shredded by the water's power.*

A multitude of torrents
No other waterfall is made up of so many separate channels as the Iguaçu Falls. From the narrow Devil's Throat, the river spreads out into numerous cascades. The San Martín Fall is the main cascade on the Argentine side, but others have been given more fanciful names such as the 'Two Sisters', 'Floriano' and 'Three Musketeers'.

IGUAÇU FALLS: THE GREAT WATER

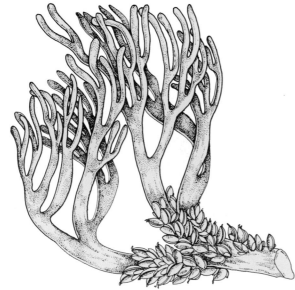

Water plants *The cliffs beneath the falls are host to a number of aquatic herbs, resembling mosses and lichens, that grow only in fast-flowing water. The flowers of these plants have no petals and bloom at the end of the rainy season. None is taller than 4in (10cm).*

Daredevil drop *Twisting like a giant silver snake through virgin forest, the Iguaçu River rises near the city of Curitiba in the Serra do Mar mountains and is fed by 30 tributaries in the course of its 800-mile (1280km) journey to the falls. As the river approaches the falls, it broadens, spreading across a wide area before crashing violently over the precipice.*

over the cliff each second. And, every 40 years or so, an excessively severe dry season causes the river to dry up completely. When this last occurred, in 1978, the falls were reduced to no more than a line of rocky cliffs and remained that way for a month, until a trickle of water appeared – a sign that they were about to come back to life.

Iguaçu means 'great water' in Guaraní, the language of the Indians who originally inhabited this watery paradise, rich in lush tropical vegetation. According to Indian legend, the origins of the falls can be traced to the vengeful action of a god who lived in the jungle near the Iguaçu River. Thwarted in love by a warrior called Caroba, who carried the god's beloved, Naipur, downriver in a canoe, he lost

Solitary splendour *The graceful jaguar, the largest cat in South America, is perfectly adapted to life around the falls, using its thick, powerful limbs not only to climb trees but also to swim across rivers. It preys on animals such as peccaries and capybara, and also eats fish, deer, otters, turtles and ground-dwelling birds.*

At home in the falls *The forest-dwelling Brazilian tapir is a frequent visitor to the waters around the Iguaçu Falls. A confident swimmer and agile diver, this stocky, short-legged creature is also sure-footed on land, no matter how rugged the terrain. The tapir feeds by night on leaves, buds, fruit and aquatic plants which it roots out with its long snout.*

his temper. To prevent the lovers from travelling too far he shattered the earth below the river, splitting its surface into a line of waterfalls.

The Indians lived here long before the Spanish explorer Alvar Núñez Cabeza de Vaca 'discovered' the Iguaçu Falls in 1541 while leading a band of 280 soldiers from the coast of Brazil to the newly founded city of Asunción in Paraguay. In line with contemporary custom, de Vaca named the falls Saltos de Santa María after the Blessed Virgin Mary, but they soon reverted to their local Guaraní name. De Vaca's discovery left him curiously unmoved. The first account of the expedition, published in Spanish in 1555, merely mentions that 'the current of the Iguaçu was so strong that the canoes were carried violently downriver, because close to that point is a large fall.... It was therefore necessary to take the canoes out of the water and carry them on land past the waterfall.'

The botanist Robert Chodat was clearly impressed, however. He was enthralled by the region's rich and thriving plant life: 'an exuberant, almost tropical vegetation, the fronds of great ferns, the shafts of bamboos, the graceful trunks of palm trees, and a thousand species of trees, their crowns bending over the gulf adorned with mosses, pink begonias, golden orchids, brilliant bromeliads and lianas with trumpet flowers....'

At the beginning of this century, Brazil and Argentina established national parks on their respective sides of the falls to protect the rich tropical and subtropical wildlife. Birds such as tinamous and parrots haunt the trees, and swifts nest in the craggy outcrops of the falls, swooping low over the river to feed on the swarms of insects that hover there. These include hundreds of species of butterfly, some with wings the size of a human hand. The lush vegetation also supports a number of larger mammals, such as ocelots, jaguars, tapirs, three species of deer and two species of peccary, members of the hippopotamus family.

From the Brazilian shore the entire sweep of the falls is in clear view, while from the Argentine banks observers can climb freely through and under the waterfalls and witness their splendour close up. The grandeur and primitive beauty of the magnificent cascades together create an astonishing spectacle of nature untamed.

BLUE HOLES: LAIRS OF THE LUSCA

The calm surface of the Caribbean Sea off the island of Andros slowly starts to rotate, whirlpools form and at their centre gaping dark blue holes begin to gulp water. For centuries, a Bahamian legend of a sinister, mythical creature called the Lusca has been woven around this strange phenomenon.

S een from the air, the low-lying island of Andros in the Bahamas is a fissured mass of inlets, channels, islets and coral shallows. Here and there, dappled patches of inky blue divert the eye from the brilliant turquoise hue of the lagoon. These are the blue holes, the notorious 'doors' to a subterranean maze of flooded cave systems interwoven with passages and galleries that by twists and turns lead to small chambers, immense canyons and cathedral-like vaults.

At each high tide, as the water rises inside the barrier reef that embraces the coast of Andros, the blue holes begin the performance that has earned them their fearful reputation. They start to slowly rotate, gulping water ever more rapaciously so that the inflowing currents create whirlpools which draw into their vortex – and thence to watery oblivion – anything that floats, from plant debris to small fishing boats. As the tide recedes, a powerful reverse action takes place and the holes spew out great mushrooms of water. Local people attribute this dramatic sequence to a mythical creature, the Lusca, that is reputed to dwell in the blue holes. Half shark, half octopus, the Lusca supposedly uses its long tentacles to drag food into its deep lair, then disgorges the remains when sated. Small wonder that Bahamian fishermen, some of whom have lost ancestors to the raging maelstroms of these deceptively calm waters, continue to treat the blue holes with circumspection.

Andros is the largest of the Bahamian islands. Some 100 miles (160km) long and 40 miles (65km) across at its widest point, the island sits on the marine plateau of the Great Bahama Bank. It is lapped on three sides by warm, shallow seas, but a channel of deep water known as the Tongue of the Ocean curls past the length of its eastern shore. In places along the wall of this abyss, colourful coral shallows suddenly give way to dark blue depths. These deep openings in the limestone bank on the margin of the island are the mysterious blue holes. Their equivalents on land are circular black lakes in wooded parts of the island.

Even today the blue holes have not been counted and relatively few have been explored; moreover, their very existence has only recently been explained. The first serious modern explorer of the area, the Canadian George Benjamin, in the 1960s made aerial surveys to chart the caves. Then, equipped with an aqualung and underwater cameras, he dived to probe their secrets. His discoveries

Mysterious seas *The dark blue Tongue of the Ocean* (RIGHT) *snakes past the shore off the island of Andros into the heart of the Great Bahama Bank. The walls of this 6000ft (1800m) deep underwater channel are composed of limestone sediments that are honey-combed with large caverns and tunnels.*

Rocky jaws *A diver penetrates the gloom of the underwater catacombs* (ABOVE) *that comprise the Blue Holes of Andros.*

BLUE HOLES: LAIRS OF THE LUSCA

HOW BLUE HOLES ARE FORMED

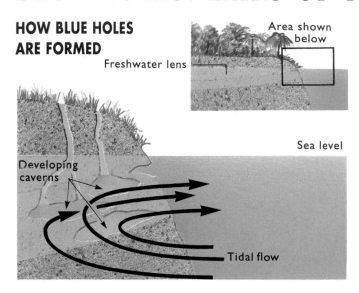

Freshwater lens

Area shown below

Sea level

Developing caverns

Tidal flow

1 Rainwater seeps through overlying rock and combines with sea water to form a brackish mixture. This is carried out by the tidal flow, eroding fissures in the rock. Over millions of years these fissures are enlarged first into channels, then caverns.

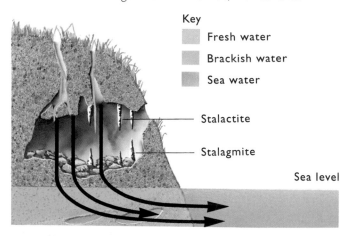

Key

Fresh water

Brackish water

Sea water

Stalactite

Stalagmite

Sea level

2 During successive ice ages, water was locked into ice caps and glaciers and the sea level fell, draining underwater caverns. Dripping water caused stalactites and stalagmites to form in many caverns, while in others roofs collapsed, creating blue holes.

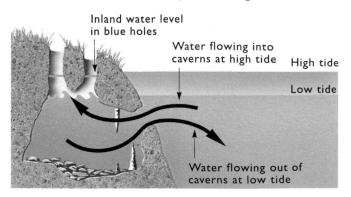

Inland water level in blue holes

Water flowing into caverns at high tide

High tide

Low tide

Water flowing out of caverns at low tide

3 Water rushes into or out of the blue holes depending on whether the tide is high or low. So powerful is the flow that divers must time their forays to coincide with the 20-minute period of 'slack water'. To miscalculate the timing of a dive could prove fatal.

provided geologists with the information they needed to begin at last to unravel the mystery surrounding the holes.

The Bahamas are part of a chain of limestone platforms, or banks, which began to form around 130 million years ago. Over the last 2 million years, successive ice ages locked water into the Earth's ice caps and glaciers, causing the sea level to fall. In the warmer periods the ice melted and the sea level rose accordingly. At the peak of the last ice age, around 20 000 years ago, sea levels were as much as 400ft (120m) lower than they are today. This meant that underwater caves – carved out of the limestone over millions of years by a corrosive mixture of fresh water and sea water – were drained. No longer buoyed by water, their ceilings started to collapse.

In many cave roofs a dome developed upwards and in some places broke through the Earth's surface, forming an open shaft. When sea levels rose again, the shafts filled with water and created the blue holes. Today, at high tide, sea levels around Andros rise above the groundwater levels of the island's water table. The pressure of the sea forces water into the blue holes, creating their strong characteristic whirlpools, and groundwater levels rise slightly. As the tide recedes and pressure of the sea water drops, the groundwater pushes the sea water down, causing it to well

out of the blue holes in great domes. The myth of the Lusca has its origins in these strong reversing currents.

Surprisingly, a wealth of creatures has adapted to life in this seemingly hostile environment; indeed, explorers have likened some of the caves to underwater zoos. Nurse sharks rest motionless on sandy floors; crayfish inhabit rock crevices; sky-blue and lavender sponges drift eerily through the indigo depths; and at certain levels the water is alive with tiny crustaceans and swimming worms. One of the most curious species of all, and previously recorded only at inland sites, is the *Lucifuga*, a blind cavefish with a pale, colourless body.

More dramatic still was the discovery, in 1991, of human bones and skulls at an inland diving site known as Sanctuary Blue Hole. These remains were attributed to the Lucayan people (an Arawak-speaking tribe which inhabited the Caribbean at the time of Columbus) who probably used the holes as burial grounds.

The prospect of being trapped in the holes discourages many divers, and there is still danger involved in exploring them. Even with the most modern safety equipment divers never venture into the blue holes alone: anyone attempting to do so at high tide would be sucked in like a cork down a drain, sustaining the legend of the Lusca.

Sudden drop *A diver prepares to investigate an inland hole* (LEFT) *using the most up-to-date diving equipment. (It allows the diver to stay down at a depth of 64ft/20m for five hours without the need for decompression.) Cave divers must move slowly since a careless stroke will disturb the sediment, reducing visibility. Divers always use a guideline that will lead them back to the cave entrance.*

Inky depths *The waters of the Black Hole on Andros* (RIGHT) *appear inky blue because they are so deep. They are yet to be explored.*

Feeding grounds *A shoal of fish forages in the area where fresh and salt water mix* (RIGHT). *There is plenty of debris to be found floating at this level, for it is supported by denser, briny waters.*

STROKKUR: THE BOILING FOUNTAIN

Iceland is a land of geysers and the greatest of all is situated in the south-west of the island. From a quiet steam-covered pool, Strokkur becomes a seething cauldron that suddenly shoots a column of boiling water high into the air, approximately every four to ten minutes.

A t regular intervals throughout the day, as if it were triggered by some underworld master of ceremonies, Strokkur hurls its column of boiling water 70ft (22m) towards the sky. After a few seconds, with a hiss of steam, the fountain subsides and the waters of the surrounding pool calm down. At these times Strokkur becomes a sheet of clear water overhung with steam. The first sign of approaching activity is a fluctuation in the level of the water. As the waters heave with ever-increasing speed, a dome of clear, scalding water wells up for a moment. Then, with a roar, the dome suddenly bursts, and Strokkur repeats its display. No wonder its name means 'The Churn' in Icelandic.

Strokkur is situated in the geothermal region beside the Hvítá River in Iceland, about 50 miles (80km) east of Reykjavík. A group of steaming pools of scalding water and bubbling mud is located in this area and it is the site of the Stori Geysir, or Great Gusher, once the most powerful geyser of the group. All other geysers were named after it – the Icelandic word *geysir* means to gush.

At one time the waters of this world-famous hot spring reached the incredible height of 230ft (70m). In 1810 it was active every 30 minutes, yet just five years later the time between eruptions was as much as six hours, and in

Healing properties
The power station sited at Svartsengi (BELOW), on the south-western Reykjanes peninsula, uses geothermal energy. Run-off water from the plant collects in the 'Blue Lagoon', a pool which has become well known for curing skin complaints, such as eczema.

Steaming pool *A huge bubble of scalding water (ABOVE) wells up on the pool's surface immediately before Strokkur explodes. The ground vibrates with a deep rumbling that accompanies the eruption and the white cloud of steam can be seen from a distance of 3 miles (5km).*

1916 all activity suddenly ceased. Then in 1935, after some water had been drained off, the geyser began to erupt again on its old schedule of every 30 minutes.

Today the Stori Geysir is quiet again, giving little hint of its past splendour. Occasionally technicians prompt it to put on a spectacular display for visitors by pouring large amounts of liquid soap into the pool. This increases the density of the water, which acts like a lid on the geyser, preventing the steam from escaping. When some of the soap solution is removed from the vent, the pressure is relieved and the geyser erupts.

Iceland owes its geysers to the fact that it is situated on the Mid-Atlantic Ridge, where two great segments of the Earth's crust, known as tectonic plates, are moving away from each other. This causes a line of weakness through which molten magma wells up from deep within the Earth. The magma heats underground water which can escape through geysers.

Hot springs and lakes of bubbling mud occur in areas where pockets of molten magma lie close to the surface near underground water, as in the Hvítá valley. The magma heats both the porous rocks and the water which has soaked down through them. If the water can escape freely, it will rise to the surface as a bubbling hot spring or mud pool. If, however, water is partially enclosed in a hollow column in these rocks, it will heat up to a high

247

STROKKUR: THE BOILING FOUNTAIN

temperature and create a geyser. The pressure of the water column itself initially prevents the water from boiling. Heat builds up and eventually the water starts to boil at as much as 6°C (11°F) above normal boiling temperature at the surface – this is known as superheating. Steam pressure builds up and forces the water above the top of the column into a dome in the pool. This, in turn, lowers the pressure allowing more water to boil until, finally, the superheated steam blasts a column of hot water out of the ground as though it were being shot from a giant cannon. When water begins to accumulate in the hollow in the heated rock, the whole cycle starts again.

Since the early 1900s, the Icelandic people have made efficient use of the heat stored below ground. They employ this energy for heating in industry, agriculture and in the home. By 1942, an extensive system of pipes and pumping stations was bringing natural hot water to large storage tanks in the hills around the capital, Reykjavík. The water sources were carefully chosen to avoid disrupting the playing of Strokkur and other geysers. Today, most homes in the city are plumbed into the natural hot-water system. In other areas, engineers use the volcanic rocks to heat cold water pumped down to them.

The town of Hveragerdhi, south-east of the capital, bears witness to the success of using natural energy. In the town, lying only 155 miles (250km) from the Arctic Circle, tropical houseplants and fruit and vegetables, such as bananas and cucumbers, flourish in glasshouses heated by geothermal waters, giving the town its reputation as 'the garden of hot springs'.

HOW A GEYSER WORKS

Geysers occur where magma, or molten rock, lies near the Earth's surface. Water seeps through crevices in the rock to form underground reservoirs. The water is heated by the hot rocks and some eventually turns to steam. A head of steam builds up until it escapes in a huge jet of water and steam, which is known as a geyser.

Explosive force *Strokkur's boiling plume* (LEFT) *consists of water droplets and super-heated steam. The Vikings believed Iceland to be the entrance to the underworld, since the contrast between fire and ice was similar to that described in the tales of the Norse gods.*

Man-made steamers
At Krafla, in north-east Iceland, engineers have drilled steam wells (RIGHT) *for use as a source of power. Geothermal energy supplies a third of the island's needs, but only five per cent of the potential power has been tapped.*

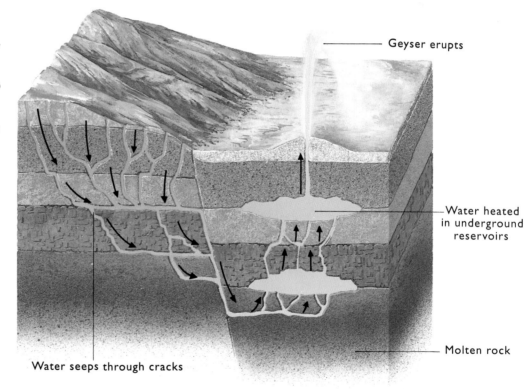

Geyser erupts

Water heated in underground reservoirs

Molten rock

Water seeps through cracks

RIDDLES AND SYMBOLS

W hen our early ancestors outlined their own hands with pigment on the walls of caves, they were making the first conscious statements of personal identity. Much later their descendants began to make their mark on the landscape itself, sometimes echoing the scale of their surroundings with sculpted earthworks and huge incised figures. The message was now more complicated, expressing the relationship between human beings and the gods and spirits they believed inhabited the land. These early expressions of the supernatural fascinate us with their primitive potency. Some, such as the Nazca Lines of Peru and earth-mound effigies of North America, are doubly mysterious, for many are animal pictures only recognisable from the air. Today some investigators believe that the neolithic stone arrangements at Stonehenge in England and Carnac in France are astronomical observatories, representing the flowering of the first human science. Prehistoric astronomers could predict with great accuracy the turning of the seasons and the longer cycles associated with the Sun and Moon. Eager to ensure that spring growth would follow the long winter, farmers of many cultures developed mazes and maze dances into symbolic rituals, which eventually the Christian Church took over, and a fertility ritual became a substitute for a pilgrimage to the Holy Land.

GIANTS OF THE HILLS

When unknown carvers scoured human and animal forms into hillsides throughout Britain, they could not have foreseen how many generations of observers would be baffled by their artistry.

T he Cerne Abbas giant, carved into a hill in Dorset in southern England, is one of the most enduring and mystifying sights of ancient Britain. Over the centuries he has weathered the elements and prevailing climates of morality alike, but for all the time that he has threatened with his club and shocked with his phallus, our understanding of the giant's purpose has advanced little.

The naked figure is 180ft (55m) tall. His head is relatively small and bald and his features rudimentary, but his nipples, ribs, penis and testicles are strongly etched. His right hand merges with a massive 121ft (37m) long notched club which overshadows the entire image.

Many legends have grown up around the Cerne Abbas giant. According to local folklore, dating back at least to the Middle Ages, he was said to represent a real giant who wreaked havoc in this area of the Dorset countryside by eating sheep and causing general destruction. One day he lay down on the hillside to digest his latest meal and fell asleep. Determined to rid themselves of the troublemaker, the local people seized the chance to kill the giant, then carved his colossal outline in the chalk.

The symbolic significance of the giant's left hand, which may once have held an animal skin, has been the subject of much debate. A pelt would be in keeping with the most enduring legend surrounding the giant – that he represents the Graeco-Roman god Hercules, who was often depicted naked, wielding a club and clutching a lion skin. There is some evidence to support this belief. A similar image was depicted on a fragment of Romano-British pottery found in Norfolk, and there was a Hercules cult in the Roman Empire under Emperor Commodus (ruled AD 180–193) which probably had devotees in Britain. The giant may have been the emblem of this cult, or the Celtic equivalent of Hercules. The name Helith, Helis or Heil was traditionally used for the giant and could be a corruption of Hercules.

There is historical proof, too, that letters and numbers may once have been carved between the feet of the giant. One theory suggests the letters were ANO, standing for *anno* – 'in the year of' – and the missing numbers 1748,

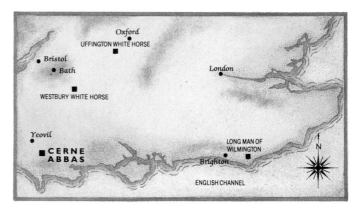

Westbury White Horse
The figure cut into a hillside on the edge of Salisbury Plain in Wiltshire is a far more conventional depiction of a horse than its Uffington counterpart (p255). Dating from 1778, the Westbury image is, in fact, a remodelling of a far earlier animal more akin, by all accounts, to the one in Oxfordshire. It is quite possible that the Westbury horse of today was shaped more to the taste of the commissioning landowner.

Giant of Cerne Abbas

The primitive, but strangely graceful, outline is framed by a trench 2ft (60cm) wide and deep, scoured into the chalk hillside. Since the early 18th century, local people have re-scoured the giant's outline and repacked the furrows with chalk every seven years. This practice continued until 1920, when the National Trust took over the care of the figure.

The Long Man At 230ft (70m) tall, the chalk figure on a hill at the eastern end of the South Downs near Wilmington in Sussex is one of the largest images of the human figure in the world. He has been variously identified as a Roman soldier, St Paul, and even a prehistoric surveyor, owing to the presence of the two staffs, which could be sighting poles. Scientific dating of the Long Man, as with the other chalk figures, is precluded since his outline has been frequently re-scoured, but he was probably carved 2000 to 2500 years ago.

the date when the figure is known to have been recut. Some commentators go further, alleging that this was the year in which the figure was first created, as a sort of quasi-historical folly.

Could the Cerne Abbas giant really be an 18th-century fake – or are its origins destined to remain buried for ever in the mists of antiquity? The local legend of a marauding sheep stealer supports the view that the giant is ancient. In addition, there is its similarity with other hill carvings: many are close to ancient burial sites, which certainly hints at their prehistoric origins.

The Uffington White Horse in Oxfordshire, for example, lies just below the Iron Age hillfort of Uffington Castle, so is possibly itself from the Iron Age. The Long Man of Wilmington in Sussex is believed to be neolithic, since it is close to a neolithic long barrow and other burial mounds, and the Westbury White Horse is situated below the Iron Age earthwork of Bratton Castle. And just above and to the right of the Cerne Abbas giant's head lies the

Trendle, a small, square Iron Age enclosure where Mayday festivities were enjoyed.

Only two hill carvings represent men – the Cerne Abbas and Wilmington figures – while the others appear to be various effigies of horses. Even here, however, appearances may be deceptive, because at least one of these famous 'white horses' – that at Uffington – may depict a dragon. The 394ft (120m) long image, so sharp that it can be seen 15 miles (24km) away, lies close to a flat-topped mound known as Dragon Hill. Legend has it that this was the very place where St George slew the dragon, its blood spilling on two patches of earth and rendering them infertile to this day. The numerous other carved white horses in the British countryside almost certainly represent more mundane quadrupeds, possibly created in honour of an ancient Celtic goddess, Epona, who was usually symbolised in the form of a horse.

Theories abound as to why ancient peoples carved these figures. The more staid suggest that they were attempts to *king. More recent analysis equates the depiction with a much earlier style – that of the Celts around 100 BC. The horse was greatly revered by the Celts, and images of animals in a similar style appear on Iron Age coins and buckets found locally.*

But the figure may not be that of a horse at all. The tail is conventionally horse-like in style, but the beak-shaped jaw is more like that of a dragon. If the figure were a dragon, it would lend credence to the legend that St George killed such a beast at nearby Dragon Hill.

Horse or dragon? *Of all England's chalk figures, the White Horse at Uffington, Oxfordshire, is the most elegant. But controversy has dogged its origins.*

In the 18th century it was thought that the horse might be a commemoration of one of the victories of a Saxon

DANCING AROUND THE MAYPOLE

The proximity of many of England's hill figures to ancient sites associated with fertility rites, such as dancing around the maypole, gives a major clue to their origin and purpose. The maypole can be thought of as echoing much of the Cerne Abbas giant's phallic symbolism, while also acting as the focus for May games such as Morris dancing.

Traditionally, maypoles were painted in red and white stripes and decorated with flags and flowers. Once these were raised, the festivities could begin.

create images of local gods, much as later Christians made statues of the Virgin. Among the more fanciful theories is the suggestion that the carvings were intended to catch the eye of space travellers. The truth is that no one knows for certain why they were created, although folklore may help to pinpoint their purpose.

Since legends of fertility rites associated with ancient sites are common throughout British folklore, the theory that the giant is a pagan fertility symbol is widely accepted. The Cerne Abbas giant's club points towards the Trendle, where fertility rituals were once enacted. Childless wives supposedly became fertile after spending the night there, and infertile couples who slept on the carving overnight were believed to be guaranteed a baby.

But it seems unlikely that the true purpose of the Cerne Abbas giant will ever be known. Like the other ancient hill carvings in the British Isles, it remains a potent image of an era that will continue to fascinate and perplex for generations to come.

STONEHENGE: A COSMIC TEMPLE?

An enduring monument to bygone mysteries of religion and science, the great megalithic circle of giant stone slabs at Stonehenge provides the modern world with a timeless puzzle, an architectural wonder and a tribute to the human imagination. Was it a sacred burial ground or a prehistoric observatory?

S tanding starkly in the middle of Salisbury Plain, Wiltshire, Stonehenge presents a riddle that seems as old as time itself. One of England's loveliest cathedrals, Salisbury, lies only 8 miles (13km) away, yet the seven centuries that have passed since Salisbury Cathedral was built are a brief span beside the antiquity of these huge and ancient stones.

The extraordinary concentric stone circles that occupy the site today represent thousands of years of archaeological changes. Bridging the Late Stone Age and Early Bronze Age, the monument was constructed in three or even four stages over a period of roughly 1500 years, though mainly between 1800 and 1400 BC. But what remains of Stonehenge today is but a shadow of its former glory. More than half the stones have either fallen, or are missing, or lie buried.

Building was begun as early as 2800 BC (some experts claim 3800 BC), when a vast circular ditch was dug and 56 pits excavated inside its earthen bank. Named Aubrey Holes after their 17th-century discoverer John Aubrey, the pits have been capped with concrete, but the first gigantic stone to be placed, the Heel Stone – marking the entrance to the earthworks – is said to stand in its original position. Two further rings of pits, the Y and Z holes – which may have had some astronomical significance – lie between the Aubrey Holes and the massive stone circles in the centre.

Around 2100 BC, 80 bluestones were brought from Wales and formed into two concentric circles. These were later replaced by a circle of 30 huge sandstone monoliths called sarsens. Within this circle stood two partial

Star gazing *Anyone who has witnessed the sun rising over the great sarsen stones at the time of the midwinter solstice can hardly doubt that Stonehenge had some ancient religious and astronomical function.*

Bird's-eye view *From an aerial viewpoint the original shape of Stonehenge can still be discerned, but many of the stones are missing.*

Mystical aura Stonehenge is one of the most frequently visited archaeological sites in the world and has been carefully excavated and restored; in 1958 one of the fallen stones was raised. The mystical aura surrounding Stonehenge attracts such great crowds, particularly during the summer solstice, that critics have expressed concern over possible damage to the monument. As a result, the site has been enclosed and public access to the stones is now limited.

Merlin the mighty A 14th-century manuscript shows Merlin the magician effortlessly positioning a massive stone lintel.

According to Geoffrey of Monmouth, a medieval writer, Merlin transported the sarsens of Stonehenge to Salisbury Plain.

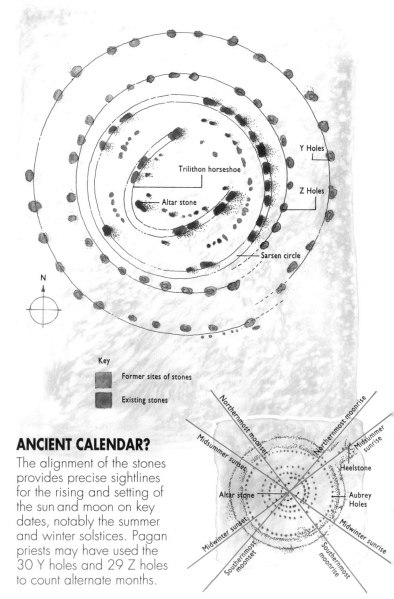

Y Holes

Trilithon horseshoe

Z Holes

Altar stone

Sarsen circle

N

Key

Former sites of stones

Existing stones

ANCIENT CALENDAR?

The alignment of the stones provides precise sightlines for the rising and setting of the sun and moon on key dates, notably the summer and winter solstices. Pagan priests may have used the 30 Y holes and 29 Z holes to count alternate months.

Northernmost moonrise

Northernmost moonrise

Midsummer sunset

Midsummer sunrise

Heelstone

Altar stone

Aubrey Holes

Midwinter sunset

Midwinter sunrise

Southernmost moonset

Southernmost moonrise

horseshoe formations, the outer made of five sarsen trilithons (two upright stones with a third placed across the top) and the inner of 19 shaped bluestones. The only digging tools of the Neolithic creators were pickaxes made from the antlers of red deer, so their architectural achievement is astonishing.

The Saxons named the megalith Stonehenge – the word means 'Hanging Stone' – while medieval scribes referred to it poetically as 'the Giant's Dance'. Although scholarly observers were in general agreed about the site's mystical associations, none was clear about its true purpose. The 17th-century architect Inigo Jones, for example, argued that the stones were the remains of a Roman temple, but 18th and 19th-century opinion held firm that the stone circle was a druid temple where sun-worship and human sacrifice were practised. This is unlikely, however, since Stonehenge was completed at least 1000 years before the druid cult flourished. The first glimmer of truth about the site only came to light in the 20th century, when archaeologists established the real age of the monument and arrived at more realistic conclusions about its original purpose. But the known facts are still few.

The sarsens of the outer ring, which stand 16ft (5m) tall and weigh around 26 tons apiece, were hauled from the Marlborough Downs, about 20 miles (32km) away, and meticulously arranged so that lintels and uprights, connected by ball and socket joints, met securely. The bluestones from the Preseli Hills in south-west Wales, each weighing up to 4 tons, were probably ferried by raft around the Welsh coast and up the River Avon, then dragged overland.

But what purpose did all this effort serve? Pointing to the number of ancient earthworks located in this area, which has the greatest concentration of circular mound tombs in Britain, most archaeologists today maintain that Stonehenge was a ceremonial burial ground. Evidence of cremations has been found in many of the Aubrey Holes, but proof also exists that the holes were dug long before any cremated remains were placed in them. They might have been intended for ritual libations, such as wine, poured into the holes by devout agricultural workers to appease the gods of nature, and the stone circles might have formed a temple of sorts for ceremonial worship.

More recently, astronomers claiming to have 'decoded' the stones propose that Stonehenge is a prehistoric computer, an astronomical calendar or an astrological calculator, since the alignments of the stones seem to bear a direct relationship to the movements of the sun, moon and planets and their ever-shifting relationships. While mathematical and statistical evidence can be produced to support nearly every new theory, no single theory has yet solved the riddle of Stonehenge's fabled past.

DRUIDS: PRIESTS OF THE ANCIENT CELTS

A privileged caste of priests who trained for up to 20 years in preparation for their duties as guardians of sacred lore, the druids were masters of magic and manipulators of supernatural forces. Besides their priestly role, the druids also administered justice and guided the actions of the ruling Celtic chiefs or kings of Britain, Ireland and France.

The name druid is Celtic for 'knowing the oak tree', and worshippers often performed their rites in densely wooded areas. Robed in white, they revered a multitude of martial gods and goddesses, offering them both human and animal sacrifices to mark seasonal festivities. In the first century BC Julius Caesar wrote extensively of

druid activities, particularly of the sinister ritual sacrifices that struck terror into the hearts of all Celts.

The Celts believed that the soul resided in the head and feared that a severed head – which retained a person's consciousness – might be used for magical purposes. Druids were known to have preserved severed heads, and dried heads have been found at some ancient druid sites.

From the early 1900s up until 1988, modern druids (who have no connection with the Celtic brotherhood) were allowed to use Stonehenge to celebrate the summer solstice.

THE ANCIENT AVENUES OF CARNAC

The earth mounds and standing stones of Carnac are some of the oldest man-made structures in Europe and comprise the largest megalithic monument on the continent. Thousands of commentators have speculated on their purpose, but it remains a mystery.

Megalithic monuments are scattered all over Europe in a broad swathe that stretches from Italy in the south to Scandinavia in the north, and arcs round to include the British Isles. The greatest assembly of all, however, is at Carnac in the heart of the pinewoods and heathland of Brittany in western France. Not only are there more stones here than elsewhere in Europe, they are also arranged in the largest-scale pattern, over the biggest area, some 5 miles (8km) long. Little is known about the people who erected the stones at Carnac, but they must have been skilled engineers with recourse to an enormous labour force, and they must have worked to a preconceived plan.

The Carnac complex comprises three major concentrations of menhirs (the word, from the Welsh *maen*, 'stone', and *hir*, 'long', refers to any tall, free-standing stone), all situated to the north of the town of Carnac: Le Ménec, Kermario and Kerlescan. At Le Ménec, 1099 stones are arranged in 11 rows, over an area of land ⅝ mile (1km) long and 110yds (100m) wide. To the east of this are the 10 rows of Kermario, which stretch ¾ mile (1.2km). Farther east still is the almost-square alignment of Kerlescan, 13 short rows of stones – 540 in all – which end with a semicircle of 39 huge menhirs after ½ mile (800m). A fourth, much smaller assemblage at Le Petit Ménec is made up of a mere 100 stones.

All these concentrations of stones are broadly similar. They are conceived in rows, aligned west–east, although the rows are not spaced equally but are placed closer together towards the outer (northerly and southerly) edges of the formation. The farther east along an assemblage one looks, the closer together and taller the stones. Occasionally, too, the stones are placed not in rows but in parallel curves. The height of the menhirs also varies: the smallest stones, at the western end of Le Ménec, are about 3ft (90cm) high; the tallest at Kermario are 23ft (7m) high.

The 3000 menhirs of the Carnac complex may represent only half the original number of stones. Some have eroded, still more have been pillaged by local farmers for their own uses and by amateur archaeologists. Earth tremors and an earthquake in 1722 toppled and smashed many of the stones, which made them even easier to carry away.

The concentrations of stones were erected at different times, between about 3500 and 1500 BC, which makes them roughly the same age as Stonehenge in England and

Ancient and modern In many areas of the Carnac complex, as at Le Ménec, houses and standing stones exist side by side, and in some cases dwellings obscure parts of the overall design. (At Le Ménec they cut across what was once a semicircle of stones.) On occasion, too, stone fragments are clearly visible in the cottages, boundary markers and outbuildings of the surrounding hamlets.

THE ANCIENT AVENUES OF CARNAC

the pyramids in Egypt. Although the 'architects' of Carnac and their methods remain a mystery, geologists are in general agreed that some, if not all, of the menhirs pre-date the introduction of the wheel to Europe (the first evidence of which dates from around 1000 BC, although it may well have been in use earlier). The stones were hewn from local granite, and presumably dragged from the place of quarrying to the site at Carnac, then hauled into position. Since some of the tallest stones are likely to weigh in excess of 350 tons, an enormous workforce must have been employed on the project. At a time when the life expectancy for men was 36 years and women 30, it is unlikely that anyone engaged at the start of one of the sections of the complex would live to see its completion.

The avenues and circles of menhirs are not the only pre-historic monuments at Carnac, nor are they the earliest. Earth mounds, or tumuli, at least two of which were built before 4000 BC, have also been discovered in the area. The alignment of Kermario points to an upright stone

that marks the entrance to the passage grave of Kercado, which comprises a large, grass-covered mound topped by a single stone. Inside, a stone-lined passage leads to a square stone chamber where successive generations were buried. Constructed around 4700 BC so that its entrance faces the mid-winter sunrise, this is Europe's oldest surviving structure.

The mounds and, in particular, the stones at Carnac have drawn thousands of visitors over the centuries, many of whom have attempted to explain the significance of the avenues of menhirs. As the 19th-century French novelist Gustave Flaubert observed: 'Carnac has had more rubbish written about it than it has standing stones.' One of the most popular theories about Carnac is that it was a religious centre, and that the stones were worshipped by the ancient Bretons. Much later, the same stones were 'adopted' by the Romans, who carved into them the names of their deities. After the coming of Christianity, crosses and other associated symbols were also carved upon the stones. Local folklore, however, holds that they are ranks of Roman soldiers, turned into stone by the local saint and former pope, Cornély, after they had chased him out of Rome and back to his native Brittany.

According to one belief (current at least until the Middle Ages) the stones could increase fertility, and so a barren woman might sleep for several nights on a cromlech (a flat stone laid horizontally across several standing ones) anointed with wax, oil and honey. Alternatively, she would raise her skirts and either squat over a stone, or slide down it to absorb its magical power. Many people apparently believed that the standing stones represented their ancestors'

Buried mysteries *Mont St-Michel, to the north-east of Carnac, is a large burial chamber with connecting galleries leading to smaller rooms. The tumulus of St-Michel (St Michael) is 65ft (19m) high and 377ft (114m) long, and has been dated to around 4000 BC. It was first uncovered in 1862.*

From pagan to Christian *The tumulus of St-Michel was originally a pagan burial ground, but it has been Christianised by the addition of a cross and a small chapel dedicated to St Michael, the dragon slayer. St Cornély, the patron saint of cattle, is more frequently associated with the region.*

spirits, petrified for eternity. Perhaps they were conceived as place markers for those attending ritual ceremonies at which druid priests blessed crops and animals. Or were they simply monuments to the dead? The word Carnac itself means 'cemetery of the dead' in Breton.

A more recent theory gives the stones a specific purpose. Studies of Carnac and other megalithic sites have led Dr Alexander Thom to conclude that the builders of the rows of menhirs had an advanced knowledge of astronomy and arranged the stones either to study the movement of celestial bodies – particularly the moon, but also the sun and stars – or to use as a huge, astronomical clock, whereby ploughing and planting times, for example, could be

deduced. According to Dr Thom, the most important stone in this lunar observatory was the now broken megalith at Locmariaquer known as *Er Grah* (the Fairy Stone). From mounds and stones up to 8 miles (13km) away, the moon rise and moon set could be observed, using the stone as a marker.

It may never be possible to say with certainty what the giant stones at Carnac signify, but that does not detract from the power that they exert over the thousands of visitors who flock to see them each year. Although the stones are covered in lichen and many are missing, Carnac provides an awe-inspiring link with the beginnings of civilisation on the continent of Europe.

Modern theorist *Dr Alexander Thom, former Professor of Engineering at Oxford University, surveyed the stones in the 1970s. He concluded that they were of astronomical significance.*

The Fairy Stone *Also known as* Le Grand Menhir Brisé *(the Great Broken Menhir), this was once the largest megalith in Europe, standing 65ft (20m) high. It may have been the keystone of a giant lunar observatory, but since the broken pieces lie at the end of a Neolithic burial mound, its purpose may have been to guard the dead. An earthquake in 1722 might have caused its fall.*

THE PUZZLE OF CHARTRES

The monumental Gothic cathedral of Notre-Dame dominates the skyline of a small market town. But the inspiration for its design continues to baffle historians.

T he magnificent 12th-century cathedral in the northern French town of Chartres is an age-old enigma. Few who visit fail to be moved by its powerful aura. For Notre-Dame is a giant riddle, an equation to be solved, yet one expressed not on paper but given form in stone blocks and glass stained with such consummate skill that even today, 800 years after the cathedral was built, its beauty still stuns visitors. Pious Christians continue to attend services here, and architects and historians visit the cathedral in an attempt to unravel its mysteries.

The present cathedral was begun after a fire in 1194, but the site on which Notre-Dame stands has long fulfilled spiritual needs. In the belief that they could somehow harness the Earth's energy, prehistoric builders had erected a dolmen (two or three sturdy, unhewn stones topped by a large flattish one) at Chartres. It was held that all who entered the dolmen's chamber would be revitalised by the Earth's natural forces. In time, the site – which also encompassed a well and a mound constructed nearby – came to be revered as holy ground.

Later, but still in pre-Christian times, the Druids (Celtic priests of Gaul and Britain) established a college at Chartres which became a centre for their teachings. In response to a prophetic vision, these ancient priests carved a wooden statue of a virgin and child which they named the Virgin Under the Earth. Christians discovered the statue, blackened with age, in the third century and thereafter worshipped it as the Black Virgin. It was on this sacred ground that the first of the churches dedicated to Our Lady was constructed, so inaugurating a series of buildings on the site, the culmination of which is the Gothic masterpiece that stands here today.

Theories abound as to the source of inspiration for the present cathedral. Legend has it that the advanced architectural knowledge necessary to build such a structure in medieval times was brought from the East by the original Knights Templars. These were nine French knights who were persuaded by Bernard of Clairvaux, founder of the Cistercian Order of monks, to abandon their worldly possessions and go in search of 'the secrets' believed to be buried in the holy sanctuary under the ruins of Solomon's Temple in Jerusalem. During their ten-year search, the knights were suspected of dabbling in the occult. When they returned to France in 1128 it was rumoured that they

Holy ground *A church
has stood on the hill of
Chartres for almost 1500
years. The present structure
is the sixth edifice. Its
graceful south spire dates
from the 12th century; the
ornate late-Gothic north
spire was added around
1507. Fires ravaged the first
five buildings: the Duke of
Aquitaine razed the first in
743; Danes set light to the
second in 858; the third went
up in flames in 962 and the
fourth in 1020. The fifth
Notre-Dame, and the first
cathedral, begun in 1134,
was almost destroyed by fire
in 1194, setting the scene for
the final act of construction.*

Carved in stone *Some
2000 sculpted figures adorn
the porches and portals of
Notre-Dame. The naturalistic
poses and the occasional
blending of sacred and
secular subjects reveal a
distinct Gothic influence.
Often the identities of the
medieval craftsmen who
created them are unknown,
but features common to
Chartres' figures are also
found in those in the
cathedrals of Angers, Le
Mans, Bourges and Senlis,
suggesting that the same
hands may have been
responsible.*

265

THE PUZZLE OF CHARTRES

had found the Ark of the Covenant, a chest reputed to contain the secrets of Divine Law governing number, weight and measure, including the so-called Golden Number, 1.618. The ratio of 1:1.618, the Golden Section or Mean, was judged to be particularly aesthetically pleasing and governs much of the art and architecture of the Renaissance and later. Certainly the knights' return coincided with the initial flowerings of Gothic architecture in Europe, and construction of the first cathedral at Chartres began six years later. Within 30 years, masons, glaziers, sculptors, geometers, astronomers and other craftsmen had created an immense shrine, whose proportions, orientation, position and symbolism have stimulated the psyche and refreshed the spirit of visitors ever since.

The 'sacred centre' of the cathedral lies between the second and third bays of the choir. This is where the altar originally stood. Some 121ft (37m) below the sacred centre is the water in the Druid's well. Towering exactly the same distance above the sacred centre is the pinnacle of the cathedral's Gothic vault.

No one knows whether this symmetry was intentional or coincidental, but that does not detract from the spiritual potency of the place. It is said to possess the power to transform people, to transmute them into a higher spiritual

266

SYMBOLIC STRUCTURE

Notre-Dame is a study in symbolism. The roof over the nave and apse presents a cross to the heavens, while the two towers may be interpreted as the fingers of God. The ground plan was probably designed using the Golden Number, 1.618. Distances between pillars, and the lengths of the nave, transepts and the choir, are all multiples of this figure.

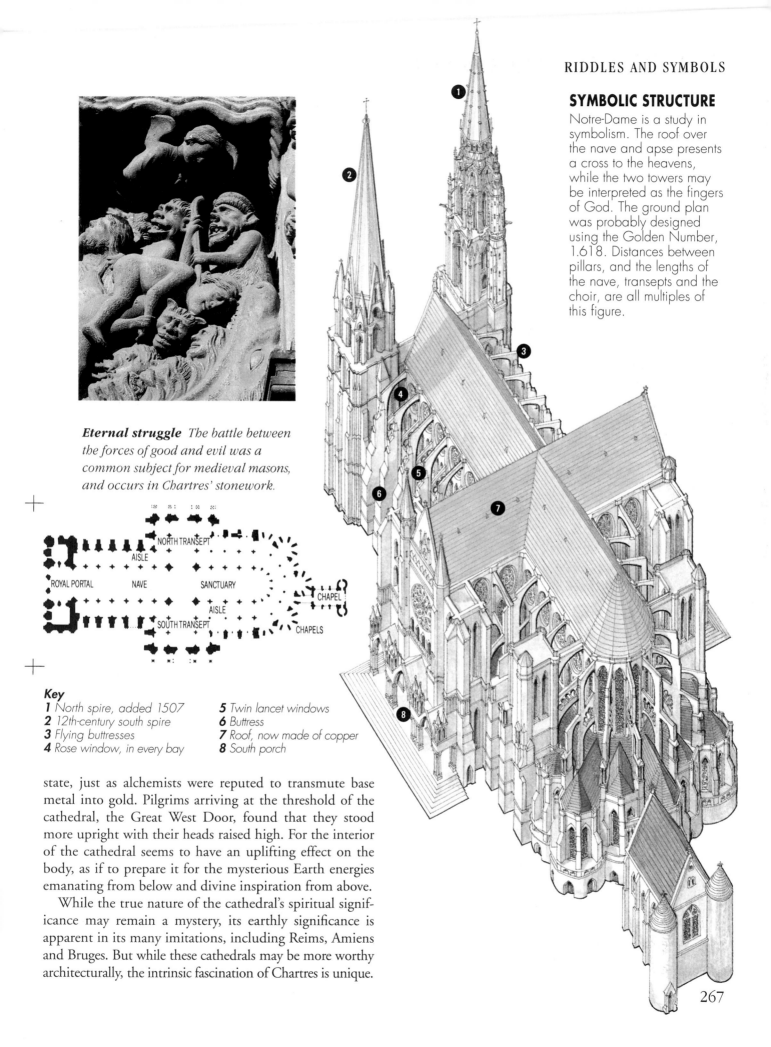

Eternal struggle *The battle between the forces of good and evil was a common subject for medieval masons, and occurs in Chartres' stonework.*

NORTH TRANSEPT
AISLE
ROYAL PORTAL NAVE SANCTUARY
CHAPEL
AISLE
SOUTH TRANSEPT
CHAPELS

Key
1 *North spire, added 1507*
2 *12th-century south spire*
3 *Flying buttresses*
4 *Rose window, in every bay*
5 *Twin lancet windows*
6 *Buttress*
7 *Roof, now made of copper*
8 *South porch*

state, just as alchemists were reputed to transmute base metal into gold. Pilgrims arriving at the threshold of the cathedral, the Great West Door, found that they stood more upright with their heads raised high. For the interior of the cathedral seems to have an uplifting effect on the body, as if to prepare it for the mysterious Earth energies emanating from below and divine inspiration from above.

While the true nature of the cathedral's spiritual significance may remain a mystery, its earthly significance is apparent in its many imitations, including Reims, Amiens and Bruges. But while these cathedrals may be more worthy architecturally, the intrinsic fascination of Chartres is unique.

THE EXTERNSTEINE: A FOREST SANCTUARY

A clump of jagged rocks, grotesquely carved by water and wind, in a north German hill forest is the site of many ancient rituals. Rich in spiritual associations, this remote sanctuary was once the focus of a bitter struggle between pagan worshippers and Christian monks.

Visitors to the Teutoburger Wald in North Rhine-Westphalia might well stop suddenly in their tracks to gaze open-mouthed in wonder at the first arresting sight of the Externsteine. Towering 100ft (30m) above the forest floor, etched dramatically against the sky, is the curious vision of five gnarled sandstone pillars riddled with caves, passages and secret chambers. The fairytale setting of the rocks – evoking a picture in a child's story book – adds to the air of enchantment. Located in an area thick with sacred ancient sites, this is a place with powerful mystical and mythological associations: according to folk tradition, the stones were raised overnight by giants and burned by the devil. The flames of the inferno were believed to be responsible for their grotesquely contorted appearance.

This remarkable natural feature holds a place in German spiritual tradition similar to that of Stonehenge in Britain. Firm evidence about the origins and significance of the Externsteine has proved tantalisingly elusive: one theory holds that it was used as a major ceremonial centre of worship in the Stone Age; another that its religious origins date no farther back than the 12th century, and that the site is a re-creation of the holy places of Jerusalem, inspired by Crusaders' tales.

When Christianity supplanted paganism in Germany around 722, sites of worship were appropriated by the new religion. In medieval times the Externsteine was used as a refuge by Christian hermits. A legacy from this period is a magnificent carving on one of the larger rocks.

An evocative site *The Externsteine has been a place of pilgrimage since prehistoric times. After the medieval age it served as a fortress, a pleasure palace and a prison. Now restored, supposedly to its original form, it is a popular tourist attraction.*

Romanticised view *The rugged crags proved an irresistible subject for artists and writers of the Romantic movement in the early 19th century. In 1836 a picturesque artificial lake was created nearby.*

THE EXTERNSTEINE: A FOREST SANCTUARY

The *Descent from the Cross* was carved around 1120 by Cistercian monks from the abbey at nearby Paderborn, who used the Externsteine's rock-cut chambers for prayer. A notable detail of the bas-relief is the *Irminsul*, or world-pillar – believed by pagan Saxons to support the universe. Symbolising Christianity's dominance over paganism, the *Irminsul* is bent double to form a foot-support on which Nicodemus (who in the biblical account helped to bury Jesus) stands to remove Christ's body from the Cross. Significantly, the feet of Nicodemus have been deliberately chipped away – a mutilation explained by locals as the pagans' revenge for the Cistercians' symbolic humiliation of their sacred emblem.

The crags of the Externsteine are riddled with man-made caves and passages which have been enlarged by successive generations. While some had uses which are obvious, such as the chapel, the purpose of others remains a mystery – there are steps that lead nowhere, odd platforms and niches, a rock-cut coffin, small drilled holes and larger apertures cut into the rock faces. The widest rock pillar contains a large, irregularly shaped chamber, accessible through two doorways. The north-eastern entrance and both the chamber's windows face the midsummer sunrise, making it likely that secret pagan ceremonies took place here. The second doorway gives entry via a narrow, bizarrely shaped carved passage. Many of the chamber's features are similar to those found in subterranean religious structures elsewhere in Europe.

A small chapel, the most evocative place in the Externsteine, has been hewn from the rock near the top of one of the pillars. Accessible only by rock-cut steps and a precarious footbridge, the chapel is roofless and, at its eastern end, there is a round-headed niche containing a pillar-altar unlike anything found in conventional church architecture. Directly above the altar is a circular window 20in (50cm) wide. Antiquarian researchers in the 19th century observed that it was aligned toward both the midsummer sunrise and the most northerly rising point of the moon – two important astronomical occurrences marked by ceremonies at many prehistoric stone circles and similar sites. The researchers maintained that the chapel had been built high above the ground to permit a clear view of the sun and moon as they rose behind specific landmarks on the horizon beyond the forest canopy. Moreover, they

Lower chapel *The strange energies (symbolised by the World Serpent in the* Descent from the Cross *carving) believed to be present at the site of the Externsteine run through the earth and are accessible only to those who enter the caves or holes in the rocks.*

Artificial crypts and chambers and deep basins in the ground (LEFT) *were made as a means of gaining entry into the very 'bones' of the earth.*

Human touch *Generations of carvers have left their mark on the rugged pillars of the Externsteine. The platforms, niches and holes that were added have suffered the effects of wind and weathering over the millennia.*

found that the Externsteine lies at more or less the same latitude as Stonehenge, so the direction of the midsummer sunrise – an important factor to Europe's astronomer priests – is identical in both places.

Wilhelm Teudt, an evangelical parson, expanded on this research in the 1920s. He found that the site of the Externsteine lies on the network of 'holy lines' that he had discovered in northern Germany. He claimed that these lines, roughly equivalent to the ley lines identified by other researchers, linked the Externsteine with ancient sites elsewhere, including the stone circle at nearby Bad Meinberg. Above the chapel, Teudt believed, there had once been other chambers and wooden structures used to observe the sun, moon and stars, suggesting that the Externsteine was a centre of an ancient solar cult. His discoveries also convinced him that the roofless and ruined condition of the observatory-chapel was the result of deliberate vandalism by Cistercian monks. He showed that a 50 ton slab lying at the foot of the rock pillar had been broken away from the chapel's side. The monks had destroyed the sanctuary to purge the site of its pagan associations, thereby rendering it fit for Christian worship.

Mystical setting *The circular window of this small, roofless chapel carved in the rock is perfectly aligned to catch the sunrise at the summer solstice.*

Christian triumph *Below the Crucifix is the* Irminsul. *This is the mythical World Serpent, symbol of the earth energies accumulated at the site of the Externsteine.*

GIZA: LEGACY OF THE PHARAOHS

The Great Pyramid of Khufu stands as a proud testimony to the extraordinary vision and engineering skills of the ancient Egyptians. It has survived virtually intact over the centuries and is the only one of the Seven Wonders of the Ancient World in existence today.

R ising starkly from the flat desert plain 5 miles (8km) outside Cairo, the three great pyramids of Giza tower over a surrounding complex of subsidiary pyramids and tombs. Nearby lies the statue of the Great Sphinx. These wonders of the ancient world have survived nearly 5000 years, but it is only since the 19th century that archaeologists have begun to piece together how and why they were built.

The town of Giza is situated at the foot of the Nile delta, which once marked the boundary between Upper and Lower Egypt. When these two kingdoms were united in about 2925 BC, the new state of Egypt established its capital at Memphis, on the west bank of the Nile. This became the home of the pharaohs, who ruled for some 3000 years through 30 consecutive dynasties.

The three great pyramids of Giza were erected during the fourth dynasty (about 2575–2465 BC). The largest, the tomb of the pharaoh Khufu, called Cheops by the Greek historian Herodotus, was the first to be built. The central pyramid, the second to be built, is slightly smaller and belongs to the pharaoh Khafre, or Chephren, Khufu's son. The third, much smaller pyramid is that of the pharaoh Menkaure, or Mycerinus, Khufu's grandson.

The pharaohs were regarded as living gods, destined at death to join the many other gods worshipped by the Egyptians. Some gods, such as Osiris, ruler of the dead, and the jackal-headed Anubis, officiated at the judgement of the dead. Egyptian rulers built themselves 'houses of death' containing a complete suite of underground rooms furnished with all the things they would need in the after-life, including food, utensils and jewellery. These tombs are strategically situated at the edge of the desert on the west bank of the Nile. (Since the west is where the sun sets, the ancient Egyptians associated it with death.)

The early pharaohs of the first and second dynasties built small rectangular tombs, or *mastabas,* such as those found at Saqqara, west of Memphis, and Abydos. But a hundred years before work began on the pyramids at Giza, Zoser, a pharaoh of the third dynasty, revolutionised tomb architecture by building the first pyramid. It rose in six magnificent steps to tower 200ft (60m) over the desert at Saqqara and, unlike any other building before it, was dressed in stone. Later pharaohs developed a smooth-sided shape, as seen in the Red Pyramid at Dashur, and

Pyramids of Giza *The tombs of the fourth-dynasty pharaohs, Khufu, Khafre and Menkaure, are Egypt's most famous monuments. (The most distant pyramid shown here is that of Khufu, the central one is Khafre's; Menkaure's, with three small pyramids in front of it, is closest.)*

Khafre's pyramid (INSET) *stands on higher ground than Khufu's and so appears taller. While the pyramids' structures remain, their smooth limestone casings were stripped off during the Middle Ages and used for buildings in Cairo, leaving the stepped surfaces to be seen today.*

Each of the pyramids is at the hub of a mortuary complex comprising several *mastaba tombs and two temples linked by a causeway. One of the temples was built on a canal cut from the Nile.*

273

GIZA: LEGACY OF THE PHARAOHS

this design culminated in the magnificent pyramids that were erected at Giza. The immense pyramid of Khufu (the top is now missing) originally rose to a height of 481ft (146.6m). It is so large that, according to one estimate, Westminster Abbey and St Paul's Cathedral in London, St Peter's in Rome and the cathedrals of Florence and Milan could all fit inside. Some 2½ million stone blocks, each weighing on average 2½ tons, were used in its construction. These blocks were put together without mortar and fitted so closely that the British Egyptologist Flinders Petrie (1853–1942) observed that 'neither needle, nor hair' could be inserted into the joins.

This massive construction, which took approximately 30 years to complete, was not only an astonishing feat of engineering but also required the transportation of tons of materials and the effective organisation of an estimated 100 000 men. Most of the stone was hewn from local quarries, but the limestone facing had to be brought from Tura on the east bank of the Nile 8 miles (13km) away, while the pink granite that lined the burial chamber came from Aswan, more than 600 miles (965km) to the south.

The first entry into Khufu's tomb since ancient times was made in the ninth century on the orders of Ma'amun, the caliph of Baghdad, who was hoping to find treasure. His men broke in through the north wall and eventually reached the King's Chamber, only to find it empty of treasure and other goods. Archaeologists are still puzzled as to why it should have been empty when there was no evidence that the tomb had previously been plundered.

Today, tourists use the same north entrance. Inside, one passage goes down to an unfinished burial chamber and another, the ascending passage, leads up to the King's chamber in the heart of the monument. Off the same passage is a corridor leading to another unfinished room known as the Queen's chamber; beyond that is a narrow passage, discovered in April 1993, leading to a small door.

Near the Great Pyramid stand the tombs of Khufu's officials and relatives. There are also rows of *mastabas* and small boat pits, long since emptied of their contents by grave robbers. In 1954, the dismantled sections of a large boat were discovered in the sand on the southern side of the pyramid and reassembled – a task that took ten years.

Eternal journey *The dismantled boat excavated near Khufu's pyramid is 142ft (43.3m) long and 19½ft (5.9m) wide at the centre. The boat pit contained 1224 pieces of wood, probably cedar from the Lebanon, arranged in 13 layers. Ropes and oars were also found.*

The boat's function is uncertain. It may have been used to carry the pharaoh's body to Giza for embalming and burial, or it could have been a 'sun boat' to ferry his soul across the heavens.

BUILDING A PYRAMID

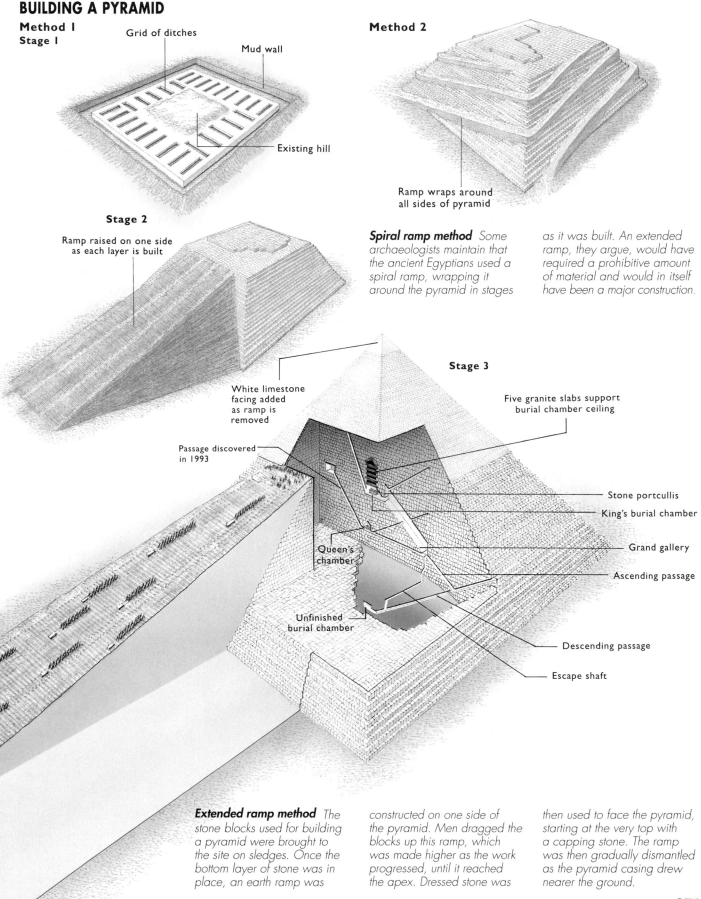

Method 1
Stage 1

Grid of ditches

Mud wall

Existing hill

Stage 2

Ramp raised on one side
as each layer is built

White limestone
facing added
as ramp is
removed

Passage discovered
in 1993

Queen's
chamber

Unfinished
burial chamber

Method 2

Ramp wraps around
all sides of pyramid

Stage 3

Five granite slabs support
burial chamber ceiling

Stone portcullis

King's burial chamber

Grand gallery

Ascending passage

Descending passage

Escape shaft

Spiral ramp method *Some
archaeologists maintain that
the ancient Egyptians used a
spiral ramp, wrapping it
around the pyramid in stages
as it was built. An extended
ramp, they argue, would have
required a prohibitive amount
of material and would in itself
have been a major construction.*

Extended ramp method *The
stone blocks used for building
a pyramid were brought to
the site on sledges. Once the
bottom layer of stone was in
place, an earth ramp was
constructed on one side of
the pyramid. Men dragged the
blocks up this ramp, which
was made higher as the work
progressed, until it reached
the apex. Dressed stone was
then used to face the pyramid,
starting at the very top with
a capping stone. The ramp
was then gradually dismantled
as the pyramid casing drew
nearer the ground.*

It may have been a state boat during Khufu's lifetime or intended for use after his death.

The perfect orientation of the Great Pyramid, whose square base was aligned almost exactly north–south and east–west, and various mystical interpretations of pyramidal measurements, have led to some strange theories about the purpose of the pyramids. Several 19th-century British astronomers claimed that the pyramids were built as astronomical observatories and could have been used as sundials. One astronomer, Charles Piazzi Smyth, used pyramidal measurements to 'prove' that the pyramids were the work of God the 'Divine Geometer' and that they contained information revealing the date of the Second Coming of Christ. Other pyramidologists believe that the pyramids were built by aliens from outer space.

Archaeological and literary evidence suggests that the pyramids were funereal monuments, but were not necessarily used as the burial places of pharaohs. One of their functions – and those of other tombs – may have been to house the *ka*, or soul, which the ancient Egyptians believed would survive after death.

The sheer grandeur of the pyramids was criticised in Roman times. Pliny the Elder (AD 23–79) called them 'vain and foolish ostentations of the fortunes of kings'. But Pliny could not foresee that in its ostentation the Great Pyramid of Khufu was to achieve its maker's dream of immortality by keeping his name alive for over 5000 years.

Access to the tomb *The majestic proportions of the grand gallery, which leads from the ascending passage to the King's chamber in the Great Pyramid* (LEFT), *have long puzzled historians. The gallery may have been used to house the huge granite blocks which were slid down the corridor to seal it after the funeral.*

THE ART OF EMBALMING

The Egyptians believed that in order to enjoy the afterlife their bodies had to be preserved intact and so they developed the art of mummification. The word mummy comes from the Arabic *mumiya*, 'bitumen', since preserved corpses blackened by age were once thought to have been soaked in tar.

The embalming process began by making an incision in the abdomen through which the intestines, lungs, liver and stomach were removed. The brain was extracted through a cut in the base of the skull. These were preserved separately and stored in jars alongside the body (in later times, they were returned to the body). To remove all the body fluids, the corpse was packed in natron, a natural salt from a dried lake in the Nile delta containing a high proportion of sodium bicarbonate. It is thought that this was the reason why after six to eight weeks the body was dry and stable. Finally, the body was wrapped in several layers of linen bandages, before being placed in a coffin and laid in the tomb.

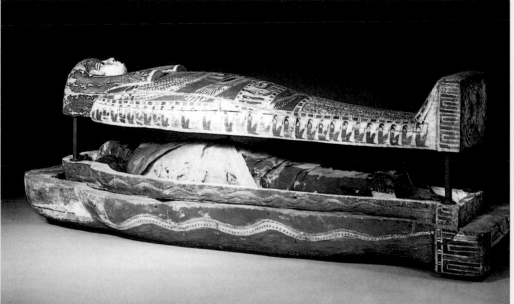

Gods of the afterlife *Jackal-headed Anubis was an ancient Egyptian god of the dead, particularly associated with the funeral cult. He was considered to be the inventor of embalming, an act he first performed on the god Osiris, who, aptly for the ruler of the dead, is often represented as a mummy.*

The mummy case *After bandaging, the face of the mummy was sometimes covered with a mask. The mummy was then placed in a contoured wooden coffin. This was plastered, then painted with an idealised figure of the deceased.*

THE CITADEL OF GREAT ZIMBABWE

For centuries, the largest stone monument in sub-Saharan Africa has puzzled historians and archaeologists. To account for its origins, various people have coupled it with such evocative names as King Solomon and the Queen of Sheba, but the ruins of Great Zimbabwe retain their secret to this day.

There were many thriving civilisations in Africa long before the arrival of Arab traders, who settled there in the 11th century. Several hundred sites of stone ruins have been discovered between the Zambezi and Limpopo rivers, but of these the most impressive is Great Zimbabwe, from which the modern state (formerly Southern Rhodesia) takes its name.

Zimbabwe is an anglicised form of an African word meaning 'stone houses', for the ruins are built in stone, which is not a common building material in Africa. The Great Zimbabwe complex is scattered over 60 acres (24ha) at the head of a valley. Dominating the site is the Great Enclosure, bounded by an elliptical outer wall 830ft (250m) in circumference. Three narrow gaps in the wall lead to an interior divided by other stone walls, passages and rooms. The most intriguing feature of the Great Enclosure is the conical tower near the outer wall. A superb example of dry-stone masonry, it stands 30ft (9m) high with a base circumference of 57ft (17m). The shape resembles the style of granary built by farmers of the local Shona tribe but, since it is completely solid, its purpose has totally baffled archaeologists.

About half a mile north of the Great Enclosure, on top of a granite hill, is another complex of ruins known as the Hill Fortress, or Acropolis. This was also built using dry-stone walling. Narrow staircases, just wide enough for one person at a time, lead into a labyrinthine interior consisting of a series of small enclosures. Seven soapstone birds, thought to have some religious significance, were found in one of these inner sanctuaries; the bird is now Zimbabwe's national emblem.

Portuguese traders, who came to Africa in the 16th century in search of gold, were the first Europeans to hear of Great Zimbabwe. A Portuguese historian, João de Barros, published a book in 1552 describing rich gold fields there, and great buildings made of dry stone called 'simbaoe' by the local inhabitants.

About 50 years later a Portuguese missionary, João dos Santos, referred to these same buildings in his writings, reporting that some Africans believed them to be the ruins of gold mines belonging to the Queen of Sheba or, perhaps, King Solomon. Dos Santos himself thought that these were the gold mines of Ophir, mentioned in the Bible as the source of King Solomon's gold.

No Portuguese had actually set eyes on Zimbabwe – the tales of its existence had been recounted by African traders. Nonetheless they thought that they had identified the Biblical land of Ophir, and this idea inspired other Europeans, who perpetuated it in their literature. The Dutch, who had settled in South Africa by the mid 17th century, attempted to find the stone ruins of Ophir but did not succeed.

In 1867, the German geologist Karl Mauch visited Great Zimbabwe and in his detailed account declared it

Zimbabwe ruins *The largest structure is the Great Enclosure (*RIGHT*). Its outer wall is made of granite slabs laid in rows like bricks but without mortar. The eastern section is the most impressive at 35ft (10.7m) high and 17ft (5m) thick.*

The Acropolis *This is the oldest section of the ruins and contains Great Zimbabwe's only surviving doorway (*LEFT*), which here leads to a passageway.*

THE CITADEL OF GREAT ZIMBABWE

THE GREAT ZIMBABWE COMPLEX

Key **1** *Hill fortress* **2** *Surrounding dwellings* **3** *Curved passage*
4 *Conical tower* **5** *Royal residence* **6** *Monoliths*

to be the ruins of the Queen of Sheba's palace. But in 1905 the British archaeologist David Randall-MacIver brusquely dismissed that idea and began to excavate the Great Enclosure and Acropolis. He proposed that, far from being ancient, the complex was started in the 11th century and completed in the 15th. Subsequent archaeological studies have confirmed this, adding that the actual site was established in the third century.

Most experts agree that Great Zimbabwe is African in origin and design, but there is no explanation as to why it was built of stone, rather than the traditional materials of wood and mud. Nearby ruins of mines (from which precious metals were obtained) indicate that the site was probably the centre of an African mining culture which declined in the 15th century. The British archaeologist Roger Summers, who examined these mines in 1958, concluded that the mining methods were the same as those used in the Kolar district of India, suggesting that there

had been an influence from that country. The discovery of Arabian and Persian artefacts proved that the inhabitants of Great Zimbabwe had contact with the outside world and that they probably traded extensively. Historians have also suggested that in the ninth century Zimbabwe was a slave centre, transporting Africans to Arab lands.

Although some facts about Great Zimbabwe have been established, they are simply odd pieces in a jigsaw which is far from complete. The identity of the people who constructed the great buildings is still a mystery and there is little clue as to why the site was abandoned. Real evidence is hard to come by without a written language. So the great stone ruins stand in their hilltop setting, the only remaining proof of a civilisation lost to time.

Within walls *Running parallel to the outer wall of the Great Enclosure is a second wall, creating a narrow passageway (LEFT). This inner wall is a section of a smaller, earlier one, less skilfully constructed than later parts.*

An enigmatic symbol *The conical tower (BELOW) remains a puzzle. Various theories have been advanced as to its purpose, including suggestions that it is a fertility symbol (an idea that derives from its phallic shape), a watch tower or a religious icon.*

Golden relics *Gold was probably the coinage used for foreign trade in Zimbabwe. Its inhabitants were skilled miners and craftsmen, as gold artefacts (BELOW) found there testify. The presence of gold gave rise to the belief that this was the site of King Solomon's mines, but most of it was plundered in the 1800s.*

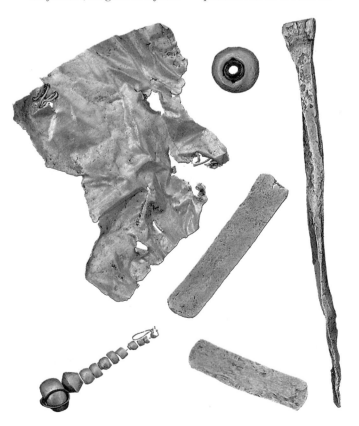

HONG KONG: CITY OF HARMONY

The ancient Chinese art of geomancy – shaping the landscape to harmonise with the Earth's energy – is still practised in one of the world's most modern cities.

Hong Kong is the most densely populated place on Earth: 5½ million people are crammed into the city's 412 sq miles (1067 sq km²). It is also one of the most vibrant places, where the pursuit of business and pleasure continues around the clock. Yet despite appearances, Hong Kong has more in common with ancient China than with the world's other modern metropolises. For Hong Kong is constructed according to the traditional principles of *feng shui*.

Translated as 'wind and water', *feng shui* is the art of geomancy, a complete system of mystical landscaping based on centuries-old Chinese wisdom and philosophy. Its major principles hold that health, wealth and prosperity only come to people who inhabit a world in which man-made forms, such as houses, places of work and even tombs, are in balance with natural forces, such as the wind in the trees and the water in rivers and streams. The task of ensuring that there is harmony in the universe falls to the geomancer; traditionally he is consulted whenever a change to the landscape is planned. His role is to make sure that any proposed new structure is sited in the right place, is orientated correctly, and is built at the most propitious time. If he feels that the edifice will upset the natural order, the geomancer advises against its construction.

Where buildings are concerned, *feng shui* ideals hold that there should be mountains or hills to the north, or back, of the site to ward off evil influences, while to the south should be a view, preferably over water. *Feng shui* is not just about how man-made changes affect the natural landscape, however; it also encompasses the effect of these changes on an individual's prosperity and well-being. For only when a person lives and works in a harmonious environment, and when his ancestors are buried favourably, will the opposing forces of *yin* and *yang*, of *chi*, the beneficial 'cosmic breath', and *sho chi*, the 'breath of ill fortune' on which personal good fortune depends, be in balance.

In a city as overcrowded as Hong Kong, where it is often impossible to position a building correctly, the role of the *feng shui* consultant is crucial. His task is to minimise the almost inevitable imbalance through such techniques as demolishing walls, bricking up windows and moving doors. Alternatively, he may recommend certain colours: red, for example, is reputed to bring happiness to the occupants of a house. Or symbols may be advocated, such as a dragon on the left and a tiger on the right of a building, which is meant to be an auspicious combination.

The geomancer is not successful in every case, however. According to local superstition, Bruce Lee, the former kung-fu master and international film star, met an untimely death in 1973 because his house was situated in the valley of Kowloon, a place avoided by traditional Chinese because it has bad *feng shui*. Lee was advised by a geomancer to install an eight-sided mirror in a tree outside his house to defuse the negative power of the site. When a typhoon blew down the tree and broke the mirror, he was

City that never sleeps

Like New York, Hong Kong is built largely on hard granite, which gives the firm foundations necessary to support its many skyscrapers (ABOVE). Even so, buildings must be strengthened against the typhoon season, which runs from June to October.

Feng shui *orientation*

Geomancers use a special compass (RIGHT) to help them determine whether natural forces and man-made forms are in complete harmony. Information on astrology, geographical direction and features of the landscape is arranged concentrically on the face.

BANKING ON THE CORRECT SITE

Making an entrance
Feng shui *expert Koo Pak Ling was retained by architect Sir Norman Foster as adviser at the planning stage of the Hong Kong and Shanghai Bank building. His original sketch shows the best place to site the entrance – angled to one side – which was followed through to the final design. Foster was so impressed by the geomancer that he retained his services for the entire project.*

The headquarters of the Hong Kong and Shanghai Bank, designed by British architect Sir Norman Foster and begun in 1979, is said to be – at £500 million – the world's most expensive building. It is certainly one of the most technologically advanced; its floors are not stacked one upon another, but suspended from eight steel pylons to create terraces of open work spaces. Despite its hi-tech modernity, the building is sensitive to Oriental custom, both visually in its lattice-work exterior and spiritually in its respect for the Chinese tradition of *feng shui*.

Foster was advised to position the escalators of the banking hall on the tail of the dragon whose shadow falls from a nearby peak. And when the bank's two bronze guardian lions were moved from the old headquarters, the *feng shui* expert advised that 4am on a Sunday would be the most propitious time; they were lowered simultaneously by two cranes to avoid showing favour.

left unprotected and died soon afterwards at the early age of 32, when he was at the height of his career.

This dependence on ancient philosophy is all the more surprising given that Hong Kong is so modern in every other respect. When the British first arrived there in the 1820s, the island was an inhospitable place, inhabited only by a few fisherman, but its natural harbour proved the ideal place to anchor British opium-carrying ships. After the first Opium War (1839–42), the Chinese ceded Hong Kong to the British. At a time when many of the world's great cities already had cultural and social traditions that stretched back for centuries, the British Foreign Secretary Lord Palmerston described Hong Kong as 'a barren island with hardly a house upon it'. Its spectacularly rapid metamorphosis has been made despite unpromising foundations, for Hong Kong has few natural assets.

Initially, its importance and prosperity depended on its sheltered deepwater harbour. In an area of south China notorious for piracy, it gave merchants and ship-owners the

Shaping the world *The picturesque landscapes of ancient China were designed by* feng shui *experts. 'The Imperial Travelling Palace at Hoo-Kew-Shan'* (LEFT) *illustrates some of the important geomantic elements: mountains behind the building and water in front. The pagoda on the hill deflects harmful influences, and ornamental devices, such as roof dragons, ward off evil.*

Bird's-eye view *From the 70th floor of the new Bank of China* (BELOW), *the harbour's natural shelter is clearly visible. At 72 storeys and 1019ft (310.6m), the bank is the tallest building in Hong Kong. It was completed in August 1988 on the 8th day of the 8th month of the 88th year, a date chosen to ensure the best possible luck. The word for 'eight' in Cantonese also means prosperity.*

security and protection of British law, and Hong Kong soon became established as the major port for European trade with China and the rest of eastern Asia. As the shipping trade grew, so did the related banking and insurance services that have today made Hong Kong one of the financial capitals of the world.

In the harbour, completely dwarfed by the surrounding skyscrapers, lie the junks of the Tanka or 'boat people'. These are fishermen and their families who live on their boats as their ancestors did and are a constant reminder of Hong Kong's origins as a fishing port. A decline in the fishing industry has meant that many of these people now have to find work on shore.

With limited natural resources, Hong Kong is dependent on imports, and it has developed as an international trading centre where goods are imported and re-exported without tariffs. In the late 1940s, an influx of refugees from the Communist take-over in China provided both labour and investment capital, and an intense programme

of factory and warehouse building was inaugurated. Today, the manufacturing industry has become the most important sector of the economy, employing 40 per cent of the work force. Hong Kong's biggest export earners are textiles and clothing, followed by electronics, watches and plastic toys. The city has also become an important publishing and printing centre. The enormous wealth created in the colony, the problems of space and, perhaps, an emphatic optimism in the face of an uncertain future after Hong Kong is returned to Chinese rule in 1997, have resulted in some of the most imaginative and innovative commercial buildings in the world.

It has taken little more than 150 years for Hong Kong to be transformed from an inhospitable island with no fresh water and a reputation as a notorious haunt of pirates to one of the most modern and wealthy cities in the world. Could it be that the geomancer's art has ensured Hong Kong's prosperity by siting its skyscrapers so that they are shielded against evil influences?

ULURU: DREAMTIME SANCTUARY

A giant chunk of red sandstone in the middle of the Australian desert is steeped in mystery and legend. This place of spiritual significance, whose every eroded scar has a meaning for its Aboriginal owners, also exerts its power on the imaginations of the thousands who visit it every year.

As the sun spreads its dawn rays across the sky, Uluru begins to lighten. Shifting from black to deep mauve, the giant monolith gradually becomes more distinct. When the first rays of the sun strike, the stone bursts into a riot of reds and pinks that chase each other across the surface with startling speed. Shadows flee the hollows until the whole rock is bathed in desert daylight. The colour changes continue throughout the day, and by evening have run the spectrum from golden and pinky reds through ruby to crimson red and purples.

Like the Sydney Opera House, Uluru has come to symbolise Australia. But unlike that modern man-made structure, the rock represents the country's far distant past, when the Aboriginal peoples were the only human occupants of the land. Uluru is the Aboriginal and now official name. Better known is the English name, Ayers Rock – which dates only from 1873 when the explorer William Gosse saw it and named it for Sir Henry Ayers, premier of South Australia, which was responsible for the government of the great expanse of the Northern Territory.

A visitor's first impression of the rock – visible from 60 miles (100km) away – is the abruptness with which it rises above the plain. Then it is its sheer bulk that amazes. Measuring 1142ft (348m) high, and with a circumference of 5½ miles (9km) at the base, Uluru is often cited as the world's largest monolith. But it is in fact just the tip of a mostly submerged 'mountain' extending to an estimated depth of 3¾ miles (6km) below ground level. Some 550 million years ago, the rock was part of the ocean floor that occupied the centre of Australia. Then the oceans receded and gradual movements and upheavals in the Earth's crust pushed the rock over on to one side.

The rock is made of arkose, a type of red sandstone that contains large quantities of feldspar. Various oxides of iron are also present. This composition accounts for the remarkable changes in colour that occur as night gives way to dawn, dawn to daylight and daylight to dusk. Many people visit Uluru simply to watch the effects of light at different times of day and during different seasons. When it rains the rock appears to have a liquid silver skin. Surface grooves become raging torrents, and the water that cascades down the rock's precipitous sides forms transient pools on the surrounding desert floor.

On close inspection, the rock reveals a delicacy of form

286

Rib of rock The kangaroo was hunted for food by the Aborigines. It is recalled at Uluru by the formation known as the Kangaroo's Tail, a huge ridge that was left after adjacent rock had flaked and fallen away, in the same manner as a snake might shed its skin.

The red giant The orange-gold rays of the evening sun catch the summit of Uluru. This bulky lump of red sandstone is gradually wearing away, but its overall shape remains the same. The Aborigines believe that the rock has not altered since the Tjukurpa (Dreamtime).

287

in features that have been carved by rain and wind. They include the caves and permanent pools that are the sacred places of the Aborigines, and the cracks, crevices and striations that have been ascribed animal or human shapes.

The forces of nature are also wearing away the rock with other clearly visible results. The alternating extremes of hot and cold temperatures, characteristic of a desert environment, bring about a process called spalling, in which flakes of rock are shed from the surface and slide down to the ground below. Not all the loosened areas fall away, however: on the north face of Uluru a colossal rocky spine known as the Kangaroo's Tail leans like a giant buttress against the steeply curved slope.

William Gosse was not the first European to set eyes on Uluru. A year earlier, the explorer Ernest Giles had glimpsed it from the shores of Lake Amadeus, some 25 miles (40km) to the north, while making one of several expeditions into the Australian interior. When he returned to the rock the following year, he found that Gosse had already reached the summit. More recently, the Australian adventurer and writer Robyn Davidson visited Uluru while journeying in the outback. In her book *Tracks* she described her first, vivid impression of the rock: 'The indecipherable power of the rock had my heart racing. I had not experienced anything quite so weirdly, primaevally beautiful.' Davidson's sentiments are echoed by most visitors, who are usually surprised by their strong emotional reaction to what is, after all, just a large lump of stone.

These impressions become more meaningful to those

Rock pool *Rainstorms in the desert are infrequent, but waterholes such as Maggie Springs are sometimes fed by water draining off the rock.*

Eroded pits *Uluru supports no vegetation: its pitted surface, the result of weathering, makes it difficult for plants to take root.*

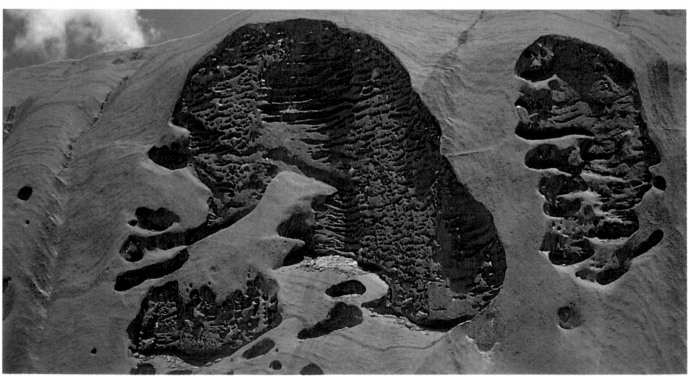

who know something of the Aboriginal myths and legends associated with the rock and its environs. According to Aboriginal legend, Uluru is a landmark on one of the Dreaming trails laid out by their ancestors during the Tjukurpa, the period when the Earth was still being formed. In the Tjukurpa, or 'Dreamtime', the region around the rock was home to the hare-wallaby and carpet-snake peoples. The carpet-snake people were attacked by the venomous-snake people, an invading tribe from the south. They were saved only by the intervention of Bulari, earth-mother heroine of the hare-wallaby people, who vanquished the invaders by breathing a poisonous cloud of death and disease around them.

The legends of the hare-wallaby people also tell of a time when their group was threatened. An evil dingo named Kulpunya, sung into existence by a rival group, was set loose on the hare-wallaby people, who managed to escape thanks to their fantastic ability to leap. For today's Aborigines, evidence of both incidents can be seen or felt at Uluru. The bodies of the venomous-snake people are locked into the shape of Uluru, and a water stain down one side of the rock shows where their blood flowed. The footprints of the escaping hare-wallaby people are visible as a series of caves around the base of the rock.

Every fissure of Uluru has powerful connotations for the Aborigines. Regardless of the numbers of people who visit the rock, Aborigines consider themselves custodians of a symbolic landscape bequeathed to them by their ancestors; Uluru is central to that landscape.

Dogs of the outback
Hardly distinguishable from a domestic dog, the dingo roams wild, killing sheep and rabbits for food. It was almost certainly introduced to Australia from South-east Asia by the Aborigines.

TJUKURPA: THE 'DREAMTIME'

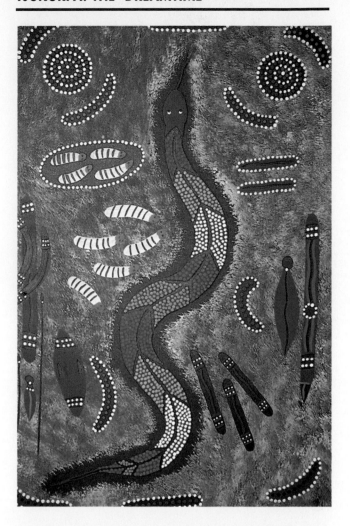

Australian Aborigines believe that their ancestors lived during a period called the Tjukurpa, the 'Dreamtime', in the course of which the amorphous Earth started to take shape. The Tjukurpa has nothing to do with dreams and dreaming in the conventional sense, however; it is more a spiritual philosophy, a religious interpretation of the landscape that refers to both the past and the present.

During the ancestral Tjukurpa, the world was inhabited by animal-humans with supernatural powers, including the Yankunytjatjara, or carpet-snake people, and the Pitjantjatjara, the hare-wallaby people, both of whom are associated with the rock itself. These peoples undertook long journeys and quests; wherever they stopped to pick fruit, hunt or even to throw away fish bones, the landscape changed. Waterholes came into existence and rock formations appeared, all of which became sacred.

In these places, different Aboriginal families, each with its own language and stories, were born. At the same time, an intricate pattern of tracks was established across the desert. These are the Dreaming trails, once vital to the survival of the Aborigines who lived and hunted there. Their whereabouts and secrets have been passed down from generation to generation in songs, in paintings, and in the ritual corroboree ceremonies. The painting (ABOVE) depicts a carpet snake and witchetty grubs during the Tjukurpa.

THE FIRST AUSTRALIANS

The Aborigines first reached northern Australia 50 000 years ago by island-hopping from South-east Asia. A brown or black-skinned people, they were neither farmers nor herdsmen but nomads who dispersed into some 600–700 tribe-nations each speaking one of 200–250 languages or dialects as distinct from each other as are French and Chinese. They existed by hunting animals – using such unique hunting weapons as the boomerang and a spear-thrower called a woomera – and by gathering fruits and roots.

A tribe-nation comprised several self-governing groups consisting of an extended family – a man and his brothers, with their wives and children. Today, as in the past, women share equally in this highly spiritual and egalitarian culture,

although both sexes have their own sacred places and ceremonies. In these are preserved the myths, songs and ritual dances that relate to particular heroes in the ancient Tjukurpa. Each of these heroes is associated, in turn, with a specific plant, animal or other natural object.

The exploits of the heroes are re-enacted at corroborees: these are ritual ceremonies of song and dance, lasting up to a week, in which usually the men, and in some tribes the women, paint their faces and bodies (generally white to symbolise male potency, death and rebirth) and may cover themselves with tufts of grass or feathers. The corroboree is a spiritual festival, but there are no priests. Everyone plays a part, although elders who can recount all the songs and

Aboriginal art *Colourful paintings adorn Nourlangie Rock in Kakadu National Park. The works at Kakadu are among the great wonders of the world and may be at least 25 000 years old. There are some 7000 rock art sites in this park alone.*

Dreamtime recalled *With their bodies painted and decorated, Aborigines meet at a corroboree (BELOW). They perform the complex rhythms of song-cycles and ritual dances to re-enact events from the Tjukurpa and initiate young men into the mysteries of life.*

Dance for the kangaroo
Legends from the Tjukurpa are passed on through dance and song: this dance tells the story of a kangaroo hunt. It is performed at Peppimenarti in the north of the Northern Territory. Once this area was a cattle station, but today the Aborigines own the land that they work.

stories are particularly revered. The elders are also responsible for the safekeeping of the sacred stones or boards, which are incised with patterns of scratches to represent the stories. These stones and boards are hidden in caves and brought out on ceremonial occasions only.

Cave paintings fulfil a similar symbolic function, but also identify the creatures associated with a particular group or person (wall paintings were generally executed in sacred Aboriginal caves, which tourists are not allowed to enter). Such beliefs, in which a person is closely linked with a particular animal, plant or even an inanimate object, are referred to as totemism. Aboriginal totems have a dual identity – half human and half non-human. An Aborigine may

indicate a depression in Uluru and call it a snake-human, declaring 'That is my grandfather'. A male Aborigine would never injure or eat his totem, which is sacred to him; to kill his totem would hold the same significance as killing a member of his family.

While women and children, and sometimes visitors, can attend boys' initiation ceremonies, as well as death rituals, religious occasions are secret, and harsh penalties are incurred by anyone who reveals their content. In the past, death was the usual sanction for law-breaking of this nature, but that form of punishment was largely replaced with trial by spear. In such trials, the accused was surrounded by clansmen who threw their spears at his thighs.

EASTER ISLAND: HOME OF STONE GIANTS

A pinprick of land in the watery expanses of the South Pacific has a history of unique sculpture. Huge stone statues, the most enigmatic in the world, were hewn from the island's extinct volcanic crater and dragged into place.

I t is said that Easter Island is one of the loneliest places in the world. This tiny island – almost 1200 miles (2000km) from its nearest island neighbours, more than twice that far from a large landmass, and just 16 miles (25km) long – prompts many puzzling questions. Where did the first inhabitants come from? How did they find the island at all? And why and how did they construct more than 600 giant stone statues, only to tear most of them down?

The first Europeans to set foot on the island, on Easter Sunday 1722, were Dutch sailors. They stayed long enough to name the island and for their admiral to note that he judged the islanders to be of two different racial types. He also wrote that they appeared to worship colossal statues carved from stone. (In fact, the statues were cut from badly eroded volcanic rock.) In 1770 a party of Spaniards from Peru rediscovered Easter Island. At that time, the island's population was estimated at 3000: just four years later, during his second Pacific voyage of discovery, Captain James Cook found between 600 and 700 men and just 30 women. The population recovered slightly in the early 19th century, but was dealt another blow in 1862, when the Peruvian government took 1000 men to work as slaves on the mainland. A few months later, the 15 survivors were returned to the island; with them they carried smallpox. Having no resistance, the islanders succumbed to the disease.

The dwindling population helps to explain why the islanders' origins are so poorly understood. There were no written records on Easter Island, and with every death the oral tradition and the culture it described became less and less clear. And, although many wooden tablets carved with pictograms have been found on the island, as yet no one has been able to interpret the symbols.

Natives told Captain Cook that 22 generations had

Sentinels The statues on the Nau Nau platform in Anakena Bay, restored in 1978, stand with their backs to the place where Chief Hotu Matu'a is said to have landed. He named the island Te Pito o te Heuca, *'the navel of the world', probably a reference to its extreme isolation.*

Variety in stone There are small differences between statues made at the same time. Most middle period statues are on the coast, but this is one of seven on a platform at Akivi, about a mile (1.6km) inland on the west coast.

EASTER ISLAND: HOME OF STONE GIANTS

passed since Chief Hotu Matu'a had led their ancestors to the island, but they could not say from where. There are two major theories, both of which may be correct to a certain extent. If they are, this would explain why visitors to Easter Island, from the Dutch admiral on, have noted that the islanders seem to be of two different racial types.

According to the first theory, put forward in the 1930s by Alfred Metreaux, the islanders' ancestors came from other Polynesian islands to the west. Many archaeologists favour this suggestion: there are cultural similarities between Easter Island and others in the Polynesian group, and the voyage would have been shorter for would-be colonisers than if they had come from the east.

The second theory was proposed by the Norwegian archaeologist and anthropologist Thor Heyerdahl. He pointed out the physical similarities between many of the long-headed Easter Island statues and some South American peoples. He argued that the staple island crop, the sweet potato, could only have come from the Amazon region, and that seed dispersal over such distances was unlikely. And, finally, by crossing the Pacific from the coast

CREATING THE STATUES

Carving, moving and raising the statues was a mammoth undertaking. It is estimated that it took 30 men a year to carve a large statue. Their fronts and sides were fashioned at the quarry. Only then was the statue separated from the rock and slid into a pit so that carvers could work on its back.

Kneeling giant The earliest statues depict kneeling men. Unlike later statues, which were made from a uniform material, different types of stone were used for early examples. The similarities between these statues and figures found in pre-Inca South America support Heyerdahl's theory that some of the islanders originated there.

Tireless eyes Many moai have eyes carved from white coral, with red scoria rock as irises. It is thought that the eyes were inserted only when the statues had been hoisted into position at their final resting place. Material for the statues was hewn from an extinct volcano at Rano Raraku in the east of the island; the red tuff rock for the topknots came from a crater at Punapau in the west.

294

The statue was roped to a sledge for transport to its final site, up to 4 miles (6km) away. This journey took 90 men around two months to complete. The topknot was secured with beams lashed to the head.

A mound of rocks built up under the statue raised it gradually. As the mound grew, a crossbeam was inserted under the head to help in the lifting process. When the statue was almost upright, ropes were attached to the head so that it could be hauled into place.

Once it was upright, ropes and sledge were removed. The raising stage is estimated to have taken 90 men three months.

Beams lashed to head

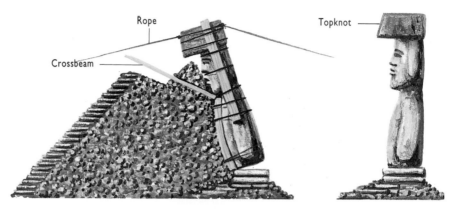

Rope

Crossbeam

Topknot

EASTER ISLAND: HOME OF STONE GIANTS

of South America to Polynesia on the *Kon-Tiki*, a raft made from balsa logs, he proved that such a journey was possible.

Whoever they were, the Easter Islanders constructed the most famous stone statues in the world. Anthropologists, by studying the remains of the statues and other man-made artefacts and by listening to fragments drawn from legend, have identified three cultural periods in the island's history.

During the earliest period, from about AD 380, most statues were of kneeling human figures carved from volcanic slag or basalt. In the second, or middle, period which began around 1100, the type of statue most commonly associated with the island became prominent. This was the *moai*, with the upper body of a man, a stylised head, inlaid eyes and elongated ear lobes. The statues stood on stepped stone platforms called *ahu*, which supported up to 12 figures. Over the centuries, ever larger statues were fashioned and a red topknot, or *pukao*, was added to the heads. These images, thought to represent chiefs deified after death, are unique.

The beginning of the third, or late, cultural period in about 1680 seems to have coincided with the outbreak of civil war between the two peoples who had previously co-existed peacefully. This may have begun when trees started to become scarce: boats for fishing could not be replaced and the soil deteriorated. As food stocks dwindled, the socially dominant 'long ears', possibly from South America, and the subservient 'short ears' from Polynesia, who eventually emerged as victors, started to fight. (Legend has it that women and children were captured and eaten, which could explain why Captain Cook found so few women on the island.) In the conflict the 'short ears' took over the various platforms and tore the statues down.

War and famine were frequently mentioned by 19th-century visitors to the island, and conditions only began to improve following its annexation by Chile in 1888. Then, the population recovered to see their home become the focus of one of the great riddles of the modern world.

Easy access *Some statues still stand with their lower halves buried in pits. The figures were tipped into holes in the ground to enable carvers to finish their backs.*

Home of the Birdman *Island houses were made from lava with a covering of turf on the roof slabs. From about 1500, the village of Oronga* (BELOW) *was the centre of the Birdman cult.*

Birdman chief *Terns nest on many of the small islands off the shore near Oronga, and the eggs of these sea birds were an important source of food for the islanders. The man who collected the first egg in spring became Birdman and supreme island chief for a year. A figure of the Birdman is carved on a large rock overlooking the islet of Motu Nui.*

EARTH MOUNDS: MAN-MADE HILLS

Dotted across North America are more than 100 000 earth mounds, dispelling the early settlers' belief that no previous culture of any significance existed on that continent. Now aerial photography has offered conclusive proof that innovative and visionary peoples lived here as early as 1000 BC.

When European explorers first ventured across the vast untamed wilderness of North America during the 16th and 17th centuries, they found no trace of prehistoric culture outside Mexico. The tribes of semi-nomadic Indians they encountered had apparently never been geographically settled, and as a result had left neither buildings nor sites containing cultural artefacts. It was not until colonists reached the Ohio and Mississippi river valleys in the 18th century that they came across unequivocal, man-made evidence of the continent's former inhabitants.

The proof came in the form of earth mounds. These vary in size, building method, shape and function, and were constructed over a long time span by a number of different peoples. So far, more than 100 000 have been identified. Shapes range from simple tumuli and elongated wall-like works to complex conical and pyramid-shaped structures.

The smallest earth mounds cover less than 1 acre (0.4ha); the largest, Monk's Mound in present-day St Louis, has a 16 acre (6.4ha) rectangular base – larger than the Great Pyramid at Giza – and is 100ft (30m) high. Unique to North America are the so-called effigy mounds, built to represent human, bird or animal forms.

Many of the effigy mounds, including Serpent Mound in Ohio, were symbolic. Serpent Mound's symbolism is disputed, but according to the most recent theory the snake represents a solar eclipse in which the separate oval mound near the head (usually referred to as the 'egg') represents the sun, which is being attacked by the snake.

The builders of the mounds also used them as foundations for other structures, including temples and fortresses. The vast majority of earth mounds, however, were tombs.

The longest snake *Serpent Mound is North America's largest effigy mound. For all of its 1330ft (405m) length, it follows the contours of a small stream, Bush Creek, but is raised 150ft (50m) above the water level, and about 3ft (90cm) above ground level. It was built of stones overlaid with clay.*

EARTH MOUNDS: MAN-MADE HILLS

Sometimes the mound was constructed over a funerary container, simply to cover an existing burial place. At others, a completely new site was excavated. A pit, large enough to hold between one and three bodies, was dug and lined with wooden logs on which the bodies were placed. Alternatively, the bodies were laid out on the logs on the ground. A pole-and-wire construction supported a covering of bark, which was in turn overlaid with the earth or stones that comprised the mound.

Some of the burial mounds were found to contain objects that the dead might have been thought to need in an afterlife. These included axes, obsidian spearheads, stone maces; jewellery and precious items such as shell beads, copper-covered masks, mica mirrors and freshwater pearls. The paraphernalia of everyday life – textiles, carved pipes and conch-shell drinking cups – has also been unearthed.

The mounds were created by three separate peoples. The earliest builders, who flourished from around 1000 to 100 BC, were the Adena. They had an almost obsessive preoccupation with death, and their mounds primarily contain graves and grave goods, including objects in copper and stone, such as pipes and decoratively incised tablets.

Although the Hopewell people, whose mounds date from about 100 BC, kept many Adena traditions, their

Rock Eagle Mound *About 1500 years ago, the Hopewell people of Georgia moved tons of boulders to construct a huge bird effigy – its wingspan is 120ft (36.5m) – from piled stones. Perhaps the most remarkable feature of effigy mounds is the concept that lay behind them: they can only be seen properly from the air.*

The excavator *The 18th-century amateur archaeologist Montroville Dickenson claimed to have investigated more than 1000 American Indian sites, and even commissioned Irish–American artist John Egan to paint him at work. The result shows how the skeletons and artefacts were arranged inside a mound.*

culture was more advanced. For almost four centuries their influence extended over much of present-day Indiana, Michigan, Wisconsin, Iowa and Missouri. They were also successful traders. The copper they used for their ornaments and armour came from around Lake Superior. Knives were carved from obsidian – a volcanic rock that has been traced to Yellowstone National Park 1000 miles (1600km) away – and the mounds contained sharks' teeth that must have come from the Gulf of Mexico.

The tradition of mound-building was continued after the decline of Hopewell society by the Mississippians, who flourished after AD 700. Their great soil mounds were like the pyramid temples of the Mayans and Aztecs, but used less often as graves, and their 12th-century city Cahokia has been called America's first metropolis north of the Rio Grande. Today, Monk's Mound is all that remains of a city that sheltered 30 000 people. Some 100 other earth mounds supporting official residences and temples, and housing the dead, were once visible from its summit. Homes built from clay-covered poles protected a society that lived by growing maize, squashes and beans, and by hunting and fishing. Cahokia offers the clearest evidence so far of the sophisticated culture that existed at least 300 years before the European 'discovery' of North America.

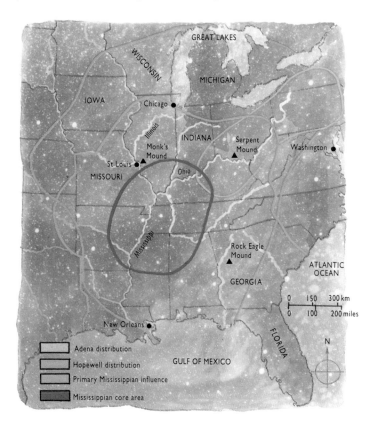

Ancient pipe *The Adena were adept stone carvers. This 8in (20cm) long tobacco pipe was carved by an Adena craftsman 3000 years ago, and found in an Ohio earth mound. It depicts a human figure wearing earrings and a loin cloth. The mouthpiece is at the top of the head and the tobacco bowl is between the feet.*

Along the waterways *The largest concentration of earth mounds in North America is found along the Ohio River valley. But they also exist along the banks of the Illinois and Mississippi rivers from the Great Lakes in the north to the Gulf of Mexico. This suggests that the early Americans traded along these rivers.*

301

NAZCA LINES: PATTERNS OF PERU

*Giant geometric shapes, enormous animal figures and ruler-straight lines extending
to the borizon: why these impressive markings are etched into the bare grassless soil
of a remote region of Peru is one of the greatest
mysteries of all time.*

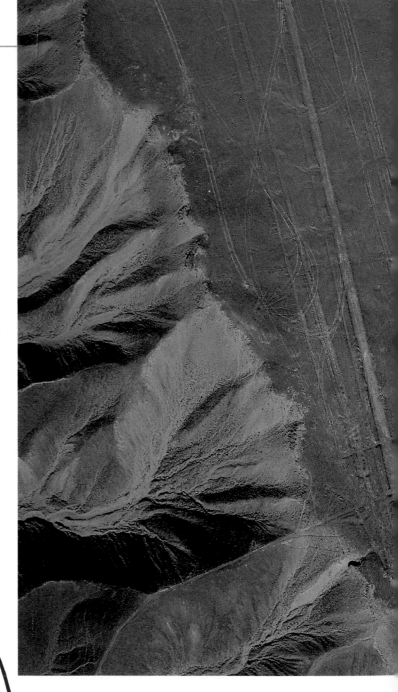

S ome 2000 years ago, a South American civilisation about which very little is known created some of the most puzzling inscriptions on Earth. Peru's Nazca Desert resembles pages from a giant's sketchbook. The red desert rock has been etched with more than 100 designs, ranging from familiar plant and animal forms to geometric patterns and strange series of straight lines. Theories abound as to what they were supposed to represent and why they were drawn at all, yet their true purpose, if they have one, remains a complete enigma.

The largest work of graphic art in the world covers an area of 200 sq miles (520km^2) in Peru between the Andes and the Pacific Ocean. Scant reference to the Nazca lines was made by 16th and 17th-century Spanish explorers, but they remained largely unknown to the outside world until the 1920s, when Julio Tello, the so-called father of Peruvian archaeology, first recorded the designs. The patterns did not become the subject of serious investigation until 1941, when the American archaeologist Dr Paul Kosok, from the University of Long Island, went to Nazca. Since then, the German mathematician and astronomer Dr Maria Reiche has devoted more than 40 years to charting and recording the inscriptions and attempting to explain their significance.

The drawings on Nazca's desert floor were all made in the same way: by scraping away the reddish gravel on the surface of the desert to reveal the pale yellow rock beneath. This appears to have been done by hand – at least, there is no evidence of the use of animals – and in such a way that, regardless of shape, size or subject, each image is made up of a single, uninterrupted line.

The subjects of the Nazca inscriptions fall into two

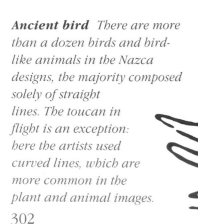

Ancient bird *There are more
than a dozen birds and bird-
like animals in the Nazca
designs, the majority composed
solely of straight
lines. The toucan in
flight is an exception:
here the artists used
curved lines, which are
more common in the
plant and animal images.*

Snake-beaded bird *The
body of the creature* (RIGHT)
*is that of a hummingbird.
But the long sinuous neck
resembles a serpent as it
snakes its way across the
desert. One suggestion is
that the creature, like the*

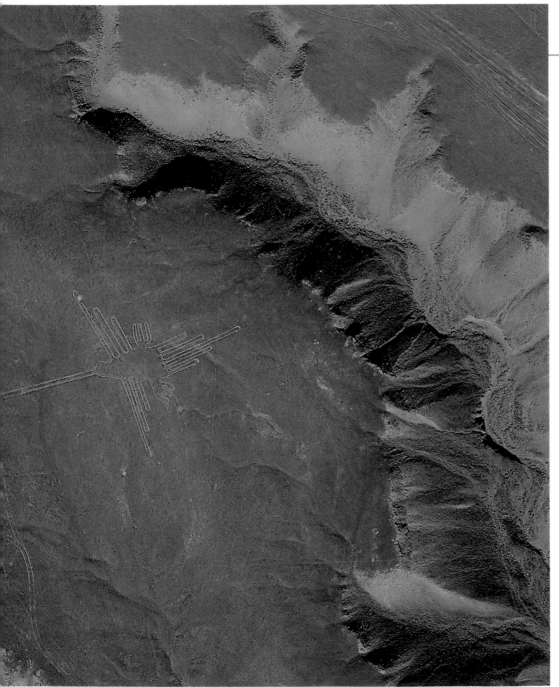

Bird's-eye view *A nectar-eating hummingbird extends its long thin beak to reach dead-straight lines that extend to the horizon. The bird appears to have been connected to the grid lines at some time, although the point of contact has been obscured by scuff marks over the years. Car tracks have also erased some of the grid lines.*

other animal figures, is intended to represent a constellation or another of the heavenly bodies revered by the Nazca Indians.

303

NAZCA LINES: PATTERNS OF PERU

4

2

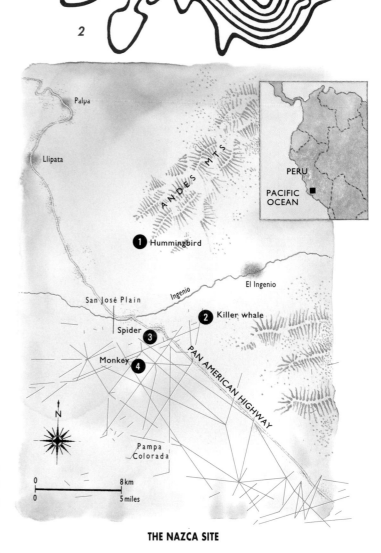

THE NAZCA SITE

broad categories: figures and lines, the latter of which are arranged either in pairs like tramlines or conceived as geometric patterns. And, since in many places lines are etched over figures, the figures were clearly made first. Among them are the leaves and branches of various plants; animal and bird figures; and strange combinations of two different forms. These include the figure of a man with the head of an owl and a bird with an over-long serpent in place of its beak.

The lines themselves are so straight that it seems likely they were set out using a series of poles aligned by eye. Yet one of the mysteries is how the builders managed to maintain such alignment over the distances involved: some lines deviate by less than 10ft per mile (2m per km) over distances of more than 5 miles (8km). In many places, series of lines fan out from a single point in all directions, formations that Maria Reiche calls starlike clusters. Often lines crisscross one another in an apparently random fashion to form giant rectangles and triangles.

The Nazca inscriptions appear to date from between 500 BC and AD 500; they were probably made by the

Nazca Indians who inhabited areas of Peru before the rise of the Inca Empire. The Nazcans were farmers who cultivated the fertile plain along the Pacific coast of Peru. These people left no evidence of a written culture: all that is known about them comes from studying their burial places and grave goods. The dead were interred in the foetal position, surrounded by multicoloured pottery and other artefacts, but many of the burial grounds, some of which contained up to 5000 graves, have been robbed.

This fragmentary knowledge of the Nazcans does not explain why they etched these patterns in the desert. One supposition was that they were ancient highways, but this is unlikely since many end abruptly on the tops of hills. The most widely accepted hypothesis was proposed by Dr Paul Kosok, who believed that the figures and lines

PICTURES IN THE DUST

Little rain falls in the Nazca region, so the majority of drawings have remained as fresh and new as when they were made. Many of the figures are huge: the spider, for example, is 148ft (45m) long. The monkey figure has been interpreted as symbolising the rising of Benetnasch, a star of the Plough constellation, in AD 1000. Hummingbirds are common on Nazca ceramics, and often appear in the markings; the whale is the only marine creature.

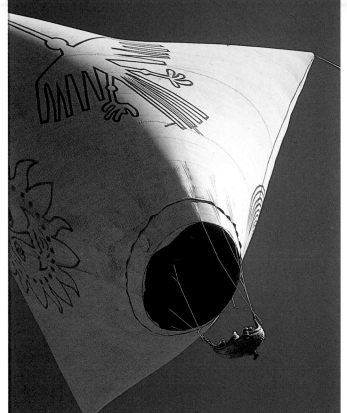

Flight of the Condor *The American explorers Julian Nott and Jim Woodman tried to prove that the people who made the designs could have seen them from the air. They built* Condor I, *a hot-air balloon, using only materials which would have been available to the Nazcans.*

Airport runways? *Many of the pairs of lines resemble landing strips. Suggestions that they were intended for spaceships have been discounted, however – not least because the desert soil could not support the presumed weight involved.*

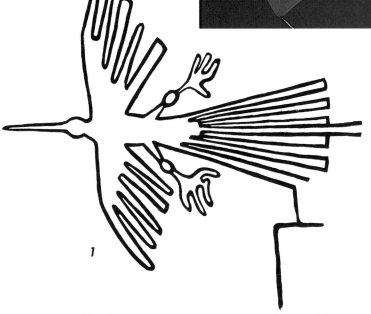

1

represent 'the largest astronomy book in the world'. Dr Reiche shares this view. She has suggested that they predict the positions of stars and constellations at various times of the year and were used to determine the seasons for sowing, harvesting and so on. The beaks of some of the bird forms, for example, are aligned with the position of the sunrise at the summer solstice.

The fact that the lines can only be fully appreciated from above prompted the theory that the Nazcans were able to fly, or at least hover above ground, as the lines were being constructed. While this fascinating idea is not wholly far-fetched – paintings on pottery show objects that bear some resemblance to both kites and hot-air balloons – it does not explain why these lines were made in the first instance.

MAZES AND LABYRINTHS

The true purpose of the maze remains a riddle to this day. Mazes come in many guises, from religious symbol to pure entertainment, and, uniquely among patterns and devices, mazes are found the world over, in all cultures.

S pirals and mazes are among the most ancient of all human abstract designs, the first pictures to represent ideas rather than depict events such as hunts and battles. They appeared at the same time in different parts of the world which, separated by vast distances, could not have influenced each other. Maze designs of a similar age have been discovered in Arizona, India and Sumatra, as well as in Europe.

The maze was associated with religious ideas of death and rebirth and became the focus of rituals to ensure the returning fertility of spring after the long winter death of the sun. Early communities in southern Europe carved pictures of mazes into the rocks of their tombs and monuments. Others, such as those in Scandinavia, created real mazes, marked out with cut turf or boulders, which were used in ritual dances at the spring solstice.

The most famous mythological maze in the Western world is the labyrinth of King Minos in Crete, once home to the Minotaur – half man, half bull. The Athenian hero, Theseus, found his way through the maze and killed the Minotaur. Excavations of the Minoan palace at Knossos in Crete have revealed no trace of the labyrinth. However, there is ample evidence of a bull cult, whose emblem is the double-headed axe, or *labrys,* which may be the origin of the word 'labyrinth'.

The earliest built maze is not known. In the fifth century BC, Herodotus, the Greek historian, visited a famous building at Fayum in Egypt, built in 1800 BC by Amenemhet III, and described it as a 'labyrinth'. Although it was a rambling structure, with 12 courts and many chambers connected by winding paths, it does not seem

Mosaic maze *The most famous maze story of all, that of Theseus and the Minotaur, is depicted on this 15ft (4.6m) by 18ft (5.5m) mosaic floor* (RIGHT), *discovered in a Roman villa near Salzburg in Austria. At the entrance on the right is a portrait of Ariadne, seated, waiting for her lover to return.*

Fabric patterns *In this portrait of a man* (ABOVE), *painted by Bartolommeo Veneto in 1510, the clothes are decorated with maze-like designs. The 'Solomon's Knots' on the sleeves are a combination of cross, swastika and labyrinth.*

Mazes for fun *Three-dimensional wooden mazes, with panels that can be moved about* (LEFT), *are popular in Japan. Runners race against the clock to see how long it takes them to reach the centre.*

307

MAZES AND LABYRINTHS

Rock carving *These two seven-ring labyrinths* (ABOVE) *were found near Tintagel, Cornwall (1). Their sharp grooves, cut at a constant angle, indicate that an iron tool was used to inscribe them, but they are difficult to date. Suggestions range from the 6th to 17th centuries.*

Maze epitaph *In the cemetery of the village of Alkborough, England (3), a tombstone bearing a maze* (BELOW) *commemorates the village squire who made sure that Julian's Bower, a medieval maze nearby, was well maintained.*

The Path of Life *In the nave of Chartres Cathedral (2) lies a maze* (reproduced BELOW), *which is probably symbolic of the Christian way to God.*

to have had the deliberate design of a true labyrinth.

One of the oldest maze-like designs in northern Europe, dating from about 2500 BC, is the triple spiral inscribed on rock inside a burial mound at New Grange, County Meath in Ireland. Other rock carvings of mazes have been found throughout Europe, showing a development from spirals at early sites to the more complex 'Cretan labyrinth' of later centuries. The latter pattern is a simple maze with one entrance and a path that winds its way to the centre through a series of seven rings.

From the end of the 12th century, mazes began to appear in churches throughout Europe, marked out in tiles on the floor. Many medieval French cathedrals are

GREECE
● *Athens*

7
CRETE

Prehistoric design *A rock carving found at the entrance to a rock tomb* (ABOVE) *at Luzzanas, Sardinia (4), dates from 2500 to 2000* BC *and may represent the world's oldest surviving labyrinth.*

Hampton Court *The oldest surviving hedge maze* (ABOVE) *in Britain – and probably the most famous in the world – is at Hampton Court (5) in Surrey. It was planted in 1690 for William of Orange, King William III.*

Scandinavian mazes *Boulder designs* (BELOW), *including the maze at Kugsoren, Sweden (6), were used in fertility rituals and dances, and in 'fishermen's magic', which was reputed to control the wind.*

Old money *Dating from the third century* BC, *a coin from the Greek island of Crete (7) shows the Classical seven-ring labyrinth design* (ABOVE) *that refers to the legend of Theseus and the Minotaur.*

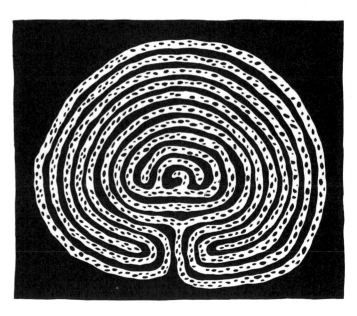

noted for such mazes, including Bayeux, Amiens, Chartres and Sens. Christian pavement mazes became integral to the act of penance, in which the faithful would follow the twists and turns of the pattern crawling on their knees. This penance was often set for those who could not make the pilgrimage to the Holy Land, and church mazes became known as *chemins de Jerusalem*, 'roads of Jerusalem'. In Italy, labyrinths were carved on pillars and walls where they could be traced with a finger while praying. One such maze can be seen in Lucca Cathedral.

Mazes were also used in folk rituals that had their roots in pagan fertility rites. In England, turf mazes, such as Julian's Bower at Alkborough on Humberside, were used during festivities at Easter and on May Day. Spiral dances, where young men and women twirl inwards to a centre point and then out again, were popular well into the 19th century. Maze dances still take place in Europe and are based on the ancient Crane Dance, or *geranos*, said to have been danced by Theseus and his companions on the Greek island of Naxos to celebrate their escape.

The enthusiasm for formal gardens incorporating a large puzzle maze gripped Europe from the 16th century onwards. Mazes were marked out with high hedges and led up several blind alleys as in the Hampton Court maze. Today, the world's largest hedge maze, first opened in 1978, stands at Longleat House in Wiltshire.

TIMELESS LANDSCAPES

T he combination of physical beauty and inherent spirituality of some landscapes has drawn like a magnet truth-seekers, from monks and hermits to pilgrims and explorers. The power of untouched environments is the most potent attraction for many: the novelist Joseph Conrad was fascinated by the primeval vigour of the Congo rainforests. In Tanzania, the huge Ngorongoro Crater, remnant of a collapsed extinct volcano, is an ecological time capsule, where great herds of herbivores survive virtually free from human disturbance, protected by the altitude and the high crater walls. Some landscapes have drawn religious communities to settle, in the hope that isolation and serenity might be conducive to meditation and spiritual growth. The slender rock pinnacles of Metéora in Greece have been the refuge of monks and hermits for more than 1000 years. In Cappadocia in Turkey, early Christian monks made their homes in strange, rocky cones, formed through the erosion of volcanic tufa, hollowing them out over the centuries to create cells, churches, and even underground cities where religious minorities could take refuge from successive waves of conquerors. But perhaps the most powerful spiritual landscapes are those, like the Himalayas, whose scale and intrinsic beauty make human visitors most aware of their own impermanence and vulnerability.

HALEAKALA: HOUSE OF THE SUN

One of the world's largest volcanic craters is situated on the Hawaiian island of Maui. The awesome spectacle of the sun rising over its rim has provided inspiration for generations of artists and writers.

The forbidding splendour and unique natural beauty of Haleakala crater at the summit of the mountain of the same name can be fully appreciated only by those who have seen it for themselves, according to the American writer Jack London. He maintained that 'Haleakala has a message of beauty and wonder for the human soul that cannot be delivered by proxy.' London is just one of generations of non-native commentators who have been moved by this dormant volcano since Captain James Cook discovered the Hawaiian islands in 1778.

Haleakala mountain, which soars to a height of some 10 000ft (3000m), dominates the island of Maui – the second largest of the tropical chain that constitutes Hawaii, 25 miles (40km) north-west of the so-called Big Island, Hawaii itself. *Haleakala* is Polynesian for House of the Sun. Local legend links the volcano to the god after whom the island of Maui is named. There was once a time when the Sun, in its haste to get back to sleep, raced across the sky, with the result that the island received fewer hours of daylight. This angered Maui's mother Hina because it prevented her from properly drying the cloth she made from pounded tree bark. Maui devised a plan: he wove a coconut-fibre rope and lay in wait for the Sun to rise at the top of Haleakala. As it rose, he lassoed the first shafts of sunlight, so capturing the Sun: Maui made the Sun promise to move at a more leisurely pace, thereby

MAP OF THE CRATER
OF
HALEAKALA

W. D. ALEXANDER, SURVEYOR,
1869.

Charting the volcano As early as 1869, maps (LEFT) of Haleakala show the two large gaps in the rim through which clouds roll into the crater. Known tracks and trails along the crater floor are also recorded.

Desolate landscape As its early morning mantle of cloud is burnt off by the sun, the floor of Haleakala's crater some 2500ft (760m) below is revealed in all its glory. The slopes and floor of the crater, which since 1960 has been part of the 28 655 acre (11 597ha) Haleakala National Park, are crossed by 30 miles (48km) of tracks and trails which enable visitors to appreciate the natural beauty at close quarters.

313

Haven for hunters *In the late 19th century, when wild goats roamed the crater floor, visitors included a group of Catholic brothers, equipped with guns and warm clothes.*

TRAVELLER'S TALES

In 1866 the American author Mark Twain (INSET), then a reporter for a California newspaper, visited the Hawaiian islands and spent some time on Maui exploring the wonders of Haleakala. In his book about his travels as a young man, *Roughing It*, published six years later, he described his experience of the mountain. He and his companions took two days to reach the summit; on their second night on the mountain, having built a fire, they 'froze and roasted, by turns, all night'.

Like many visitors who stand on the volcano's eastern rim (which has eroded far more than any other part of the crater), Twain was 'aggravated' by the curious sensation he experienced as dawn broke of looking up at, rather than down on, his surroundings. Undeterred by what he called 'this singular fraud perpetrated upon the eye by isolated great altitudes', Twain and his companions gazed down at the 'yawning dead crater, into which we . . . tumbled rocks half as large as a barrel [captured by a member of the party in an engraving used in *Roughing It*, RIGHT] from our perch. . . . It was magnificent sport.'

Into the abyss *The most impressive view into the crater is said to be that from Kalahaku Overlook* (LEFT).

Unique beauty *The silversword plant grows only in Hawaii, and survives in the crater owing to its large, tightly packed cluster of spiky, sabre-like leaves. Like those of desert-dwelling yucca plants, these can store water.*

solving Hina's problem and ensuring a full day of sunlight for the islanders.

Haleakala last erupted in 1790, and is the largest dormant volcanic crater in the world: the rim measures some 20 miles (32km) in circumference. Unlike many volcanic mountains, Haleakala is not perfectly symmetrical. Its eastern slopes are badly eroded and gouged by deep valleys and gorges that were formed by molten lava pouring from the crater down existing river valleys. The western slopes, by contrast, are crisscrossed by small, rain-fed streams. Climbers reach the summit by following a winding road through green meadows and groves of eucalyptus. When the sky is clear the road offers sweeping views over plantations of sugar cane and, south-eastwards, across the Pacific to the mountains of Hawaii.

At its rim, the crater is 7 miles (11km) across, while its floor covers an area of more than 19 sq miles (49km²). The terrain differs from one part to another, and the crater includes areas of forest, desert, meadow and a lake. The northern and eastern areas are used as grazing land, but the western and southern sections are arid, their surface consisting of sands that range in colour from deep chocolate brown to the palest of beiges, or thick layers of grey, russet, brick-red and purple ash and cinders streaked with black lava. Deposits of reddish cinders, 16 in all, some of which rise as high as 1000ft (305m), are dotted across this part of the floor like miniature volcanoes.

These differences in the nature of the terrain of the crater floor are due to the irregularities in the rim. The low eastern sections, which include two huge gaps, Koolau and Kaupo, allow rain-bearing Trade Winds into the crater to water this area of the floor. These clouds, which swirl below the rim of the crater, are also responsible for a curious visual effect, known as a Brocken bow, whereby the shadow of an observer standing on the rim is reflected in the bank of cloud hanging over the higher northern portion of the crater's rim.

Nothing grows on Haleakala's steep-sided inner walls, but a variety of grasses and shrubs have gained a foothold in the ash and cinders on the crater floor. Among them is the silversword plant which, after anything up to 20 years of growth, produces a thick stem that can measure as high as 9ft (2.7m). This is briefly crowned with exquisite purple flowers, after which the plant dies. Some years ago it was in danger of extinction, partly due to grazing by wild goats, and partly because of human collectors: it is now a protected species. Resident animals and birds include goats, pigs, petrels and the Hawaiian goose.

Haleakala holds a special place in Hawaiian culture. Native peoples used to place offerings of food in the crater to appease the gods, and it may once have been a burial ground for Hawaiian chiefs. For modern visitors, however, the crater's multicoloured yet austere beauty and the swirling clouds inside its rim leave the longest-lasting impression.

GIANT'S CAUSEWAY: STAIRWAY TO THE SEA

A promontory off the coast of northern Ireland provides the world's most spectacular example of what can happen when volcanic lava cools slowly: tens of thousands of geometric columns set together in a honeycomb pattern comprise a unique stairway down to the sea.

A ccording to legend, the Irish giant Finn MacCool built a road across the Atlantic waters from his home on the coast of County Antrim in northern Ireland to the Hebridean stronghold of his sworn enemy Finn Gall. He collected hundreds of long stone stakes and hammered them in a course along the seabed, then went home to rest before the assault on Finn Gall. The Scottish giant, however, craftily seized the initiative by crossing from his island of Staffa to Ireland. When MacCool's wife persuaded Finn Gall that the sleeping giant was her infant son, he grew worried about just how big the father might be and fled in terror. As soon as he was safely out to sea he started to rip up the road behind him so that it could not be used again.

Although scientists have now explained the formation of Giant's Causeway, it is easy to understand how the legend came about. Its size alone gives the impression that the causeway is the work of superhuman hands. Viewed from the air it does indeed resemble a paved pathway along 900ft (275m) of the coastline and projecting as far as 500ft (150m) northwards into the Atlantic Ocean. Most of the columns are around 20ft (6m) high, although in places they soar to more than twice that height. Its composition, too, is awesome: some 40 000 basalt columns, all of which are regularly shaped polygons, the majority six-sided hexagons, fit together so precisely that it is difficult to slide a knife between them.

And at the other end of MacCool's road, 75 miles (120km) away, the island of Staffa is ringed by 135ft (40m)

Stepping stones *The view towards the Antrim coast at low tide reveals many of the 40 000 step-like columns that comprise the Giant's Causeway. There may once have been more columns – broken remains litter the beach – and some have probably been carried out to sea. The columnar formation, which covers 5 acres (2ha), may well continue beneath the Antrim soil.*

Battered by rough seas
The Giant's Causeway is composed of hard igneous basalt, low in silica and rich in magnesium and iron, which not only gives the pillars their dark colour but also makes them extremely tough. This reduces the rate at which they are eroded by the turbulent North Atlantic waters that separate northern Ireland and the Scottish Hebrides.

GIANT'S CAUSEWAY: STAIRWAY TO THE SEA

Rocky wonderland
Natural wonders abound along the entire coastline of County Antrim. Among the features that line the shores are fine beaches, dramatic headlands, sea caves that reverberate to the sound of the pounding surf, and towering cliffs composed of black basalt columns similar to those of the causeway itself.

Basalt patchwork *The symmetry of the columns of the causeway is more apparent from above. Some have four, five, eight or ten sides, but most are regular hexagons which range in size from 15 to 20in (38 to 50cm) across and fit together perfectly.*

high cliffs, composed of the same sheer basalt columns as the causeway. There, Fingal's Cave, named by the English naturalist Sir Joseph Banks after Finn Gall, cuts into the island for a distance of 200ft (60m). Its floor, walls and roof are all made of black basalt columns.

The columns at Giant's Causeway are grouped into three natural platforms, known as Grand Causeway, Middle Causeway and Little Causeway. Within these groups, certain formations have been given fanciful names, including the Wishing Chair, the Fan, Chimney Tops and the aptly named Giant's Organ, which towers 39ft (12m) above the ground like a set of church organ pipes.

Giant's Causeway was discovered by a Bishop of Derry in 1692 and, although a few observers made their way there during the 18th century, it remained largely unnoticed until the end of the century. Then, a series of accurate drawings and paintings commissioned by Frederick Hervey, Earl Bishop of Derry, from members of the Dublin Society and Britain's Royal Society, alerted both the scientific community and the world at large to this strange collection of rocks. Among visitors in the early 19th century was the novelist William Thackeray, who wrote that the rocks looked 'as if some old old princess of an old old fairy tale were dragon guarded within'.

Legends apart, various theories have been proposed to account for the origins of the causeway. It was once thought to have been a petrified bamboo forest, or to have been the result of the precipitation of minerals from sea water. Today, however, most geologists agree that it is volcanic in origin. Around 50 million years ago, much of northern Ireland and western Scotland became volcanically active. Vents in the Earth's crust opened time and time

again, pouring lava over the landscape to a depth of more than 500ft (180m). As the lava cooled it solidified, to be overlaid by yet more lava as a fresh eruption occurred. Where molten lava overlays a flat bed of solidified basalt, it cools and contracts very slowly and evenly. The chemical composition of the lava means that the pressure built up in the cooling layer acts equally around a central point and pulls the lava apart in a regular shape, usually a hexagon. This need occur only once for the pattern to be set, and the hexagon is then repeated throughout the entire layer. As cooling extends into the sheet of basalt itself, a series of hexagonal columns results.

In the topmost layer, which cooled first, the rocks shrank and cracked into regular prismatic patterns, rather like the mud on a dried riverbed. As cooling and shrinkage continued, the cracks on the surface extended downwards through the entire lava mass, splitting the rock into upright columns. Over thousands of years, the power of the sea has gradually eroded the tough basalt columns so that today they stand at different heights. The speed of cooling was also responsible for the colour of the columns. As the rock lost its heat, it oxidised, turning from red to brown to grey and, finally, to black.

The causeway has inspired generations of artists and writers – some of the most eloquent were the early 19th-century Romantics. One of their number called it 'the altar and temple of Nature…executed with a symmetry and grace, a grandeur and a boldness which Nature alone could accomplish'. Perhaps the most fitting epithet however, is that of explorer and naturalist Sir Joseph Banks: 'Compared to this, what are the cathedrals or palaces built by man?…mere models or playthings'.

Musical cavern *The most lasting testimonial to the volcanic activity that created both the Giant's Causeway and Fingal's Cave on the island of Staffa was the music composed by the German Felix Mendelssohn. After his stay on Staffa in 1829, he transformed the rhythmic sounds as the Atlantic breakers swirled around the cave into his* Hebrides Overture, *more popularly known as 'Fingal's Cave'.*

MÉTÉORA: PINNACLES OF HISTORY

For more than a thousand years tall spines of sheer rock, fixed in the shadow of the Pindhos Mountains in Greece, have provided sanctuary for monks seeking peace and solitude to contemplate the will of God.

On the flank of the Pindhos Mountains, at the western edge of the plain of Thessaly in the heart of northern Greece, 24 gigantic perpendicular rocks rise from the ground. Etched by wind and rain into curious shapes, these monoliths echo to the chants and prayers of a religious brotherhood, for since the ninth century, an ascetic community of monks has chosen to live perched precariously on these ancient pinnacles.

The rocks of Météora are composed of a mixture of sandstone and conglomerate (waterworn fragments of rock bound together by a natural cement). They were formed about 60 million years ago as the rocky bed of a sea that covered what is now Thessaly. A series of violent earth movements in the area then thrust the seabed upwards, forming a high plateau and causing numerous fault lines to develop in the thick layer of sandstone. Subsequent weathering of the fractured sandstone by water, wind and

extremes of temperature left behind the huge pillars of rock, marked by horizontal seams which geologists maintain were made by the waters of a prehistoric sea.

The Greek historian Herodotus recorded in the fifth century BC that local people believed the plain of Thessaly had once been flooded by sea water and encircled by rocky shores. If this is accurate, there was probably an inundation at the end of the last Ice Age, around 8000 BC. However, Herodotus failed to mention the rocky pinnacles of Météora, and they are not recorded in the writings of any other ancient Greek authors. This somewhat surprising omission has been taken as evidence in some quarters that the pinnacles did not exist 2000 years ago – a theory dismissed by modern geologists.

The first people to inhabit Météora were hermits, who sheltered from the elements in hollows and fissures in the rock towers, several of which reach 1800ft (550m) above the plain. This great height, combined with the sheerness of the cliff walls, deterred all but the most determined visitors from interrupting their meditations. Initially the hermits led a life of solitude, meeting only on Sundays and special feast days to worship and pray in a chapel built at the foot of the rock known as Dhoupiani. By the end of

Natural formation *Earth movements and erosion created the huge monoliths at Météora. Some of the pinnacles, which average 1000ft (300m) in height, are needle-like, others resemble giant tusks, still more have been described as vast grey stalagmites.*

Out of this world *A Greek word, Météora means literally 'in the heavens above', an apt description of the monastery of the Holy Trinity, which was built in 1458.*

METÉORA: PINNACLES OF HISTORY

Etched by erosion
Metéora has been called 'the rocky forest of Greece'. Vertical grooves in the mighty masses of dark grey stone that form its pinnacles have been scoured out by rainwater trickling down the face of the cliffs. The horizontal lines are much older and were formed by the lapping of waves against the rocks when the plain of Thessaly lay under the ocean.

the 12th century, a loosely organised ascetic community had evolved, whose members still respected the ideals of solitude.

By the 14th century, the Byzantine Empire's 800-year supremacy over northern Greece was being increasingly threatened as Serbian kings and Turkish raiders vied for control of the fertile plain of Thessaly. Peaceful monastic communities were particularly vulnerable, and in 1344 Athanasios Koinovitis, from the community on Mount Athos, led a group of followers to Metéora. Between 1356 and 1372 he founded the Great Meteoron monastery on the pinnacle of Broad Rock, a place ideally suited to the monks' needs, for they were safe from political upheaval and had complete control over access to the monastery. Visitors could reach it only by climbing a long ladder, which was drawn up whenever the monks felt threatened.

In the 15th and 16th centuries, the few simple dwellings became inadequate to house the numbers of men seeking refuge at Metéora and larger, more sophisticated buildings were constructed. The ladder, too, was replaced – by a nerve-racking net-and-rope device operated by a windlass from a gantry overhanging the rock.

A Russian religious scholar described his trip in the net in 1896. It was, he stated, 'an agonising lift, the rope was going here and there all the time, dragging me along until at last it reached the top'. But even then his terrifying adventure was not over because '. . . as they pulled me towards the wooden platform, they overturned me over the abyss. Horrified, I closed my eyes and nearly lost consciousness.' Today, 115 steps hewn out of the rock provide a slightly less precarious access to the summit.

In 1517, the monks Nectarios and Theophanes built the monastery of Varlaám, named after a 14th-century hermit who had chosen this place as his retreat. They established one of the most austere religious orders at Metéora; among its principal practices were long, nocturnal prayer sessions and ritual flagellation. The monastery was reputed to house two holy relics, the finger of St John and the shoulder blade of St Andrew.

Although the design of the monastery is simple, the chapels of All Saints and the Three Hierarchs are adorned with frescoes. Those in the Chapel of All Saints, painted in 1548 by Franco Catellano, depict scenes from the lives of Jesus Christ and the Virgin Mary. Together with equally beautiful works of art painted on the walls of the monastery of St Nicholas by Theophanes the Cretan in 1527, these frescoes provide a powerful insight into the style and techniques of artists of the Byzantine Empire.

In spite of the restricted space, between the 13th and 16th centuries 24 different monasteries were founded at Metéora, each comprising one or two houses in which were located the monks' cells, a refectory, a church or chapel, and – in some instances – a library. Today, all but five are uninhabited. Varlaám, Great Meteoron and Holy Trinity house monks, while St Stephen and Roussanou are home to communities of nuns.

The eerie fascination of Metéora's geology and the spiritual pull which the place exerts are largely responsible for its current demise as a religious centre. As Metéora increasingly becomes a museum piece which attracts thousands of tourists each year, aspiring young monks and nuns are unwilling to join the monasteries, while older devotees flee from them, to seek solitude elsewhere.

Building achievement
Bathed in early morning sunlight, the structures of Great Meteoron stand out on the Broad Rock. The monks who built them in the late 14th century used only ropes and nets to haul up every block of stone and each piece of timber from the plateau more than 1300ft (400m) below.

Restored to glory The monastery of Varlaám was damaged in World War II and the subsequent civil war in Greece. Like the other Metéora monasteries, it has been rebuilt and is now a major tourist attraction.

Simple life The stark interior of the wooden and stone living quarters at the monastery of Varlaám reflects the humble way of life led by the monks who dwelt there. By contrast, the monastery's two chapels – the Chapel of All Saints and the Chapel of the Three Hierarchs – are decorated with well-preserved, brightly coloured frescoes and finely detailed icons.

MOUNT ARARAT: THE PAINFUL MOUNTAIN

The towering summit of Ararat remained unconquered until the 19th century, for monks believed that no one should attempt to reach the 'sacred top' where the remains of Noah's Ark were said to rest.

The dazzling summit of Mount Ararat, capped by a permanent layer of glistening snow, soars towards the heavens like a magnificent silver-beaked bird. The peak that is known locally as Ağrı Dağı, 'the painful mountain', rises in solitary splendour from the plain of the River Aras, providing a dramatic contrast to the dusty, rugged surrounding landscape. Mount Ararat's fame rests not on the natural beauty of its symmetrical, deceptively smooth flanks and brilliant white crest, however, but on its Biblical associations, for this mountain is held to be the first to have pierced the receding waters of the Great Flood and offer a safe berth for Noah's Ark.

Mount Ararat in fact comprises two peaks 7 miles (11km) apart connected by a rough-topped ridge: Great Ararat – at 16854ft (5137m) the highest mountain in Turkey – and Little Ararat, which rises to 12782ft (3896m) above sea level. Both are volcanic in origin, and composed of layers of ash and lava, although there is no longer any sign of a crater on either of the summits. The flanks, however, are still covered in the small cones and fissures usually associated with volcanic activity. Many of the rocks of the valley floor are likewise partly composed of ash.

The upper and lower slopes of Mount Ararat are largely barren. Despite a permanent snowline at around 14500ft (4420m), water is scarce on the mountain and a few birch trees are the only vegetation that can survive. Around the middle slopes, however, from 5000 to 11500ft (1500 to 3500m), the terrain is lusher, and Kurdish farmers graze their sheep on the good pastureland. Few other animals make their home here, although there were certainly greater numbers in the early 19th century when the British diplomat James Morier, reported 'bears, small tygers, lynxes and lions'. Wild cats and snakes may have inhabited the mountain in medieval times, giving rise to rumours of dragons, but colourful local tales of small snow worms so cold they could cool a large bowl of sherbert have never been substantiated.

These legends of fantastic beasts roaming its slopes may have contributed to Ararat's reputation as unclimbable. Its daunting mystical aura and the physical hazards involved, which included avalanches, blinding mists, falling boulders and sudden, severe changes in the weather, meant that it was not scaled until 1829, when Johann Jacob von Parrot, a 37-year-old German professor, reached the summit at

Gentle giant *One of the epithets that has been applied to Ararat refers to its size: 'the Armenian Giant'. The mountain dominates its surroundings, in terms of both its height and bulk, measuring some 25 miles (40km) in circumference.*

Ararat is not only beautiful, it also brings considerable benefit to the land at its feet. Meltwater from the peak flows freely down the hillsides, making this part of the Anatolian plain, near the boundaries of Turkey, Iran and Armenia abundantly fertile.

his third attempt. He celebrated his achievement by planting a wooden cross there. Others followed, including, in 1876, the British scholar and statesman James Bryce. Gazing from the summit across the dusty plain to territories ruled for centuries by tsars, shahs and sultans, he was overwhelmed by a sense of history and declared: 'If it was indeed here that man first set foot on the unpeopled earth, one could imagine how the great dispersal went as the races spread themselves down from these sacred heights... No more imposing centre of the world could be imagined.'

Mount Ararat's mystical reputation stems from the Bible. God, so disgusted by the wickedness of the human race that he decided to wipe it out with a cataclysmic flood, spared only the righteous Noah, his family and a male and female specimen of every bird and animal – all of whom sheltered in a great ark. 'And in the seventh month, on the seventeenth day of the month, the ark came to rest upon the mountains of Ararat' (*Genesis* 8:4). Once the waters subsided, Noah, his family and the animals left the vessel.

The Bible is not specific about which mountain of the ancient land of Ararat was the resting place of the Ark. The legends of the Armenian and Persian peoples living in this area of eastern Turkey, and predating the Christian era, firmly place the landing site at Ağrı Dağı. The Armenians believed that they were the first people to

Inspired to climb *In his book* Transcaucasia and Ararat, *James Bryce described the 1876 ascent of Ararat. He was encouraged, he said,* 'by the sight of the glittering peak above... like an Eastern beauty, beginning to draw over its face the noonday veil of cloud...'

Building Noah's Ark

According to Genesis, *God chose the 600-year-old Noah to be saved because he was a 'just man'. He gave precise instructions: the Ark was to be made of gopher wood and lined inside and out with pitch so that it would be water-resistant. It was to be 300 cubits long, 50 cubits wide and 30 cubits high. (A cubit, traditionally the length of a man's forearm from the elbow to the tip of the middle finger, measured between 17 and 22in/ 43 and 56cm.)*

Noah, his wife, his three sons, Ham, Shem and Japheth, and their wives were the only members of the human race God thought worthy of survival.

Nec mora continuo exequitur Noe iussa tonantis
Materies abiegnus erat fortissimus asser.

Sic qui feruenti Christum veneratur amore,
Permanet incolumis curis neq; subiacet ullis.

populate the Earth after the Flood, while the Persians called the land around Ararat the 'cradle of the human race'.

Sightings of the Ark on the mountain have been recorded since the fifth century BC, when Chaldean (Babylonian) priests are said to have scraped the carbon coating from pieces of wreckage. Medieval travellers brought back tales of having seen relics of the Ark, and over the centuries additional claims of sightings have been made. Bryce himself discovered a possible relic: 'amid blocks of lava, a piece of wood about four feet long and five inches wide, which had obviously been shaped by means of a tool'. In 1916, a Russian pilot flying over the mountain reported seeing the remnants of a large ship. Tsar Nicholas II sent out a search party, which returned with notes and photographs, all of which disappeared during the Russian Revolution.

Scientific examination – including carbon dating – of existing wooden fragments indicates that none of the remains is old enough to date back to Noah. One theory proposes that they are all that is left of a centuries-old monastery (once a place of pilgrimage), destroyed by an earthquake in 1840. No conclusive physical proof of the Ark's existence has yet been found. Ararat continues to enthral those who witness its splendour nonetheless: in the words of James Morier, writing in 1818: 'It is perfect in all its parts…everything is in harmony.'

Artistic vision *The Flood – with its scope for drowned bodies – has long influenced makers of still and moving images. The 19th-century* French engraver Gustave Doré included the flight of the dove (ABOVE); in his 1929 film Noah's Ark (BELOW), Michael Curtiz has bodies to the fore.

THE CONES OF CAPPADOCIA

Needles of rock thrust upwards from the plain of Cappadocia, in central Turkey, to create a startling, almost unearthly landscape. The early Christians, who made their homes in this desolate terrain, adapted their living conditions to the environment in the most extraordinary ways.

I n the uplands of Turkey's Anatolian heartland lies the ancient region of Cappadocia. Riven with valleys and dotted with extinct volcanoes, the Cappadocian plateau was once a major trading crossroads, traversed by merchant caravans and warring armies alike. South of the capital, Kayseri, is a broad territory of strange, haunting landscapes dominated by rock cones sculpted by driving wind.

The process that shaped this unique landscape began when the volcanoes of Cappadocia erupted about 8 million years ago. They deposited countless layers of ash, lava, debris and mud, raising the altitude of the land by more than 1000ft (300m) to form a prominent plateau.

Millions of years of compression turned the volcanic ash into a soft, pale rock called tufa. This was overlaid by a thinner layer of dark, hardened lava known as basalt. As the basalt cooled, it contracted and split, laying itself open to the erosive action of the weather. Streams and floods crisscrossed the plateau, cutting ever deeper, and earthquake shocks and winter frosts helped break up the layers of tufa and basalt.

Today, the process of erosion continues, slowly wearing down the pinnacled landscape and exposing the multi-coloured layers of earth. These range from the palest tufa, through tones of ochre, russet and deep chestnut (caused by mineral impurities), to the black of the basalt.

The desolate appearance of the terrain belies the fertility of a soil rich in mineral nutrients. If carefully irrigated, the valleys can produce abundant crops of fruit, cereals, and vegetables. A closer look at this extraordinary landscape

Bizarre landscape
Curious-looking rock cones rise up from the plain near Ürgüp (RIGHT). *The pinnacles grow higher as the valley floor at their base is worn away by water and frost. They are then whittled down by the wind until, finally, they collapse.*

Fairy chimneys *A few miles north-east of Göreme lies Zelve, noted for its Christian churches carved into the cliffs and its capped pinnacles known as fairy chimneys* (LEFT). *These are tall pillars of soft rock that are partly protected from erosion by the black conical boulders of weather-resistant basalt resting on top of them.*

THE CONES OF CAPPADOCIA

Rock chapels *The Christian builders of the churches of Göreme* (LEFT) *carved domes, arches, columns and even benches and tables out of the soft tufa, then decorated the interiors with murals.*

A traveller's tale *In the early 18th century, Paul Lucas, a Frenchman, visited Cappadocia. His account of his findings, including an etching of inhabited cones* (ABOVE), *was widely disbelieved.*

reveals the most unusual signs of human habitation, for the soft tufa has been carved and tunnelled to create womb-like spaces where people lived and worshipped long ago. The greatest concentration of these rock dwellings is 56 miles (90km) south-west of Kayseri.

The most famous inhabitants of the cliffs and cones of Cappadocia were the early Christians. Christianity was brought to Anatolia by St Peter in the first century AD. In the fourth century – the early years of the Byzantine Empire – a native Cappadocian, Basil the Great, was made Bishop of Caesarea (now Kayseri). He encouraged new monastic settlements in the valleys of Cappadocia and for the next thousand years the monks carved away at the tufa, creating numerous churches and hermitages.

These masons imitated the free-standing architecture of the Byzantine era. Early churches were based on the simplest plan, with barrel-vaulting, a rectangular nave and a small apse, the whole no more than 26ft (8m) long. Larger churches were built in the 10th and 11th centuries on the Byzantine cross model, with central and side domes. They were all decorated in Byzantine style, and their murals depicting the life of Christ and the saints have

survived to the present day, thanks to the darkness and dryness of the church interiors. In the eighth century, the Iconoclasts, a Christian sect which forbade the worship of icons, destroyed many of the early frescoes and replaced them with geometric patterns, but by the tenth century there was a return to rich and colourful representations. Patrons vied with each other to hire the best mural artists and some of the most magnificent paintings from this period can be seen in the churches of the Göreme and Ürgüp valleys. The Turkish invasions of the 13th century dealt the death blow to church building.

South of Nevsehir are a number of underground towns carved on many levels out of the tufa. These warren-like excavations, whose inhabitants were known as troglodytes, could each house several thousand people hiding from enemy armies. Early Christians used these underground refuges, but their last occupants were Turks escaping from Egyptian troops in the 19th century.

Carved-out churches and underground cities add a human dimension to Cappadocia, but essentially it is the vast landscape of extraordinary rock shapes, created over millions of years, that takes the observer's breath away.

CITY IN THE ROCK

The Cappadocia settlements were extremely advanced. Shafts gave entrance to the city, and were used for ventilation, while water came through a shaft sunk down to the water table. Streets connected one area with another; wheel doors blocked 'no entry' zones. Rooms were cut into the tufa, with major furnishings such as beds also hewn from the solid rock. Niches provided storage space and housings for oil lamps.

Key
1 Air shaft 2 Box bed
3 Tunnel street 4 Wheel door
5 Room used as chapel

Underground city

Derinkuyu (RIGHT) *was a subterranean refuge for early Christians hiding from Roman, Arab and Turkish armies. There were many underground cities in Cappadocia, some connected by tunnels several miles long. They had storerooms, living quarters, wells, air shafts, pits to catch invaders and a maze of interconnecting passages. With doorways sealed by large boulders, they made impregnable, if dark and uncomfortable, underground fortresses.*

NEFTA OASIS: GARDEN IN THE DESERT

A startling patch of green in a sea of sand, Nefta Oasis is a luxuriant garden of palm trees, mimosa, vines and succulent fruit. White-domed mosques and shrines are studded across the emerald landscape, for Nefta is also one of Tunisia's major religious centres.

A ccording to Arabic legend, the first spring of fresh water to issue from the earth once the Great Flood had abated was discovered at Nefta by Kostel, one of Noah's grandsons. From that spring developed a fertile oasis which today is encircled by the barren, rolling hills of south-west Tunisia.

While the blazing desert sun bakes the surrounding land, water wells up from beneath Nefta's soil. A combination of natural forces and human ingenuity has created Nefta Oasis and La Corbeille – a verdant, palm-embroidered hollow lying immediately to the north of the oasis. At Nefta, water that has accumulated in the permeable rock layer below ground is forced upwards along more than 150 fault lines in the underlying rock strata. (Since the 1960s, engineers have sunk artesian wells in the rock strata to tap into this natural resource.) At La Corbeille, cracks and fissures in the sides of the crater itself send water bubbling to the surface.

An intricate network of irrigation ditches distributes spring water to Nefta's fertile gardens, where orderly rows of date palms – 35 000 of them in all – are planted in square plots. Around one-third of the trees are of the Degla variety, said to be the finest in the world. The delicious, energy-rich fruits (which have been likened to 'fingers of

Water of life *In desert areas such as Nefta, underground water may have accumulated more than 40 000 years ago. Some reserves are unlikely ever to be replenished.*

Ancient way station
Nefta lies among desert hills near Tunisia's border with Algeria, 250 miles (400km) south-west of the capital Tunis. The oasis is not only a haven for desert travellers crossing the Sahara, it is also a shelter for pilgrims and a stopping point for birds migrating to and from the African continent.

NEFTA OASIS: GARDEN IN THE DESERT

light and honey') are not the only product of the palms. Their leaves are cut into strips and dried, then woven into baskets and other containers; date stones are ground and fed to animals, and the tree sap is used to make a wine known as *lagmi*. Once the tree itself has become unproductive (which may only be after 200 years) it is harvested for timber. In addition, date palms play an important part in protecting other, more vulnerable, species. Their mature height of 100ft (30m) provides a screen against the strong desert winds, and their large, spreading leaves moderate temperatures that can exceed 46°C (115°F) in the shade. In this sheltered environment, farmers grow vegetables and fruits such as pomegranates, figs, peaches, apricots, oranges and lemons.

To the south, on the edge of the town of Nefta, lies a vast and treacherous seasonal salt lake known as the Chott el Djerid. During summer, the sun bakes the surface of the dried-up lake to a hard crust, and at its centre salt deposits gleam like snow. When the water table below Nefta's oasis rises in autumn, however, the Chott is flooded. In spring, as the water level falls again, the area is transformed into a colossal swamp of salty mud.

In the 1980s a highway was built to transport people and vehicles across the Chott. Before the road was constructed travellers could cross only by keeping to a narrow path marked by palm trunks (the Chott was once known as 'the Lake of Marks'). Those who ventured off this trail did so at their peril. In the 12th century an Arabic writer recorded the loss of a caravan of a thousand camels which was completely engulfed by mud when one of the leading animals strayed from the path.

The open basket *Date palms flourish in the depression known as La Corbeille (French for open basket). Water seeps out of the ground there, and is directed southwards along a tree-lined channel to the main oasis at Nefta. In 1912, the British travel writer Norman Douglas described La Corbeille as 'a circular vale of immoderate plant luxuriance, a never-ending delight to the eye'.*

As well as a sanctuary and a source of succulent produce, Nefta has also been for 1000 years the centre of the mystical Islamic sect known as the Sufis. The association between Nefta and Sufism (the word comes from the Arabic for 'mystic') started shortly after the Muslims conquered the region in AD 670. Ibrahim ibn Adham, the sect's founder, went there in search of solitude – to study the Koran and contemplate the will of Allah. Tunisian Sufis established *zaouias*, or 'fraternities', in many rural areas. There, local

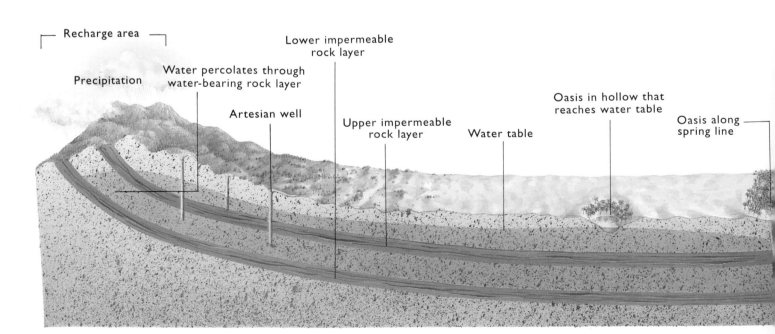

Recharge area

Precipitation

Water percolates through water-bearing rock layer

Artesian well

Lower impermeable rock layer

Upper impermeable rock layer

Water table

Oasis in hollow that reaches water table

Oasis along spring line

Sweet water *The pure liquid from Nefta's springs provides the town's drinking water. Many of the pools are also used for bathing, although scorpions abound.*

people were offered shelter and education, and sometimes justice. At Nefta, the Zaouia of Sidi Ibrahim, overlooking La Corbeille, consists of a series of tombs (including those of the saint and his son), courtyards and reading rooms. As the holy reputation of the oasis grew, so other men of religion were attracted to Nefta, further enhancing its spiritual stature. As a result, the old quarter of Nefta today harbours more than 100 shrines and 24 mosques, whose white cupolas shimmer in the brilliant desert sunlight.

Recharge area

Water-bearing rock   Lake in depression

Water table   Impermeable rock layer

Spring line

Fault line

Succulent harvest *The date palm, one of the world's oldest cultivated plants, takes 15 years to mature, after which it yields up to 200lb (90kg) of fruit a year.*

BURIED WATER

Fertile patches occur in the desert in areas where water is trapped in rocks below the surface. Rain falling over distant hills percolates down and seeps horizontally through porous rock. Where it is restricted between two impermeable layers, pressure builds up and at weak spots or fault lines in the rock water is forced up to the surface. Artesian wells are often sunk in these places.

GREAT RIFT VALLEY

*From the Middle East to southern Africa the Earth
is being torn apart along a vast fissure in its crust.
In the Rift Valley, remains of the earliest known
ancestors of modern humans have been unearthed.*

The longest continuous crack on the surface of the planet contains the lowest point on land and is flanked by some of the world's highest volcanic mountains. It holds several of the Earth's largest lakes and provides a seaway between Europe and the Orient. The scar that is the Great Rift Valley is of awesome proportions, measuring up to 60 miles (100km) across, and with walls falling to depths of between 1500 and 2600ft (450 and 800m) from the surrounding plateaux.

From Syria in the north to Mozambique in the south the Rift passes through 20 states and stretches 4200 miles (6750km) – almost one-fifth of the circumference of the globe. It is a spectacular example of what happens when two of the Earth's crustal plates (one bearing the Arabian Peninsula and East Africa, the other the remainder of the African continent) separate under land: constant shifting along the line of the Rift widens lakes and rivers and deepens gullies. In time, the sea may flood in, cutting off East Africa from the rest of the continent.

The term valley is a misnomer, since the course of the Great Rift is invaded by mountains and plateaux, and in southern Ethiopia it even splits into two branches before

Depths and hollows *Once a volcanic peak, Ngorongoro in Tanzania is now a crater some 12 miles (20km) across and 2000ft (600m) deep.* *Even in times of drought, the springs and saltwater lake that make the crater so attractive to animal and bird life can be relied upon.*

336

Red Lake *Lake Natron in Tanzania, stained red by the seasonal growth of algae, provides one of the most uncanny sights on Earth. Vast spirals of sodium carbonate, thrust* *up from the bowels of the Earth by geysers, bubble to the surface of the lake and crystallise into slabs of natron that float across the waters of the lake like miniature icebergs.*

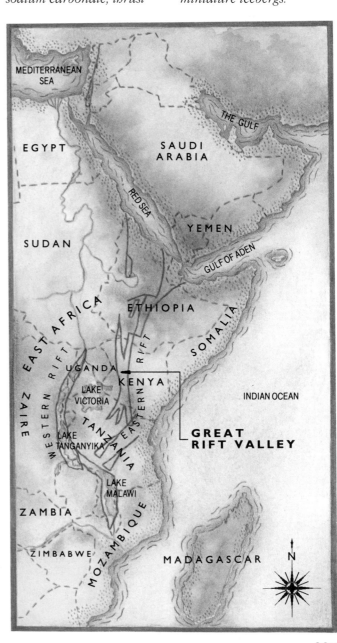

337

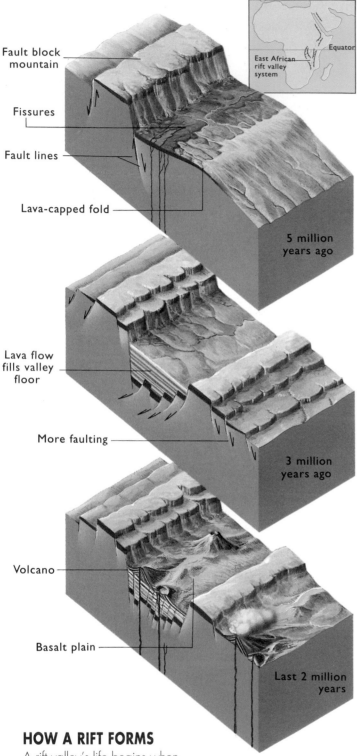

Fault block mountain

Fissures

Fault lines

Lava-capped fold

5 million years ago

East African rift valley system

Equator

Lava flow fills valley floor

More faulting

3 million years ago

Volcano

Basalt plain

Last 2 million years

HOW A RIFT FORMS

A rift valley's life begins when magma heats the Earth's crust, making it expand and bulge outwards. Eventually part of the crust collapses to form a steep wall, or fault block mountain, along a fault line. Further upward movement of the crust creates a series of fault block mountains resembling a staircase. In the faulting process the central block of land subsides to form a flat-bottomed trench (graben). Magma reaches the surface via the faults, pouring out through volcanoes or fissures in the valley floor to form basalt plains.

re-forming in the area of Lake Victoria on the Tanzania–Uganda border. The lakes, seas and depressions that line its path, however, give the clearest indication of its progression.

The Rift, starting in Syria, forms the valley of the River Jordan and the Dead Sea. The surface of the Dead Sea, at 1312ft (400m) below sea level, is the lowest point on all the continents. At such depths the valley acts like a giant basin into which water flows, but from which it rarely drains. Instead, in the high temperatures of this region, rapid evaporation makes any large body of water such as a lake very salty. The salinity of the Dead Sea (some 30 per cent, ten times that of ocean water) enables bathers to float easily in its waters.

Around 500 miles (800km) from the Rift's beginnings, ocean floods in, and the scar travels the length of the Gulf of Aqaba and the Red Sea before swinging into the continent of Africa at the broad, fan-shaped Danakil Depression in Ethiopia. Salt waters akin to those of the Dead Sea once flooded this 2000 sq mile (5000km²) flat plain, some 510ft (155m) below sea level. But all the water evaporated, leaving behind deposits of rock salt that in places are 3 miles (5km) thick.

Of all the lakes that have been carved along the Rift, the freshwater 'Great Lakes' of East Africa – Tanganyika, Malawi and Victoria – offer a marvellous illustration of evolution in action. Just as the isolated continent of Australia boasts several unique species of animal, so the waters of these lakes, separated by vast expanses of dry, barren land, contain several hundred fish species that do not exist anywhere else in the world.

Victoria, which at 330ft (100m) deep is the shallowest of the three lakes, is also the youngest, having existed for some 750 000 years. It was formed when land to its west rose, damming the course of several rivers. As each river expanded and deepened to form a small lake, in addition to the fish that already existed new species evolved by taking advantage of the different habitats on offer. Lake Victoria itself also changed, at times flooding to take in creatures from what had been isolated waters, at others drying out, returning species to seclusion. In the case of the narrow, deeper and much older lakes of Malawi and Tanganyika – over two million years old – it seems more likely that new species simply evolved from populations that became isolated because of their habits.

Since rift valleys occur above 'hot spots' in the Earth's crust, where differences in temperature and density cause molten magma to rise towards the surface of the planet, volcanic activity along their length is common. So it is in East Africa, where several massive volcanoes dot the landscape. Mounts Kilimanjaro (on the Kenya–Tanzania border) and Kenya (in Kenya), the highest peaks on the continent,

White gold *The Danakil Depression glistens white with rock salt, an important commodity in an area where bodies lose their own salt fast, and where the infertile land makes growing crops impossible. Working in temperatures that often exceed 52°C (125°F), men use poles to pry chunks of salt away from the rock bed.*

sit along the line of the Rift. In northern Tanzania, the collapsed crater of a third volcanic summit, Ngorongoro, provides one of Africa's premier wildlife sanctuaries.

The Serengeti plain to the west supports 100 times more animals than Ngorongoro. But since the crater benefits from a natural irrigation system and is almost never dry, it can provide water and grazing all year round. The 2 million animals that make their home on the Serengeti, by contrast, must migrate to fresh pastures in the dry season.

Sandwiched between these two wildlife havens lies Olduvai gorge, a cleft within a cleft that is more than 330ft (100m) deep and nearly 10 miles (15km) long. Millions of years ago, as silt and sand drained from the seasonal lakes and streams that watered what was then the Serengeti plateau, they were laid down in the valley. Volcanic activity contributed lava, ash and cinders to the layers of accumulated debris. Finally, when the land configuration changed yet again, the rushing waters of a new stream carved the gorge, the walls of which revealed not only strata of natural materials, but also fossil bones and artefacts.

Owing largely to the work of British archaeologist and anthropologist Louis Leakey, his wife Mary and their son

Family of man *Louis Leakey's son Richard* (RIGHT) *continued his father's work at Olduvai. Skulls excavated here include those of the most recent ancestor of modern humans,* Homo erectus, *which existed from 1.6 million to 200 000 years ago, and of* Australopithecus, *which is between 3.7 and 1.6 million years old.*

Grazing ground *The rich grasslands of Ngorongoro crater floor provide permanent pastures for 25 000–30 000 herbivorous animals. In addition to zebras and wildebeest, Ngorongoro supports a huge population of black rhino. It is thought that the abundance of shrubs, herbs and clover on which they feed more than outweighs the lack of the bush cover that they generally prefer.*

Pink paradise *Like Lake Natron, Lake Magadi in Kenya resembles a vast cauldron bubbling with soda and alive with algae. Only flamingoes can profit from these intensely alkaline waters, sieving them through their horny beaks for the teeming plant life that constitutes the major part of their diet.*

Pseudotropheus auratus
3¼in (9cm) herbivore

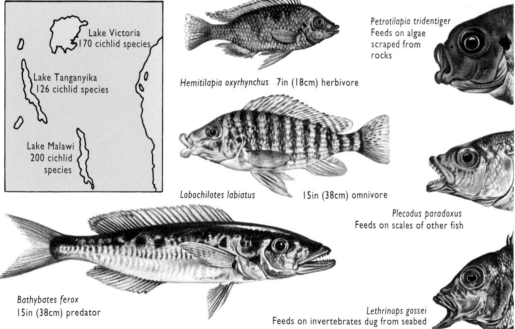

Lake Victoria
170 cichlid species

Lake Tanganyika
126 cichlid species

Lake Malawi
200 cichlid species

Hemitilapia oxyrhynchus 7in (18cm) herbivore

Petrotilapia tridentiger
Feeds on algae scraped from rocks

Lobochilotes labiatus   15in (38cm) omnivore

Plecodus paradoxus
Feeds on scales of other fish

Bathybates ferox
15in (38cm) predator

Lethrinops gossei
Feeds on invertebrates dug from seabed

UNIQUE ISOLATION

The Great Lakes of Africa contain an extraordinary diversity of fish species, most of them the bright freshwater tropical fish of the Cichlidae family. A large number of cichlids are unique to the lakes and provide a perfect example of the evolution of species. Their varying jaw and teeth configurations are adapted to the type of food they eat and they have evolved a range of body forms: predators, for instance, are torpedo-shaped for speed. To attract mates, many are also highly patterned or coloured.

Richard, Olduvai has yielded portions of the rich tapestry of human evolution. In 1959, the Leakeys came upon the first almost complete skull of a human-like creature of the genus *Australopithecus* ('southern ape'), trapped between layers that can be precisely dated at 1.9 and 1.7 million years old. This hominid had a small cranium that enclosed a brain only one-third the size of that of a modern human, but the shape of the base of his skull revealed that he walked upright on two feet, rather than using his forelimbs for extra stability as do apes. More than 50 hominid skulls have been uncovered at Olduvai, and other, even older, finds farther north in Ethiopia suggest that this part of Africa was the birthplace of the human species.

The Great Rift Valley is many things: cradle of humankind, wildlife sanctuary, scenic wonder. The most spectacular feature of the greatest crack on the Earth's surface is that it is constantly shifting and, as it does so, water invades more and more of the land. Eventually the crack may become a tear, and East Africa will finally separate from the mainland, an island continent in a vast new ocean.

341

GLISTENING KILIMANJARO

Rising majestically from the grassy plains of East Africa is the continent's highest mountain and one of the largest extinct volcanoes in the world. The snow-capped peak of Kilimanjaro stands proud against a vivid turquoise sky.

J ust 200 miles (320km) south of the equator is a place where the snow never melts and ice sheets hold fast all year round. That place is the summit of Kilimanjaro, at 19 340ft (5895m) the highest point in Africa. Its very name, Swahili for 'the mountain that glistens', derives from the fact that, although its foot lies in the tropics, the climate at its head resembles a Siberian winter.

Kilimanjaro is in Tanzania, very near the Kenyan border, in East Africa. Its sheer bulk – it is some 60 miles (100km) long and 47 miles (75km) across – is all the more impressive because the mountain stands alone, with no range of adjoining peaks to detract from its splendour. It was formed two million years ago when a period of volcanic activity resulted in continuous streams of lava rising from the Earth's core. As the lava from one eruption cooled and solidified, it was overlain by a fresh stream when renewed turbulence ripped the Earth apart. Consequently, Kilimanjaro today comprises three separate summits, which correspond to three periods of upheaval: Kibo is the central, highest cone, flanked by Mawenzi to the east and Shira to the west. This is not the whole story of Kilimanjaro's birth, however. Once the volcanic activity had ceased, the forces of erosion began to play their part in shaping the mountain.

The lowest of the peaks, Shira, resulted from the initial eruption that gave rise to the original summit. The collapse and subsequent erosion of that summit formed a plateau

Solitary magnificence
Kilimanjaro's snowy summit rises dramatically above the canopy of rain forest trees that cover its lower slopes. Like Mount Kenya farther to the north, the mountain is held sacred by the people who live in its vicinity. According to legend, the souls of the dead reside on the mountain's slopes.

African glaciers
*Early morning sunlight illuminates the eastern side of Kilimanjaro's main crater rim, and the formidable ice cliffs in the foreground (*LEFT*). In all Africa, only Mount Kenya and Mount Ruwenzori have similar snow fields.*

Klipspringer *This nimble, quick-footed antelope, measuring about 22in (55cm) high at the shoulder, has a coarse yellow and grey coat and practically no tail.*

High-altitude vegetation consists mainly of dwarf everlastings, lichens and mosses. Some larger mammals, such as buffalo, duikers and even leopards, sometimes venture to this level, and rock hyraxes run nimbly up and down almost vertical cliff faces. Mountain chats nest in holes under rocks and alpine swifts on steep rock cliffs. Several species of sunbird, notably the red-tufted malachite sunbird, are found almost up to the snow line.

Everlasting *This robust plant with stiff yellow flower heads retains its form and colour when dried.*

Moorland vegetation includes mosses and tussocks of sedge, particularly in the wetter valleys. Many herbaceous plants grow in areas of open moorland, including white-flowered saxifrage and giant gladioli. Wild dogs can be found in some areas, and in this region leopards prey on rats, hyraxes and duikers.

Giant groundsel *The curious felt-like covering on the stem of this 13ft (4m) plant is in fact a mass of dead leaves. At night, a rosette of leaves closes to protect the plant's delicate central bud.*

Leopard *The leopard commonly sits in wait in the branches of a tree, ready to pounce and capture passing prey, such as small mammals and birds. It takes its kill back up into the tree branches, where it is safe from scavengers.*

Giant lobelia *The leaves of this 12ft (3.6m) high plant curl inwards at night to protect the central bud from the cold. Water is stored in the base of each leaf.*

The tropical rainforest is mainly characterised by camphor, cedar and red stinkwood trees, which can grow to 100ft (30m) and more. Trees here are often covered with orchids, parasitic creepers and beard lichens. The forest supports a variety of wildlife, such as elephants, black rhinoceroses, leopards, giant forest hogs, mountain gorillas, colobus and vervet monkeys, jackals, nocturnal suni and two varieties of small antelope. Birds include flycatchers, robin-chats and small hornbills.

that now stands 12 395ft (3778m) above sea level. From a distance, Mawenzi appears to be a lump on the side of Kibo, but it is a precipitous, jagged rock crest, some 17 564ft (5353m) high. A flat saddle 7 miles (11km) long links Mawenzi to Kibo, the youngest of the peaks. Kibo's dome is a crater 1½ miles (2.5km) across and 984ft (299m) deep. Within its rim is a smaller crater containing an ash pit that still exudes sulphurous gases. Kibo is the only one of the three above the snow line: an ice field tops its northern rim and extends into the crater, while another hangs from its south-western face. This ice sheet reaches down to around 15 000ft (4500m), making it the most extensive glacier in Africa.

Kilimanjaro's height and isolation relative to its surroundings mean that the mountain exerts a powerful influence over its own weather systems. As easterly winds from the Indian Ocean reach Kilimanjaro, they are forced upwards by its sheer bulk. Whether they release their moisture as rain or snow depends on how high they are deflected (most of the snow that blankets the summit falls not from overhead clouds but from clouds sucked up from farther down the slopes). As a result, and in contrast to the savanna grassland of the surrounding plains, Kilimanjaro boasts several vegetation zones.

The lowest slopes have been cleared for cultivation. The dense tropical rain forest, which begins at around 6500ft (2000m), shelters perhaps the greatest variety of creatures: tall trees house many forest birds; and dense ground-cover plants protect small animals from large predators. At around 11 500ft (3500m) the vegetation is typical of moorland, dominated by heathers and mosses, while just below the snow line the flora becomes more alpine. Large animals, such as buffalo, and leopards on their trail, are often sighted on the snow line, where they are unlikely to survive for long.

Kilimanjaro draws thousands of visitors every year. One of the best known was the American writer Ernest Hemingway, who wrote his short story 'The Snows of Kilimanjaro' after a trip in 1938. His description of the mountain is an eloquent summary: 'As wide as all the world, great, high and unbelievably white in the sun'.

VEGETATION ZONES OF KILIMANJARO

Blue monkey *Fruit, flowers, nectar, leaves, shoots, buds and insects are the staple diet of this shy-looking greyish-blue monkey, which measures about 20in (50cm) high. Its prey includes bush babies and wood owls.*

Rüppell's griffon *The dark plumage of this 35in (89cm) high vulture is interspersed with pale patterning. One of nature's most efficient scavengers, this vulture feeds entirely on large carcasses and may have to fly for more than a day in search of food.*

Giant heather *The gnarled trunk and branches of this massive species, which measures up to 20ft (6m) high, are swathed in yellowish moss and lichens.*

Forest buffalo *The buffalo roams in herds of up to several hundred animals wherever there is water to drink and mud in which to wallow.*

These once forested lower slopes have been cleared for the cultivation of subsistence and cash crops. Today an effective intensive system of irrigation is practised on terraced fields, ensuring permanent cultivation.

Banana *Along with millet, bananas are the primary subsistence crop on Kilimanjaro.*

Coffee plant *Kilimanjaro's most important cash crop, coffee is cultivated on the fertile southern slopes.*

The wildlife of the savanna is a major tourist attraction. Families of warthog and rhinoceros and herds of elephant, wildebeest, gazelle, impala and giraffe roam these plains, and Africa's major predators, namely lions, leopards and cheetahs, are found here. Smaller predators, such as the jackal, hyena, bat-eared fox and mongoose, and some species of vulture also inhabit this region.

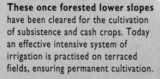

Herds of elephant *roam the plains of the savanna.*

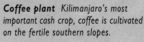

Acacia tree *Elephants feed on the pods and seeds.*

ft | m
6000

18 000 — 5000

16 000

14 000 — 4000

12 000

10 000 — 3000

8000 — 2000

6000

4000 — 1000

0 — 0

BARE

HIGH-ALTITUDE DESERT

GRASSLANDS AND MOORLANDS

TROPICAL RAINFOREST

CULTIVATED SLOPES

SAVANNA

345

Peer groups The structure of Masai society revolves around groups of males of a similar age who have been initiated, or circumcised, at the same time. From that moment on, they form a cohesive 'set' whose members move through a series of grades in the tribe's hierarchy, each of which lasts an average of 15 years. The grades include junior warrior, senior warrior, junior elder and senior elder. Senior elders are empowered to make decisions on behalf of the rest of the tribe.

Personal adornment Both men and women spend many hours decorating their bodies, the women favouring jewellery such as large necklaces, silver earrings, headbands and bracelets. Their hair is usually cut very short or completely shaved (BELOW). This is in total contrast to the warriors, who wear their hair long, finely plaited and interwoven with strands of ochred threads.

THE MASAI

In the late 19th century, cattle-rustling made the Masai, the semi-nomadic warriors of Kenya and Tanzania, notorious among fellow Africans and Europeans alike. And yet Masai custom holds that rustling is a justifiable means to an end, since cattle were put on the Earth only shortly after the Masai, given to them by the creator. Masai warriors believe they are simply taking back what is rightfully theirs.

The Masai have grazed their herds on the grassy plains around the foot of Kilimanjaro for some 300 years – they are thought to have moved south down the Great Rift Valley from the Upper Nile region. They comprise a loose collection of related peoples, but the true Masai, who depend on their herds of cattle, sheep and goats, spurn those who have settled in one place and have chosen to plant crops.

The staple of the Masai diet is cow's milk (although goat's milk is also drunk). Animals may be slaughtered and eaten on ceremonial occasions, most of which are held to mark the passage of a group of males into a higher social grade, but at other times cattle are considered too precious to be eaten. Cows are also traditionally given as a dowry. After marriage, a man may allow his wife guardianship of some of his cows, but they still belong to him. Children are usually entrusted with the care of the smaller animals.

Home is never permanent. The Masai live in a *manyatta*, consisting of a number of wooden-frame huts overlaid with mud and dung, and enclosed in a thornbush fence. The animals live in similar thornbush enclosures inside the main outer fence. Every three or four years, when the pasture and enclosures have been exhausted, the tribe moves on.

In the shadows of the mountain The majority of the Masai – some 100 000 in all – inhabit the border regions of Kenya and Tanzania, an area whose landscape is dominated by the snow-capped mass of Kilimanjaro.

The mountain has a special place in Masai mythology, for it was the home of Ngai, husband of the moon and creator of all things, including the Masai people and the cattle which they revere. The Masai justification for cattle-raiding is that they are the rightful guardians of such God-given bounty.

As brave as a lion After circumcision, Masai warriors leave the safety of their homes, armed only with clubs, spears and swords, to spend time on the plains tending herds of cattle. Lions abound in open country; a warrior who successfully spears a lion is entitled to wear the lion's mane headdress on ceremonial occasions (LEFT).

Blood of life Ox blood is traditionally mixed with milk or drunk alone, particularly during the dry season, to eke out the milk and help warriors keep up their strength. The animal's jugular vein is tapped, a container, usually a gourd, is filled, and the ox is then left to recover. It is more usual today to supplement milk with maize flour to make a porridge.

347

THE VALE OF KASHMIR

*Once the summer residence of Mogul emperors and the families
of the British Raj, the Vale of Kashmir has been likened to paradise.
To the Irish poet Thomas Moore it was 'the Eden of the Earth'.*

Between snowcapped Himalayan peaks and the summits of the Pir Panjal lies the Vale of Kashmir, one of the most beautiful, fertile and temperate parts of the Indian subcontinent. It was once held in such great esteem that when, on his deathbed, the Mogul emperor Jahangir (1605–27) was asked if there was anything he desired, he replied, 'Only Kashmir.'

Around 60 million years ago, the Vale of Kashmir was the basin of a lake some 3000ft (900m) deep, 85 miles (140km) long and 20 miles (30km) wide, fed by melted waters from glaciers and rain-swollen mountain rivers. The lake eventually disappeared, leaving behind the fertile valley that is now drained by the meandering Jhelum River, which leaves Kashmir at Baramula.

According to Hindu mythology, the lake was once the home of a water demon, Jalodbhava, whom the gods wished to destroy. While he remained in the water the demon was invincible, and the conflict was only resolved when a holy man (the grandson of Brahma, the creator god) used his magic sword to cut a passage through the mountains at Baramula. The waters of the lake drained away and Jalodbhava was left defenceless.

Although part of Kashmir is now in Pakistan, the Vale of Kashmir is in the northern Indian state of Jammu and Kashmir. It lies at an altitude of 5300ft (1600m) and is sheltered by mountains which safeguard its inhabitants from the worst of the monsoon. Because it is so high, its climate is far milder than that of nearby regions, and it was to Kashmir that many of the heat-weary British flocked in the summer months during the days of the Raj.

Srinagar, the capital, was a particular favourite. But the Maharajah refused to allow the British to buy land here on which to build houses, so they took to the water instead and constructed wooden houseboats on Lake Dal by building frame houses on long boat hulls. The British have gone, but the houseboats remain, rented out to tourists.

The lake is also famous for the gardens that float on its surface, covered in blooms. Farmers tend the gardens from shallow-draught boats, wending their way between them to gather tomatoes and pumpkins or vividly coloured flowers. Each floating garden is made of topsoil laid on strips of reed about 6ft (2m) wide which are anchored to poles that can be moved around and moored in different parts of the lake. This ingenious method of harvesting

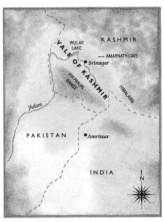

City of canals *The Jhelum River runs through the heart of Srinagar, serving as its main thoroughfare, where waterways crowded with small boats and taxis far outnumber the roads. It is a city built on water and has thus earned the title 'Venice of the East'.*

THE VALE OF KASHMIR

extra crops in a country where flat land for cultivation is limited is both efficient and highly picturesque.

Srinagar was founded in the third century BC, when King Ashoka sent Buddhist missionaries to Kashmir. From then until AD 144, the country was ruled by 52 kings, after which time various rulers introduced the religions of Hinduism and Islam in turn. Then, in 1585, Kashmir was conquered by the Mogul emperor Akbar and became part of the Muslim Mogul Empire. During the summer Akbar took up residence in Kashmir. It was an ideal location, since it was relatively close to his power base in Delhi and to the trade routes over the mountains; it also provided a respite from the heat and dust of the plain.

Akbar declared Kashmir his own 'private garden', and believed that the purpose of its inhabitants was to tend it. It was he who instigated the building of the magnificent palaces and their grounds in Srinagar. All Mogul gardens conform to a set design comprising a series of rectangular stepped terraces. In those of Srinagar, water rushes over stone parapets, runs beneath the pavilions and flows in a series of waterfalls through the length of the gardens until it joins Lake Dal. The largest of Srinagar's gardens, covering an area 1797ft (548m) by 1109ft (338m), is Nishat Bagh (*bagh* means garden in Hindi). It was laid out in 1633 to a design by Asaf Khan, brother-in-law of Shah Jahan, the builder of the Taj Mahal. Shah Jahan also created Kashmir's Shalimar Bagh, reputedly the most magnificent garden in the world, with splendid pavilions, cascading waterfalls and a profusion of exotic flowers.

Beyond the bustle of the city lie farmlands where rice, wheat and maize and a wide variety of fruit are cultivated. Above the fields, in the isolated foothills of the Himalayas that can only be reached by pony or on foot, semi-nomadic Gujar and Bakharval tribes herd buffalo and goats.

Kashmir is known as the 'happy valley' because its isolation seems to cut it off from the troubles of the rest of the world. In reality this is not so. Kashmir is in such a desirable position that neighbouring rulers have fought over it for thousands of years. The present conflict between predominantly Hindu India and Muslim Pakistan over who should rule Kashmir started in 1947, after the British left. To complicate matters, the Maharajah of Kashmir was a Hindu while most of his subjects were Muslims, and at first he refused to hand over Kashmir to either country. Then Pakistan invaded and, in return for military aid, the Maharajah formally ceded Kashmir to India.

A ceasefire was declared in 1949, but sporadic fighting between India and Pakistan continues to break the peace of the 'happy valley' of Kashmir, and many Kashmiris want independence from both those countries.

LAND OF SAFFRON AND CASHMERE

One of Kashmir's key industries is the production of saffron, the world's most expensive spice; it is used as a dye as well as a food flavouring. Saffron is hand picked from autumn-flowering crocuses grown 8 miles (13km) south-east of Srinagar. Within each flower lie three stigmas; their orange tips yield the best saffron, that from the stems is of lesser quality. It takes more than 4500 blooms to make 1oz (30g) of the spice.

Kashmir is also renowned for its high-quality woollen carpets. Intricate floral designs in unusual blends of colours are woven, often by children, on looms in factories. Soft, warm, embroidered or woven shawls made from the finest 'cashmere' wool, spun

from the downy undercoat of a special breed of goat, are also produced here. On these, the early pine-cone motif has lost its floral form and become the abstract shape we know as paisley.

Procession of pilgrims
Each year in midsummer, pilgrims flock to the cave of Amarnath. Here Shiva, the Hindu god of creation and destruction, was said to have revealed the secrets of the universe to his wife, the goddess Parvati. Inside the cave is a large column of ice, formed by a steady trickle from a natural spring. As they pray to Shiva, pilgrims shower the column with flower petals.

Mogul emperor *In this mid-17th-century painting, Emperor Akbar crosses the Ganges with a colourful retinue. Akbar introduced irrigation to India and drew up the earliest rules for the game of polo.*

Taking to the hills *From April to October, while their husbands remained in the sweltering heat of Delhi and the plains, many of the British Raj wives went with their children to the cool hill stations of Kashmir and Simla, among others. On the plains, temperatures could remain at an oppressive 40°C (104°F) for days on end.*

351

HIMALAYAS: THE ROOF OF THE WORLD

If Everest, the highest mountain in the world, were anywhere else but central Asia, it would dwarf everything around it. Yet in the rugged land of snowy peaks soaring between steep-sided valleys that is the Himalayas, it is just one feature of a landscape conceived on a giant scale.

The mighty peaks of the Himalayas rise above the line of perpetual snow, by day glistening purest white in the brilliant sunlight. When the sun slips towards the western horizon, its rays bathe the summits in a soft red glow, and shadows chase each other across pink crests. As the light dims and night thickens, the jagged black peaks are outlined against an inky, starry sky. This is not just a land of supreme natural beauty on an immense scale, where colossal mountains tower skywards; it is also a region steeped in religion and myth, the dwelling place of Buddhist and Hindu deities. It was once an impenetrable barrier between the south and the fabulously wealthy towns along the Silk Road to the north – Samarkand, Bukhara, Kashgar and Kotan. Even today, the Himalayas evoke an image of a lost land, untouched by human hand and home only to solitary ascetics and abominable snowmen. In this century the mountains have also come to represent the ultimate goal for climbers everywhere.

Nowhere on the surface of the earth are there peaks like those of central Asia, where six mountain systems interlock in a broad curve 100–150 miles (160–240km) wide along the neck of the Indian subcontinent. The greatest of these is the Himalayas (Sanskrit for 'abode of the snow'). They extend westwards from the cold white pyramid of Namche Barwa in the forests of northern Assam along the edge of the Tibetan plateau through Bhutan and Sikkim, Nepal and Ladakh, to their great western bastion, Nanga Parbat in Pakistan, a total distance of some 1500 miles (2400km). Peaks of the Outer Himalayas to the south rise to a maximum of 5000ft (1520m) above sea level. Northward these abut the Lesser Himalayas, which average 15 000ft (4570m) in height; between them lie steep valleys with altitudes of some 3000ft (900m).

The Great Himalayas are the backbone of the whole system and reach their maximum heights in Nepal. There cluster nine of the world's fourteen highest peaks, including Everest, at 29 022ft (8846m), Kanchenjunga, 28 208ft (8598m) and Annapurna 26 503ft (8078m). North of the Great Himalayas is the range known as the Tethys, or Tibetan, Himalayas, which borders the southernmost part of the great Tibetan plateau.

Fossils of fish and other sea creatures found in the Himalayas prove that the rocks that comprise these massive mountains originated as marine deposits: between

Rocky summit *Seen from the alpine region of Gokyo, 20 miles (32km) south-west of Everest, the jagged peak of the planet's highest mountain extends into an unusually cloudless sky. Straddling the border between Nepal and Tibet, Everest is seldom totally covered by snow at its top, and mountaineers who accept the challenge of Everest must be rock climbers, rather than snow and ice specialists, to complete the final assault on the summit.*

353

HIMALAYAS: THE ROOF OF THE WORLD

Holy family *Shiva and his family* (LEFT) *are prominent figures in Hindu mythology. His wife Mahadevi is also known as 'the daughter of the mountain'.*

Temples in the snow *Against a backdrop of snow-clad peaks, rows of Buddhist prayer flags flutter in the breeze* (ABOVE) *at a mountain shrine in Nepal.*

65 and 570 million years ago they formed the floor of the ancient Tethys Ocean. As the crustal plate bearing India drifted north towards the mainland of Asia and collided with it, the Himalayan mountain chain was thrust upward.

Geological studies have concluded that the mountains were uplifted in at least three distinct and widely separated phases. The first phase, roughly 38 million years ago, produced the Great Himalayas. The second phase, between 7 and 26 million years ago, formed the Lesser Himalayas; and the third phase, around 7 million years ago, created the Siwalik Hills. Movement along the plate boundary is a continuous process; over the last 1½ million years the mountains have grown 4500ft (1370m) higher.

The names with which these remote, other-worldly

THE ABOMINABLE SNOWMAN

The Himalayas, particularly the region surrounding the Tso Rolpa glacial lake between Everest and the Nepalese capital Kathmandu, are reputed to be the home of the yeti, known to the Tibetans as the 'demon of the snow'. Many explorers and mountaineers claim to have seen either the ape-like creature itself or its footprints, or to have heard a strange scream-like call. Nicknamed the abominable snowman, the yeti has not so far been accepted as a known species by the scientific community, despite having been the subject of much investigation. Some experts say the footprints are those of a bear or even a mountain goat, distorted as the snow melts then freezes over again. Nonetheless local belief in the yeti is so strong that in the 1950s the Nepalese government banned the killing or smuggling of yeti. No one has yet been tried for either crime.

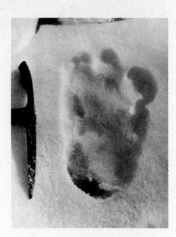

Walking snowman *Footprints provide some of the most compelling evidence in support of the existence of the yeti. A row of prints on a glacier (LEFT) prove that a creature, probably walking upright, passed this way. A close-up (RIGHT) reveals the size and ape-like character of the prints. Both pictures were taken by the British climber Eric Shipton in 1951. Since then, plaster casts of prints some 14in (35cm) wide and 17in (43cm) long have added some credence to eyewitness reports.*

peaks have been endowed testify to the awe which they inspire in all who gaze upon them. Several are associated with goddesses, including Chomo Lhari, 'goddess of the holy mountain', and Annapurna, 'goddess of food'. It is to be expected therefore that the Himalayas should figure in the most ancient sacred writings.

In Hindu mythology, this region is known as Deviabhumi, the country of the gods. Here on Gaurisshankar lived the great god Shiva and his consort Mahadevi, daughter of Himavat, himself the personification of the mountains. Shiva is one of the supreme trinity of Hindu gods and lord of agriculture. It is fitting that from his abode in the permanent snowfields of the Himalayas flow the life-giving waters of three of Asia's major rivers, the Indus, the Brahmaputra and the Ganges.

Shiva and his consort are not the only deities to have inhabited the Himalayas. According to both Hindu and Buddhist legend, at the centre of the earth stood the mountain of Meeru, around which the sun, moon and stars revolved. Hindus identify Mount Kailas in the Tibetan Himalayas with Meeru. Here lived Kubera, god of riches,

lord of the Earth's treasures and king of supernatural beings known as Yaksas. On Meeru too lived Indra, the most supreme of early Hindu gods, lord of the thunderbolt and bringer of rain and fertility to the land.

The mountains' spiritual associations led the first recorded traveller to the region in AD 400. Fa-Hsian, a Chinese monk, came in search of religious truth. The earliest accurate map was produced in the 1730s by a French geographer, Jean-Baptiste Bourguignon d'Arville, although he failed to determine correctly the heights of many of the mountains. In the early 19th century, big-game hunters from British India visited the area seeking tigers and bears, and brought back local tales of strange footprints in the snow. These were the first hint of the existence of the yeti.

In the 1850s, the world's highest mountain was known in the Western world simply as Peak XV. To the Indian population it was Sagarmartha, 'summit of heaven', and to the Tibetan people it was Chomo Lungma, 'mother goddess of the land'. It was named Everest by the British in 1862, in honour of Sir George Everest, Surveyor-General of India, who six years earlier had led an expedition to chart

HIMALAYAS: THE ROOF OF THE WORLD

the heights of the mountains in the Himalayan range.

Towards the end of the 19th century, Tibet and Nepal closed their borders to Europeans, and although the Dalai Lama permitted an expedition to visit in 1921, the party only had time to reach the foot of Everest and map its lower slopes. A member of that team was George Mallory, who three years later attempted the awesome climb to the top of the world's highest mountain.

Mallory, the leader of the 1924 expedition, and fellow climber Andrew Irvine may have been the first to stand at the summit of Everest. Certainly they were within reach of the peak when they were enveloped by cloud and disappeared from the view of their colleagues below, never to be seen again. The earliest authenticated conquest was made nearly 30 years later by a British expedition, led by John Hunt. The final assault was made on 29 May 1953 by the New Zealander Edmund Hillary and the Nepalese Sherpa Tenzing Norgay. Hillary later wrote of his thoughts on standing where no other human being had ever been known to have stood: 'My initial feelings were of relief – no more ridges to traverse and no more humps to tantalise us with hopes of success. I looked at Tenzing... and there was no disguising his infectious grin of delight.'

Climbers continue to attempt the ultimate summit, although so far only about 400 people have succeeded in standing on the roof of the world: the Himalayas, and Everest in particular, protect their secrets well. They are still the abode of snow, the exclusive domain of the gods and perhaps, as time may yet reveal, the yeti.

On top of the world
Sherpa Tenzing stands proud as Edmund Hillary documents for history a moment of ultimate glory: reaching the summit of Everest. Sherpas are renowned for their endurance on Himalayan expeditions and have been dubbed 'tigers of the snow'. They regard Everest as the 'goddess of the universe'.

Conquering heroes
Tenzing and Hillary relax at base camp after their climb. Improvements made during the 1940s in oxygen supplies, clothing and kit played a part in the successful ascent.

356

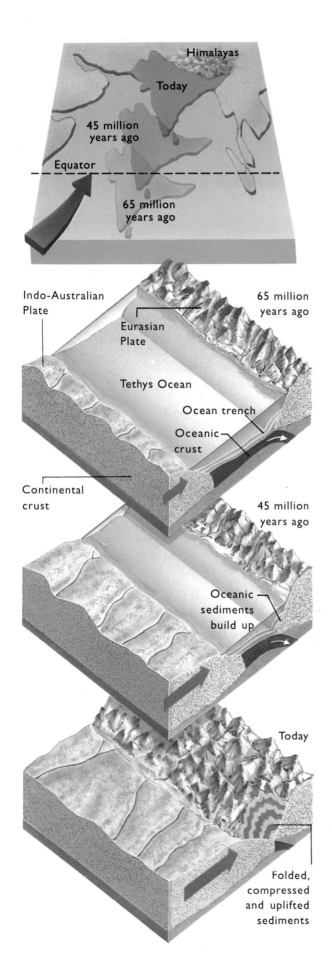

Himalayas

Today

45 million
years ago

Equator

65 million
years ago

Indo-Australian
Plate

Eurasian
Plate

65 million
years ago

Tethys Ocean

Ocean trench

Oceanic
crust

Continental
crust

45 million
years ago

Oceanic
sediments
build up

Today

Folded,
compressed
and uplifted
sediments

MAKING MOUNTAINS

When the supercontinent of Pangaea broke up some 250 million years ago, the Indo-Australian Plate began to drift northwards. It moved quickly, in geological terms, and about 45 million years ago smashed into the larger, heavier Eurasian Plate, giving rise to the Himalayas. The floor of the Tethys Ocean, which had separated the two landmasses, was forced upwards, over the margins of the folded plates, where it sits today.

Eventually the two plates will become fused together, but today they are still moving, continuing to push the Himalayas ever higher. Everest is 'growing' by about 2in (50mm) a year.

Summit of heaven *The attraction of Everest (on the left) for mountaineers is undeniable, and the climbing season short if they are to avoid the freezing temperatures, tempestuous gales and deep snow that characterise the mountain for most of the year. Although many attempts to reach its summit have ended in failure and sometimes death for expedition members, climbers remain undeterred. In recent years there have been successful ascents by climbers from all over the world, including teams of women and teams who have chosen not to use oxygen.*

357

MOUNT FUJI: SACRED SHRINE

The highest mountain in Japan was born from fire and may perish in the same way, yet its fragile beauty has been compared to that of a flower. Mount Fuji is not only a natural wonder, it is also a sacred place that has drawn pilgrims and inspired artists and poets alike for generations.

The perfect symmetry of Mount Fuji's silhouette has long been the ultimate Japanese symbol of beauty. Indeed, in Japan the mountain is 'that which is without equal'. It is a place for all seasons and all times of day, singularly beautiful when viewed from any angle. But to climb to its snow-capped summit in spring and gaze down at the plum and cherry trees that blossom at its foot is said to surpass any other experience of Fuji's grandeur. At 12388ft (3776m), the mountain looms large in more than just the country's landscape. It has provided inspiration for poets and artists for at least 12 centuries and has come to be identified with Japan itself. Moreover, it holds a special place in the country's official religion, Shinto, and is also significant to Buddhists, who believe that a path encircling the mountain at 8200ft (2500m) marks the gateway to another world.

The artist Katsushika Hokusai recorded many views of Fuji, and it is these changing moods as much as its inherent beauty that have beguiled first native, and later foreign, visitors to the mountain. The Japanese poet Basho (1644–94), for example, found majesty in Fuji in all seasons: 'Though Fuji is hidden,/In the rain and mist of winter,/On such a day, too,/There is joy.' More recently the American writer Lafcadio Hearn (1850–1904), whose love of the country prompted him to become a Japanese citizen, called the mountain merely 'the most beautiful sight in Japan'.

Fuji is the holiest mountain in Japan, and has been accorded that status for centuries. It was first worshipped by the aboriginal Ainu people (who still live on the most northerly of Japan's principal islands, Hokkaido), who bestowed the name of their fire goddess Fuchi on the mountain. The Japanese continued to venerate Fuji, and retained the Ainu name. According to Shinto belief, higher spirits, or *kami*, exist in all works of nature, but mountains are deemed particularly sacred. Fuji, as the highest and most beautiful mountain in the country, is especially revered; it is worshipped as the home of the gods, the symbolic link between the mysteries of heaven and the realities of earth.

The Shinto shrine just below the summit dates back 2000 years to a period of particularly intense volcanic activity during which the emperor ordered it to be built in an attempt to appease the gods. Even as late as the end of World War II, many Japanese considered it their sacred duty to climb the mountain. Eyewitness reports from the

Views of Japan *Fuji rises from a plain that is almost at sea level and, on a clear day, it can be seen from a distance of some 50 miles (80km). Once the mists clear after the sun rises, the mountain itself offers breathtaking views of the surrounding countryside, peninsulas and islands, and of the Pacific Ocean.*

SEA OF JAPAN

HONSHU

Tokyo

MOUNT FUJI

Osaka

PACIFIC OCEAN

Artistic impetus *Fuji has inspired countless artists. Katsushika Hokusai (1760–1849) is probably the best known in the West. His series of woodblock prints entitled '36 Views of Mount Fuji', produced between 1828 and 1833, mark the zenith of the Japanese landscape print, in which sympathy for the subject is matched by artistic skill.*

359

MOUNT FUJI: SACRED SHRINE

Eye of the crater *Today,
Fuji's crater measures 1659ft
(505m) across and 660ft
(200m) deep. It has been*
*compared to a lotus flower,
since it is ringed by eight
crests, known as the* Yaksudo
Fuyo, *the eight petals of Fuji.*

THE THIRD BORN

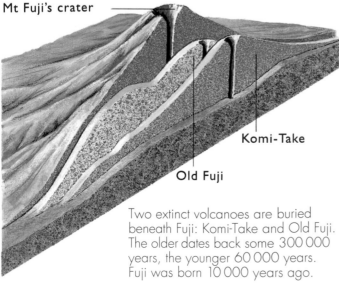

Mt Fuji's crater

Komi-Take

Old Fuji

Two extinct volcanoes are buried
beneath Fuji: Komi-Take and Old Fuji.
The older dates back some 300 000
years, the younger 60 000 years.
Fuji was born 10 000 years ago.

last century describe thousands of the faithful, dressed in
white tunics, sandals and straw hats, ascending one of the
six paths to the summit. The pathways were often littered
with cast-off sandals, which were so flimsy that several
pairs might be needed to complete the nine-hour trek.
Today an estimated 400 000 people – mostly Japanese
tourists – climb Fuji every year, the vast majority during
the months of July and August, when the snow relinquishes
its grip on the summit.

From the top, the sides of the mountain slope away at
an angle of 45°, then level out before reaching the ground.
There, Fuji traces an almost perfect circle 78 miles (126km)
in circumference. In an arc around the northern slopes of
the mountain are the Five Lakes. In spring, when the fruit
trees and azaleas are in bloom, this area is a riot of colour;
likewise in autumn, when the part-primeval forest around
the lakes flames into brilliant reds, then myriad shades of
brown. Many of the best views of Fuji itself can be had
from these interconnecting lakes, whose still waters perfectly reflect the mountain's natural symmetry. Like Fuji,
the lakes are volcanic in origin.

According to Japanese Buddhist tradition, the mountain
appeared overnight in 286 BC when the ground opened to
form Bava, Japan's biggest lake; Fuji was made from the
displaced earth. The legend is not without foundation
since the whole Japanese archipelago is riddled with tectonic
fault lines, along which are situated many mountain ranges
and lakes. The island of Honshu sits astride the major fault
line, where 25 volcanic cones are clustered: the largest of
these is Mount Fuji, whose origins date back some 10 000
years, not 2300 years, as claimed in Buddhist legend.

The wide plain that surrounds Fuji has a history of
intense volcanic activity. Some 300 000 years ago it erupted,
spewing lava from the earth's core. Outpourings from
several cones have helped to fashion Fuji's present shape
by building up alternate layers of solidified lava and a
conglomerate composed of cinder, ash and lava. These
layers reflect the sequence in which a volcano erupts: huge
volumes of molten lava spread out evenly over the
mountain slopes; violent explosions then follow in which
clouds of cinder, ash and lava pellets are ejected high into
the air, before falling to cloak the slopes.

The first recorded eruption of Fuji was in AD 800, the
latest eruption (Fuji is not dead, simply dormant) was in
1707, when the city of Edo (modern-day Tokyo) 60 miles
(100km) away was covered in a dense layer of cinders and
ash. The unique place that Fuji holds in the Japanese
consciousness and the romanticism that surrounds the
mountain may be due to the knowledge that its beauty
might not endure. Tradition holds that it was born overnight; it may one day perish as suddenly in a ball of fire.

Daybreak in the east
Watching the sunrise – the goraiko – from the summit is one of the most moving experiences associated with Mount Fuji. Immediately before the sun moves above the horizon, its disc is reflected perfectly in the atmosphere, causing a wash of colours that evaporates once the sun rises.

Snow kingdom Fuji's summit is covered with snow for ten months of the year, and even during the two summer months patches of white cling to its slopes. Only the high rocky crags perched on the crater's rim escape the glistening blanket: high winds prevent snow gaining a foothold.

THE ROLLING SHENANDOAH

The melodious American Indian name Shenandoah evokes a sad song and the strife of the Civil War – the Shenandoah Valley was where the Confederate General 'Stonewall' Jackson launched his campaign. Today it is an area of outstanding natural beauty and a national park.

The American writer Washington Irving, who died in 1859, described the Shenandoah Valley as 'equal to the promised land in fertility and far superior to it for beauty'. Just five years after Irving's death a local farmer deemed it 'a desert'. In the interim, the most beautiful valley in Virginia had become the focus of some of the fiercest fighting of the American Civil War, which culminated in 'the Burning' of 1864, when General Philip Sheridan and the Federal Army laid waste to the valley, leaving it a smouldering wilderness.

Shenandoah (meaning 'daughter of the stars') was the name the American Indians gave to the river that flows along the bottom of the valley. In fact there are two rivers, the North Fork and South Fork, which flow on either side of Massanutten mountain before converging at the town of Front Royal. They continue as one for some 50 miles (80km) across the border into West Virginia, then join the Potomac River at Harpers Ferry. From the misty heights of the Blue Ridge Mountains there are breathtaking vistas over the lazy loops of the Shenandoah's South Fork; nonetheless it is the North Fork, twisting like a serpent as it approaches Front Royal, that is traditionally regarded as the 'rolling river' of the famous sea shanty.

Shenandoah Valley is some 150 miles (240km) long and averages about 25 miles (40km) wide. More than a century elapsed between the arrival of white settlers in Virginia in 1607 and their discovery of this region. In 1716, an expedition across the Blue Ridge Mountains under the leadership of Alexander Spottiswood, the Governor of Virginia (who drank a toast in champagne and claret to the party's good fortune in uncovering an area of such beauty), opened the way for white settlement. Until then, the valley had been the exclusive domain of the Shawnee and Iroquois native American peoples (who hold that the word Shenandoah derives from their language). The trail that they created along the bottom of the valley became a major route for further expansion westwards and is today an interstate highway.

The settlers who were attracted to the valley itself from the 1720s onwards were of three racial origins but came from two main areas; most were German Lutherans and Scottish-Irish Presbyterians from Pennsylvania, and there was a trickle of English from eastern Virginia. What they all had in common was their reliance on the family unit

Meeting point *The Shenandoah joins the Potomac at Harpers Ferry, named after a local farmer Robert Harper, who lost his house in the so-called great pumpkin flood, when scores of pumpkins floated downstream from gardens farther up the river.*

From a bluff known as Jefferson's Rock at Harpers Ferry, the former US president Thomas Jefferson viewed the confluence of the North and South Forks of the Shenandoah and the surrounding hills and cliffs. He pronounced the scene 'worth a voyage across the Atlantic'.

THE ROLLING SHENANDOAH

as a workforce (there was almost no slavery in the Shenandoah Valley) and their dedication to an agricultural way of life – the fertile soil was suitable for dairy and livestock farming, and for growing both fruit and grain.

The valley's natural advantages made it an obvious location for the Confederate Army under General Thomas J. Stonewall Jackson – a Virginian himself – to shelter during the Civil War (1861–65). Its soil provided all the food the soldiers needed (indeed they called the valley their breadbasket); the old Indian trails along its floor offered an ideal means of moving troops and supplies quickly and in secret; and the whole valley, sheltered by the Shenandoah and Allegheny Mountains to the west

and the Blue Ridge Mountains to the east, was easily defended. In addition, whoever held the valley held one of the few viable north–south highways. Having suffered several crushing defeats in the Shenandoah Valley in 1862, and dismayed at renewed fighting in the area, on 29 September 1864 Sheridan ordered his cavalry to burn anything that might be of use to the Confederates. His troops took him at his word: crops, mills and granaries, farms, livestock and homes were all set ablaze.

It must have seemed to the survivors of the war that the valley would never bloom again. But the healing forces of nature, combined with the perseverance and hard work of local people, in time re-created the landscape. Today, the

Theatre of war In 1862 the peace of the Shenandoah Valley was shattered by war (BELOW). General Stonewall Jackson won lasting fame for his Valley Campaign, during which he inflicted five defeats upon Federal troops in less than three months. New Market (LEFT) was the scene of the last Confederate victory in the valley, in 1864. Against a much larger force under General Sheridan, the Southern troops won, thanks to 225 teenage cadets, who plugged a breach in the Southern battle line.

 Union General Philip Sheridan    Confederate General Stonewall Jackson

valley's orchards provide more than half of Virginia's apples, its pastures produce all the state's poultry and the majority of its beef and vegetables, and its vineyards yield many fine wines. Most of the trees in the valley have become re-established. The only exception is the chestnut, which recovered from the war, but was ravaged by blight at the turn of the century. Even today, new shoots on the trees are struck by the disease. As a result, the forest comprises chiefly oak, white pine, willow and sycamore trees.

In 1926, 194 000 acres (78 000ha) of the Shenandoah Valley were designated a national park. In addition to woodlands and meadows, the park includes some 60 peaks over 2000ft (600m) in height, and every year thousands of visitors flock to enjoy the spectacular scenery only 75 miles (120km) from the nation's capital city, Washington D.C.

The garden of Virginia, Shenandoah possesses many of nature's bounties and it is a cradle of history. But, above all, it is proof of the power of nature which, in little over a 100 years, has restored what was ravaged so thoroughly.

Tranquillity regained
The 105 mile (169km) long mountain-top Skyline Drive (BELOW) *affords spectacular views over the Shenandoah Valley. There are now more than 700 plant species here, including trees, shrubs, vines and as many as 80 different wild flowers that provide food and shelter for up to 200 varieties of bird.*

LEGENDARY REALMS

W hen the workaday world fails us humans, we dream – and many dreams have been converted into legends of dream lands, ever out of reach. In all cultures, mythological lands are often described as having sunk beneath the waves. The story of the Flood related in the Old Testament is echoed far beyond the Middle East, and the Greek philosopher Plato was the first to describe the mysterious island continent of Atlantis, destroyed by the sea-god, Poseidon. Such myths and stories of sinking islands may have their origins in folk memories of volcanic eruptions, earthquakes and tidal waves, which are known to have destroyed some island cultures. The destruction of Thera (modern Santorini) by a volcanic explosion had a dire effect on lands around the Aegean Sea, particularly Crete, the centre of Minoan culture. Arthurian legends, with their half-pagan, half-Christian stories of a warrior king, gave rise to a number of sites associated with him. Glastonbury is thought by some to be the isle of Avalon, Arthur's resting place; others identify the fifth-century fort of Cadbury Castle in Somerset with Arthur's court at Camelot. While some yearn for knights in shining armour, others lust for gold. Spanish conquistadors tried in vain to find El Dorado, the mythical realm of a king who was coated in gold dust then rowed out into a lake, into which he hurled gold as an offering to the sun god.

THE ENCHANTED CITY OF CAMELOT

The dream of Camelot, the golden city where peace and harmony reign, first gripped the popular imagination in the Middle Ages when war and disease were rife. The desire to believe in the existence of this ideal city has inspired a search for a real place that can be identified as Camelot.

The mythical realm of Arthurian legend has kept people enthralled for eight centuries. At its heart lies Camelot, the towered city where King Arthur held court and where he and his knights lived by the codes of chivalry and courtly love.

The name 'Camelot' was coined by the 12th-century French poet Chrétien de Troyes. Inspired by troubadours at Eleanor of Aquitaine's court, he had introduced into Arthur's story the theme of courtly love, whereby a lady could become the object of devotion of an honourable knight who would dedicate himself to her. This provided the knights with motives for their chivalrous deeds and gave the story immediate appeal to ladies.

Chrétien's Camelot lay in a timeless land of enchanted forests and castles where marvels and magic abounded. From here the knights set out on their quests, rescuing damsels in distress, risking physical and supernatural perils and eventually returning home to Camelot. The epitome of stability in an unpredictable universe, Camelot symbolised civilisation versus barbarism, order amid chaos, a golden future and a glorious past.

The story of Camelot begins and ends with Arthur. There is some evidence that behind the legendary king lay a real person, a fifth-century British warlord who kept the Germanic tribes at bay following the departure of the Romans. After the Saxon conquest, tales of this warlord became part of Celtic folklore, passed down through generations among those who lived in the west of England, Wales and Brittany, beyond the Saxon reach. The search for Camelot thus began in the lands of the Celts.

The historian Geoffrey of Monmouth first popularised Arthur in the 12th century. In his account of the king he

Candidate for Camelot
The site of Cadbury Castle (RIGHT) is one of the places that has been identified as Camelot, seat of King Arthur's court. According to one tradition, every Midsummer Eve and Christmas Arthur and his knights ride over the hill and down to a spring nearby to water their horses.

Round Table *This oak table, which is displayed in Winchester Castle, was once believed to be Arthur's Round Table, but it has proved to be medieval. Its importance lay in the fact that when the knights sat at the table they were all equal in position, and so it became a symbol of unity.*

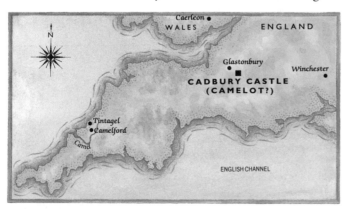

CAMELOT

placed Arthur's court at Caerleon in South Wales, the site of an important Roman fortress and amphitheatre. In Geoffrey's time, the remains of a once magnificent city were still visible, so it seems appropriate that he should have set his story there. Caerleon lies on the River Usk, which could have transported kings and queens to Arthur's city of golden-gabled palaces.

Cadbury Castle at South Cadbury in Somerset is the most probable location of Camelot. Here, during the period when Arthur is supposed to have lived, was the largest of known British strongholds, the headquarters of a king who could marshal resources unmatched by anyone else. The first person to identify Cadbury with Camelot was John Leland, antiquarian to King Henry VIII, who wrote: 'At the very south end of the church of South-Cadbyri standeth Camallate, sometime a famous town or castle...'.

There is some archaeological evidence to back Leland's claim. In the 1960s, excavations led by archaeologist Leslie Alcock found that the Iron Age fort of South Cadbury had been reoccupied and strengthened at the end of the fifth century, when Arthur may well have been active. The fort had been built in the first century BC, stormed by the Romans in AD 83 and left unoccupied for 400 years before its reconstruction. Only a few traces of the timber buildings remain, including a hall 63ft (19m) long. Could this have been where the Round Table once stood?

Another claimant with a strong suit is Tintagel Castle on the north coast of Cornwall, supposedly Arthur's birth-place. A castle has stood here since 1145, which is far too recent to be Camelot. But excavations have revealed that a Celtic monastery once occupied the site, and shards of pottery found here indicate that it was inhabited in the fifth century. Whatever the link between Camelot and Tintagel, its reputed Arthurian connection still draws the tourists.

The story of King Arthur best known today appeared in 1485 in *Le Morte d'Arthur* by Sir Thomas Malory, who identified Camelot with Winchester simply because this had been the Saxon capital from 849 to 1066. Another tradition holds that Arthur lived in the north of Britain, in a kingdom called Dalriada (now Argyll), and that the site of the battle of Camlan (Arthur's last battle) was Camboglanna, a Roman fort on Hadrian's Wall.

If there is no certainty about the location of Camelot, then that is most probably because it existed, like its ruler, only in the imagination of the story-tellers. If it were based on a real location, Cadbury Castle seems to be the most plausible. But Camelot's true appeal lies in what it represents – a place where honour and courage prevailed, where the strong protected the weak, and where harmony reigned. The poet Tennyson aptly wrote of Camelot: 'Lord, there is no such city anywhere, but all a vision.'

Scottish resting place
One popular legend holds that Arthur is not dead but asleep. The location of his resting chamber is thought by some to be under the Eildon Hills in the Scottish Borders (ABOVE).

THE STORY OF KING ARTHUR

King Arthur was first mentioned in a tenth-century Welsh poem, but he was popularised by Geoffrey of Monmouth in the 12th century. Various elements were added to the legend – courtly love by Chrétien de Troyes, the Holy Grail by Robert de Boron – but it was Sir Thomas Malory who pulled the story together.

Malory's Arthur is in the heroic tradition, fighting against odds to win his kingdom. Raised by the magician Merlin (LEFT), as a young man he showed himself to be the true heir to the throne by pulling a sword out of a stone, a deed no one else could perform. Once he had secured his kingdom, he was given the enchanted sword Excalibur by the Lady of the Lake. He then married Lady Guinevere, receiving the Round Table as part of her dowry, and established his court at Camelot.

The knights underwent tests of valour, culminating in the search for the Holy Grail. However, Arthur's downfall was finally brought about by the love for Guinevere of the greatest knight of all, Sir Lancelot. Harmony could not be maintained and the king's nephew, Mordred, tried to seize power. Arthur and Mordred met in battle at Camlan, where both were destroyed – and with them the kingdom of Camelot.

Excalibur After the battle of Camlan, King Arthur was carried dying from the battlefield by Sir Bedevere. Legend relates that the knight took the king to a lake, where Arthur ordered him to throw the magical sword Excalibur into the water. In this 14th-century Dutch manuscript (LEFT) *the Lady of the Lake holds aloft the sword. The lake is reputed to be Dozmary Pool in Cornwall* (RIGHT).

The story may have had its roots in prehistoric religious beliefs. It is thought that Bronze Age man may have appeased the river gods in a ritual which involved 'burying' weapons of war in lakes and rivers.

AVALON: KING ARTHUR'S RESTING PLACE

The island of Avalon belongs to the realm of the imagination, yet its location has been eagerly sought. The discovery of King Arthur's grave has linked it inextricably with the English town of Glastonbury.

Many of the Celts believed that the dead lived on, and that their saints and heroes were transported after death to the idyllic island of Avalon. Consequently, when the 12th-century scholar Geoffrey of Monmouth came to write his popular *History of the Kings of Britain,* he linked Avalon with the Celtic hero King Arthur. According to Geoffrey, the mortally wounded king was borne to Avalon, where his sister, the sorceress Morgan le Fay, promised to heal him if he stayed with her.

The Arthurian legend in addition asserted that one day Arthur would return to liberate the Welsh from the yoke of the English kings: after all, was he not the once and future king? The chronicler William of Malmesbury, in common with other early commentators, wrote in 1125 that Arthur's place of burial 'is nowhere to be seen, whence ancient rhymes fable that he is yet to come'.

The English kings of the 12th century were faced with an unruly Welsh nation which openly espoused the hope that Arthur would return from Avalon and defeat the royal oppressors. In particular, the Plantagenet King Henry II felt it would be prudent to dash these hopes once and for all by finding Arthur's burial place, thereby proving beyond doubt that the Celtic hero was dead. Henry had been told that Arthur might be buried at Glastonbury and instructed the Abbot of Glastonbury to start searching for the grave.

The monastery at Glastonbury, founded in 705, had become a Benedictine house in the tenth century. In 1184 the abbey was destroyed by fire and Henry II initiated its reconstruction. But Henry died in 1189, and soon afterwards the monks – probably prompted by a financial crisis – started to dig, hoping to find relics of Arthur that would bring fame and fortune to their abbey.

What the monks discovered must have seemed highly satisfactory to those who were keen to link legend with reality. Working behind curtains, the diggers reached a depth of 7ft (2m) and finally found what they were looking for: a stone slab and a lead cross on which was inscribed *Hic jacet sepultus inclitus rex Arturius in insula Avalonia* ('Here lies buried the renowned King Arthur on the isle of Avalon'). Deeper still was an oak tree hollowed out in the shape of a coffin, inside which were two skeletons: one tall with its skull smashed by a heavy blow, the other smaller and with a fragment of blond hair still

'Isle of glass' *This name from Celtic mythology refers to Glastonbury when it was almost an island. The remains of Iron Age lake villages nearby confirm that this area of Somerset once lay under water and boats could have sailed to Glastonbury. The Tor rose from undrained marshes covered in sheets of water that reflected the sky.*

The Fortunate Isle *This was Geoffrey of Monmouth's name for Avalon, now identified with Glastonbury. In his second book,* Life of Merlin, *he described Avalon as a place where the earth 'of its own accord brings forth all things in superabundance'.*

AVALON: KING ARTHUR'S RESTING PLACE

attached. Surely these were the bodies of King Arthur and his queen, Guinevere?

The monks must have rejoiced, for the discovery of the bodies would once again draw pilgrims to Glastonbury and help fill their dwindling coffers. An additional bonus was that the burial clearly linked Glastonbury with the legendary island of Avalon, an identification which has become an accepted part of the abbey's tradition.

The bones were placed in two caskets, painted with the portraits of Arthur and Guinevere and their coats of arms, and were added to the abbey's treasury of relics. In 1278, while in the process of subduing the Welsh, King Edward I had Arthur's bones removed from the casket and put on display as a reminder that the king was dead and would not come again. They were then transferred to a tomb and placed in front of the high altar, where they remained until the dissolution of the monastery in 1539.

It is tempting to suppose that the discovery of the bodies was engineered by the abbot to raise funds for the rebuilding of Glastonbury Abbey. The story is, however, backed by archaeological evidence. In 1934, the remains of the empty second tomb were found where the high altar had once stood, and a plaque now marks the spot. A second archaeological excavation, led by Dr Ralegh Radford in 1962, rediscovered the original grave and confirmed that a cavity had existed there; but it could find no evidence as to the grave's occupant. This site lies some 50ft (15m) from the south door of the Lady Chapel.

The lead cross originally found at the grave has also given rise to doubts. There are several different versions of the inscription on the cross, which disappeared more than 200 years ago. Early descriptions say it mentioned Guinevere as well as Arthur, but a drawing of the cross in William Camden's *Britannia* in 1607 makes no mention of her name.

It has been suggested that the cross was made by the monks in 1190, but this is hard to accept. The lettering is crude and points to an earlier date, while the Latin version of Arthur – *Arturius* – was not in use at that time and has only been found in a seventh-century document. If the cross was a fake, its maker was remarkably consistent.

Mystery also surrounds the final resting place of the cross. It survived the Dissolution and 200 years ago was known to have been in the possession of a member of the clergy at Wells Cathedral. The rediscovery of the cross, which is by no means impossible, would open up the whole debate again.

Glastonbury is an ancient site which has always been imbued with myth and legend. In pre-Christian times pagan rites were practised on Glastonbury Tor, and excavations have uncovered traces of Christian buildings that predate the foundation of the monastery in 705. Legend has it that the early church, or 'Old Church', was built by Joseph of Arimathea, the rich man who wrapped up the body of Jesus and carried it to his own tomb. Joseph's staff was supposed to have taken root and become the Glastonbury Thorn, which still flowers at Easter and Christmas in the abbey grounds. With such a history, it seems fitting that Glastonbury should provide the setting for Arthur's death and the identification with Avalon.

THE GLASTONBURY ZODIAC

In 1929, a wave of controversy was caused by the publication of a book *The Glastonbury Temple of the Stars*, written by the English sculptress Katharine Maltwood (1878–1961). The author (RIGHT) claimed to have discovered a group of huge figures outlined by the natural contours and man-made features of the Somerset countryside in a 30 mile (48km) circle around Glastonbury. She believed that the area's hills, watercourses, ancient tracks and earthworks represented the 12 signs of the zodiac, with the 525ft (160m) Tor itself as the zodiac's centre. By the association of place names and legends, she then linked the whole zodiac with the story of King Arthur.

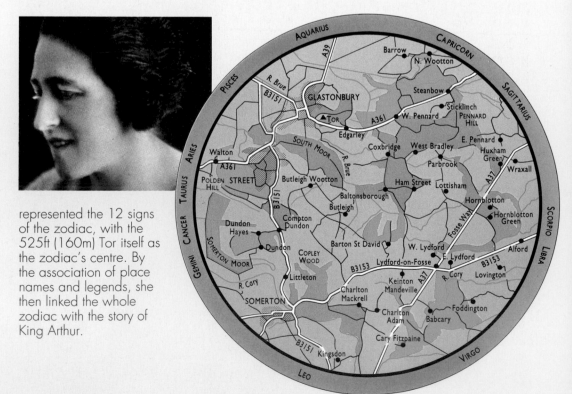

374

The Death of King Arthur In the painting of the death of Arthur by the 19th-century British artist James Archer, the dying king is tended by two queens. In Malory's tale, a single queen, and other black-hooded women, bore Arthur in a barge to Avalon, where according to Geoffrey of Monmouth's account he would be healed of his wounds. This idea may have had its origins in the legend of a sanctuary off the Brittany coast – where enchantresses were reputed to cure the ills of all who came there.

The living dead The Celts envisaged the dead as living on a distant island, which is probably how the Avalon legend arose. This belief led to the practice of burying the dead on islands. One sixth-century historian wrote that Britain served as such a place for the Franks. Bardsey Island (ABOVE), off the coast of North Wales, was another burial ground, reputed to contain the graves of 20 000 saints. Glastonbury, which was once virtually an island, may also have been a burial place for the dead.

Legendary site There are many stories and traditions associated with Glastonbury and its ruined abbey. Joseph of Arimathaea was supposed to have settled in Glastonbury, and both King Arthur and St Patrick are said to be buried in the abbey grounds. Legend has it that Glastonbury Tor was once the entrance to a realm of the underworld.

ELSINORE: CASTLE OF HEROES

The impressive fortress of Kronborg once struck fear into the hearts of foreign sailors. But its fame rests on its connection with two great figures of legend, Hamlet, prince of Denmark, and Holger the Dane.

N orth of Copenhagen, on a promontory overlooking the sea, stands the great castle of Kronborg, its elegant copper-clad pinnacles contrasting dramatically with its massive fortifications. The castle's history is one of contrasts too – over the centuries it has served as a royal residence, a garrison and, latterly, a museum. However, its fame chiefly rests on its connection with two great figures of legend.

The first of these is Hamlet, prince of Denmark, the eponymous hero of the play by William Shakespeare (1564–1616). Kronborg was the setting for this drama, but the playwright called it Elsinore, using the anglicised form of Helsingør, the name of the town at the foot of the castle walls. The other legendary hero is Holger the Dane, one of the 12 knights-companion, or paladins, of Charlemagne (742–814), Emperor of the West. Like the British King Arthur, Holger is supposed to be sleeping until the hour of his country's greatest need, when he will rise to defend it.

Eric of Pomerania, king of Denmark, Sweden and Norway, built the citadel of Krogen, on Elsinore's outermost spit of land, in about 1420. The fortress defended the waters of the Sound (both sides of which were Danish territory until 1660) and enforced the payment of the Sound Dues, a toll paid by ships passing through on their way to the Baltic.

King Frederick II decided to rebuild the fortress in 1574, when his country declared war against Sweden. He chose the most fashionable style of the period – Dutch Renaissance – and by 1585 the new castle, renamed Kronborg, was complete. Four years later, Kronborg Castle provided a romantic setting for the honeymoon of James VI of Scotland (later James I of England), following his politically expedient marriage to Frederick's daughter, Anne of Denmark. Since the English generally regarded the castle as Denmark's best-known landmark, it is not surprising that Shakespeare chose it as the dramatic backdrop for his setting of *Hamlet,* which he wrote between 1600 and 1601.

As was his usual practice, Shakespeare based his tragedy on an existing story. In the late 12th century, the Danish historian Saxo Grammaticus had written a Latin history of Denmark. In it he described the tumultuous career of Amleth, prince of Denmark, whose father was murdered by Amleth's uncle. The uncle then married the widowed

Magnificent fortress
Kronborg Castle stands at the narrowest part of the Sound between Denmark and Sweden. Between 1425 and 1857 foreign ships had to anchor at Kronborg to pay a toll before they were allowed to pass through the Sound. The revenue went directly to the king, whose large bronze cannon on the seaward side of the castle ensured that ships always paid their dues.

ELSINORE: CASTLE OF HEROES

Delineatio Arcis CRONENBURGENSIS

Strong defence *During the reign of King Christian V (1670–99), massive new fortifications were built on the landward side of Kronborg Castle, seen in an engraving of c.1696. On and off for a century, Denmark had been at war with Sweden, which menaced her from Bremen and Pomerania to the south.*

Gerutha and usurped the throne. Grammaticus set the story in Jutland, but Shakespeare moved it to Kronborg Castle; he may even have heard a detailed description of the castle from actors who had performed there for the Danish court.

Certainly King Frederick had created a landmark to inspire, a place to be both feared and revered by foreign visitors, but this fortress did not stand undisturbed after his extensive renovations. In 1629, during the reign of King Christian IV, it was badly damaged by fire, but was meticulously rebuilt in the same style. (The chapel, which escaped the fire, still has its original gilded oak furnishings.) Between 1658 and 1660, Kronborg was occupied by the Swedes, who carried off many of the paintings and

figures from the fountain in the castle courtyard when they eventually departed.

In the late 18th century, part of the castle became the prison of the young English princess Matilda, who was forced to marry the mad Danish King Christian VII. Wrongly accused of infidelity, she was imprisoned for the rest of her short life, first in Kronborg, then in Hanover, where she died in 1785, aged 23. In that same year the castle was requisitioned for use as a barracks and it served this purpose until 1922.

Kronborg has attracted many tourists over the last 200 years. A whimsical garden was created towards the end of the 18th century, where visitors could wander to the Kingdom of Heaven, passing on the way a Hermit's Hut

Holger the Dane, sculpted by Hans Peder Pedersen-Dan in 1906, sits in the dungeons beneath Kronborg. Regarded as the Danish national hero, he was known as one of Charlemagne's paladins and was said to have lived with the enchantress Morgan le Fay in Avalon for 100 years before returning to court. This probably gave rise to the legend – enshrined in one of Hans Andersen's fairytales – of his sleeping under the castle until needed by his country.

Playing the part The leading British actor John Gielgud (RIGHT) played Shakespeare's melancholy Dane, Hamlet, at Kronborg in 1939. The very first performance of the play at the castle took place in 1816.

The mad prince The Danish prince Hamlet (BELOW), shown in this 17th-century portrait, is the subject of Shakespeare's tragedy. In the earliest written Danish version of the legend, the prince feigns madness and eventually wins back his kingdom. Shakespeare used the idea of Hamlet's pretending to be mad to cover up his plot to avenge his father's death.

and make-believe grave, marked by a broken column. This garden became known as Hamlet's Garden and the grave as Hamlet's Grave. In 1857, an enterprising local man obtained permission 'to arrange Hamlet's Grave in a manner corresponding to legend'. He moved the pillar elsewhere and charged 32 skillings to see it. Although this is no longer on view to visitors, most tourist guides continue to offer a 'Hamlet tour'.

Visitors still flock to the castle, which now houses a maritime museum, to walk on the ramparts and to enjoy a stroll in the pleasant seaport of Elsinore with its cobbled streets and old houses. It is a fitting tribute to Shakespeare and Kronborg that the 180-year-old tradition of performing *Hamlet* in the castle courtyard continues today.

ATLANTIS: A LOST CONTINENT

The wealthy island of Atlantis was supposedly peopled by virtuous citizens, boasted golden walls and silver temples, pleasure gardens and a racecourse, but was destroyed in anger by the god who had fashioned it. The story of Atlantis is well known, yet when and where this utopia existed, if ever it did, remains a mystery.

For more than two millennia, the legend of an idyllic golden age enjoyed by the citizens of a fabulously wealthy island continent – swept away in an overnight cataclysm – has gripped the Western imagination. The Greek philosopher Plato's description of the rise and fall of Atlantis has inspired some 2000 books and untold years of investigation. And, although more than 40 sites have been suggested for this legendary utopia, there is still no evidence that it existed at all.

In his dialogues *Timaeus* and *Critias*, penned in the fourth century BC, Plato gave the first written account of an island 'larger than Libya and Asia Minor together' and the people who profited from its bounty. Atlantis was given to Poseidon, god of the sea and earthquakes, at the sharing out of the earth. The Atlanteans were all descended from the god and Clerio, the mortal woman whom he married.

According to Plato, Atlantis was a great maritime nation, lying beyond the Pillars of Hercules (the present-day Strait of Gibraltar) and dominating the Mediterranean as far as Egypt and Turkey. It was a place rich in natural resources, with an abundance of food. High mountains provided shelter from the northerly winds, and animals – including elephants and horses – roamed its meadows and drank from its lakes and streams. Ten kings reigned over the ten regions of this island paradise, whose citizens coexisted in perfect harmony. 'They despised everything but virtue... giving little thought to the possession of gold and other property.' Not only were they model citizens, the Atlanteans were also great horsemen and skilful helmsmen.

In time, however, the people of Atlantis grew discontented with their many blessings and tried to extend their domain throughout the entire world. In the climactic battle that ensued, Athens stood alone against Atlantis, and prevailed. Poseidon turned his wrath on the island: around 9500 BC a terrible cataclysm struck and Atlantis disappeared beneath the waves, along with all trace of its existence.

Plato was adamant that the story was true, and quoted as his source a tale told to an Athenian statesman, Solon, 200 years earlier and then passed down orally. Viewed as history (although even Plato's pupil Aristotle did not accept the truth of the narrative), the rise and fall of Atlantis poses two problems: its date and location.

The earliest known civilisation developed in the region of present-day Iraq around 3500 BC, and there are no

Volcanic landscape
Sheer cliffs bear witness to the cataclysm that befell the island of Thera (Santorini) around 1500 BC. Since 1967, excavations on the island have revealed remains of a rich Bronze Age civilisation, with frescoes and artefacts similar to those discovered on Minoan Crete, 75 miles (120km) to the south. Items associated with a bull cult fit Plato's description of the Atlanteans' religious preferences.

Eye of the storm *The rim of a crater (RIGHT) some 31 sq miles (80km²) in extent is all that remains of the once towering volcano of Thera. Evidence suggests that the blast was felt as far away as Crete and the western coast of Turkey, and it is likely that the ash from such an*

eruption blocked out the sun over the whole of the eastern Mediterranean for several days. In addition, the eruption of Thera is contemporary with, and almost certainly related to, the collapse of the powerful and prosperous Minoan civilisation on Crete.

ATLANTIS: A LOST CONTINENT

traces of settled communities at all before 7000 BC. There was no Athenian city-state to wage war against Atlantis in 9500 BC. Nor were horses known in Europe until the Bronze Age (around 3000 BC), yet they are mentioned frequently in Plato's Atlantis.

The principal difficulty in siting Atlantis is Plato's insistence that it lay beyond the Pillars of Hercules, which is inconsistent with both of today's preferred locations: the Greek island of Thera (Santorini) and Troy. In 1992 Dr Eberhard Zangger, a German geoarchaeologist – that is, a practitioner of the science of linking archaeology to changes in the landscape – published the result of a ten-year study into the location of Atlantis, entitled *The Flood from Heaven*. He maintains that Troy on mainland Turkey fits Plato's description of the site of Atlantis. It stands to the north of a plain adjacent to narrow straits, is buffeted by strong northerly winds, and there are hot and cold springs nearby. More persuasively, he believes that the epithet 'Pillars of Hercules' was applied to the Strait of Gibraltar only around 500 BC. Before that time, he says, the term was used to describe the Dardanelles, the strait separating Europe and Asia, leading to the Black Sea. As for Plato's contention that Atlantis drowned (while Troy did not), he argues that around 1200 BC flash floods did indeed submerge those parts of Troy located on the plain.

Dr Zangger's theories have yet to be evaluated fully; until they are, the favourite site for Atlantis remains Thera. There are many similarities between Plato's description

Golden age existence
Landscaped gardens and an exercise ground for horses (ABOVE) *are depicted in Gerald Hargreaves'* Atalanta *(1949), one of many books on Atlantis.*

and the archaeological remains of the Bronze Age civilisations of the Aegean (3000–1500 BC). Excavations at Akrotiri on Thera by the Greek archaeologist Professor Marinatos have uncovered the remains of a large Bronze Age city thought to be an important commercial centre of the Minoan civilisation. Houses two or three storeys high and richly decorated with frescoes bear witness to Thera's prosperity. Around 1500 BC calamity befell the island: Thera's volcano erupted with great force and the whole island was 'swallowed by the sea'.

Neither Troy nor Thera fits the date '9000 years before Solon' of Plato's Atlantis. One theory supposes that this is due to the simple mistake of adding a nought. If Plato had meant '900 years before Solon', the date would have coincided neatly with the eruptions on Thera.

It may never be possible to say whether Plato was describing fact or fiction. If it could be proven beyond doubt that an error was made in the date, and that the Pillars of Hercules did not always refer to the Strait of Gibraltar, the riddle of Atlantis might be solved.

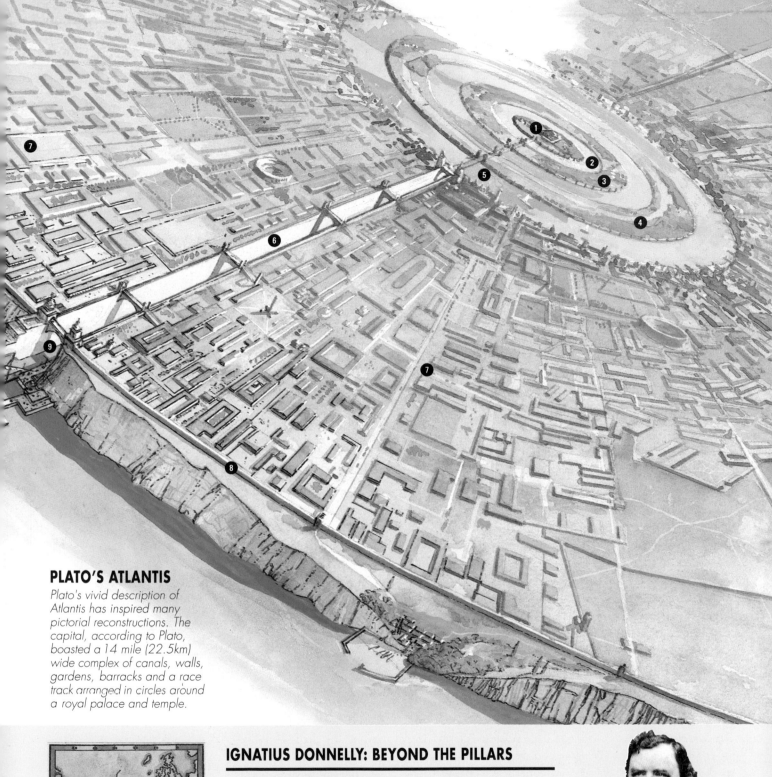

PLATO'S ATLANTIS

Plato's vivid description of Atlantis has inspired many pictorial reconstructions. The capital, according to Plato, boasted a 14 mile (22.5km) wide complex of canals, walls, gardens, barracks and a race track arranged in circles around a royal palace and temple.

IGNATIUS DONNELLY: BEYOND THE PILLARS

An Irish-American scholar and politician, Ignatius Donnelly (1831–1901), published *Atlantis: the Antediluvian World* in 1882. Much of his theory about the lost continent was fanciful, but his location of the island in the mid-Atlantic (LEFT) fits Plato's description. He looked at the similarities between mythologies, languages and customs of ancient civilisations on both sides of the Atlantic, such as the Ancient Egyptian and pre-Colombian cultures, and suggested that Atlantis – sunk midway between the Old and New Worlds – provided the cultural bridge between them. He also dated the destruction of Atlantis to the final retreat of the last great Ice Age, around 8000 BC, when glaciers melted and the oceans rose to unprecedented heights.

SHANGRI-LA: A HEAVENLY ABODE

A harmonious community situated somewhere in Asia, a dream world to fulfil all human aspirations: James Hilton's Shangri-La captured the imagination of the Western world in the early 20th century.

W hen the English novelist James Hilton chose to locate the action of his romantic adventure *Lost Horizon* in Shangri-La, he gave his native language a new word. The novel, published in 1933, and to an even greater extent the film made soon afterwards, caught the public imagination. Shangri-La and the isolated utopian community it supported were presumed to be real.

The community into which Hilton's two stranded airmen stumbled was situated in an unexplored and inaccessible region of Tibet. There, in a lamasery perched high on a mountain, 50 lamas (monks) spent their days in the pursuit of knowledge and the arts; at their head was the High Lama, who had discovered the secret of longevity and who could foretell the future. One of his prophesies was that Shangri-La would be threatened by barbarians from outside.

Guided by the principles of moderation in all things, the lamas ruled over 1000 Tibetans, who lived in peace and harmony in the fertile valley below. Here, in a stretch of land some 12 miles (20km) long and 5 miles (8km) wide, they grew a variety of crops. A rich gold seam meant that anything that could not be produced in Shangri-La could be bought from elsewhere. No strangers ever entered the city, however; villagers left the valley and met their contacts at prearranged points.

Precedents for Shangri-La are not difficult to find. There are many traditions of a hidden earthly paradise in Eastern cultures. Early Buddhist writings call it Chang Shambhala and describe it as a source of ancient wisdom. Belief in it was once widespread – in China, the Kunlun Mountains were said to shelter a valley where immortals lived in perfect harmony, while Indians sought a place called Kalapa, north of the Himalayas, home of 'perfect men'. By following the path of the Tartars back to Mongolia, Russian legend held that one would reach Belovodye, where holy men lived apart from the world in the Land of White Waters. Tibetan and Mongolian legends, too, told of such a paradise.

If Shangri-La were to exist in reality rather than myth, then Tibet would be one of the most likely locations. The country could rightly be considered the most remote on Earth, almost impossible to reach, and unwelcoming to foreigners. There, from his monastery-citadel at Lhasa (from 1904 a 'forbidden city' to Europeans), the Dalai Lama presided over the spiritual and material well-being of his subjects. The very fact that so few Westerners had

Hidden utopia *Seemingly impassable mountains wreathed in mist hiding lush valleys are central to almost every legend of a perfect place removed from civilisation, including Hilton's Shangri-La. It is not surprising that Hilton sited his Shangri-La in a part of the Far East where the landscape is dominated by high mountains sheltering fertile green valleys.*

SHANGRI-LA: A HEAVENLY ABODE

seen Lhasa fostered the belief that those who could visit the city would witness marvels. And certainly Buddhist monks and mystics were credited with extraordinary powers. One dramatic training was that of *lung gon*, reputed to allow adherents to overcome gravity and reduce their body weight so that they could move along at fantastic speeds.

The British traveller Alexandra David-Neel spent 14 years in Tibet at the beginning of this century. She recorded seeing a lama travelling at an incredible speed without running: 'He seemed to lift himself from the ground, proceeding by leaps. It looked as if he had been endowed with the elasticity of a ball.' She was prevented from

stopping him by her Tibetan companion, who told her that to break his meditation would most certainly kill him.

David-Neel belonged to the Theosophical Society (a religious sect with roots in Buddhism, founded in 1875), which may have coloured her perceptions of Tibetan life. But her experiences are echoed by the Russian traveller Nicholas Roerich, who made many visits to the country and recorded what he had seen in *Shambhala*, published in 1930. (Shambhala has become a synonym for Shangri-La.) In devising *Lost Horizon* Hilton undoubtedly drew on this work and on David-Neel's journals.

The Buddhist tradition of a subterranean paradise

Medium and message
The 1937 film of Lost Horizon *(LEFT), for which Hilton himself wrote the screenplay, found a responsive audience.*

Hilton was not the first to write about an ideal community isolated from the corruption and barbarism of modern civilisation. The ability to see into the future and to enjoy an abnormally long life span are also common in such tales. But at a time of political and economic turmoil, Hilton and director Frank Capra did make an opportune comparison between the materialistic and war-torn West and the wisdom and peace of the mystical East.

Tibetan sanctuary
Banners and tapestries (ABOVE) illustrate Shambhala, 'a northern place of quietude' in or to the north of Tibet, where mountains enclose secret valleys.

Mountain paradise *The Himalayas were the setting for Nicholas Roerich's* Abode of Light. *In the preface, the publisher calls Roerich a 'mystic-dreamer'.*

known as Aghartha has also been linked with Shambhala. On his 1924 expedition through the Altai Mountains in Mongolia, Roerich was told by a lama that Shambhala was a great city at the heart of Aghartha where 'the king of the world' ruled. He became convinced Aghartha was linked to all the nations of the world by subterranean tunnels.

In his novel *The Coming Race* (1871), the English writer Edward Bulwer Lytton also describes a world under the earth's crust populated by a superior race, the *Vril-ya*. Through the exercise of *vril* – a psychokinetic energy, more highly developed in the female, dominant, sex – the *Vril-ya* plans to conquer the 'upper world'.

This notion of a master race equipped with mystical powers proved a powerful attraction to both occultists and the Nazis. Adolf Hitler believed in the existence of a superior race living underground and even sent expeditions to search in German, Swiss and Italian mines for the entrance to their kingdom.

It is ironic that barbarians akin to those foretold by *Lost Horizon's* High Lama should seek for their own ends the secret utopia, where holy men live in peace and harmony. Shangri-La continues to symbolise for people a serenely tranquil place, within the boundaries of which all human desires are satisfied.

387

GARDEN OF EDEN: PRIMAEVAL PARADISE

The existence of a paradise on Earth where all was perfection has been part of human belief from earliest times. Its location may never be known, but the Garden of Eden has been a most fruitful source of artistic inspiration.

The account in the book of Genesis of the creation of Adam and Eve, their fall from grace and expulsion from the paradise on Earth that God made for them, lies at the heart of the Jewish and Christian traditions. The idea of the Garden of Eden has captured the creative imagination of generations of artists and writers, throughout the centuries.

The world's most famous garden was idyllic, well-watered and abundant with food. For company, Adam and Eve had 'every beast of the field and fowl of the air'. Trees provided ample shade; a sparkling river flowed through the garden and, once outside, divided into four streams – the Pishon, Gilon, Tigris and Euphrates. That much was documented. Shape, size and location were left open to interpretation. The only tree whose presence can be inferred with any degree of certainty is the fig, although later tradition identified the date palm with the tree of life and the banana plant as the tree of knowledge of good and evil.

The garden was usually conceived of as enclosed, although this may be because the word *paradisos*, the Greek translation of Garden of Eden, means 'an enclosed piece of land'. From these scant beginnings, poets and painters, commentators and theologians fashioned images of Eden, often drawing on other traditions of the earthly paradise to round out their own interpretations.

Probably the oldest account of such a paradise dates from the second millennium BC. The Sumerian Dilmun, situated where the sun rises, was the abode of the gods, a place where grieving, sickness and old age were unknown and where 'the raven's croak could not be heard'. There is more specific reference to a magical garden (albeit bearing more resemblance to 'God's garden' of the book of Ezekiel than to the Eden of Genesis) in the Sumerian *Epic of Gilgamesh*. Here, the hero Gilgamesh journeyed to a mountaintop 'garden of the gods', where the bushes glittered with gems: fruits of carnelian and leaves of lapis lazuli.

The non-Biblical descriptions of paradise that had most influence on later Christian visions were those of the Classical poets. In the eighth century BC, the Greek epic poet Homer wrote of a place he called Elysium, situated at the world's end. There was no snow in Elysium, nor any strong winds, just a gentle refreshing breeze. Homer's contemporary Hesiod, by contrast, focused on idyllic existence, rather than the place itself, evoking a lost

golden age when people were at peace. Like Adam and Eve before the Fall, they never grew old, but lived, free from toil, on the ample bounty of the fruits of the land.

Homer and Hesiod, and the later Roman poets Virgil and Ovid, influenced visions of the garden from the early Christian era to the Renaissance and beyond. In his epic work *Paradise Lost*, the English poet John Milton (1608–74), for example, described the Garden of Eden in vivid detail. His paradise was a walled plateau on a craggy, wooded mountain, reached by climbing a steep path. Scented plants such as myrtle and balm perfumed the air, which was filled with birdsong; trees provided shade, and

Vision of heaven *The plan showing paradise divided into four parts is from an 18th-century Indian manuscript and is faithful to the Koranic vision. In earthly gardens, streams separated the four quadrants.*

THE GARDEN OF EDEN?

Renaissance Eden *Jan Bruegel followed an artistic tradition stretching back centuries when he painted his vision of a lush paradise in 1620. He had some advantages over earlier artists in that he was able to include exotic birds such as parrots, which he could paint from life, or at least from illustrations by those who had seen such creatures in the flesh. In addition, his animals, while not necessarily native to Europe, did not have to be conjured from fantasy. He chose to take the story of the apple literally, incorporating an abundant crop.*

GARDEN OF EDEN: PRIMAEVAL PARADISE

streams and fountains offered an ample water supply. Milton's genius was to take material from both Biblical and non-Biblical sources and weave it into a coherent whole. The perpetual spring that the garden enjoyed and its fertile soil were both firmly rooted in Classical Elysium.

The garden as a feast for the senses is also a feature of the Islamic paradise which, unlike the Garden of Eden, exists in heaven rather than on earth. According to the Koran, steadfast Muslims will be rewarded in the afterlife with gardens containing gushing fountains and flowing springs, shade-giving trees (including the palm and the pomegranate) and soft couches on which to recline. Dressed in green silk robes, the blessed, attended by virgins 'as fair as rubies and corals', will be served food in silver dishes.

While Islamic scholars were more concerned with recreating paradise on Earth by constructing idyllic gardens, their Christian counterparts, as late as the Middle Ages, became obsessed with the idea of finding the Garden of Eden. Some believed it must have been destroyed in the Great Flood; others that the garden was sited on a mountain and so survived. A popular view was that it was located in the east, on an island: Sri Lanka became the preferred site. When Christopher Columbus deduced that the world was not flat but pear-shaped, this prompted the conclusion that the garden was situated on its 'stalk'.

As more and more of the world was charted, but with no sign of the garden, scholars returned to Genesis looking for clues as to its whereabouts. Mesopotamia (the ancient name for Iraq) seemed the obvious place to start since the Tigris and the Euphrates, named in the Bible, flow

Rivers of life *Islamic gardens, whether in Iran, India, Moorish Spain or elsewhere, have in common pools of water blue with the reflection of the sky, playing fountains, scented flowers and shade-giving trees, in accordance with the Koranic description of paradise. The garden at Fin in Iran was created in 1550 and, following tradition, is enclosed, rectangular and divided into four quarters by water channels that mirror the four rivers of life.*

The four continents *Traditionally, the botanic garden was conceived as an attempt to recreate the Garden of Eden by bringing together flowers, shrubs and herbs from all over the world. The Oxford Botanic Garden in England was laid out in 1621 in four quadrants to symbolise the four rivers of life and the four known continents – Europe, Africa, Asia and America.*

through the area. But Mesopotamia is huge, and the other two streams, the Pishon and the Gihon, could not be located and so were of no help in pin-pointing the site of the garden. Jerusalem, and Golgotha, where Jesus was crucified, were also associated with the garden. Since Jesus was often typified as the second Adam, it was satisfying to link the place of His death with the site of Adam's banishment.

It is thought that the inability to locate the Garden of Eden prompted Christians to follow the Islamic lead and try to recreate it. They drew on the Bible and Classicism rather than the Koran; nevertheless, in the botanic gardens of Padua, Paris, Oxford and elsewhere laid out in the 16th and 17th centuries, they succeeded in fashioning paradise on earth.

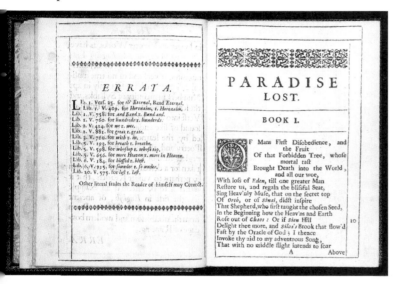

Lost for words *In his great epic,* Paradise Lost, *first published in 1667, John Milton* (LEFT) *sited Eden on top of a mountain. His version of the garden featured cascading streams, palms, cedars and scented shrubs. It was a paradise for the senses.*

Artistic inspiration
The lack of any detailed description of the garden has given artists free rein over the centuries. The Dutch painter Hieronymous Bosch (1450–1516) envisaged a rural idyll, where Adam and Eve lived in harmony with exotic animals and birds. Bosch's well-watered Garden of Eden supported an abundant and luxuriant plant life.*

EL DORADO: CITY OF GOLD

For more than four centuries adventurers have sought the legendary city of El Dorado in the mountains and jungles of South America. It has never been found, for it did not exist, and yet the power embodied in the tale of a place of inestimable riches remains undiminished.

People have been obsessed with gold since it was first discovered. This is partly due to its rarity: the total mined in all the world to date amounts only to some 100 000 tons. Gold is also one of the most constant metals, neither corroding nor tarnishing, therefore it has long been the choice of kings, the ultimate measure and symbol of wealth.

This association with riches beyond man's wildest dreams guaranteed its place in fact and fiction, but gold has also acquired mythic status. The most potent golden legend – that of the fabulously wealthy city of El Dorado, where even the cooking pots were made of gold – has attracted generations of adventurers to South America. All have been disappointed, since they were drawn by a myth.

Like most myths, the story of El Dorado has some basis in fact, and its genesis can be dated fairly precisely. When Christopher Columbus returned from his voyage of discovery in 1493 with tales of having seen unlimited supplies of gold, he unleashed gold fever in Europe. Within 50 years, the enormous stocks of gold owned by the Aztecs of Mexico and the Incas of Peru had been plundered by the conquistadors. No one in Europe who witnessed the unloading of ships stacked high with golden artefacts, ingots (many objects were melted down before transportation) and gemstones can have doubted that there was wealth for the taking in the New World. Tales of the conquistadors' good fortune were legion. In 1530, for example, Francisco Pizarro held the Inca emperor Atahualpa to ransom for a roomful of gold and two of silver; his demands were met.

In 1539, the Spanish entered the territory of the Muisca people and founded the city of Bogotá. Here they heard of the traditional ceremony performed on the shores of

Lady of the water
Surrounded by desolate hills, Lake Guatavita, the favoured location for the mythical city of El Dorado, is situated 30 miles (50km) north-east of the Colombian capital, Bogotá. On one bank the lake still bears the scars of Antonio de Sepulveda's attempts to drain it in the 1580s. The lake was once sacred to the local Muisca people, who made offerings to a former chieftain's wife, said by legend to dwell in the depths of the lake with a terrible monster.

Scientific curiosity
Alexander von Humboldt published the first illustration of Lake Guatavita in 1810. He calculated that if 1000 Indians each threw five gold trinkets, as some accounts held, annually into the lake over 100 years, then 500,000 gold objects lay at the bottom.

The men who travelled to South America may have failed to locate a city of gold, but there was gold, and plenty of it, in the tombs and temples of the New World. The Muisca and other peoples had for centuries made golden masks of their leaders, many of which were encrusted with gemstones, particularly emeralds for the eyes. Although enormous numbers of masks and other artefacts were melted down and formed into ingots before shipment back to Europe, many escaped the conquistadors' grasp.

Lake Guatavita to the north-east to acknowledge a new Muisca king. Furthermore, it was claimed that there were people still living who had witnessed the last occasion when a king had been so honoured.

The ceremony took place at dawn so that the king and his entourage could salute the sun god. At the designated moment, the naked king was covered in gold dust so that he became, literally, a golden man, *el dorado*. He was placed on a rush raft, while courtiers arranged gold and emeralds at his feet for him to offer to the sun god. Four chiefs, also naked except for golden crowns, bracelets and other jewellery, joined him on the raft, each carrying an offering. When the raft reached the middle of the lake, a banner was raised as a signal for silence, whereupon the king and his chiefs cast their offerings into the waters.

The prospect of so much treasure within apparently easy reach gripped the Spanish imagination. In 1545 an attempt to dredge the Lake Guatavita yielded nothing. Undeterred, in the 1580s a Bogotá merchant, Antonio de Sepulveda, tried to drain it. With a labour force of 8000 Indians, he managed to cut a huge swathe in the shore-line, which is visible even today. A surge of water lowered the level of the lake by about 60ft (18m) before the banks collapsed, killing many of the labourers in the process. Sepulveda was partially successful, however, and the king of Spain was presented with a gold breastplate and staff as

Engraver's fancy *The new Muisca king is prepared for the sacred ceremony on Lake Guatavita* (RIGHT). *One attendant smears resin on to his body, while a second blows gold dust through a pipe: in this way he is totally covered in gold to become* el dorado, *'the golden man'. The Muisca costumes are the invention of the engraver Theodore de Bry, who lived in Germany and published the illustration there in 1590.*

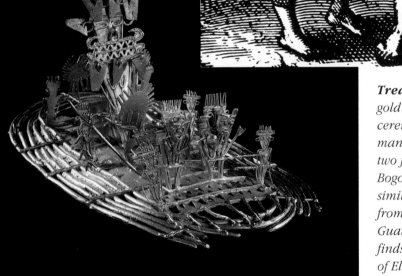

Treasure trove *A solid gold model depicting the ceremony of 'the golden man'* (LEFT) *was found by two farmers in a cave near Bogotá in 1969. It was similar to a piece recovered from Lake Siecha, near Guatavita, in 1856. Such finds ensure that the legend of El Dorado endures.*

Breath of life *The rivers of South America often yielded gold nuggets, and panners* (BELOW) *were a familiar sight to the conquering Spanish. In 1589, the Spaniard Juan Castellanos wrote of the inhabitants of Buritica, north-east of Bogotá: 'Gold is what gave them breath.'*

EL DORADO: CITY OF GOLD

well as an emerald the size of a hen's egg, found in the lake.

A century later the story started to change. As the tale was retold with embellishments, El Dorado ceased to be a person and became a place. In addition, its location shifted, first to the lower Orinoco, then to the Amazon, some 1500 miles (2400km) from Lake Guatavita. This was the legend that tempted the Englishmen Walter Raleigh and Colonel Percy Fawcett, the Spaniards Gonzalo Jiménez de Quesada and Sebastián de Belalcázar and the German Nicolaus Federmann to try to locate the golden city.

Lake Guatavita became the focus of renewed – largely fruitless – activity after 1799, when a party of scientists led by the Prussian Alexander von Humboldt spent 18 months tracing the course of the Orinoco River, which for part of its length flows along the Colombia–Venezuela border, deep inside the territory that had originally spawned the myth. Reports of the lake's existence brought a fresh wave of adventurers to the area. When, in 1807, Humboldt returned to the lake and publicly calculated that 500 000 gold objects must lie at its bottom, the search began again.

It seems likely that the vast majority of gold and jewels deposited in Lake Guatavita during the 'golden man' ceremony went into the Spanish treasury in the 16th century. Certainly the last major attempt to drain the lake, in 1912, yielded only a few small ornaments whose worth in no way compensated for the engineering costs. Those who searched for the city of El Dorado, on the other hand, were doomed to failure: in spite of the volumes dedicated to describing it, the golden city never existed.

In search of untold wealth *The routes taken by the majority of early explorers led to Lake Guatavita. Colonel Fawcett, who set out from Cuiabá,* *disappeared in mysterious circumstances. According to some reports he was discovered living in an Indian village, but his remains were never found.*

An empire for England *Sir Walter Raleigh realised that friendship with the Indians was essential if* *he was to achieve his goals of gold and territory for Britain. In this illustration he receives an Indian chief.*

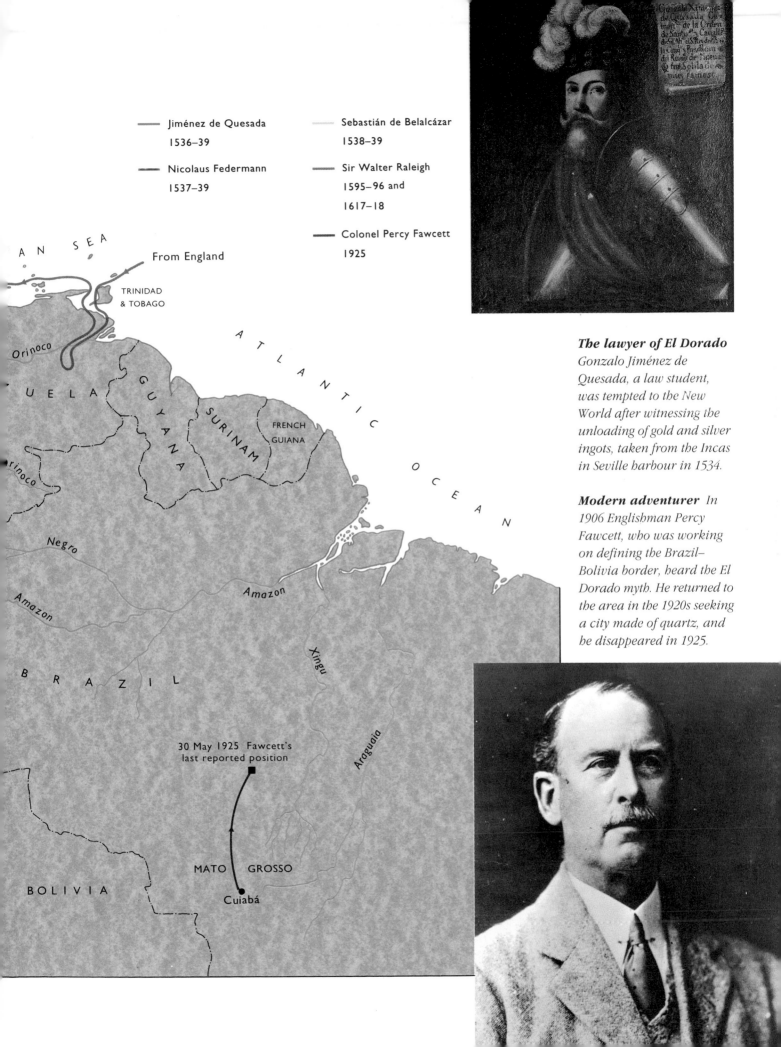

Jiménez de Quesada
1536–39

Nicolaus Federmann
1537–39

Sebastián de Belalcázar
1538–39

Sir Walter Raleigh
1595–96 and
1617–18

Colonel Percy Fawcett
1925

From England

The lawyer of El Dorado
Gonzalo Jiménez de Quesada, a law student, was tempted to the New World after witnessing the unloading of gold and silver ingots, taken from the Incas in Seville harbour in 1534.

Modern adventurer *In 1906 Englishman Percy Fawcett, who was working on defining the Brazil–Bolivia border, heard the El Dorado myth. He returned to the area in the 1920s seeking a city made of quartz, and he disappeared in 1925.*

30 May 1925 Fawcett's
last reported position

MATO   GROSSO

BOLIVIA   Cuiabá

GAZETTEER

Under the same headings as the chapters in the book – *Our Incredible Earth, Monumental Wonders, Watery Worlds, Riddles and Symbols* and *Timeless Landscapes* – the gazetteer gives information about other strange and amazing places in the world. The sites are arranged alphabetically; each is briefly described and its geographical location given. Where relevant, its historical significance is explained.

The symbol ◉ is used to indicate World Heritage Sites: sites considered under the World Heritage Convention of 1972 to be of unique natural and cultural value.

Bold page numbers in brackets refer to main articles; italic page numbers in brackets refer to gazetteer entries.

OUR INCREDIBLE EARTH

The Earth's natural features – timeless in their slow progression, yet shocking in the suddenness with which they can change – enforce our awareness of the fleeting and fragile quality of human endeavour. We can but marvel at the beauty and power of great mountains, volcanoes, deserts, canyons and caves, and the ingenious fitness of plant and animal life to survive in them.

Aconcagua   ARGENTINA
Cerro Aconcagua, at 22 834ft (6960m), is the highest mountain in the western hemisphere – 2513ft (766m) higher than Mount McKinley in Alaska, the tallest peak in North America. The summit of the mountain is situated in the Andes of Argentina, 70 miles (112km) from the city of Mendoza, but its western flanks lie in Chile, north of the capital Santiago. In the south, the mountain slopes sweep down to one of the most important passes in the Andes, the Uspallata Pass. A statue of Christ, erected in 1902 to commemorate the boundary agreement between Argentina and Chile, is located at the pass.

Statue of Christ

Ahaggar Mountains   ALGERIA
The mountain range in southern Algeria, known as the Ahaggar (or Hoggar), lies at the heart of the Sahara some 900 miles (1500km) south of Algiers. It is bounded on the north, south and east by steep sandstone cliffs that form the outer limits of the Tassili Plateau. From the plateau, which lies at an average height of 6500ft (2000m), the mountains rise to 9573ft (2918m) above sea level at Mount Tahat, the highest point in Algeria. The mountains are composed of metamorphic rock some 2000 million years old and are part of the ancient bedrock of the African continent. Some of the peaks are no more than volcanic cores, the rugged remains of volcanoes exposed by erosion. The tallest of these, the Ilamen, reaches an altitude of 8760ft (2670m).

Akan National Park   JAPAN
◉ Established in 1934, Akan Park on Hokkaido was named after one of two active volcanoes on the island. It covers 3346 sq miles (8666km²) within a subarctic zone of moors, virgin forest and spectacular lakes. The waters of Lake Ashu are said to be among the clearest in the world. The lake is also notable for a unique freshwater plant, the velvety green Marimo weed.

Amazonia National Park   BRAZIL
In 1974, a national park covering 4000 sq miles (10 360km²) was established in the Amazon rainforest of Brazil. It exhibits the rich variety of wildlife typical of tropical rainforests, with many ferns, herbs, vines, bromeliads, lianas and orchids flourishing among the mangrove, palm and rubber trees. Manatee and freshwater dolphins inhabit the river. Deer, capybaras, armadillos, tapirs and numerous species of monkeys live on the forest floor and among the trees. Bird species, as varied and colourful as they are numerous, include the toucan, parrots, macaws and the iridescent hummingbird.

South American hummingbird

Armand Cave   FRANCE
In 1897, the French potholer Louis Armand, exploring in the limestone hills of the Cévennes 50 miles (80km) north-west of Montpellier, discovered the deep cavern later named after him. After making his way down a vertical shaft 246ft (75m) deep, he entered a vast chamber, now known as La Grande Salle, which measures 330 by 180ft (100 by 55m). The floor is covered with what has been described as a 'forest' of stalagmites, formed from the percolation of water through the roof of the cave; the tallest of these is 100ft (30m) high.

Atacama Desert   CHILE
Reputedly the world's driest region, the Atacama Desert in northern Chile extends for 596 miles (960km), from the Peruvian border to the River Copiapû. It lies at an average altitude of 2000ft (610m) above sea level.

The desert, a series of dry salt basins in which there is almost no vegetation, contains rich deposits of nitrates, copper, iodine and borax. Water is piped from the Cordilleras (low mountain ranges to the east and west) to supply nitrate fields, copper mines and desert towns, such as Calama. This town experienced a drought that lasted 400 years, ending only in 1971.

Badkhyzsky Nature Reserve   TURKMENISTAN
◉ In 1941, when the Badkhyzsky Nature Reserve in southern Turkmenistan was established, the population of wild asses in the region was threatened with extinction, but since then it has made a remarkable recovery. Wild goats, wild pigs, honey badgers and hyenas, among other animals, live under the protection of the reserve, which covers an area of 514 sq miles (1330km²).

Banff National Park   CANADA
◉ Situated in the Rocky Mountains (*p404*) of southern Alberta, in Canada, Banff National Park covers an area of 2564 sq miles (6641km²). It borders Jasper National Park to the north and Yoho National Park to the west. Banff includes part of the Columbia ice field, the largest sheet of glacial ice in North America outside the Arctic Circle.

The park is famous for its grand scenery, particularly its glacial lakes, and for the hot springs on Sulphur Mountain. The forests are full of spruce, fir, pine, aspen, larch, balsam poplar and paper birch. There is also an abundance of wildlife. Bird species include the golden eagle, grosbeak, ptarmigan, Bohemian waxwing and Canadian jay. Grizzly and black bears, moose, mountain caribou, elk, mountain goats and bighorn sheep are among the larger mammals.

Moose

Bayerischer Wald National Park   GERMANY
This park occupies 46 sq miles (120km²) of mountainous terrain on the German border with the Czech Republic, where the granite mountains range in altitude from 2400 to 4800ft (730 to 1450m). Spruce trees dominate on the

higher slopes, with mixed forest, including pine, maple and beech, lower down. Within the park there is a small reserve at Neu Schönau, where bears, wild cats, buffaloes, lynx, grey wolves and other animals that once roamed wild in the region now lead a protected life.

Grey wolf

Blue Ridge Mountains   USA

The Appalachian range runs for more than 1200 miles (1930km) from Quebec in Canada south-west to Alabama. The Blue Ridge Mountains make up some 650 miles (1050km) of this mountain chain, beginning in southern Pennsylvania and running through Maryland, Virginia and North Carolina to Georgia. The range is noted for its wooded scenery and includes two outstanding national parks – Great Smoky Mountains National Park on the Tennessee–North Carolina state border and Shenandoah National Park (p362) in Virginia.

Brecon Beacons   WALES
National Park

The mountains, forests, moors and lakes of the Brecon Beacons National Park, established in 1957, lie between two sandstone ranges in Dyfed and Powys in southern Wales. To the west is Black Mountain and to the east are the Black Mountains; the highest mountain is Pen-y-Fan (2907ft/886m) situated in the centre of the park.

During the last Ice Age, glaciers poured from rock basins known as cwms, between the mountains. Some of these hold deep lakes, such as Cwm Ilwch below Pen-y-Fan which, according to local legend, is bottomless. In the south, there are many caves and wooded gorges.

The park is home to a wide variety of animal and plant life,

including alpine plants that grow on some of the high north-facing slopes. Polecats and badgers hunt on the lower hills, and the lakes harbour huge pike and eels.

Bryce Canyon   USA
◉ A network of ravines, running for 20 miles (32km) along the eastern edge of Paunsaugunt Plateau, makes up Bryce Canyon in southern Utah. The ravines were formed by erosion, which carved the plateau into thousands of rock towers, columns and spires. The shales, sandstone and limestone of the plateau are rich in minerals – iron compounds, copper and manganese – which contribute to the array of colours, from fiery red, through orange to deep purple, seen in the geological formations. Today the canyon is preserved as a national park.

Cacahuamilpa   MEXICO
Caverns

In a huge limestone formation near Taxco, about 90 miles (145km) south-west of Mexico City, underground streams and rivers have dissolved calcium carbonate from the rocks to form a series of caverns. The grandest of these is Cacahuamilpa. The main gallery here is 4528ft (1380m) long, 325ft (99m) wide and as much as 230ft (70m) high. Slowly dripping water has embellished the cavern walls with fantastic mineral formations, and stalagmites rise from the floor to a height of 130ft (40m).

Canyonlands   USA
National Park

A wilderness area, situated at the confluence of the Colorado and Green rivers in Utah, constitutes Canyonlands National Park. The rivers have carved two deep gorges into the red sandstone, and action by water and wind has created spectacular landforms, including mesas, spines and arches varying between 3600ft (1100m) and

Sego lily

almost 7000ft (2100m) high. Near the water, cottonwood and similar plants are found, and in the rainy season, from May to August, many wildflowers bloom, among them the Sego lily.

There is a wide variety of birds and other animals, including a herd of desert bighorn sheep indigenous to the area. Many ancient native American rock paintings decorate the walls of Horseshoe Canyon. The park was established in 1964 and covers 527 sq miles (1365km²).

Carlsbad Caverns   USA
National Park

A fabulously decorated system of underground chambers, Carlsbad Caverns lie beneath the arid Guadalupe Mountains of New Mexico. The caves also contain one of the largest colonies of bats in the world: 11 species make their homes here, including western pipistrelle, pallid, lump-nosed, fringed myotis and Mexican free-tailed bats.

Not all the caves have been explored, but those that have form a labyrinth some 23 miles (37km) in length. The Big Room (14 acres/5.6ha) is the biggest chamber in the USA; the deepest of the major caverns lies at 1013ft (309m). There is also an underground lake in which the water remains fresh because it does not support any life forms.

As an entity, the caverns contain a matchless array of spectacular limestone formations: stalagmites, stalactites and the rarer epsomite needles, soda straws, cave pearls and lily pads. In 1923, the Carlsbad Caverns became a national monument, and in 1930 they were designated a national park covering an area of 73 sq miles (189km²).

Carnarvon   AUSTRALIA
National Park

This park is sometimes referred to as the 'Grand Canyon of Queensland', for it is centred on an enormous gorge 20 miles (32km) long and 150–1200ft (45–370m) wide. In some places the sandstone walls rise vertically for 590ft (180m). The gorge, on the eastern face of the Great Dividing Range, was carved out by the waters of Carnarvon Creek. Many smaller gorges, branching

off the main one, contain caves, and in some of these fine examples of Aboriginal art have been found. Around the gorges are open forests of spotted eucalyptus, interspersed with cabbage palms and tree ferns up to 40ft (12m) high. Notable animals include koalas, pretty-face and brush-tailed rock wallabies, vulpine phalangers, the little northern dasyure and the platypus.

Koala

Cheddar Gorge   ENGLAND
Situated at the western end of the Mendip Hills in Somerset, the Cheddar Gorge lies some 15 miles (24km) south-west of Bristol. The gorge is famous for its systems of caverns and the fantastic natural limestone formations within them. The largest and most spectacular system was discovered in 1890. It extends some 3750ft (1145m) into the hills and contains remarkable limestone constructions which resemble natural and man-made wonders. These include petrified waterfalls, cathedral vaults and rushing rivers of 'marble'.

Chobe National   BOTSWANA
Park

The park covers 4180 sq miles (10 830km²) and is located in the valleys of the rivers Chobe, Ngwezumba and Savuti. Swamp, marshland forest and grassland dominate, with fauna typical of these ecosytems – including hippopotamuses, elephants, lions, leopards, cheetahs, zebras, giraffes, 18 species of antelopes and numerous bird species. A fossil lake-bed is among Chobe's most notable features.

Corbett National Park   INDIA
Established in 1935, Corbett National Park covers 201 sq miles (520km²) in the broad valley of the Ramganga River in Uttar Pradesh, near the foothills

of the Himalayas (p352). Open plains and hills, gorges and ravines are host to an astonishing variety of animals, including leopards, hyenas, jackals, wild pigs, hogs and barking deer, rhesus monkeys, common langurs, red junglefowl, ospreys, tortoises, crocodiles and Indian salmon.

The park was named after Jim Corbett, a well-known tiger hunter turned conservationist, and the presence of tigers is one of the park's outstanding features. Two other animals of note are the fish-eating gavial (a relative of the crocodile) and the marsh crocodile, or mugger.

Cotopaxi ECUADOR

An almost perfectly symmetrical volcanic cone, Cotopaxi is permanently covered with ice and snow. It rises to 19 344ft (5896m) above sea level in the Central Cordillera of the Andes, 30 miles (48km) from Quito, the capital city of Ecuador.

Cotopaxi is the highest active volcano in the world. Its first recorded eruption occurred in 1533, its last major eruption – and one of the worst in terms of casualties – in 1877. In that year, thousands of people were killed by gigantic avalanches of mud and meltwater created by the volcano's intense heat.

Devils Tower USA

The monolith known as Devils Tower is an excellent example of a volcanic intrusion that has been exposed by erosion. It is 865ft (263m) high, and its base is 1000ft (305m) in diameter. It is faced with fluted columns and has a flat top 275ft (85m) across, so the whole structure resembles a giant tree stump. This rock tower, situated in north-eastern Wyoming, near the Belle Fourche River, was declared a national monument in 1906, the first such designation in the USA.

Devils Tower

Dinosaur CANADA
Provincial Park

Situated in the southern part of Alberta, near the town of Brooks, Dinosaur Park is one of the world's most important sites for fossil remains. Extensive deposits of dinosaur skeletons and fossilised bones have been found here. More than 300 complete skeletons of 35 different dinosaur species have been uncovered, as well as the fossils of over 80 species of other vertebrates, including frogs, lizards, turtles, mammals and birds. Despite its seemingly harsh terrain, the park's 16 380 acres (6628ha) support a fragile and unique ecosystem containing many rare and endangered species. Lake Newell is on the flight path of migratory ducks.

Eisriesenwelt AUSTRIA

The Eisriesenwelt, meaning 'world of the ice giants', is a cave system in the Austrian Alps 30 miles (48km) south of Salzburg. The air temperature inside the cave, which lies 3300ft (1000m) above the valley floor, remains constantly at or below freezing point, so water dripping into the cave soon becomes frozen. As a result, the interior is filled with stalactites, stalagmites, 'curtains' and other formations made entirely of ice. Extending 26 miles (42km) into the mountains, the Eisriesenwelt is the largest permanently ice-filled cave in the world.

Gir Lion INDIA
National Park

Established in 1965, Gir Lion National Park in Gujarat covers 545 sq miles (1412km²) of open hilly country on the Kathiawar Peninsula of western India. The vegetation includes arid jungle of mixed deciduous teak forest and belts of thorn scrub.

The park is famous as the last sanctuary of the rare Asiatic lion, which has been protected in the Gir forest since the beginning of the century, when there were only about 12 left in India. At the end of the 1980s there were estimated to be some 300 lions in the national park. Other animals of note include leopards, hyenas and antelopes, wild pigs, sloth bears, deer, monkeys and numerous bird species.

Gobi Desert CENTRAL ASIA

One of the world's great desert regions, the Gobi Desert stretches in an arc 1000 miles (1600km) long from northern China to south-eastern Mongolia. It covers an area of some 500 000 sq miles (1.3 million km²) – about the size of the US state of Alaska. The desert lies on a plateau at altitudes between 3000 and 5000ft (900 and 1500m) and is largely composed of bare rock, particularly in the east, with sandier areas in the west.

Wildlife includes camels, horses and asses, and rodents such as the marmot and gopher. The fossil remains of dinosaurs and mammals and prehistoric implements have been found in central regions of the Gobi.

Gorge du Verdon FRANCE

In the middle reaches of the Verdon River, which rises on Mont Pelat in the Alpes Maritimes and merges with the Durance, a tributary of the Rhône, lies a great gorge. The Gorge du Verdon, about 30 miles (48km) north-west of Cannes, is the largest in France: 12 miles (19km) long and 2300ft (700m) at its maximum depth. In some places, the gorge is only 20ft (6m) wide at the bottom. The gorge was formed by the river eroding the limestone plateau over which it flows and is one of the most spectacular in the series of gorges formed by the Verdon in this way.

Gorongoza MOZAMBIQUE
National Park

Lying between a mountain range and a plateau region in central Mozambique is the Gorongoza National Park. The 1456 sq miles (3771km²) of the park include marshy areas, savanna, subtropical palm jungle and open grassland with many waterholes. This is one of the last refuges for the

Black rhinoceros

dwindling numbers of black rhinoceroses, with many other grassland animals well represented, among them lions (some of which have taken up residence in a group of derelict houses), leopards, zebras, elephants, hippopotamuses, antelopes, baboons, monkeys, crocodiles, storks, spoonbills and crowned cranes.

Gran Paradiso ITALY
National Park

Set amid the scenic mountain ranges of north-western Italy, Gran Paradiso borders France's Vanoise National Park (p406). The spectacular scenery comprises mountain ranges with peaks rising to 13 323ft (4061m), extensive glaciers, and forests of silver fir, pine and larch. In the alpine meadows, violas, saxifrage, campanulas, sedum and other

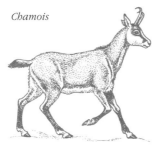

Chamois

plants make a colourful display in June, attracting a variety of butterflies. Ibex and chamois are present in such numbers that the populations must be artificially controlled. Smaller mammals include hares, foxes, badgers, otters, ermine, martens and weasels, with golden eagles, woodpeckers, snow finches, ptarmigans and white grouse among the bird species.

Great Basin USA
National Park

A nature reserve 120 sq miles (310km²) in area, Great Basin National Park was established in 1986. It occupies a region of great scenic beauty in the old Humboldt National Forest of Nevada. The mountainous landscape comprises the forested slopes of the southern Snake Mountains; the highest point, Wheeler Peak (13 063ft/3982m), is covered with ice and snow even in summer. On its eastern slopes are the Lehman Caves, a national monument since 1922.

Spectacular stalagmites and stalactites adorn the network of tunnels and galleries, inside which prehistoric native American artefacts and burial sites have been found.

Great Victoria Desert　AUSTRALIA

A vast, arid wasteland of ever-shifting sand hills, the Great Victoria Desert of south-west Australia has little vegetation other than spinifex grass. The desert lies between Gibson Desert in the north and the Nullarbor Plain to the south. It extends eastwards from Kalgoorlie almost as far as the Stuart range. Much of the Great Victoria's eastern extremity is Aboriginal territory.

Greenland　ATLANTIC/ ARCTIC OCEANS

Greenland is the largest island in the world. It is separated from Canada's Ellesmere Island by 16 miles (26km), with the nearest European country, Iceland, 200 miles (322km) away across the Denmark Strait. Greenland covers an area of about 800 000 sq miles (2.1 million km²), of which only about 5 per cent is habitable. Most of the island is covered with an ice cap, in some places as much as 14 000ft (4300m) thick; beneath the ice lie some of the Earth's oldest rocks, dating back around 3700 million years. The coast is so deeply indented that its length of 24 430 miles (39 315km) is roughly the same as the distance

Polar bear

around the equator. At Gunnbjørn Fjeld, in the south-east, the coastal mountains rise to 12 145ft (3702m).

Greenland was settled *c.*2500 BC by seal-hunting Inuit from North America; today it is a self-governing province of Denmark with a mainly Inuit population of some 55 400. Wildlife includes polar bears, polar wolf, reindeer, Arctic hares, lemmings and the rare musk ox. Arctic terns fly from Antarctica, where they spend the southern summer, to breed here. The tundra vegetation of mosses, lichens, grasses and sedges is augmented by dwarf trees on the warmer, rainy south-west coast.

Gunung Lorentz Nature Reserve　INDONESIA

The highest mountain in south-east Asia is Mount Jaya (16 532ft/5039m) in the Indonesian territory of Irian Jaya, which occupies the western half of the island of New Guinea. From the mountain's snow-capped peak, near the centre of the territory, to the tropical beaches on the coast extends a vast area of 7700 sq miles (20 000km²), which in 1978 was designated the Gunung Lorentz Nature Reserve.

Small marsupials, more often associated with Australia and New Zealand, live among the lush vegetation in this hot, humid region, as do huge multicoloured butterflies and birds of paradise. Bowerbirds, cassowaries and various species of cockatoo, parrot and lory are among other exotic birds that thrive in the nature reserve.

Hautes Fagnes Natural Park　BELGIUM

Situated in the forests of the Ardennes on the border with Germany, Hautes Fagnes Natural Park is linked to the neighbouring German–Luxembourg Nature Park. With an area of 190 sq miles (500km²), it is the largest state reserve in Belgium. In the north there are forested hills of beech and spruce, and in the central part, fields and hedges. Most of the southern part lies in the valley of the River Our, which flows southwards into Luxembourg.

A level area of marshy moorland has been set aside as the Hautes Fagnes Nature Reserve. Here, bog asphodels and insect-eating sundews are among the unusual plants that grow in the peat bogs. Wild boar, wild cats and deer roam the wooded areas that also provide nesting sites for a wide variety of birds.

Hindu Kush　CENTRAL ASIA

The Hindu Kush – after the Himalayas the highest mountain range in the world – is an extension of the Himalayan system. In an arc 500 miles (800km) long, it sweeps from central Afghanistan across the northern border of Pakistan to merge with the Karakoram range in north Kashmir. More than 20 of its peaks exceed 23 000ft (7010m). The highest, Tirich Mir, rises to 25 229ft (7690m).

Several passes give access across the range – it was by way of these that Alexander the Great and Timur (Tamerlane) crossed the Hindu Kush to India. Now the main break in the system is the Salang Tunnel, 8780ft (2676m) long, linking Kabul to the north.

Alexander the Great

Hoge Veluwe National Park　NETHERLANDS

Established in 1930, Hoge Veluwe National Park is an area of inland dunes on which trees have been planted to stabilise the sand. Grassland and heath have also become established, so the relatively small area of only 18 sq miles (47km²) today supports a wide range of wildlife.

Red deer, roe and fallow deer, and introduced mouflon graze on the rich grasses, and badgers, foxes, pine martens and polecats hunt among the trees. Scots pines now greatly outnumber the original oaks and beeches, and all provide nesting sites for many species of bird, including honey buzzards, black woodpeckers and the rare white-tailed sea-eagle.

Hohe Tauern National Park　AUSTRIA

Spruce, silver fir, pine and larch trees clothe the mountains and valleys in this beautiful alpine region. Red deer, ibex, chamois, marmots and hares have made

their home here, along with birds such as ptarmigans, alpine pipits, snow finches and Bonelli's warbler.

Meltwater from the glaciers tumbles towards the valleys over many waterfalls; Krimml Falls, with a drop of 1247ft (380m), are the largest. The Grossglockner–Hochalpenstrasse, the highest road in Europe, reaches 8218ft (2505m); Grossglockner itself (12 457ft/3797m) is Austria's highest peak. Hohe Tauern National Park occupies more than 1000 sq miles (2590km²) in Salzburg, Carinthia and East Tirol provinces.

Hölloch Cave　SWITZERLAND

This immense cave (whose German name means 'hellhole'), stretches beneath the Swiss Alps and belongs to the longest cave system in Europe; it is the third longest cave in the world. It was formed over millennia by the dissolving action of water as it percolated from the meltwater of retreating glaciers, as well as from numerous underground springs, through the limestone formation of central Switzerland.

Exploration began in 1875 and recommenced at the turn of the century, but the cave proved so difficult to probe that by 1954 only about 30 miles (48km) of tunnels and chambers had been surveyed. Explorations continued, and in 1976 expeditions revealed an underground network 83 miles (133km) long. But even today parts of the cave system have yet to be explored.

Huascarán National Park　PERU

This ruggedly beautiful park, stretching for more than 100 miles (160km) along the Cordillera Blanca, the eastern branch of the huge Andean mountain chain, consists of a range of titanic, perpetually snowcapped peaks. There are no fewer than 27 summits over 19 500ft (5950m), the highest, at 22 205ft (6768m), being Huascarán itself.

The area is prone to seismic disturbances, which occur regularly. One severe tremor in 1970 caused an avalanche that buried ten villages and most of the town of Yungay, killing some 20 000 people in one of the worst natural disasters of this century.

Jean Bernard Cave   FRANCE

The Jean Bernard Cave, in the foothills of the Alps south of Lake Geneva, is the deepest known cave in the world. It was discovered in 1963 and named after its finder. Exploration in 1969 revealed many new tunnels, chambers, shafts, galleries and underground rivers. Then, its maximum depth was estimated at 2044ft (623m); it is now known to be 5256ft (1602m).

Kakadu National Park   AUSTRALIA

◈ One of the largest parks in the world, Kakadu National Park covers some 5000 sq miles (12 950km²) east of Darwin in the Northern Territory. It was established in 1979, three years after the whole area of flood plains, plateaux and escarpments was designated an Aboriginal homeland. Some of the earliest evidence of human settlement has been found at Obiri Rock.

Many indigenous and migratory birds breed in the tropical wetlands, and the rivers provide a home for estuarine and freshwater crocodiles and some unusual fish, such as a rare and primitive archer fish. In all, a third of Australia's bird species and a quarter of its species of fish can be found in Kakadu. The park's environment was once threatened by large numbers of water buffalo, descendants of animals taken to the region by 19th-century settlers. The buffaloes have now been virtually eradicated.

Aboriginal handprints on rock

Kaziranga National Park   INDIA

◈ The game reserve at Kaziranga, in Assam, was established in 1908. In 1974, when it became a national park, the reserve held the country's remaining 12 great Indian one-horned rhinoceroses;

but over the years, with the protection offered by the park, their numbers have increased to more than 1000. One factor in this success is the annual flooding of the Brahmaputra River, for the resulting swampland is not accessible to humans. Other animals that thrive in the marshes, with their scattered clumps of elephant grass and thickets of trees, include deer, buffaloes, elephants, leopards and tigers, as well as pelicans and other water birds.

Keoladeo Ghana National Park   INDIA

◈ Once the duck-hunting preserve of the Maharajas of Bharatpur, this small 11 sq mile (28km²) site in Rajasthan is now a sanctuary with one of the most spectacular concentrations of breeding and migratory birds in the world. Part woodland, part swamp, the area is a winter refuge for white storks, the Siberian goose and the European wild duck, or mallard. The natural depression that forms the park becomes a shallow lake in summer, providing a home for openbill storks, white ibises and Sarus cranes, among other birds. The critically endangered Siberian crane is also dependent upon the park for its survival.

Kootenay National Park   CANADA

On the western slopes of the Rocky Mountains in British Columbia, Kootenay National Park lies astride 70 miles (112km) of Highway 93 between Windermere and Banff. The 537 sq miles (1390km²) of the park contain a host of natural wonders, ranging from snowcapped mountains more than 10 000ft (3000m) high to waterfalls, hot springs, canyons and lush valleys. Among the major sights are Radium Hot Springs, which each day spew out 500 000 gallons (2.3 million litres) of water at a temperature of 46°C (115°F), and Marble Canyon, a gorge 200ft (60m) deep whose walls are lined with marble.

Kruger National Park   SOUTH AFRICA

◈ Originally known as the Sabie Game Reserve, this park in the

eastern Transvaal was renamed in 1926 in honour of the Boer statesman Paul Kruger. With an area of 8000 sq miles (20 700km²), it is among the world's largest national parks and was one of the first natural areas in South Africa to be protected by law. Some 4000 species of birds, including the ostrich, have been recorded in the park, which is also home to some of Africa's rarest animals (including black and white rhino ceroses and red jackals) as well as hippos, elephants, lions, leopards, cheetahs, giraffes and antelopes.

Cheetah

Madagascar   INDIAN OCEAN

This island in the south Indian Ocean is the fourth largest in the world, with an area of 226 658 sq miles (587 009km²). Most of the forests on the highland plateaux have been cut down, but the remnants provide a home for some unique animals. These include 15 species of lemur – long-tailed primates resembling monkeys – and 30 species of spiny-coated, insect-eating tenrec. There are also many types of birds and lizards, including 27 species of chameleon.

Unusually, in view of its proximity to Africa, only 250 miles (400km) away across the Mozambique Channel, the island has no monkeys, no native hoofed animals and no carnivores other than two types of civet cat. Present until recent times, but now extinct, was the huge, ostrich-like and flightless elephant bird.

Ring-tailed lemur

Mammoth Cave   USA

Some 90 miles (144km) south of Louisville, Kentucky, is the world's longest cave system – Mammoth Cave – with 330 miles (530km) of passageway. Europeans discovered the caves in 1797, and today the amazing stalactites, stalagmites, curtains of limestone cascading like waterfalls, and delicate, flower-like white gypsum crystals still capture the imagination. Some 360ft (110m) underground, the Echo River shelters a number of species of fish, crayfish and shrimp, all blind and colourless, the result of generations spent in total darkness.

Mana Pools National Park   ZIMBABWE

◈ Occupying 859 sq miles (2225km²) of woodland along the Zambezi River, Mana Pools National Park was established in 1963. It is one of the last of southern Africa's truly wild places. Huge escarpments fringe the river's flood plain, and pools of clear water lie hidden among the trees. During the dry season animals, including cheetahs, elephants, wild dogs and rare black rhinoceroses, migrate from as far as 60 miles (100km) away to find water in the Mana Pools park, which remains always damp and green, with lush vegetation.

Mauna Loa   HAWAII

The world's tallest active volcano, Mauna Loa towers 13 677ft (4169m) above sea level and occupies more than 2000 sq miles (5180km²) of the island's surface. It erupts every 3½ years on average and, due to its very high temperature and low silica and gas content, the lava is extremely fluid and can flow 20 miles (32km) or more before it cools. Mauna Loa, in Hawaii Volcanoes National Park, is one of the few active volcanoes where one can peer into the crater.

Meru National Park   KENYA

Forests, palms, grasslands and swamps characterise Meru Park, established in 1967 just 93 miles (150km) north-east of Kenya's capital Nairobi. Vegetation in the park's 339 sq miles (880km²) is lush all year round, thanks to several rivers – including the

402

Rojewero, famous for its turtles.

In 1978, Meru's rare white rhinoceroses, reintroduced from South Africa after having been extinct in Kenya for thousands of years, were all shot by poachers. Today, buffaloes, elephants, zebra and giraffes roam the park.

Mojave Desert   USA

Located north-east of Los Angeles, the Mojave Desert occupies about 15 000 sq miles (39 000km²) of southern California. The Mojave is almost completely surrounded by mountains, most notably to the north and west by the Sierra Nevada; to the south-east it merges with the Colorado Desert. The desert floor is made up of sedimentary rocks that are rich in minerals; vegetation is limited mainly to cacti and other succulents, since only 4½in (115mm) of rain fall annually, the majority in winter.

Mount Etna   ITALY

At 10 902ft (3323m), Mount Etna is Europe's highest active volcano. Located 18 miles (29km) north-west of Catania in Sicily, Etna stands in isolated splendour, snowcapped for nine months of the year. It covers an area of 600 sq miles (1550km²) and is 93 miles (150km) around its base. On the fertile lower slopes of the mountain, citrus fruit, olives and vines are grown.

Higher up are forests of beech, oak, chestnut, pine and birch; above them is a zone of sand, ashes, fragments of slag and lava. The centre of volcanic activity has changed often, resulting in the formation of some 200 subsidiary cones, the most important of which are the twin peaks of Monti Rossi (3110ft/948m).

The first recorded eruption, in 475 BC, was noted by the Greek tragic poet Aeschylus, who was living in Sicily. Evidence suggests that between 1500 BC and AD 1669 there were 71 eruptions, that of 1669 lasting from March 11 to July 15 and sending some 990 million cu yd (757 million m³) of lava streaming down the side of the mountain. Etna's major eruptions this century took place in 1928, 1949, 1964 and 1971, with lesser eruptions in 1979 and 1992.

Mount Kenya   KENYA

⊛ In central Kenya, 70 miles (112km) north-east of Nairobi, rises Mount Kenya. The highest mountain in Africa after Mount Kilimanjaro (p342), it has three major peaks: Batian (17 057ft/5199m), Nelion (17 021ft/5188m) and Lenana (16 355ft/4985m).

From Mount Kenya, the summit of Kilimanjaro can sometimes be seen 200 miles (320km) away: one of the longest confirmed lines of sight on Earth. In 1949 the Mount Kenya National Park was established to protect its unusual plant and animal life.

Mount Mayon   PHILIPPINES
National Park

The unique feature of Mount Mayon National Park, covering a relatively small area of 21 sq miles (55km²), is that it is centred on an active volcano 8077ft (2462m) high. The unpredictable Mayon volcano has erupted more than 20 times in the last 200 years (the last was in 1984). It is located in the south-eastern part of the main island of Luzon, and its perfectly symmetrical cone has earned it its name, which means 'beautiful'.

Mount Meru-Arusha
National Park   TANZANIA

⊛ Established in 1962, Mount Meru-Arusha National Park occupies 53 sq miles (137km²) near the border with Kenya. It can be divided into three regions. North of Ngurdoto crater is woodland and bush, in which buffaloes, elephants, giraffes and rhinoceroses roam; in the centre are the Momela lakes with their lush surrounding grassland; in the south is the crater of Mount Meru (14 977ft/4565m), Africa's fifth highest peak. Rainforest surrounds Ngurdoto crater, which is 1½ miles (2.4km) across,

Giraffe

and the rim is a good spot from which to view the wide variety of wildlife it supports. The Momela lakes, where many animals go to drink, are also a good vantage point for observing wildlife.

Mount Vesuvius   ITALY

Some 9 miles (15km) south-east of the city of Naples, in Campania, Mount Vesuvius rises 4190ft (1277m) above the Bay of Naples. It is the only active volcano on mainland Europe and

Cast from cavity in ash

consists of a crater 4593ft (1400m) in circumference and 709ft (216m) deep. The remains of the original volcano, known as Monte Summa, form a semicircular ridge around the existing younger cone. Vesuvius's most famous eruption, and the first to be recorded (by Pliny the Elder), occurred in AD 79, when volcanic debris overwhelmed the cities of Pompeii (p411), Stabiae and Herculaneum. The most recent eruption was in 1944.

Nahanni   CANADA
National Park

⊛ In 1976 Nahanni National Park was declared the first World Heritage Site. Covering 1840 sq miles (4765km²) of 'limitless wilderness' on the eastern side of the Mackenzie Mountains in the Northwest Territories, the park can be reached only by floatplane or by boat up the Liard River. As a result, few people get to see some of the most remarkable scenery in North America.

The terrain consists mainly of limestone karst, sculpted by the elements into undulating surfaces, deep sinkholes and underground rivers and caverns. At Rabbitkettle Hot Springs (p416), for example, the precipitation of minerals from warm spring water has built up a terraced mound 90ft (27m) high. At the Devil's Kitchen, the

sculpting agent is the relentless wind, which has carved strange shapes in the sandstone.

Nahuel Huapi   ARGENTINA
National Park

The cold, clear lake of Nahuel Huapi is in the Andes Mountains of west-central Argentina. It plumbs a depth of 985ft (300m), has an area of 205 sq miles (528km²), and gives its name to the surrounding park. This was established in 1903 and became the country's first national park in 1934; today it occupies 1275 sq miles (3300km²). In addition to many snowcapped peaks, it includes glaciers, fast-flowing rivers, waterfalls, lakes and areas of dense forest. On the lower slopes and around the lake, wild flowers proliferate. Dominating the region is Mount Tronador (11 660ft/3554m), one of the highest mountains in Patagonia.

Nanda Devi   INDIA
National Park

⊛ The second-highest mountain in India, Nanda Devi (25 645ft/7817m) lies in the Garhwal Himalayas of Uttar Pradesh, 205 miles (330km) north-east of Delhi. The mountains here surround a high-altitude basin of lush pastures covering 243 sq miles (630km²). The area was made a game reserve in 1939, and in 1982 became the Nanda Devi National Park. The inaccessibility and isolation of the park mean it is left to blue sheep, gorals (goat-like antelope), musk deer and tahrs (wild goats), which are a source of food for snow leopards.

Snow leopard

The Negev   ISRAEL

Covering an area of about 4700 sq miles (12 200km²) is the dry hilly region of the Negev. It resembles an inverted triangle, with its southern point at the Red Sea port of Eilat measuring only 6 miles (10km) across. In the north, the Negev stretches from the Mediterranean to the Dead

Sea; it is bordered to the west by the Sinai Peninsula, and in the east by the Wadi Araba, a dry riverbed running 100 miles (160km) from the Dead Sea as far as the Gulf of Aqaba.

The northern region of rolling hills, the most arable part of the Negev, is irrigated by a conduit from Lake Tiberias (Sea of Galilee), and contains many settlements, or kibbutzim. In the south the hills reach a height of 3396ft (1035m). The central area is characterised by elongated eroded depressions, oriented north-east to south-west, the largest of which is 984ft (300m) deep, 23 miles (37km) long and 5 miles (8km) wide.

Niokolo-Koba National Park   SENEGAL

◉ Centred on the village of Niokolo, Niokolo-Koba National Park, established in 1962, occupies a huge area of 3525 sq miles (9130km²) in east Senegal, near the border with Guinea. Most of the region is savanna, which remains habitable even in the dry season because of the water provided by the River Gambia and its tributaries. Forests line the river banks, and there are many ponds and lakes in the grassland. The park shelters a vast range of wildlife: more than 300 bird species, 70 species of mammals (including the rare Darby's eland and bubal hartebeest), and some 30 species each of reptiles and fish. This area has been occupied by humans for at least 100 000 years.

Nullarbor Plain   AUSTRALIA

The name Nullarbor is derived from the Latin for 'no tree', an apt description of the vast plain, 100 000 sq miles (260 000km²) in extent, that stretches for 600 miles (965km) from Ooldea in South Australia to Kalgoorlie in the west, and 175 miles (280km) from north to south, from the Great Victoria Desert (p401) to the Australian Bight. Part of the plain is a national park. A railway crosses the plain; one stretch of the line runs dead straight for 310 miles (500km).

Formerly a seabed, today the Nullarbor consists largely of sand dunes, with no surface streams. The annual rainfall is only 10in

(25cm), but a large system of caverns lies beneath the plain, some of which hold percolated water. Saltbush and blue bush are the dominant vegetation, and rarely, after winter rain, there are flowers and grasses. Wildlife includes the thorny devil – a lizard, bristling with sharp spines.

Thorny devil

Ojos del Salado   CHILE

The Pacific Ocean is encircled by the 'Ring of Fire' – a chain of volcanoes on the edges of the tectonic plates that make up this area of the Earth's crust. The Andes form part of the chain, and it is on Chile's mountainous border with Argentina that Ojos del Salado (22 664ft/6908m), the world's tallest volcano, is found. Although it has not erupted recently, it has fumaroles and cannot be regarded as extinct.

Ordesa National Park   SPAIN

Established in 1918, Ordesa is one of the oldest national parks in Spain. Its 60 sq miles (155km²) adjoin the French Pyrenees National Park to the north, and together the two make up the largest protected region in Europe. The park, which is about 110 miles (180km) east of San Sebastian, is dominated by Monte Perdido (11 004ft/3354m). Among the animals to be seen is the unusual Pyrenean desman, a small mammal that resembles a mole but has a long, rat-like tail. Plants unique to the park's gorges and forests include the Pyrenean aquilegia and saxifrage.

Pyrenean desman

Paparoa National Park   NEW ZEALAND

The first national park in New Zealand (Tongariro, p406) was established in 1887; 100 years later the event was celebrated with the opening of Paparoa National Park on the north-western peninsula of South Island. It occupies only 108 sq miles (280km²), yet includes mountains, forests and a coastal strip of craggy headlands.

The intervening karst (limestone area), sculpted by slightly acidic rainwater into holes, crevasses and underground galleries and caverns, is the park's most unusual feature. This type of terrain is rare in New Zealand, and is nowhere better seen than at Paparoa. Since receiving protection in 1987, wildlife has proliferated in the park.

Peneda Gerês National Park   PORTUGAL

Mountainous terrain with lush valleys make up the 190 sq miles (500km²) of Peneda Gerês National Park, established in northern Portugal in 1970. The highest of the granite peaks is Mount Nerosa (5069ft/1545m). Heavy rainfall in the mountains feeds fast-flowing rivers, and many unusual plants grow in the fertile valleys. Unique to the area is the rare Schreiber's green lizard.

Redwood National Park   USA

◉ Redwood National Park covers an area of 88 sq miles (228km²) along the coast of northern California. It was established in 1968 in order to conserve the tallest tree species in the world (right), the coast redwood (*Sequoia sempervirens*). Many of these trees grow more than 325ft (100m) high, with a girth of 26ft (8m) – the bark alone is almost 1ft (30cm) thick. The tallest tree in the park, also the world's tallest, is 367ft (112m) high. In the distant past, the coast redwood was found in many parts of the world, China and Greenland included; it is now confined to coastal California and south-west Oregon.

Rocky Mountains   CANADA/USA

The Rocky Mountains extend from the Bering Strait, north of the Arctic Circle, through British Columbia and Alberta and across the US–Canadian border as far south as New Mexico, a distance of about 3000 miles (4800km). The tallest peaks in the Rockies are found in Colorado, where there are 50 summits over 4000ft (1200m), including Mount Elbert, the highest at 14 432ft (4399m). The loftiest peak in the Canadian Rockies is Mount Robson (12 972ft/3954m).

The Rockies form the Continental Divide: rivers on the west of the mountains flow into the Pacific Ocean, those on the eastern side flow into the Atlantic. The mountains are renowned for spectacular scenery, particularly in the national parks, including Grand Teton, Yellowstone (p407), Rocky Mountain, Banff (p398), Jasper, Yoho, Kootenay (p402), and Gates of the Arctic.

Rondane National Park   NORWAY

Established as a nature reserve in 1962, Rondane became Norway's first national park in 1970. It is a mountainous area of 221 sq miles (572km²), which includes canyons, moraines and other glacial features, and ten peaks of more than 6525ft (1990m). The highest of these is Rondeslottet, which rises to 7146ft (2178m). There are some Iron Age sites in the park where bog ore, which is still to be found in marshy areas, was smelted.

The soil is poor and most of the vegetation alpine, but there are some scattered dwarf trees and a small forested area. Yellow-white reindeer moss, a type of lichen, covers much of the ground and provides food for the animals after which it is named. There are also elk, foxes, hares, stoats, weasels, wolverines and otters. The many bird species include golden plovers, ptarmigans, meadow pipits, snow buntings, phalaropes and white dotterels.

Coast redwood tree

Royal Chitawan National Park   NEPAL

In 1973 this national park was established in the Himalayan foothills in southern Nepal. It is an area of forests, grasslands, lakes and swamps drained by the slow-moving Chitawan River, and covers 210 sq miles (550km²). Each year the river overflows its banks, maintaining the swamps, and both are home to the marsh crocodile. There are also gaurs (wild oxen), peacocks, leopards, sloth bears and a thriving tiger population. But the main attraction is the rare great Indian one-horned rhinoceros, whose numbers nearly doubled, to 375, in the ten years after the park was opened.

Indian peacock

Ruhuna National Park   SRI LANKA

◉ About 185 miles (300km) from Colombo, on the south-east coast, lies Sri Lanka's second-largest national park, established in 1938. Known locally as Yala, the park covers 421 sq miles (1090km²) of thorny scrub, open jungle, rocky outcrops and grassy plains, with scattered lakes and lagoons. Animals include deer, buffaloes, elephants, leopards, bears and wild boars: two species, the golden palm civet and the rusty-spotted cat, are unique to Sri Lanka. Typical birds of the plains are peacocks and quail; barbets, flycatchers, hornbills and orioles nest in the forests, and there are ibis and pelicans in the nearby Kumana bird sanctuary.

Samaria Gorge National Park   CRETE

This small park, only 3 sq miles (8km²) in area, covers 10 miles (16km) of an amazing deep gorge. In places only 11ft (3.5m)

wide, yet up to 1970ft (600m) deep, it extends from the southern edge of the plain of Omalos to the coast. A large white-flowered peony is regarded as the most striking of the park's 14 unique species of plant. The commonest animal is the sure-footed Cretan wild goat, which is able to climb the craggy escarpments. The park was established in 1953.

Sarek National Park   SWEDEN

Part of Swedish Lapland, Sarek and four neighbouring reserves make up the largest wilderness area in Europe. The region has remained virtually undisturbed because it is so remote and difficult to reach.

There are more than 90 mountains over 5900ft (1800m) high and nearly 100 glaciers within the park's 749 sq miles (1940km²); the highest is Sarektjåkkå (6854ft/2089m). Fast-flowing rivers with many waterfalls thread through deep gorges; wildlife thrives in the bogs and forests on the lower ground.

Animals include arctic foxes and elks, with some bears, wolverines and lynx; wolves, which were fairly common when the park was established in 1909, are now hardly ever seen. The mountains provide nesting sites for golden eagles, and the high tundra for long-tailed skuas. Plants include the white-flowered mountain avens, or geum.

Serengeti National Park   TANZANIA

◉ Covering about 5700 sq miles (14 800km²) of north-central Tanzania, the Serengeti National Park contains extensive acacia woodland savanna as well as some of the best grazing pasture in Africa. It is well known as a refuge for the black rhino and for the huge herds of herbivores that inhabit the plains. There are an estimated 1.5 million wildebeests,

Wildebeest

or gnu, 200 000 zebra, and more than 200 000 other herbivores in the park, including Thomson's gazelles, impalas, buffaloes, elands, topis, giraffes and elephants.

Above all, the park is famous for the massive seasonal migrations of these animals, particularly wildebeests and lions, leopards, cheetahs and other animals that prey on them. The grazers spend the wet season on the plains and in May or early June, at the start of the dry season, move down a corridor, which extends north for 100 miles (160km) along the rivers that feed Lake Victoria, to the rich grassland just beyond the border with Kenya.

Simpson Desert   AUSTRALIA

The Simpson Desert is an inhospitable region of scrubland and dunes in the heart of the Australian Outback. It stretches from the Macdonnell Range in the south-eastern corner of the Northern Territory down to Lake Eyre in north-eastern South Australia and across into south-west Queensland, an area of some 29 700miles (77 000km²).

The sand dunes, which run north-east to south-west, are remarkable for their dark red colour, caused by particles of iron oxide on the grains of sand, and for their size and formation. Some are as much as 180 miles (290km) long and 100ft (30m) broad, with depressions between them up to 1000ft (300m) wide.

Stolby Zapovednik   RUSSIA

Occupying 182 sq miles (472km²) in Siberia, Stolby Zapovednik (Reservation) covers regions of taiga (forest and woodland) between the rivers Mana and Yenisey, on the eastern side of the Sayan Mountains. The trees, mainly larch, pine, spruce and birch, with smaller rhododendron shrubs, provide homes for many species of small mammal as well as bears, lynx, musk deer and Siberian stags.

The reservation, which was founded in 1925, is also noted for its strange pillars of rock (known as *stolby* in Russian), which are outcrops of granite or of the silica-based igneous rock syenite. Some of the pillars are as much as 330ft (100m) in height.

Swiss National Park   SWITZERLAND

Located in the Engadine valley, the Swiss National Park is justly renowned for its beautiful green valleys, fast-flowing streams, extensive forests and high peaks – the highest the permanently snowcapped Piz Pisoc (10 414ft/3174m). Trees, largely mountain pines, cover about a third of the park's 65 sq miles (169km²), and in summer flowers, such as yellow

Golden eagle

Alpine poppies, gentians, orchids and rock roses, bloom in the alpine meadows. Among the 30 species of mammal are blue hares, marmots, chamois, ibexes, foxes and red deer. The reintroduction of reindeer, which had vanished from the park soon after it was founded in 1914, has caused overgrazing. The forests provide nesting sites for some unusual birds such as the black woodpecker, capercaillie, eagle owl and golden eagle.

Tai National Park   IVORY COAST

◉ Situated in the south-west of the Ivory Coast, near the border with Liberia, this 1300 sq mile (3400km²) national park is one of the last remaining areas of primeval forest in west Africa. It contains many endemic species of flora, including several varieties of ebony and palm tree. The diversity of wildlife that the area supports, including the rare pygmy hippopotamus and the pangolin, is under threat from poaching, as well as from the destruction of the habitat by deforestation, especially in the northern part of the park.

Talamanca Range – Amistad Reserve   COSTA RICA

◉ Jaguars and pumas roam this 747 sq mile (1934 km²) park on the border with Panama, while the harpy eagle patrols its skies. Rain and cloud forest provide a home for many other animals and more than 400 bird species. Flora includes more than 130 orchid species, to be found in the south-west of the park. In the rugged Talamanca Mountains, tracks and trails soon peter out in the largely unexplored territory, much of which is over 8000ft (2440m) in height. The terrain is studded with granite peaks – the highest mountain, Cerro Chirripó Grande, reaches 12 861ft (3920m).

Tongariro National Park   NEW ZEALAND

Situated in the centre of North Island, Tongariro were established as long ago as 1887, when it became New Zealand's first national park. The 307 sq miles (795km²) of land was presented to the government by the chief of the Tuwahare people, Te Heuheu Tukino IV, to safeguard the volcanic mountains of Ngauruhoe, Ruapehu and Tongariro, which were sacred to the Maoris. The volcanoes are still active, and many hot springs bubble forth near Ketetahi on the northern side of Mount Tongariro (6457ft/1968m). The terrain around the peaks is bare except for dry scrubby areas; lower down there are waterfalls, lakes, forests and alpine meadows.

Tsavo National Park   KENYA

With an area of 8039 sq miles (20 821km²), Tsavo in south-eastern Kenya is one of the world's largest national parks. Tsavo East is a flat, dry bush region, much of which is closed to prevent poaching of elephants and rhinoceroses. In the dry season, bush fires are common, but after even a slight fall of rain the dormant vegetation bursts into life. Tsavo West has a hillier, volcanic landscape, with a higher rainfall and consequently lusher vegetation, and there are waterholes and springs among the acacia and baobab trees.

Wildlife includes lions, zebras, hippopotamuses, buffaloes, many species of antelopes and the elephants for which Tsavo National Park is famous. But overgrazing by the elephants has recently caused such serious environmental problems that the population is now controlled by culling some of the animals every year.

Ujung Kulon National Park   JAVA

The 302 sq miles (782km²) of this park comprise a remote hilly area on a peninsula at the western end of the Indonesian island of Java; the island of Panaitan, 6 miles (10km) offshore; and a group of islets to the north, all that remains of the volcanic island of Krakatoa (p34). By 1921, when the peninsula became a nature reserve, jungle had once more taken over the land that had been covered with volcanic ash, and in 1980 it was given national park status.

Because of its isolation, an unusual variety of animals has flourished here, including 60 Javan rhinoceroses, the only survivors of this species. Other threatened species are the banteng (wild ox), Javan gibbon, leaf monkey and wild dog.

Banteng

Urewera National Park   NEW ZEALAND

The largest area of native forest in New Zealand's North Island, covering some 770 sq miles (1995km²), forms the Urewera National Park, established in 1954. Ancient hardwood trees grow on the mountains and in the valleys, but the highest point, Mount Manuoha (4603ft/1403m), supports alpine grasses and scrub. There are also fast-flowing streams and lakes, such as Lake Waikaremoana, home of the rare blue duck. Other birds include bush canaries, grey warblers and kiwis. The most common indigenous animals are small marsupials known locally as opossums, and there are also many introduced cats, goats, pigs, sheep and red deer that have reverted to the wild.

Vanoise National Park   FRANCE

Located in south-eastern France on the border with Italy, Vanoise

National Park is the oldest in France (established 1963). It occupies 204 sq miles (528km²) between the rivers Arc and Isère, and adjoins the Gran Paradiso National Park in Italy (p400).

The whole area is one of mountains, glaciers, lakes and moraines. There are more than 100 peaks over 10 000ft (3000m), the highest being Pointe de la Grande Casse (12 667ft/3861m). Trees include fir, pine, larch and spruce. Cowberries, rock campions and alpine types of asphodel and groundsel grow in sheltered hollows. Black grouse, buzzards, citril finches, golden eagles, ptarmigan and ring ouzels are among the wide variety of birds to be found, and badgers, foxes, chamois, ibex, marmots and mountain hares abound.

Virunga National Park   ZAIRE

Located in the Kivu region of north-eastern Zaire, Virunga is famous for its wildlife, especially its colonies of mountain gorilla. Other mammals present in significant numbers are wild dogs, chimpanzees, aardvarks, lions, elephants and antelopes.

Geological features of particular note include both active and extinct volcanoes, lava flows, hot springs and glaciers, while vegetation ranges from bamboo forest on the slopes of extinct volcanoes through wooded savanna to tropical jungle. The park, established in 1925, covers 3124 sq miles (8090km²) and borders Volcanoes National Park and Ruwenzori National Park (p30) in Uganda.

Waterton-Glacier   CANADA/USA International Peace Park

The peace park, established in 1932 and the first of its kind, is the result of amalgamating two adjoining national parks, Waterton Lakes National Park in Alberta, Canada, and Glacier National Park in Montana, USA. The latter covers 1584 sq miles (4102km²) of mountainous terrain and includes more than 40 glaciers and virgin coniferous forest. Waterton Lakes National Park (203 sq miles/526km²) is located on the east side of the Rockies and features many glacial formations such as trough valleys, cirques and glacial lakes.

Wen Chun Wolong   CHINA Nature Reserve

Covering an area of 772 sq miles (2000km²) and embracing both subtropical and temperate regions, the Wen Chun Wolong Reserve in Sichuan Province has a mixture of mountainous and forested habitats. Since the reserve was established in 1969, giant pandas have maintained a

Giant panda

precarious existence in the stands of bamboo, their only food plant. Takins, a variety of antelope, and golden monkeys are among the other endangered species that find sanctuary here.

Western Ghats   INDIA

The mountain range known as the Western Ghats runs almost continuously for 1000 miles (1600km), from the mouth of the Tapti River north of Bombay to Cape Comorin at the southern tip of India. Anai Mudi Peak (8842ft/2695m) in the Cardamom Hills is the highest point. The range forms the western boundary of the great Deccan Plateau that occupies most of south-central India. The plateau slopes towards the east; so rivers such as the Krishna and Godavari, which rise in these mountains, flow eastwards across the plateau to empty their waters into the Bay of Bengal.

Western Tasmania Wilderness National Park   TASMANIA

Comprising three national parks (the Southwest, the Franklin-Lower Gord Wild Rivers and the Cradle Mountain-Lake St Clair), this area covers some 3125 sq miles (8094km²) of the last remaining temperate wilderness regions of the world. Dominating landforms include Precipitous Bluff and Tasmania's highest mountain, Mount Ossa (5305ft/1617m). The flora and fauna include many endemic and endangered plants, as well as two-thirds of the island's 32 mammal species. The parks may also harbour the Tasmanian wolf (thylacine), once believed to have died out in the 1930s.

Wood Buffalo National Park   CANADA

◉ A vast area of prairie, marsh and forest, extending over 17 300 sq miles (44 800km²) on the border of the Northwest Territories and Alberta, constitutes the largest national park in Canada – and in the world. The chief watercourse is the Peace River, and there are many lakes. When the park was established in 1922, one of the main aims was to protect the habitat of the great whooping crane, which today survives only in the park, and then in only very small numbers.

Wood Buffalo also has the world's largest herd of bison (about 15 000 animals) and a wide variety of other mammals: beavers, black bears, grizzly bears, moose, caribous, porcupines, wolverines and wolves.

Yellowstone National Park   USA

◉ The first national park in the world to be so designated (1872), Yellowstone has the distinction also of being the largest national park in the USA. It is situated in the Rocky Mountains (p404) in high plateau country of rugged mountain peaks, lakes and forests. The majority of its 3472 sq miles (8992km²) fall within the state of Wyoming, but there are portions in southern Montana and eastern Idaho. The many and varied attractions of the park include cliffs of black obsidian (volcanic

Old Faithful

glass); Yellowstone and Jackson lakes; Electric Peak (10 991ft/ 3350m), the park's highest mountain; and thousands of steam vents and hot springs, including Mammoth Hot Springs with its terraces of travertine. There are also hundreds of geysers, among them Old Faithful, whose watery eruptions occur at intervals of roughly 33 and 93 minutes – this frequency has hardly altered in the last 100 years. Yellowstone Park is also the location of the largest forest of petrified logs in the USA, which is to be found near Specimen Ridge.

Yosemite National Park   USA

◉ This area of great natural beauty and varied landscape, from forest, waterfall and river to alpine meadow, glacial lake and ice field, covers 1189 sq miles (3080km²) in the Sierra Nevada in California. It includes the Yosemite Valley, 7 miles (11km) long, with natural granite monoliths; Mount Lyell (13 090ft/ 3990m), the highest point in the park; and Half Dome Mountain. The park also takes in Yosemite Falls (2425ft/739m), North America's highest waterfall, and the 2700-year-old redwood known as Old Grizzly. This is a Sierra sequoia tree (*Sequoiadendron giganteum*), one of many growing in the park's three sequoia groves.

Zion National Park   USA

This landscape of multicoloured sandstone mesas and canyons in southern Utah was formed by the surging waters of the Virgin River and by wind erosion. The park is 229 sq miles (593km²) in area and contains some spectacular and colourful rock formations, including one of the largest free-standing arches in the world, Kolob Arch, which has a span of almost 310ft (95m).

Zion Canyon, 15 miles (25km) long, lies at the centre of the park. Ferns flourish along the banks of its streams, desert vegetation is evident on the canyon floor, and forest – largely Douglas fir, white fir and pine – grows along the canyon rim.

The park is populated by many species of small animals and birds, but its special feature is the array of fossils – seashells, fish and trees – to be found in the rocks.

MONUMENTAL WONDERS

From the earliest times, humans have been builders. In part, this has been a celebration of a hard-won ascendancy over nature, but it has also been due to the need to express a deep-felt spiritual or emotional commitment, often inspired by a site's beauty or its character. Such buildings have an inherent appeal that is as potent today as when they were erected centuries ago.

Abu Simbel   EGYPT

◉ Abu Simbel is situated 168 miles (270km) south of Aswan on the west bank of Lake Nasser. This is the site of two huge rock temples, carved out of a cliff of solid sandstone on the order of the Pharaoh Rameses II (1304–1273 BC). Originally the temples were located 98ft (30m) down river, but during the construction of the Aswan High Dam, completed in 1971, they

Rameses II

were dismantled and reassembled at their present site.

The larger of the two temples has a facade 105ft (32m) high and 118ft (36m) long. It is fronted by four seated figures of Rameses II, each more than 65ft (20m) tall. The second, smaller, structure, the Temple of Nefartari, honours Rameses' favourite wife. Six giant statues measuring 33ft (10m) in height stand along the front: four figures of Rameses II and two of Nefartari.

After the beginning of the Christian era the temples fell into disuse and were eventually covered by sand. They were discovered by the Swiss explorer Johann Ludwig Burckhardt in 1813.

Agra   INDIA

◉ The city of Agra in Uttar Pradesh was founded in 1566 and was the Mogul capital until 1659. Best known for the Taj Mahal (p150), built by Emperor Shah Jahan as a mausoleum for his much-loved wife, the city also contains the Emperor Akbar's 16th-century fort, within which are the Pearl Mosque (Moti Masjid) of Shah Jahan and the Mirror Palace (Shish Mahal).

Altamira   SPAIN

◉ The caves at Altamira, near Santander on the north coast of Spain, contain masterpieces of Ice Age art. Lifelike paintings of deer, boars, horses and bison, some more than 6½ft (2m) long, cover the ceiling of the main chamber, which is 59ft (18m) long and 26ft (8m) wide. The animals were drawn with charcoal and painted in vivid earth colours of red and violet; figures, both engraved and painted in black, appear in smaller galleries. The paintings were discovered in 1879 by a local landowner, Marcellino de Sautola, who also found flint tools and animal bones. Initially, Spanish and foreign authorities dismissed the paintings as forgeries and it was only in 1902 that they were authenticated and dated to *c*.13 500 BC.

Anthony Island   CANADA

◉ The Queen Charlotte Islands, off the coast of British Columbia, were for 2000 years the home of the Haida people, a North-west Pacific group of native Americans who lived by hunting and fishing. The Haida are particularly well known for their intricately carved totem poles, which often reach a height of 65ft (20m) and are among the largest wooden sculptures known. Many of these were destroyed by missionaries or sent to museums around the world, but on Anthony Island, now a provincial park, a typical Haida village with longhouses and totem poles has been preserved as testimony to the culture of these people who predate the arrival of Europeans.

Baths of Caracalla   ITALY

Begun in AD 211 by the Emperor Caracalla, and completed five years later, the Baths of Caracalla are the finest remaining example of Roman public baths. As well as large open-air pools, the baths include indoor frigidarium, caldarium and tepidarium (cold, hot and tepid baths) to accommodate 1500 bathers, a sophisticated hot-air heating system, mosaic floors, and vaulted halls that served as inspiration for the naves of medieval churches.

Blenheim Palace   ENGLAND

◉ One of the largest mansions in Britain, Blenheim Palace was given by a grateful nation to the 1st Duke of Marlborough after his victory over the armies of Louis XIV of France at the Battle of Blenheim in 1704. The Baroque palace, at Woodstock near Oxford, was designed by Sir John Vanburgh and built in 1705–22. The great hall, with its splendid ceilings and murals, leads to the state apartments, which house a fine collection of paintings and antiques.

The large gardens form part of an estate of 2000 acres (810ha) and comprise a formal ornamental garden with parterres, pools and fountains, laid out by the Frenchman Achille Duchêne early in the 20th century; and a natural, informal garden of trees, woods, lawns and a large lake designed by the best-known English landscape gardener, Lancelot 'Capability' Brown, in the mid 18th century.

Borobudur   JAVA

The Buddhist temple complex of Borobudur is a masterpiece of Asian art. It was built between AD 750 and 850 on a small hill, into which were cut eight stepped terraces. The lower five are square and enclosed by high walls carved with bas-relief sculptures; the upper three are circular and open, and set with 72 bell-shaped stupas, each containing a sculpture of the Buddha. The complex is surmounted by a shrine with an unfinished statue of the Buddha. Borobudur was abandoned c.1000 and the Western world did not learn of it until the 19th century.

Seated Buddha

The overgrown site was restored between 1907 and 1911, and the second phase of restoration was completed in the 1980s.

Carthage   TUNISIA

◉ The remains of the ancient city of Carthage are situated in suburban Tunis. Founded by the Phoenicians, reputedly in 814 BC, it was taken by the Romans in 146 BC, following the Punic War. The Romans rebuilt the city. Between AD 439 and 533 it was occupied by the Vandals and in 698 destroyed by the Arabs. The remains of the imperial Roman city include a circus, an amphitheatre, the Roman baths of Antonius (AD 86–161) and an aqueduct, built in Hadrian's reign (AD 117–38), which carried water from a source 82 miles (132km) away. Little remains of the original Phoenician city.

Catacombs of Rome   ITALY

In the extensive honeycomb of underground passages in Rome known as the catacombs lie the remains of early Christians martyred in the 2nd to 5th centuries. The passages, some 3–4ft (1–1.2m) wide and 7–10ft (2–3m) high, were constructed on several levels; scenes from the Bible were painted on the walls, and holes in the walls or shelves held bones or urns containing crematorium ashes. Many of the remains were later moved to the better security of various Roman churches. The catacombs were then forgotten until, in the early 17th century, about 30 of them were found by Antonio Bosio,

Catacombs fresco

an amateur archaeologist. By the 19th century, the burial chambers of five 3rd-century popes had been discovered.

Chaco Cultural/National   USA
Historical Park

◉ In a remote corner of New Mexico, 100 miles (160km) from Albuquerque, there is a desert canyon that contains 13 major pre-Columbian native American ruins. Because of its importance as the cultural centre of the south-west Anasazi Indians from 950 to 1300, Chaco Canyon has gained international status.

There is a 400 mile (640km) network of roads linking more than 100 pueblos. One of the largest and most extensively excavated of these is Pueblo Bonito, a vast building, five storeys high in places, which had 500 rooms and would have housed 1000 people. Artefacts that demonstrate the Anasazi's skill in agriculture, weaving, pottery, masonry and tool making have also been found.

Château Gaillard   FRANCE

The remains of Château Gaillard overlook the River Seine at Les Andelys, 40 miles (65km) down river from Paris. The fort was built in 1196–97 by Richard I, King of England and Duke of Normandy, to prevent French forces under Philip Augustus from reaching Rouen, capital of Normandy. Constructed along the lines of the Crusader castles in Syria and Palestine, it was impregnable. Only after a long siege was it captured by Philip Augustus in 1203–04. Large portions were demolished in 1603 during the Wars of Religion.

Congonhas   BRAZIL

◉ The town of Congonhas, situated 2850ft (870m) up in the Brazilian Highlands, is famous for its fine 18th-century church, the Sanctuary of the Bom Jesus, its chapels and gardens. The church was designed, built and decorated by the sculptor and architect Antonio Francisco Lisboa (1738–1814). The church's most famous carvings are Lisboa's soapstone sculptures of the Twelve Apostles. The chapel of Bom Jesus attracts thousands of tourists and pilgrims every year.

Coventry Cathedral   ENGLAND

The first cathedral at Coventry, St Michael's, was built in 1433 and destroyed by incendiary bombs in 1940 during World War II. Little of the medieval building other than the tower, the spire and part of the walls remained standing. The decision to build a new cathedral was made almost immediately, but Coventry Cathedral was not consecrated until 1962. The architect, Sir Basil Spence (1907–76), physically and symbolically united the old and the modern by siting the new cathedral adjacent to the ruins of St Michael's. Many of its treasures were created by eminent British artists: Elizabeth Frink's bronze eagle; Jacob Epstein's sculpture of St Michael; and Graham Sutherland's massive tapestry.

Cuzco   PERU

◉ The ancient capital of the Inca empire, Cuzco is situated in southern Peru at an altitude of 11 500ft (3500m). It was built by the Emperor Pachacuti after he came to power in 1438, although the site was settled by the Incas around 1200 and had been occupied even earlier (it is the oldest continuously inhabited city in the Americas). In the centre of the city were the Sun

Cuzco water jar

Temple, or Coricandra, and a central tower, the Sunturnvasi; around the Huacapata Plaza (the Holy Place) stood the houses of the elite, shops and potteries.

Cuzco lay at the hub of an extensive road network that ran all over the Inca empire, covering some 2500 miles (4000km). In 1533 the city was taken by the Spanish. Extensive ruins of the ancient city remain in modern Cuzco, which is noted for its churches and monasteries.

Fontainebleau FRANCE

◉ This magnificent chateau, one of the largest built by the French kings, was also used as a palace by Napoleon Bonaparte. The original building, a medieval hunting lodge in the forest of Fontainebleau, 40 miles (65km) south-east of Paris, was enlarged by Louis IX in the 13th century and entirely renovated in the Italian Mannerist style by Francis I in 1528. The finest apartments are the Gallery of Francis I, which was decorated by artists brought from Italy by the king, and the Council Room, refurbished by Louis XV. The spacious gardens were designed by the French landscape architect André Le Nôtre at the end of the 18th century.

Fountains Abbey ENGLAND

◉ The abbey, near Ripon in Yorkshire, was founded by Cistercian monks in 1132. It was twice reconstructed – in 1148 and 1179 – after being destroyed by fire. The Chapel of the Nine Altars was built at the east end of the church between 1203 and 1247; the north tower was added in 1479–94. Fountains Abbey was once the richest Cistercian house in England and its ruins are the most complete to have survived the Dissolution of the Monasteries by Henry VIII. The entire ground plan exists, as do the medieval plumbing and drainage systems. The abbey now stands in the magnificent water gardens of Studley Royal, laid out in 1727.

Great Mosque SPAIN

◉ Although La Mezquita, the Great Mosque, at Córdoba has been a Christian cathedral since 1236, it retains much of the splendour of the original Moorish building. It was built in AD 784–6 by Abd-ar Rahman I and extended during the 9th and 10th centuries. The structure is rectangular and contains a deep sanctuary, in which 850 marble columns support double tiers of horseshoe-shaped arches. The seven-sided mihrab (prayer niche) is lined with marble and gold mosaics. In the 16th century, a central high altar, chapels, a cruciform choir and a belfry 300ft (90m) tall were added.

Hadrian's Wall ENGLAND

◉ In AD 122-8, on the orders of the Emperor Hadrian, a wall was built across northern England from the Solway Firth in the west to the River Tyne in the east, a distance of 75 miles (120km). Made of stone and turf, it was intended to prevent tribes from the north invading Roman-held England. The wall utilised natural defences, such as cliffs, and in places was 14ft (4m) high. There was a forward defensive ditch and along the wall were 17 stone forts with block-houses, or milecastles, every 1000 paces – the Roman mile. One of the best preserved forts is at Housesteads. The wall was attacked and overrun in 139 and 367 and finally abandoned c.400–10.

Hermitage Museum RUSSIA

The original Hermitage complex, a series of buildings in St Petersburg which includes the Winter Palace, was built in 1764 by Catherine the Great to hold her private art collection and to serve as a place of retreat. Today it is one of the world's greatest art galleries, where the marble, malachite, jasper and agate of the setting vie for attention with works by Michelangelo, Titian, Leonardo, Rembrandt, Rubens, Degas and Renoir. There are rooms dedicated to Russian history and galleries containing Scythian relics and artefacts and other prehistoric finds.

Catherine the Great

Horyu-ji Temple JAPAN

The Horyu-ji is a five-storey wooden pagoda built at the beginning of the 7th century just outside Nara, Japan's first capital. It was built in the Chinese style, with elaborate overlapping tiled roofs, and is the oldest surviving Buddhist temple in Japan and one of the oldest wooden buildings in the world. The pagoda and kondo (golden hall) in its grounds house many paintings and carvings.

Hrădcany Castle CZECH REPUBLIC

Built high on a hill on the banks of the River Vltava, Hrădcany Castle in Prague is the largest in the world. It was founded in the middle of the 9th century and from 894 Czech kings were crowned here. Behind massive walls, on a site which covers 18 acres (7ha), several buildings are arranged around three courtyards. The architecture shows a sequence from medieval (the Dalibarka and White towers) to Gothic, Renaissance and Baroque. Other well-known buildings include St Vitus' Cathedral (designed by Matthias of Arras in 1344), the Royal Palace and the vast 243ft (74m) long Valdislav Hall.

Italian Chapel SCOTLAND

Situated on the small Orkney island of Lamb Holm, the Italian Chapel is not a grand building of vast proportions, but rather a monument to the triumph of the spirit and to human ingenuity. Built during World War II by Italian prisoners of war, the chapel was created from two prefabricated (Nissen) huts joined end to end and from scrap found nearby. The facade is concrete, with a two-pillared porch, the rood screen is wrought-iron, and the two candelabra are made from wood from a sunken ship. On either side of the altar are painted glass windows depicting St Francis of Assisi and St Catherine of Siena.

Karnak EGYPT

On the east bank of the Nile in Upper Egypt, across the river from the Valley of the Kings, lies Karnak, part of the ancient city of Thebes. The ruins at Karnak occupy an area of about 5 acres (2ha). To the north is the temple of Mont, the god of war, and to the south the temple dedicated to Mut, wife of the ram-headed Amun, god of Thebes.

Between the two is the temple complex of the king of gods, Amun-Re. One of the largest temples in the world, it has been termed a 'great historic document in stone'. Separated by courts and halls are ten pylons (gateways), two of which form a processional way, linking this temple with Mut's and, through an avenue of sphinxes, with the temple of Luxor. A hypostyle (pillared) hall built by Rameses I lies between the second and third pylons; 14 gigantic columns, 78ft (24m) high, support the roof of the central nave and on either side are seven more aisles with another 126 columns.

Khajuraho INDIA

◉ The historic town of Khajuraho, in Chhatarpur region of Madhya Pradesh, is famous for its 20 Hindu temples, all that survive of the 85 dedicated to Shiva, Vishnu and Jaina which were built there in 950–1050. Constructed mainly of sandstone, each temple is richly decorated inside and out with sculptures in high relief; those in the interior are regarded as masterpieces of erotic art. The most notable temple, the Kandarya Mahadeva, is dedicated to Shiva and contains his statue, along with some 872 other figures carved into the walls.

Kinkaku-ji JAPAN

The Golden Pavilion, or Kinkaku-ji, in Kyoto on the island of Honshu, was built in 1394 as a retreat for the shogun Ashikaga Yoshimitsu, who was responsible for the reform of the civil service and for a cultural revolution that swept Japanese court life. A three-storey building of great grace and beauty, it extends over a lake on pillars and incorporates elements of the Chinese Zen style; the walls are completely covered in gold leaf. In 1950, the pavilion, now a temple, burned down, but an exact replica was completed five years later.

Kinkaku-ji, Kyoto

Kremlin   RUSSIA

A triangular-shaped site of 90 acres (36ha) on the banks of the Moscow River houses the Kremlin. The original wooden citadel, or kremlin, erected in 1156, was rebuilt in brick in the 14th century. Later alterations and additions have resulted in a rich variety of palaces and cathedrals which reflect the architectural styles of their period: Byzantine (St Basil's Cathedral), Russian, Baroque and classical among them. The home of the Tsars until 1712, in 1918 the Kremlin became the administrative and political headquarters of the USSR.

St Basil's Cathedral

Lalibela Churches   ETHIOPIA

◉ The original name of this holy city in north-central Ethiopia was Roha, but in the late 12th and early 13th centuries it was ruled by King Lalibela, and the city was renamed after him. It was also Lalibela who reputedly undertook the construction of 11 impressive churches from rocks which were completely buried.

The method of construction was to dig a deep rectangular trench to expose a block of stone, which was then carved externally and hollowed out in such a way that the individual churches appear to be built from separate blocks. The largest church, the Beit Medhane Alem (the House of the Saviour of the World), is 109ft (33m) long, 77ft (23m) wide and 35ft (11m) deep. Today the churches are tended by more than 1000 Coptic priests of the Chabbe tribe.

Lascaux   FRANCE

In 1940, at Lascaux in the valley of the Dordogne, four schoolboys discovered a cave containing Paleolithic paintings dating from *c.*15 000 BC. In the skill of their

Prehistoric paintings, Lascaux

execution, these cave paintings are equal to those at Altamira *(p407)*; they lack the vibrant colour but are more dynamic. In the Hall of the Bulls, four jet-black bulls, three times life-size, cover the roof; elsewhere a herd of stags swims across a lake.

About 2000 paintings and drawings have been found in the caves, some of which make up compositions 20ft (6m) long. The caves were opened to the public in 1947 but were closed again in 1963 because the paintings were deteriorating due to atmospheric changes and attack by fungus. In 1983 a replica of the caves and the paintings was opened nearby.

Leaning Tower of Pisa   ITALY

This Romanesque, white marble tower is renowned for the fact that it leans 17ft (5.2m) from the perpendicular. Building of the eight-tiered structure, 179ft (55m) high, was begun in 1174 by Bonanno Pisano, and accounts vary as to whether the tower started to lean after the completion of the first or the third storey.

To compensate for the tower tilting, Pisano made the upper stories slightly taller on the short side, but the structure sank even further. A variety of further attempts were made to improve its balance, but without success, and when the final phase of building was completed in 1350, the tower continued to lean. It is now closed to the public.

Leptis Magna   LIBYA

◉ The most spectacular Roman remains – and some of the least well known – are to be found at Leptis Magna (now Labdah), 40 miles (65km) from Tripoli on the north-western Libyan coast. For centuries the site lay buried beneath the sand, so it is perhaps the best preserved of all ancient cities. Leptis Magna was founded by the Phoenicians possibly as early as the 7th century BC.

It reached its height as a trading centre, with a population of about 80 000, in the 3rd century AD, when Septimus Severus (193–211), a native of the city, became Roman emperor. Some time after the 3rd century the Vandals captured Leptis Magna and it was later briefly occupied by Byzantine Christians. The magnificent remains include the forum, amphitheatre, basilica, triumphal arch, temples and the baths built by Hadrian in AD 127.

Masada   ISRAEL

On the western shore of the Dead Sea, rising almost sheer out of the desert, is an immense hill 1424ft (434m) high. On the 18 acre (7ha) summit, Herod, king of Judea from 37 to 4 BC, created one of the wonders of the ancient world. Fortifications, palaces, cisterns, aqueducts, storehouses and Roman baths were built on three levels and joined by hidden stairways. Excavations in 1963–5 revealed also a ritual bath and synagogue, evidence of the Jews' occupation and tragic resistance to a Roman siege in AD 70–2.

Mogao Caves   CHINA

Between the 4th and 14th centuries, 496 Buddhist cave temples, known as the Mogao caves, were chiselled out of the rock cliffs 15 miles (24km) south of Tunhuang. This small town in north-central China is situated in the 'Ganzu Corridor', which formed part of the ancient trade route linking China with the West, the Silk Road *(p426)*.

The caves were decorated with religious wall paintings and then closed up, and it was not until 1900 that chance revealed a treasury of artistic and literary works. These include statues, a fine library of Buddhist texts, murals and paintings on silk, wood and paper dating from the Wei, Sui and T'ang dynasties.

Most of the objects were carried off, but the wall paintings and some statues remain. Many depict parables or episodes in the life of the Buddha; a few are abstract designs based on figurative motifs. Forty or so of the caves are currently open to the public.

Monastery of Batalha   PORTUGAL

◉ The Dominican monastery of Santa Maria da Vitória at Batalha, just south of Leira in west-central Portugal, was founded in 1388. Designed by Alfonso Domingues, it is one of the best examples of Christian Gothic architecture in Europe. The abbey complex includes the Founder's Chapel (with the tombs of King John I of Castile and Prince Henry the Navigator) and the Unfinished Chapels begun in the 1500s. In 1840 the monastery was declared a national monument.

Monticello   USA

A Federal-style home in Virginia, Monticello is a landmark of American architectural and domestic mechanical innovation. Begun by Thomas Jefferson in 1770, it took some 40 years to complete and combined aspects of a classical Roman villa with modern English and French design. The entrance hall served as a private museum of the natural sciences. The seven-day calendar clock which Jefferson designed still hangs above the door. He cut a hole in the floor to permit the rise and fall of the weights, which indicated the day of the week against marks on the wall. The doors to the parlour also show his love of all things mechanical: when one is pushed, the other opens too, propelled by a connecting loop of chain under the floor.

Mount Rushmore   USA

On the north-eastern side of Mount Rushmore (6375ft/ 1943m) in the Black Hills of South Dakota, the heads of four American presidents have been carved 60ft (18m) high into the

Mount Rushmore

granite. The mountain is a national memorial, for each president represents an aspect of the country's ideology: George Washington, the founding of the nation; Thomas Jefferson, political philosophy; Abraham Lincoln, preservation; and Theodore Roosevelt, expansion and conservation. The carvings were executed in 1927–41 under the direction of the American sculptor Gutzon Borglum.

Mount Vernon   USA

The home and burial place of George Washington (1732–99), Mount Vernon and its 8000 acres (3200ha) of landscaped grounds overlooking the Potomac river in Virginia have remained largely intact since the president's death. The splendid mansion, still with many original furnishings, provides a fascinating insight into the aristocratic life of the founding fathers of the USA. The main block of the building was begun in 1754. It has 19 rooms, the most interesting of which are the library and the bedroom, which still houses the four-poster bed in which Washington died.

Paestum   ITALY

The ancient Greek city of Paestum is situated 22 miles (35km) south-east of Salerno. It was probably founded *c.*600 BC by colonists from the Greek town of Sybaris in the south. In 390 BC it was taken over by the Romans and remained a Roman colony until 273 BC. Paestum is best known for its three Doric temples, the remains of which can still be seen, and for frescoes in the classical style discovered on the walls of a tomb in 1969.

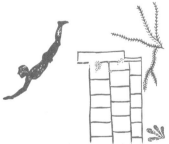

Painting on stone tomb, Paestum

Pantheon   ITALY

Built by Hadrian *c.*AD 118 on the site of an earlier temple, the Pantheon in Rome was dedicated

to seven of the chief Roman deities: Jupiter, Mars, Neptune, Venus, Mercury, Pluto and Saturn. It is remarkable both for its design and for the methods used in its construction.

It consists of a rotunda, with a portico of Corinthian columns supporting a gabled roof with a triangular pediment, surmounted by a dome. The rotunda, made of concrete faced with brick, has a diameter of about 130ft (40m); the dome, also of concrete, is 130ft (40m) in diameter at its widest point and 71ft (22m) high. An oculus, or 'eye', 27ft (8m) across, in the centre of the dome is the sole source of natural light. The marble-lined interior wall is broken by seven evenly spaced deep recesses. In AD 609 the building was dedicated as the church of Santa Maria Rotonda. It houses, among others, the tomb of the artist Raphael.

Paphos   CYPRUS

⊙ The ruins of the old city of Paphos are located in south-western Cyprus, in the modern town of Pirgos. Paphos was settled in Mycenaean times by Greek colonists and conquered by Ptolemy I of Egypt in 294 BC. A new city, built at the port of Old Paphos, then became the capital of Cyprus and remained so following Roman conquest; it was destroyed in AD 960 by Muslim raiders. Paphos was the legendary birthplace of Aphrodite, who was born from the sea foam, and her temple was built here. The entire area contains many ancient remains, including the mosaic floor of a Roman villa and an early Christian basilica associated with St Paul.

Parque La Venta   MEXICO

The ceremonial city of La Venta, perhaps the greatest Olmec site, was a complex of platforms, plazas, mounds of earth and clay and a great pyramid 112ft (34m) high. From 900 to 400 BC, it was the most important city in central America. Parque La Venta, in Tabasco province, stands near the site of this ancient city, and contains some of the relics and artefacts revealed during archaeological excavations at La Venta, which has recently been destroyed by oil operations.

Among the priceless antiquities are colossal stone heads, carved stone pillars and figurines of jade, basalt and serpentine.

Parthenon   GREECE

⊙ A Doric temple dedicated to Athena, the Parthenon on the Acropolis of Athens is one of the great architectural wonders of the Western world. It was built in 447–433 BC by the architect Ictinus, with sculptures by Phidius. Beneath the roof, which was supported by 46 columns, ran a sculpted frieze some 550ft (170m) long, parts of which are now in the British Museum. The gold and ivory statue of Athena Parthenos was 30ft (9m) high. The Parthenon later became a Christian church, then a mosque. During the Turkish–Venetian War it was used to store ammunition, and in 1687 was almost completely destroyed by an explosion. The temple is currently being restored.

The Parthenon

Patan   NEPAL

Also called Lalitpur (City of Beauty), Patan is situated 3 miles (5km) south-east of Kathmandu. Founded in AD 650, it was the capital of the Nepali kingdom in the 17th century and is now the centre of the Banra sect of gold and silversmiths, which has earned it the title 'city of artists'. Patan features a large Buddhist stupa on each of the four sides of the town; legend has it that they were built by the Indian emperor Asoka when he visited Patan in 250 BC. Other buildings include some fine Buddhist temples, the 16th-century Palace of the Malla Kings, the Royal Bath and the Temple of Lord Krishna.

Polonnaruwa   SRI LANKA

This once-magnificent ruined city lies 105 miles (170km) north-east of Colombo. It was in use as a royal residence in

AD 368, but the city was most influential in the 11th and 12th centuries when it was the Sinhalese capital. The main ruins date from the reign of Parakrama Bahu I (1164–1197), the most famous Sinhalese king.

The city's most important ruins are the Jetawanarama temple, whose walls are 170ft (52m) long, 80ft (25m) high and 12ft (4m) thick, and a statue of the Buddha, 46ft (14m) high.

Pompeii   ITALY

The ancient city of Pompeii, 12 miles (20km) south of Naples, was held in turn by Greeks, Etruscans, Samnites and, after 89 BC, by the Romans. At this time, it was an important port and a centre of agriculture, wine and perfume production. In AD 79, the eruption of Mount Vesuvius buried it in volcanic ash more than 20ft (6m) deep. Excavations began in 1748, and in 1763 an inscription (*vei publicae Pompeianorium*) was found that identified the city. Systematic excavation began in the 1860s; today some two-fifths of the ruins are still buried.

The remains that have been unearthed reveal a city of irregular shape, with walls enclosing some 155 acres (63ha), three areas occupied by public buildings, including the forum and amphitheatre, and hundreds of private houses. The earliest houses date from the 4th and 3rd centuries BC, the most luxurious, lavishly decorated with wall paintings and mosaics, from 280–200 BC. Among these is the House of the Faun, which occupies an entire block.

Puebla   MEXICO

⊙ The full name of this city in south-central Mexico is Puebla de Zaragoza, although it was founded as Puebla de los Angeles in 1532. The city centre is famous for its architecture and for the glazed tiles on the domes of many of its 60 churches. Among the most notable are the 17th-century cathedral, embellished with marble, onyx and gold, and the Church of Santo Domingo (1659), housing the Chapel of the Rosary, which is decorated with gold leaf. Other fine buildings include the 16th-century archbishop's palace, the

17th-century Casa del Alfeñique, now a museum, and the Téatro Principal, built in 1790.

Sagrada Familia   SPAIN
Barcelona's most famous building is the Sagrada Familia (the Expiatory Temple of the Holy Family), the design of which has been the subject of controversy almost since building began in 1882. It was designed as a neo-gothic structure by the Catalan architect Antoni Gaudi (1852–1926), and its early construction was directed by the architect Franceso P. Villar. Gaudi took over in 1891, after which the whole structure of the building changed. At Gaudi's death, only one of the four towers was finished. Today the three existing

Sagrada Familia

towers soar to a height of 450ft (137m); when it is completed, the central tower will rise another 200ft (61m) above them.

St Peter's Basilica   ITALY
The design of the 'new' St Peter's in Rome, said to be the most magnificent church in the world, is largely the work of Bramante, then of Michelangelo. Building began early in the 1500s, and by 1564, when Michelangelo died, construction of the 452ft (138m) high dome was well under way. Later, the nave was extended to 615ft (187m), and in 1655–67 Bernini's colonnaded piazza was added in front of the basilica. St Peter's is filled with works of art; the most famous are the *Pietà* by Michelangelo, Bernini's baldachin over the main altar and the bronze statue of St Peter.

Salisbury Cathedral   ENGLAND
This is the finest English Gothic cathedral and the only one conceived and built as a single unit on a brand-new site. It was

founded in 1220, and took only 40 years to complete. Its 404ft (123m) spire is the tallest to be constructed anywhere in the world in the Middle Ages, while the cloisters are the best preserved in England. To the north-west of the cathedral is an 18th-century close.

Shushan   IRAN
The Biblical city of Shushan, present-day Susa, is situated at the foot of the Zagros Mountains near the bank of the Karkheh River in Iran. In the 2nd millenium BC it became the capital of Elam (south-west Iran) and from 522 BC was the centre of the Achaemenid empire.

The archaeological site, identified in 1850, comprises four mounds, one of which included the palace of Darius I. The earliest levels excavated date from about 5000 BC. Antiquities found on the site include a temple tower, fine pieces of painted Neolithic pottery and a 3860lb (1750kg) bronze statue of Queen Napirasee, now in the Louvre in Paris.

Sistine Chapel   ITALY
The Sistine Chapel in the Vatican Palace in Rome is a remarkable example of renaissance art and architecture. It was built in 1473–81 by Pope Sixtus IV (hence 'Sistine') for meetings of the Sacred College of Cardinals. Best known of its many treasures is the barrel-vault ceiling covered in frescoes depicting Old and New Testament figures, painted by Michelangelo in 1508–12 at the command of Pope Julius II. The frescoes were completely restored in the 1980s.

Skara Brae   SCOTLAND
The almost perfectly preserved Neolithic village of Skara Brae on the Orkney island of Mainland was exposed in 1850 when a storm removed the sand dunes that had buried it for nearly 4500 years. The village was a tight cluster of nine stone houses, all of which were once covered with turf roofs. Each house had a central hearth, stone box-beds, dressers, storage recesses and access to both latrines and water tanks. Bone and stone tools, pottery fragments and food remains have also been found. All the evidence indicates that

the 30–40 people who occupied Skara Brae from 3100 to 2500 BC comprised a highly organised and cooperative community.

Statue of Liberty   USA
⊛ France presented the Statue of Liberty to the United States as a token of friendship marking the centenary of US independence. It stands on Liberty Island in New York harbour and was dedicated by President Grover Cleveland on 28 October 1886. The idea for the statue – 305ft (93m) from the base to the tip of the torch – was conceived by the French historian Edouard de Laboulaye after the American Civil War. The sculptor, Frédéric Auguste Bartholdi, directed its construction, which consisted of hammering copper sheets by hand and assembling them over a framework of four huge steel supports. The statue was dismantled and reassembled in New York. It was declared a national monument in 1924.

Temple of Heaven   CHINA
(T'ien T'an)
Beijing contains the most famous Chinese temple, the Temple of Heaven, built to reflect the traditional Chinese belief that heaven is round and the Earth square. No nails were used in the entirely wooden structure, which contains three main chambers – the Hall of Prayer for Good Harvests, the Imperial Vault of Heaven, and the Circular Mound Altar. When the emperor went from the Forbidden City to the temple to perform ceremonies, all windows and doors along the route had to be closed and complete silence maintained.

Tikal   GUATEMALA
⊛ This ancient Maya city in the Petén rainforest of northern Guatemala was settled in 250 BC. The earliest dated monument bears a date corresponding to 6 July AD 292, but the city was at its peak in the 7th and 8th centuries AD. It has been

estimated that Tikal contained 3000 buildings and a population of 20 000–30 000, all within an area of 6 sq miles (16km²). There were palaces, ten reservoirs, wide plazas and six temple pyramids, the largest 230ft (70m) high. Artefacts unearthed at the site include fine objects carved from jadeite, bone, shell and flint.

Tintern Abbey   WALES
Located on the west bank of the River Wye, in Gwent, near the border with England, Tintern Abbey is a majestic ruin of a church originally built for Cistercian monks. The present building, which replaced an earlier one built in 1131, was constructed mainly in the late 13th and early 14th centuries. It is a fine example of architecture representing the transition between the Early English and Decorated styles. The monastic buildings lie north of the main church. After the Dissolution of the Monasteries by Henry VIII, Tintern Abbey passed into private hands in 1537, and many years later (in 1900) the ruins were purchased by the Crown. The abbey has inspired several artists and poets, particularly the painter Joseph Mallord Turner, and William Wordsworth, who, in 1798, immortalised the ruins in his poem, *Lines written a few miles above Tintern Abbey.*

Todai-ji Temple   JAPAN
When Buddhism was adopted as Japan's state religion, it was commemorated by Emperor Shomu in 745 by the founding in Nara of Todai-ji, the temple of the Imperial Family. The wooden building, finished in 752 contained a bronze Buddha, 53ft (16.2m) tall, which survived the building's destruction in 1180 and was rehoused in the present temple in the early 1700s. The Shoso-in, a wooden treasure store supported on 40 pillars almost 8ft (2.5m) tall, contains more than 9000 works of art dating from the time of Shomu.

Tintern Abbey

Toledo — SPAIN

Formerly the capital of the Visigothic kingdom, then of Castille and of Spain, Toledo is often said to be the city most representative of Spanish culture. The old city, famous for its fine swords, contains many historic buildings. Among them are the medieval castle of San Servando, parts of which date from the Roman and Moorish periods; the cathedral, begun in 1226 and reputedly the most Hispanic of all Spain's Gothic cathedrals; the churches of St Thomas and St Romanus; and the house of the 16th-century artist El Greco.

Tula — MEXICO

An ancient American city, Tula lies 40 miles (65km) north-west of Mexico City. Founded c.750 AD, and destroyed in 1168, it was the most important of the Toltec centres, from which they ruled central Mexico in 900–1150. The population has been estimated at 30 000–40 000, living in an area of 5½ sq miles (14 km²). The ruins occur in two sites at opposite ends of a low ridge and comprise two civic centres. The main centre includes a large plaza, a palace complex, ball courts, pyramids and a five-tiered temple, topped by a two-roomed temple and decorated with paintings and sculptures.

Versailles — FRANCE

The grand Palace of Versailles, built in the classical style by the 'Sun King', Louis XIV, took 50 years to construct (1661–1711). The palace gardens, laid out by André Le Nôtre, cover 250 acres (100ha). Versailles became a place of extravagant entertainment and the centre of the French government. In 1793, during the Revolution, the palace was ransacked, but it was restored by King Louis-Philippe and turned into a national museum in 1837. After a period as the seat of parliament, it reverted to a palace, and there, in 1919, after the end of World War I, the peace treaties were signed. Today the palace of Versailles attracts thousands of visitors who flock to see, among other marvels, the 238ft (72m) Hall of Mirrors, designed by Jules Hardouin-Mansart in 1678.

WATERY WORLDS

The fascination water holds for many people – whether the silky stillness of a tranquil lake or the power of a turbulent ocean – surely stems from their primeval past, for life on Earth would not exist without water. No other element moves us so deeply, and these emotions find expression in the legends, beliefs and religious practices of all peoples.

Angel Falls — VENEZUELA

Almost 18 times the height of Niagara, Angel Falls have a total drop of 3212ft (979m), making them the highest in the world. From a grassy plateau, the water cascades 2648ft (807m) onto a rocky projection and then plummets a further 564ft (172m). The falls, set amid rainforest on a tributary of the River Caroni in south-east Venezuela, are accessible only by boat or plane. They were named after the American airman Jimmy Angel, who first saw them while flying in the area in 1935.

Aran Islands — IRELAND

For centuries, fishermen and subsistence farmers have lived on the Aran Islands, located 5 miles (8km) off the west coast of Ireland in Galway Bay. Sheer limestone cliffs up to 295ft (90m) high face the Atlantic Ocean.

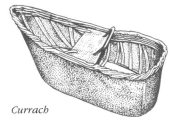

Currach

The fishermen put to sea in currachs: tarred canvas boats which also serve as ferries between the islands. Farmers grow potatoes and other crops on fields formed by spreading sand and seaweed on level areas of limestone. One of the Aran Islands' most famous residents was the playwright J.M. Synge (1871–1909), who spent part of each year there, recording the language and culture.

Band-e Amir Lakes — AFGHANISTAN

In the arid foothills of the Hindu Kush, some 50 miles (80km) west of Bamian, a chain of six lakes has formed in the bed of the Band-e Amir River, which is fed by meltwater carried down from the mountain peaks in the spring. The lakes are situated in a narrow valley near the head of the river, in a barren, rocky landscape that is otherwise largely devoid of water.

They were created by the accumulation of water behind natural stone dams, formed by the deposition of travertine (a type of limestone) in the river bed. The walls of the dams average 33ft (10m) in height and 10ft (3m) in width. The smallest lake, Band-e Panir, is about 330ft (100m) in diameter and the largest, Band-e Zulficar, about 4 miles (6.5km). The lakes vary in colour from milky white to dark green and are located at different elevations, so they appear one above the other like vast puddles on a gigantic staircase.

Bora-Bora — SOUTH PACIFIC

This jewel in the ocean is the epitome of the castaway's desert island. At its heart, draped with tropical forest, stand the remnants of a volcano. This is ringed by a turquoise lagoon, its waters stilled by the almost circular coral reef that keeps the Pacific breakers at bay. With its tallest peak, Mount Otemanu, reaching just 2379ft (725m), it is difficult to believe Bora-Bora once towered 4000ft (1200m) above sea level and 18 000ft (5400m) above its bed.

Caspian Sea — ASIA

The world's largest body of inland water, the Caspian Sea has an area of 152 100 sq miles (393 900km²). It has no outlets and no tides, and lies in a huge depression with its surface some 92ft (28m) below sea level. Its depth varies from a maximum of 3215ft (980m) in the south to an average of 17ft (5m) in the flat, sedimentary sea bed of the north. The River Volga, which drains the northern uplands, supplies 75 per cent of the sea's water. To the south, the sea is bordered by the forested slopes of the Elburz Mountains in Iran, to the west by the Caucasus and to the east by the Karakum Desert.

Congo Basin — CENTRAL AFRICA

At the heart of the 'Dark Continent' lies the Congo Basin, an area of rainforest that covers most of northern Zaire and whose river, the Congo (or Zaire), drains some 13 per cent of Africa.

This rainforest represents almost a tenth of the world's total of this rich and varied habitat and provides a home for monkeys, chimpanzees and birds such as the African grey parrot and yellow-casqued hornbill. Lower down in the trees live pythons and vipers, fruit bats and the striped squirrel, and on the floor lives one of the jungle's most impressive creatures, the gorilla.

Crater Lake — USA

This is an excellent example of a lake created by water filling a caldera (sunken volcanic crater). Crater Lake is situated in Crater Lake National Park, Oregon. It lies at an altitude of 6165ft (1880m) in the collapsed summit of the once-volcanic Mount Mazama, part of the Cascade Range that stretches north from California to British Columbia, Canada.

The lake is 6 miles (10km) wide and covers an area of almost 20 sq miles (52km²), with a maximum depth of 1932ft (590m). Rising to 778ft (237m) above the water, near the western shore, lies Wizard Island, the small cone of a volcano that formed after Mount Mazama collapsed. The lake has no inlet and no outlet, but the water level is kept fairly constant because the input from rainfall and melting snow is roughly equal to the amount of water that is lost through evaporation.

Crater Lake

Danube Delta Nature Reserve   ROMANIA

◉ Marshes, lagoons, reedbeds, lakes and islands are some of the varied habitats supporting the wildlife of the Danube Delta, where the river runs out into the Black Sea. The 150 sq mile (400km²) nature reserve was established in 1963 to conserve the numerous species of duck, geese and waders from Asia and other parts of Europe that migrate here to overwinter in the comparatively mild climate the region enjoys.

Dead Sea   ISRAEL/JORDAN

Although no friend of nature itself, the Dead Sea is one of the natural wonders of the world. Birds do not cry there nor trees overhang these mineral-laden waters. Normal sea water has a salt content of 3.5 per cent; the salinity of the Dead Sea is some 28 per cent, sufficient to kill all forms of life with the exception of a few extraordinary micro-organisms that are actually dependent on this ordinarily toxic level of salt. It is impossible to sink in the dense waters of the Dead Sea – plunging an arm in to commence a swimming stroke simply results in another limb bobbing to the surface.

Everglades   USA

◉ The entire swampy, subtropical region of the Florida peninsula south of Lake Okeechobee comprises the Everglades. Some 100 miles (160km) long and 50–75 miles (80–120km) wide, they extend over an area of 5000 sq miles (13 000km²), of which 2200 sq miles (5700km²) in the south is now a national park and World Heritage Site. Much of the Everglades is sawgrass savanna, dotted with freshwater pools and small wooded islands, with mangrove swamps along the

Flamingos

coast. In places, there are forests of tropical trees which are host to ferns, orchids, bromeliads and other epiphytes. Everglades National Park, in particular, is noted for its rich and varied fauna, including wood storks, spoonbills, flamingos, ibis, egrets, pelicans, turtles, tree frogs and alligators.

Great Lakes   CANADA/USA

The five Great Lakes that span the border between the USA and Canada form the largest group of freshwater lakes in the world, their surface waters covering an area of about 94 700 sq miles (245 300km²). Lake Superior is 31 692 sq miles (82 103km²), which makes it the world's largest lake after the Caspian Sea (*p413*). Lake Ontario (7338 sq miles/19 011km²) is the smallest and the only one which is ice-free in winter. The other lakes are Huron, Michigan and Erie; only Lake Michigan lies entirely within the USA.

Connected by navigable straits and canals, the lakes provide important transportation links between Canada and the USA, and between these nations and the rest of the world via the St Lawrence River, which flows into the North Atlantic.

Great Salt Lake   USA

The remnant of an enormous prehistoric lake that extended from Utah into Nevada and Idaho, Great Salt Lake is about 75 miles (120km) long and 50 miles (80km) wide. It is fed by three rivers – the Bear, Weber and Jordan – but it has no outlet. Water loss through evaporation exceeds the inflow from the rivers, resulting in the concentration of the mineral salts that cause the high salinity of the lake's water – between 20 and 27 per cent.

The size of the lake fluctuates, depending on the rate of evaporation and the amount of water flowing into it. In 1963, for example, the area of the lake was 950 sq miles (2450km²), while in the 1980s it averaged 2000 sq miles (5200km²).

The ancestral lake, Lake Bonneville, was about 20 times the size of the present one, and traces of its shoreline can be seen on the surrounding mountains at

elevations up to 1000ft (300m) above the present surface.

Huangguoshu Falls   CHINA

Guizhou Province, in which Huangguoshu Falls lie, is renowned for its caves and spectacular cascades. These falls are the finest in the region and also the largest in China. Hikers in this demanding terrain are rewarded by the sight of the falls' 165ft (50m) wide and 240ft (75m) deep drop into Rhinoceros Pool and can cool off with a visit to Water Veiled Cave, a recess behind the falls themselves. Altogether there are some 18 waterfalls in the area, notably Steep Slope Falls about ⅔ mile (1km) upstream of Huangguoshu, and Star Bridge Falls 5miles (8km) downstream.

Hunlen Falls   CANADA

Among the natural attractions of Tweedsmuir Provincial Park – a vast, beautiful wilderness of deep canyons and glacier-clad mountain peaks in British Columbia – is the Hunlen Falls, nearly seven times the height of the Niagara Falls. At the end of its 20 mile (32km) course the Hunlen River plunges, uninterrupted, for some 1200ft (365m) over a sheer precipice, foaming and seething into the narrow gorge below.

The river makes this monumental leap near Turner Lake, the last in a chain of glacial lakes bounded by dense forests along its course. The river is fed by runoff from glaciers and winter snows, and mule deers and bears can be seen along its banks.

Königssee   GERMANY

This small but beautiful lake lies at an altitude of 1975ft (600m) in the spectacular setting of the Bavarian Alps. It is situated 3 miles (5km) south of the resort at Berchtesgaden and 15 miles (24km) from Salzburg in Austria. The lake is 5 miles (8km) long, and only 1 mile (1.6km) across at its widest point; it has a maximum depth of 617ft (188m). The mountains that ring it, rising steeply from the water's edge, include the Watzmann, at 8901ft (2713m) the highest peak in the area, and the Hochalter (8553ft/2607m), the site of the Blaueis Glacier.

Lake Baikal   RUSSIA

The deepest lake in the world, Lake Baikal (5380ft/1640m) was created when a deep rift in the Earth's crust filled with water 25 million years ago. It is a huge inland sea, some 400 miles (640km) long and an average of 30 miles (50km) wide, which contains one-fifth of all the Earth's fresh water. More than 300 rivers supply this natural reservoir, while just one, the Angara, drains it. The lake supports a wide variety of plant and animal life, 75 per cent of which is unique, most notably the only freshwater seal in the world.

Lake Chad   CENTRAL AFRICA

At the meeting point of Niger, Cameroon, Chad and Nigeria, on the southern edge of the Sahara, lies Lake Chad. This shallow freshwater lake provides a haven for many species of bird. At its height, following seasonal rains, it covers an area of 8000 sq miles (20 800km²) and at low water, 4000 sq miles (10 400km²); but its maximum depth is little more than 25ft (8m). The present lake is all that remains of an ancient sea which, two million years ago, covered an estimated area of 100 000 sq miles (260 000km²).

Little black bustard, Lake Chad

Lake Eyre   AUSTRALIA

This lake in the Great Artesian Basin in central South Australia is, in fact, two lakes joined by the narrow Goyder Channel. Lake Eyre South is 38 miles (61km) long and 6 miles (26km) wide; Lake Eyre North (90 miles/145km long and 40 miles/65km wide) is not only the larger of the two but also the largest lake in the continent. Rainfall in this area, the driest in Australia, averages less than 5in (13cm) a year, and for much of the time the lakes are merely dry beds with a crust of glistening salt. It is estimated that as a result of seepage of underground water after freak rains in the Simpson Desert to the north, the lake fills completely only twice a century. Since its discovery by the British explorer Edward John Eyre in 1840, Lake Eyre North has been filled with water just three times. In 1964 the lake became famous when the Englishman Donald Campbell set a new land speed record there of 403.1mph (648.7km/h).

Lake Maggiore ITALY

Narrow, long and surrounded on three sides by the foothills of the Alps, Lake Maggiore is Italy's largest lake after Lake Garda. It measures 37 miles (60km) in length, 1½–3 miles (3–5km) across and 1220ft (370m) deep. In the north, the lake stretches beyond the Italian border into the Swiss canton of Ticino, the location of the resort of Locarno. In the south, on its western arm, are the popular resort of Stresa and the Borromean Islands, which include the enchanting Isola Bella.

Lake Nakuru National Park KENYA

The salty waters of Lake Nakuru in west-central Kenya attract huge flocks of pink flamingos, which congregate to feed on algae that grow in the lake. The park, established in 1961, occupies 72 sq miles (188km²) of the eastern and southern shores and is primarily a bird sanctuary. Among the 400 species recorded here are cormorants, kingfishers, pelicans and many other fish-eating birds. Mammals that live within the park's boundaries include impala, waterbuck and hippopotamuses.

Lake Titicaca BOLIVIA/PERU

⊛ Covering an area of almost 3400 sq miles (8800km²), Lake Titicaca is the largest body of fresh water in South America. It straddles the border between Bolivia and Peru and provides a home for the Uru and Aymara Indians, some of whom live on the lake itself on floating rafts which they build from totora reeds. The reeds are also used to build the Indians' distinctive boats which, in the eyes of the

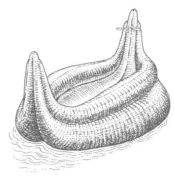

Lake Titicaca boat

Norwegian ethnologist and adventurer Thor Heyerdahl, bore such a close resemblance to the boats of ancient Egypt that he built his own craft *Ra II* from similar reeds. He then sailed across the Atlantic in it in order to prove that the Egyptians could have made the voyage in such boats.

Lake Toba SUMATRA

With a surface area of 635 sq miles (1645km²), Lake Toba is the largest lake in Indonesia, located in the Barisan Mountains in the north of the island of Sumatra. It was created 6000 years ago when an eruption destroyed a volcano's cone, forming a caldera that is now the lake basin. Later eruptions on the floor of the caldera threw up ash and other debris, creating the mountainous island of Samosir that lies within the lake.

The Batak peoples make their home on the lake shores.

Batak house

Lake Vänern SWEDEN

The largest lake in Sweden and the third largest in Europe, with an area of 2156 sq miles (5585km²), Lake Vänern lies in the south-west of the country 144ft (44m) above sea level. It is fed by the Klarälven and several other rivers, and itself drains via the River Göta into the Kattegat, the sea channel between Sweden and Denmark. Except in the south, which is largely farmland, the lake is fringed by woods that cling to the rocky terrain. The

Göta and Lake Vänern form part of the Göta Canal, which cuts across Sweden, connecting the Kattegat in the west with the Baltic Sea in the east.

Las Marismas SPAIN

The region in Andalucia known as Las Marismas (The Marshes) covers 450 sq miles (1165km²) on the estuary of the Guadalquivir River at its entry into the Gulf of Cadiz. Silt carried down by the river's powerful currents has created a haven there for wildlife. While parts of the marsh are always submerged, others are flooded only seasonally, and the diverse habitats include low-lying islands, sand dunes, grassland, heath and cork oak forest.

Las Marismas was for many centuries a hunting ground for the dukes of Medina-Sidonia. In 1963, it was granted nature reserve status and in 1969, with the adjoining Guadiamar Reserve, it became part of Coto Doñana National Park. This is one of Europe's finest wilderness regions, home to several mammal species, some of them rare, and hundreds of birds; it is also a noted resting ground for migrating birds.

Marianas Trench PACIFIC OCEAN

East of the island of Guam and north of the Caroline Islands, in the floor of the North Pacific, lies the Marianas Trench. It is a deep, curved depression 1585 miles (2560km) long with an average width of 43 miles (70km). The trench plunges to the greatest ocean depth recorded on Earth, Challenger Deep, which is 36 200ft (11 035m) below sea level. This sounding was taken in 1960 by Lieutenant Don Walsh, an oceanographer in the US Navy, and the Swiss engineer Jacques Piccard, who descended to 35 800ft (10 910m) – a record dive – in the bathyscaph *Trieste*.

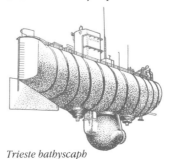

Trieste bathyscaph

Matsushima Bay JAPAN

Located in north-eastern Honshu, Matsushima Bay is one of Japan's most popular scenic attractions. Lying within the bay is an archipelago of hundreds of islands and islets, many of which are covered with pines (the name Matsushima means 'islands of pine') and some of which are linked by bridges. Only a few of the islands are inhabited, but there are Buddhist shrines and temples on several of the uninhabited ones. Protected as they are from the force of Pacific storms by the natural barrier of the archipelago, the waters of the bay are calm and still.

Mekong River ASIA

Some 340 miles (550km) of the 2500 mile (4000km) long Mekong River are navigable. Its journey to the sea starts on the Tibet (Xizang) Plateau as two streams, the waters of which combine to form the Langcang Jiang. This river flows south and south-west, forming the boundary between Laos and Burma, then swings to the south-east to mark the Laos–Thailand border.

Along the northern Thai border the river's name changes to the Mekong; there it passes through narrow defiles, over churning rapids and across plains. As it enters Cambodia it becomes a typical lowland river, broad and lazy and congested with river traffic. At Phnom Penh it divides, then one branch divides again as it enters Vietnam. Here the river forms a huge delta, one of the largest rice-growing areas in Asia, and enters the South China Sea. In the wet season at the end of summer, when the river swells, much of the water backs up into the Tonle Sap *(p417)* in central Cambodia.

Mississippi-Missouri River USA

From its source in Lake Itasca in Minnesota to its mouth in the Gulf of Mexico in south-east Louisiana, the Mississippi River is 2348 miles (3779km) long, making it the second-longest river in North America. The longest, the Missouri (2466 miles/3969km), is the main tributary of the Mississippi. The headwaters of this river lie in Montana, high in the Rocky Mountains. It flows across the Great Plains, taking up so much silt that it has been given the name Big Muddy, and joins the Mississippi north of St Louis, the so-called 'gateway to the West'. Together these rivers make up the major waterway of the USA and the largest river system in the world after the Nile, Amazon and Yangtze. From the headwaters of the Missouri to the mouth of the Mississippi is a distance of 3740 miles (6020km).

Gateway Arch, St Louis

Niagara Falls   USA/CANADA

Between lakes Erie and Ontario lies the awe-inspiring spectacle of the Niagara Falls. The curving Canadian, or Horseshoe, Falls are 2215ft (675m) wide and 176ft (54m) high; the American Falls 1060ft (323m) across and 184ft (56m) high. Visitors can walk behind the curtain of water at the foot of these falls to the Cave of the Winds, a cavern caused by erosion. Though much water is diverted above the falls to generate hydroelectricity, below them, the river is still an impressive sight as it thunders over a series of rapids into a narrow gorge 300ft (90m) wide.

Okefenokee Swamp   USA

The Okefenokee Swamp covers an area of 680 sq miles (1760km²), mainly in south-eastern Georgia, but part lies in northern Florida. In the west, the swamp is drained by the Suwannee River, which

American Alligator

flows into the Gulf of Mexico, and in the south and east by St Mary's River, which flows into the Atlantic Ocean.

The wetland supports swamp cypress trees, waterlilies and other aquatic plants; birds include yellow-bellied sapsuckers, ospreys, herons, sandhill cranes and egrets; frogs, lizards, snakes, toads and American alligators abound.

The water is shallow – less than 3ft (1m) in most places – but fish such as bass, chain pickerel and bluegill are plentiful. In the 1930s the federal government made this unique wetland habitat a wildlife refuge in order to conserve its rich flora and fauna.

Orinoco River   VENEZUELA

With a drainage basin of 366 000 sq miles (948 000km²) and a length of 1336 miles (2150km), the Orinoco is one of South America's major rivers. It rises in the Guiana Highlands, in the Serra Parima which lie along the border between Venezuela and Brazil, and then sweeps north through Venezuela, at times forming the border with Colombia. Curving towards the east, it flows down to the Atlantic, entering the ocean near Trinidad. In its upper reaches the river is joined to the Amazon by the Casiquiare (**p224**), a navigable natural canal.

Pamukkale Springs   TURKEY

These hot springs issue from the side of the mountain of Cal Daği 12 miles (20km) north of the city of Denizli, in western Anatolia. Streams of water flow down over a series of terraces, each terrace containing a pool of water supported by a wall of travertine, or solidified calcium carbonate. The travertine forms when water cascading down the edges of the terraces evaporates in the heat of the sun, leaving behind mineral deposits.

Near the modern town of Pamukkale are the remains of a Roman health spa, Hierapolis, evidence that these mineral-rich waters were thought to be therapeutic even in Roman times. Today the waters are recommended for the treatment of many nervous and skin disorders, as well as for several circulatory problems.

Plitvice Lakes   CROATIA

⊙ A series of more than 16 lakes in the thickly forested mountains of western Croatia are the main attraction of a large national park. Linked by spectacular waterfalls up to 250ft (75m) high, the lakes descend like a series of steps for 3 miles (5km) along a valley, then spill over into the canyon of the River Korana. Water is kept in the lakes by natural 'dams' of limestone deposited out of solution at the top of each waterfall. In winter, much of the surface water freezes and the waterfalls are converted into masses of convoluted icicles.

Rabbitkettle Hot Springs   CANADA

In the Nahanni National Park, in Canada's Northwest Territories, a layered dome of limestone 90ft (27m) high and 225ft (70m) across constitutes the remarkable site of Rabbitkettle Hot Springs. At the top, warm thermal water saturated with dissolved calcium carbonate spills out. As it trickles down the rocky terraces, the water evaporates, leaving solid deposits of the mineral that gradually build up more and more limestone rock. Farther down the valley from the springs, the South Nahanni River plunges over a 294ft (90m) cliff in the spectacular double cascade of Virginia Falls.

Rhine Gorge   GERMANY

Between Bingen and Koblenz the River Rhine flows through a gorge 90 miles (145km) long. The scenery is spectacular, with terraced vineyards and medieval castles – like Katz Burg, above the village of St Goarshausen – on the rocky cliffs. Near St Goar, where the river narrows, the Lorelei, a precipitous rock 433ft (132m) high, juts out. A hazard to sailors, it is noted for its echo; this may be the origin of the

Katz Burg

myth of a Siren whose song was reputed to lure sailors to their death in the treacherous currents around it. Downstream are the Siebengebirge (Seven Mountains) which, legend has it, were formed when the giants who dug out the river bed dropped some of the earth. On one of these, Drachenfels (Dragon Rock), the Wagnerian hero Siegfried is said to have slain his dragon.

Rotorua   NEW ZEALAND

Known as 'Sulphur City', for the air is always full of its pungent smell, Rotorua is in the centre of the Thermal Region on the North Island of New Zealand. To the south is Whakarewarewa, the site of the country's largest geyser,

Mud pool patterns

Pohutu (Maori for 'splashing'), which, at intervals varying from minutes to months, produces a fountain of boiling water up to 100ft (30m) high. To the east is Tikitere, an area of boiling pools and hot mud flats; at Orakei-Korako there are huge silica terraces and a fern-framed cave that holds a bright blue pool.

Saiwa Swamp National Park   KENYA

The smallest park of its kind in Kenya (only 474 acres/192ha in extent), Saiwa Swamp National Park was established in 1974 for the specific purpose of providing a protected habitat for the semi-aquatic sitatunga antelopes. These large-eared, red-brown animals spend most of their time wading neck-deep in the swamp, prevented from sinking in the mud by their large splayed hoofs.

Sinamaica Lagoon   VENEZUELA

Some 27 miles (45km) north of Maracaibo on the Guajira Peninsula, which borders the

Gulf of Venezuela, lies Sinamaica Lagoon. Here, in a paradise of coconut trees and mangroves, the people live in *palafitos*, houses built on stilts, as they did 500 years ago. These villages built above the water prompted Spanish colonisers to call the coast 'Little Venice' – Venezuela – from which the whole country took its name. The Indians use reeds cut from the fringes of the lagoon to make the roofs, walls and floors of their houses, as well as sleeping mats and baskets.

Tigris River   IRAQ, SYRIA, TURKEY

The Euphrates and the Tigris form the major river system of south-west Asia. The Tigris, 1180 miles (1900km) long, rises in the mountains of eastern Turkey, and is fed by meltwater from winter snows. By the time it reaches northern Iraq, only a broad triangle of desert separates it from the Euphrates. The rivers then enter Mesopotamia, where the vast quantities of silt they deposit create fertile land that has been farmed for thousands of years. At Qurnah, 40 miles (65km) from Basra, they join to form the Shatt al'Arab, which flows into the Gulf through a vast delta, the home of the Marsh Arabs.

Tonle Sap   CAMBODIA

Lying in a basin on the Cambodian Plain, Tonle Sap is the largest expanse of fresh water in South-east Asia. The Tonle Sap River, some 80 miles (130km) long, links it to the great Mekong River *(p415)* at Phnom Penh. When the Mekong floods during the monsoon, the lake acts as a natural reservoir for that river, whose flood waters are forced back up the Tonle Sap River to the lake, raising its depth from 10ft (3m) to 30–45ft (9–14m) and extending its width from 22 to 65 miles (35 to 105km). In the dry season, the flow is reversed, and water from the lake runs down into the Mekong.

Victoria Falls   ZAMBIA, ZIMBABWE

One of the world's greatest waterfalls, the Victoria Falls lie on the Zambezi River, the natural boundary between Zambia and Zimbabwe. It comprises five main falls: the Eastern Cataract, Rainbow Falls, Devil's Cataract, Horseshoe Falls and Main Falls, which are 5540ft (1690m) wide and 200–350ft (60–100m) high. Facing the cliff over which the river drops is a second cliff, only 250ft (75m) distant, creating a gorge into which the water pours. Its only outlet is a narrow channel 200ft (60m) across. Spray rising from this gorge reaches a height of 1000ft (300m) and at times is visible 25 miles (40km) away, while the roar of the water can be heard long before the falls are seen. Both features give rise to the local name Mosi-oa-Tunya, which means 'the smoke that thunders'.

Volga River   RUSSIA

With a length of 2194 miles (3530km), the Volga is Europe's longest river. It drains an area of some 525 000 sq miles (1.4 million km²) – about one-third of European Russia. The river rises north-west of Moscow in the Valdai Hills and flows more or less south-east until it enters the Caspian Sea *(p413)*. It is linked by canals to Moscow, the Baltic, the White and Black Seas and the Sea of Azov, and is important commercially and as a source of hydroelectricity and irrigation.

Waddenzee   NETHERLANDS

A shallow arm of the North Sea, the Waddenzee forms a saltwater zone on the north coast of the Netherlands. It is separated from the Ijsselmeer, a large freshwater lake, by a 20 mile (32km) long dam that was constructed in 1927–33 as part of an ambitious land reclamation project. At low tide the waters of the Waddenzee ebb away almost completely, exposing an area of sand flats interlaced with narrow channels. This is an important wetland habitat that serves as a sanctuary for migrating waterfowl: it is estimated that 500 000 birds or more, of various species, gather there at the height of the season.

Yangtze River   CHINA

The Chang Jiang, or Yangtze, is the longest river in China and the third longest in the world. It rises in the Tanglha range on the Tibetan Plateau and enters the East China Sea near Shanghai, 3900 miles (6300km) away. The river is navigable for 580 miles (935km) and forms one of the major transport routes between east and west China.

The Grand Canal, built by Kublai Khan in the 13th century, connects the Yangtze to the Yellow River *(below)*, and the city of Beijing to the north. The river's drainage basin covers an area of some 695 000 sq miles (1.8 million km²). It provides water for about 25 per cent of China's agricultural land and generates 40 per cent of its electricity.

Yellow River   CHINA

The Yellow River, or Huang He, is China's longest river after the Yangtze *(above)*. It runs for 3395 miles (5465km) from the Bayan Har mountain range in west-central China to the gulf of Bo Hai, north of the Yellow Sea. The river takes its name from the yellow silt it carries in its waters from the hard loess rock of the Shanxi region through which it passes on its long journey.

Yellow River gravel boat

RIDDLES AND SYMBOLS

Many mysterious structures of ancient civilisations remain to puzzle and intrigue us. While we marvel at huge earthworks and figures etched into hillsides, we can only speculate as to why our ancestors felt compelled to create them. Were they made to express a personal identity, or for magical purposes? And were the vast stone megaliths related to the ingenious first flowering of astronomy – a means of tracking the seasons and even predicting eclipses?

Abalessa   ALGERIA

Near the oasis of Abalessa, deep in the Sahara desert, lies the tomb of a queen named Tin-Hinan. It was discovered in 1925 by a French archaeologist excavating an ancient fort. The tomb, which had several chambers, contained coins and artefacts dating from the 2nd to the 4th centuries AD. No one knows when Tin-Hinan lived, but she was buried wearing a leather dress and gold and silver bracelets. Some people believe her to have been the ancestress of the nomadic Tuareg people.

Alexandropol   UKRAINE

When the Scythian nomads roamed the plains of the Ukraine, they established a reign of terror with acts of ritual brutality. From 700 to 400 BC, at the height of their power, they built huge funeral barrows, rising from the steppes like hills, in which to bury their chiefs; the barrow at Alexandropol, south-east of Kiev, is nearly 60ft (18m) high and contains several separate burial chambers.

The barrows often contained men mounted on horseback, with their servants and wives – all ritually slain to accompany their dead leader – as well as vast quantities of fine gold jewellery and embroideries.

Avebury   ENGLAND

The largest henge monument in England is situated at Avebury in Wiltshire, some 70 miles (112km) west of London. It was used as a ceremonial centre c.2600–1600 BC and comprises an earthwork 1400ft (430m) in diameter edged by a high chalk bank. Cut into the chalk on the inside of the bank is a 30ft (9m) ditch with steeply sloping sides and a base 15ft (5m) wide. Within the enclosure are three stone circles: a large circle of 100 great slabs of sarsen, the

Avebury

local sandstone, with two smaller circles adjacent to one another inside it. Four entrances to the large stone circle lie at the four cardinal points. The monument is approached by an avenue 1½ miles (2.5km) long, defined by 100 paired sarsen stones. The village of Avebury lies in the centre of the monument.

Babylon
IRAQ

The ruins of Babylon, ancient capital of the Babylonian Empire, are some 50 miles (80km) south of modern Baghdad. The city is reputedly the site of the Tower of Babel, the ruins of which are claimed to be those of a ziggurat (stepped tower) within the city walls. Babylon also contained fine temples and palaces, including the great palace of Nebuchadnezzar II, and the Hanging Gardens, one of the Seven Wonders of the Ancient World. The Ishtar Gate is the only structure that has survived intact to the present day.

Ishtar Gate

Ban Chieng
THAILAND

The remains of a mysterious early civilisation were discovered at this site, 450 miles (725km) north-east of Bangkok. Bronze items, including weapons and jewellery, that were unearthed gave rise to the theory that bronze making originated here as early as 3600 BC. It was previously thought that bronze making was first developed in the Middle East around 3000 BC.

Bhubaneshwar
INDIA

On the swampy coasts of Orissa, about 12 miles (20km) south of the Mahanadi river, stands one of the wonders of India known as the 'City of Temples'. It is said that several thousand temples were built in the area, although only 30 now remain, together with some 500 tombs. The

temples were constructed between the 7th and 15th centuries, the most famous, Lingaraja, being built c.AD 1000. Although it is stark inside, the exterior features highly decorative sculptures, created by an unknown hand in homage to an unknown god or goddess, perhaps Shiva.

Bighorn Medicine Wheel
USA

The stone circle known as the Bighorn Medicine Wheel lies near the summit of a peak in the Bighorn Mountains of Wyoming. It is constructed of individual stones laid out in a pattern resembling a wheel with 28 spokes. Six cairns have been built around the circumference of the wheel, which has a diameter of 80ft (24m). The design laid out in stone is similar to that of the medicine lodges used by the Cheyenne, a group of native North American plains people, for the Sun Dance ceremony. The origin and purpose of the stone circle are unknown, but it may have been used as an astronomical observatory.

Biskupin
POLAND

Not far from the modern town of Biskupin, 140 miles (225km) north-west of Warsaw, is a Bronze Age village, dating from around 550 BC, which for centuries lay buried under deep mud. The ancient village of Biskupin, covering an area of about 100 acres (40ha) on a peninsula in Lake Biskupin, consisted of wooden houses built of tongued-and-grooved timber and thatched with reed. They were ringed by fortifications made of earth-filled timber frames. Logs were laid down to make streets, while a causeway 450ft (135m) long connected the island to the shore. Glass and amber beads, iron and bronze tools, one of the earliest ploughs in Europe and carved bone articles were found on the site, which was probably abandoned because of flooding.

Blarney (An Bhlarna)
IRELAND

To hang head downwards and kiss the Blarney stone is to acquire great eloquence, at least according to this most appealing of legends. The stone is built into the southern wall of the 15th-century Blarney Castle,

just below the battlements. It acquired its reputation after Queen Elizabeth I described the loquacity of the Lord of Blarney, Cormac McCarthy, in frustrating the attempt to introduce land reforms as 'Blarney, what he says he never means'.

Blythe Figures
USA

About 15 miles (24km) north of the town of Blythe in California, giant figures of men and animals have been carved into rocky bluffs rising from the Colorado River. Nothing is known of the origin of the figures or when they were made. The largest man is 167ft (51m) tall; there is a ring 140ft (43m) in diameter and an animal 36ft (11m) long that resembles a horse. This presents an additional mystery: the native American horse became extinct 10 000 years ago and the Spanish did not introduce the horse from Europe until 1540.

Bryn-celli-Ddu
WALES

Along a farm track near Llanddaniel Fab, about 4 miles (6km) from the Menai Strait on the Isle of Anglesey, lies the site of a chambered cairn, built perhaps 4000 years ago. The bones found in this ancient burial chamber may be the remains of the last Druids, killed in battle in the 1st century AD by the conquering Romans. The mound marking the site covers only a fraction of the prehistoric construction; this had a base some 160ft (50m) in diameter, marked by a stone circle, or henge. Three more concentric circles have been found within the cairn itself.

Byblos
LEBANON

The seaport of Byblos (present-day Jbayl), on the Mediterranean coast north of Beirut, is one of the oldest continuously inhabited towns in the world. It was founded before 3000 BC and was the main trading centre of the

Early Neolithic pottery, Byblos

Phoenicians, from which cedar and other timbers, papyrus and ceramics (some of the earliest known such items in the world) were shipped all over the Mediterranean. Byblos flourished into Roman times and was taken by the Crusaders in 1103. Many of the ruins have been excavated. They include Phoenician ramparts, necropolis and temples; a Roman colonnade and theatre; and a Crusader gate and ramparts.

Caere
ITALY

Known today as Cerveteri, the ancient Etruscan city of Caere is located 30 miles (48km) north-west of Rome. The Etruscan civilisation flourished from the 9th to the 2nd centuries BC, and in 253 BC Caere, one of the most important cities in Italy, was partially incorporated into the Roman state. Excavations have revealed elaborate chambered tombs containing frescoes, low relief carvings and artefacts,

Painted relief of satyr's head, Caere

including gold and silver objects from the 7th century BC. At the nearby port of Pyrgi (now Santa Severa), three sheets of gold leaf have been found, one inscribed in the Phoenician language and the other two in Etruscan.

Callanish
SCOTLAND

On the west coast of the Isle of Lewis, near the village of Callanish, there is a group of standing stones that predates Stonehenge (p256). The stones are all that remains of a larger group erected between 3000 and 1500 BC. An inner circle is made up of 13 stones; the rest are arranged in three short rows and one longer, double row. For hundreds of years the significance of the monoliths has been debated and many theories have been put forward, including one which postulates that the stones were once part of a druidic temple. Today, however, most authorities favour the theory that they formed part of a lunar observatory.

Stone group, Callanish

Castelluccio   ITALY

On the road between Ragusa and Syracuse, in southern Sicily, is the prehistoric village of Castelluccio, noted for more than 200 tombs cut from rock. Such tombs are widely distributed throughout the Mediterranean region; they were carved into the cliff face and mainly used for communal burials.

The tombs at Castelluccio date from the Bronze Age and were carved out of the rock between 1800 and 1400 BC. They are peculiar in that they show no evidence of human remains, although pottery fragments and debris have been unearthed on the site. Carvings appear on the stone slabs that served as doors to the tombs, but their meaning is not apparent.

Çatal Hüyük   TURKEY

The prehistoric settlement at Çatal Hüyük, near Konya, is the largest known Neolithic site in the Near East. Excavations have revealed 12 layers of adjoining mud-brick houses, courtyards and shrines. The buildings lay beneath a mound 65ft (20m) high and covering 32 acres (13ha). Çatal Hüyük was a city with no streets, and entrance to each doorless dwelling was through the roof.

The interiors were decorated with spectacular wall paintings and plaster reliefs, and bull's-head effigies and figurines of the Mother Goddess were found. It is thought that the city housed some 5000 people and had a well-developed agricultural system.

Chavín-de-Huántar   PERU

The Chavín culture, whose origins are disputed, dominated central and northern Peru from 1200 to 300 BC. Its main urban and ceremonial centre was at Chavín-de-Huántar in the fertile Mosna Valley of the east Andes. The city covered 125 acres (50ha), and its ruins include those of the main temple, a pyramid-shaped stone building 42ft (13m) high, with a base 230ft (70m) square.

Inside, a maze of galleries and chambers are connected by ramps and stairways, with bas-relief carvings on pillars and lintels and three large carvings of the major deities. Ceramic bottles, bowls and other objects found at the site also demonstrate the remarkable artistic ability of the first Andean civilisation.

Chichén Itzá   MEXICO

The ancient Maya/Toltec city of Chichén Itzá is situated 77 miles (123km) south-east of Merida. It was established by the Maya *c.*AD 600 and was a major centre of the Toltecs in 1000–1200, after the decline of the Maya. The main complex covers an area of 1¾ miles (3km) by 1¼ miles (2km) and includes a large ball court, temple, pyramids and a causeway 900ft (275km) long. This leads to the cenote, or well, into which human sacrifices and jade and gold ornaments were thrown to appease the rain-cloud god, Chac. The reasons for the city's collapse in the 13th century are not known.

Effigy of Chac

Cumae   ITALY

The city of Cumae lies 12 miles (19km) west of Naples. It is the oldest Greek colony in mainland Italy, settled around 750 BC. Although the city was destroyed in 1205, the acropolis and the area around it contain the ruins

of graves and fortifications, including many from Roman times. Then, Cumae was famous as the haunt of the Sibyl, who was supposed to dwell in a cave there. Early this century, two caves were discovered: the first, excavated in the 1920s, was a work of Roman military engineering; the second, found in 1932, is believed to be the Sibyl's cave.

Dilmun   BAHRAIN

On the barren desert island of Bahrain in the Persian Gulf, lie the remains of some 100 000 single-chamber burial mounds. Known as 'the island of the dead',

Bronze bull's head, Dilmun c.2250 BC

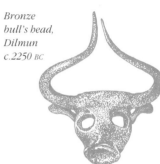

Bahrain was also the site of a Bronze Age city, with broad streets and a harbour. Houses, walls, temples, pottery and tools dating back to 4000 BC have been found on the island, as well as decorative items in cast bronze. All attest to its significance and add credence to the claim that it was Dilmun, the Sumerian paradise.

Drenthe   NETHERLANDS

In a strip of land, bordered on both sides by marshes and concentrated between the towns of Assen and Emmen, lie more than 50 so-called *hunebedden* (Huns' graves), or long dolmens, dating from 3400 to 2300 BC. Each dolmen consists of an extended chamber with a row of trilithons (two upright stones joined by a lintel) over it, and is surrounded by a circle of smaller stones. The chambers show signs of collective burials. It is thought that the style of construction originated in Poland or central Germany, but who built the dolmens here remains a mystery.

Dunadd   SCOTLAND

A natural fortification, Dunadd rises above the flat, marshy countryside between Kilmartin

and Lochgilphead in Strathclyde. By tradition, this was the capital of Dalriada, the kingdom of the Scots. In the rock near the summit there are carvings of a boar with an undeciphered inscription in a linear script and, in the rock, a bowl-shaped indentation and the imprint of a foot. It is said that this was used during the inauguration of the king.

There is evidence to show that Dunadd housed a fair-sized community in AD 500–900; among the items found are metal-working tools and quern stones.

El Panecillo   ECUADOR

Quito, the second-highest capital in the world, nestles in a high mountain valley. About 600ft (180m) above this old Inca city is a building shaped like a beehive, which is entered through an underground masonry tunnel. The top of the beehive has an opening through which the sun's light enters. This fascinating structure was built around AD 1500, possibly as an observatory.

El Tajin   MEXICO

The city of El Tajin, about 125 miles (200km) north-west of Veracruz on the Gulf of Mexico, flourished from AD 600 to 900 but was abandoned in the 13th century. Its most famous constructions are 12 ball courts, more than at any other Central American site, and the Pyramid of the Niches. In its external walls are 365 alcoves, each of which reputedly held an idol – perhaps one for every day of the year. The Totonac people, who lived in the area at the time of the Spanish conquest, claimed to have built El Tajin, but there is no clear evidence that this was the case.

Évora   PORTUGAL

On the Guadiana River, east of Évora, an ancient Portuguese city, lies one of the oldest cemeteries in Europe – a group of seven round-chambered mounds. Pottery bowls and flint blades found in the tombs date the site to 4000 BC. The sides of the tombs were formed by stone slabs about 5ft (1.5m) high, and the roofs were arched. The builders remain unknown, but it is thought that the megalithic tradition spread outwards from this region.

Filitosa CORSICA

The Mediterranean island of Corsica has some fine examples of Neolithic structures. One of the best-known megalithic sites is at Filitosa, between Ajaccio and Propriano. The structures consist of an elliptical wall of massive uncut stones, held in place with rubble and pebbles instead of mortar and, enclosed within it, three stone towers built around 1200 BC. During excavations in 1954, five standing stones, or menhirs were found and re-erected. These may represent dominant males in the community who had been elevated to heroic status.

Gotland SWEDEN

In the Baltic Sea, off the south-east coast of Sweden, lies the 1210 sq miles (3140 km²) island of Gotland. It is a rich storehouse of historical remains, which include some 400 Bronze Age cairns, 70 Iron Age forts and 100 or more Romanesque and early Gothic churches. Three outstanding relics are the Viking memorial, or picture, stones dating from the 1st millennium AD; Trojeborg, Scandinavia's best-known stone maze (date unknown), near Visby, the island's capital; and the Bronze Age ship graves. These comprise standing stones in the outline of ships, and are thought to symbolise the ships of the souls sailing to the land of the dead.

Harappa PAKISTAN

The ancient city of Harappa is one of the major sites of the Indus Valley Civilisation that arose in the 3rd or 4th century BC. It lies in the Punjab in the dry bed of the River Ravi, 200 miles (360km) south of Islamabad, and covers several hundred acres. Its massive citadel, with mud-brick walls, enclosed public buildings and a huge granary. East of this is the residential area, laid out on a grid plan and covering 1 sq mile (2.6km²). The city, with a population of around 25 000, was inhabited from 2300 to 1750 BC. There was an efficient system of mains drainage and

Carved torso of a dancer, found at Harappa

each house had a washroom. Small and exquisite naturalistic carved figures, and seals bearing an as yet undeciphered script, have also been excavated.

Hatra IRAQ

A fortress city, lying between the Tigris and Euphrates rivers in northern Iraq, Hatra was founded in the lst century BC. It was part of the Parthian empire and a religious and trading centre. The city included temples and vaulted chambers within the rectangle of the defensive walls. The Persian Sassanids destroyed Hatra c.AD 240 and ultimately overthrew the Parthians. Human and animal sculptures and fine jewellery have been found here.

Hattusas TURKEY

Around 1700 BC, the Hittites took over an Assyrian colony in central Turkey, some 100 miles (160km) east of present-day Ankara. Here they built their capital city, Hattusas (now Boğazköy). The ancient ruins, surrounded by massive defensive walls, were discovered in 1834; among the finds were 10 000 clay tables with cuneiform inscriptions. The city was destroyed c.1200 BC by marauders known as the Sea Peoples, who may have come from the Mycenaean world.

Heuneburg GERMANY

On a promontory overlooking the River Danube near Binzwagen in southern Germany stands the Heuneburg, a major prehistoric hill fort. It was occupied by a succession of peoples from the late 7th to the 5th centuries BC and reached its peak under the Celts during the 6th century, when there was a strong Greek influence in this area of Europe. In the early part of the century, the great 10–13ft (3–4m) high defensive wall was built of unbaked clay brick. Finds at the Heuneburg include Attic black-figure pottery and gold and bronze objects from local barrow graves.

Huari PERU

The site of the ancient city of Huari lies in the centre of the Ayacucho river basin, in the Andean highlands. It was once the capital of a powerful pre-Inca state controlling much of Peru,

and reached its peak c.AD 650–800 at around the same time as the civilisation based at Tiahuanaco *(p423)* in Bolivia, with which it shows similarities in art styles.

The city centre occupied about 0.6 sq miles (1.5km²) in which 70–80 rectangular compounds, laid out in a grid pattern, housed a population of some 20 000. Artefacts and remains found at Huari include pottery pieces on which human and supernatural figures often appear as motifs, turquoise miniatures ½–4in (13–100mm) high, gold masks and a copper statue of a cat.

Ife NIGERIA

From the 11th century, Ife, 100 miles (160km) north-west of Benin City, was the religious and trading centre of the Yoruba people of south-western Nigeria. It is renowned particularly for naturalistic heads crafted in terracotta and exceptionally fine figures, which date from the late 14th and early 15th centuries, cast in bronze.

To the Yoruba, Ife remains a holy city and the legendary birth place of humankind, founded by

Terracotta head

the son of the deity Oduduwa. It is thought that the related Benin tradition, which flourished from the 13th to the 19th centuries, may have derived from that of Ife.

Jericho WEST BANK

On the west bank of the River Jordan, 14 miles (22km) north-east of Jerusalem, lies Jericho, the world's earliest known town. It was occupied continuously from 9000 to 1850 BC. Excavations have revealed 20 successive layers of settlements containing mud-brick houses, which today form a tell, or mound, 10–12 acres (4–5ha) in extent. The tell is surrounded by a 10ft (3m) wall

with a 28ft (8.5m) defensive tower. Jericho was destroyed by Joshua in the 13th century BC when the Israelites conquered Canaan. According to the Biblical account, the walls of Jericho fell down when a shout went up from Joshua's army.

Karmir-Blur ARMENIA

Founded in the 7th century BC by the Urartian ruler Rusa II, the citadel of Karmir-Blur formed part of a defensive network of castles for an empire based in the mountainous regions of what is now Armenia, near the Turkish border. At its peak, the Urartian Empire was the largest state in western Asia, stretching from the Colchis and Georgia in the north to Syria in the west.

Karmir-Blur was one of the citadels built to defend the imperial capital Erebuni, now Yerevan. Half its area was occupied by a 120-room palace, within which jewellery, ivory and bronze artefacts have been found.

Kit's Coty House ENGLAND

Three upright stones supporting a sandstone block, or capstone, 12ft (3.5m) long are all that remains of Kit's Coty House, a Neolithic chamber barrow at Aylesford in Kent. The earth mound (estimated to have been more than 170ft/52m long) that originally covered the barrow has disappeared. It is said that at one time a great stone, known as the General's Tomb, stood at one end of the structure, but that it was blown up in 1867 because it interfered with ploughing. The name of the barrow is thought to derive from the Celtic for 'the tomb in the wood'.

Kong Asgers Høj DENMARK

On the island of Møn, facing across the sea to Zealand, stands 'King Asger's House', one of the best preserved mounds of the passage-grave type. Both the mound and the chamber, measuring 33ft (10m) long, are remarkably complete. Dating from 3000 BC, they may be the work of people of the Funnel-Beaker culture, but whether they were used for religious purposes alone or for some kind of astronomical activity remains a matter for speculation.

La Grotte des Fées · FRANCE

In the low-lying marshlands of the Rhône delta is situated one of Europe's greatest known rock-carved chambers. The tomb, 2½ miles (4km) north-east of Arles, has a 40ft (12m) antechamber and, at its far end, an immense burial chamber, 80ft (24m) long and 10ft (3m) wide. There are also two smaller side chambers in this impressive construction, which dates from 4000–3500 BC.

Li Muri · SARDINIA

In the fertile farming area of northern Sardinia, about 5 miles (8km) from Arzachena on the road to Luogosanto, are the oldest megalithic monuments in the island, dating from 2500 BC.

The site consists of five intersecting circles, each of which contains a small chamber of stone slabs and is surrounded by upright slabs and standing stones. Human bones, knives, pottery and beads have been found there and it is thought the site may have been used for celestial observation.

Loch Ness · SCOTLAND

The murky waters of Loch Ness (23 miles/37km long, with a maximum depth of 735ft/224m) have long been thought by many to conceal a 'monster'. Those who claim to have seen this creature describe it as 25–30ft (7.5–9m) long, with a snakelike head and neck, a sinuous body and a large tail. They believe that it might be akin to a plesiosaurus, a fish-eating reptile that died out 70 million years ago. Despite attempts to track it underwater with cameras and sonar, the monster's existence has not been proved.

Los Millares · SPAIN

The fortified settlement of Los Millares, dating from the Iberian Copper Age (3500–2000 BC), is an important archaeological site in south-eastern Spain. It is located on a promontory several miles inland from the town of Almería on the Mediterranean coast. The 7ft (2m) thick stone walls, with circular bastions at regular intervals, enclose an area of 12 acres (5ha), in which there are rectangular and circular huts. Notable features of Los Millares include the large cemetery with elaborate stone passage graves and a number of forts situated outside the walled settlement. Artefacts found in the graves include copper tools, objects made from ivory and ostrich shell, bone and stone idols, and painted pottery and figurines.

Lourdes · FRANCE

In south-western France, in the foothills of the Pyrenees, is the town of Lourdes. It is an important place of pilgrimage and attracts many thousands of Roman Catholics each year.

The springs at the Grotte de Massabielle, said to have miraculous healing powers, are deemed by the faithful to have been revealed to Bernadette Soubirous in 1858 by the Virgin Mary. The medieval castle on the

Basilica, Lourdes

river bank was a strategically important stronghold that played an important role in the Hundred Years' War; after an 18-month siege, the French captured it from the English in 1406.

Maiden Castle · ENGLAND

Regarded as the most spectacular hill fort in England, Maiden Castle occupies some 44 acres (18ha) of land near Dorchester in Dorset. It consists of a series of earthworks and ditches that were built after 350 BC on the site of an earlier Neolithic causeway and camp about 10 acres (4ha) in extent, which was gradually enlarged and altered. The existing defences date from 150 BC, with the remodelled entrances dating from 70 BC. The fort was abandoned in AD 43 following the Roman invasion of Britain.

In the eastern part of the fort the foundations of a Romano-Celtic temple and priest's house can still be seen. Excavations have also revealed, among other items, Neolithic and Iron Age pots and a store of slingstones, indicating that the slingshot was an important Iron Age weapon.

Meroë · SUDAN

On the east bank of the Nile, some 4 miles (6km) north of Kabushiyah in what is now the Sudan, lie the remains of an ancient city. Excavations begun in 1902 revealed buildings and streets, a temple to Amun, palaces and a quay. This once-important place was inhabited by the Kushites after their flight from Egypt in 600 BC. With them they brought their knowledge of pyramid building but, in contrast to the Egyptians, they used burial chambers underneath – rather than inside – these structures as tombs for their ruling families.

The people of Meroë were also well known for their skill in rendering iron. They survived a Roman invasion, but c.AD 350 were overrun by a Christian people from Aksum in Ethiopia, and their race died out altogether.

Mohenjo-daro · PAKISTAN

⊘ One of the two main cities of the Indus Valley Civilisation, apart from Harappa *(p420)*, is Mohenjo-daro. It is situated on the west bank of the River Indus, 200 miles (320km) north-east of Karachi and 400 miles (640km) south-west of Harappa.

The city comprises two mounds of mud-brick buildings. The eastern mound is the lower city of two-storey houses that accommodated most of the population of between 30 000 and 40 000. The mound to the west is a walled citadel 42ft (13m) high, which contained the religious and administrative buildings. It includes the Great Bath, also constructed of bricks and with a depth of 10ft (3m), which was probably used for ritual ablutions: like Harappa, this city too had a sophisticated drainage system. The city was inhabited from 2500 to 1500 BC, when it was abandoned.

Monte d'Accordi · SARDINIA

There is a strange ritual monument dating from 1700 BC at Monte d'Accordi on Sardinia. Situated beside the road to Sassari, 4 miles (6km) south-east of Porto Torres, the site comprises the remains of a mound some 40ft (12m) high, which appears to have no entrance. A standing stone, or menhir, is placed close to the approach ramp to the mound and a chambered tomb to one side. Nearby is an egg-shaped boulder, with a curved cut right through it.

Monte Albán · MEXICO

Around 600 BC, a huge complex of ceremonial buildings was built on a steep hill known today as Monte Albán, in Mexico's Oaxaca state. On the site, south of the great ancient city of Teotihuacán *(p176)*, is one of the most oddly shaped structures of the ancient world. No two sides or angles of the building are the same, and slabs on the outside are inscribed with symbols and hieroglyphs that even now cannot be fully deciphered. Was this particular building used for astronomical purposes? Why was it constructed in such an odd way? Both questions remain to challenge future scholars.

Mystery Hill · USA

Strange stone structures similar to those found in Europe give Mystery Hill in New Hampshire the name 'America's Stonehenge'. The site, which dates back 4000 years, may be an astronomical complex. Celtic-style inscriptions have led to speculation that it may have been built by people who came originally from Europe. It consists of drystone walls, standing stones up to 5ft (1.5m) high, dolmen-like stone slab chambers and a 4½-ton slab which has been described as a 'sacrificial table'.

Nemrut Daği · TURKEY

Silent and impassive, the heads of great stone statues, long since toppled from their shoulders, stand on a mountain-top near Lake Van in Turkey. The statues were made on the orders of King Antiochus I who ruled this earthquake-stricken area in the 1st century BC. Originally the statues were some 30ft (9m) high. Although the heads now stand alone, little of

Stone head

the majesty of these impressive stone sculptures has been lost to the ravages of time.

New Grange   IRELAND
In the valley of the River Boyne, Co. Meath, 25 miles (40km) north of Dublin, is a megalithic passage grave dating from 3200 BC. It is covered by an earth mound, 36ft (11m) high and 260–280ft (80–85m) long, and is retained by kerbstones and sheathed with sparkling white quartz pebbles.

Abstract decorations, including lozenges, spirals and chevrons, have been engraved on the kerbstones and on stones lying on the site. They are regarded as being among the finest examples of prehistoric art in Europe.

Beneath the mound is a cross-shaped burial chamber that is entered via a 60ft (18m) passage, roofed and lined with stone slabs; the chamber itself is an arched vault. Both chamber and passage are decorated with engravings. Over the single entrance, which faces south-east, is a slot through which the sun's rays illuminate the burial chamber at the winter solstice.

Together with nearby passage graves at Knowth and Dowth, New Grange forms the Bend of the Boyne site.

Engraved rock, New Grange

Old Sarum Ley   ENGLAND
This mysterious ley line (ley lines are believed by some to connect certain ancient sites) is one of many found across the English landscape. All challenge our perceptions of our ancestors' knowledge of geometry and astronomy. While it may seem inconceivable that deep under-standing of these subjects existed several thousand years ago, it seems more than coincidence that leys such as that of Old Sarum can link so many ancient monuments in an unwavering line.

Starting at an ancient tumulus, Old Sarum Ley runs north by north-west to south by south-

east across the countryside of Wiltshire and Hampshire, straight through Stonehenge, an Iron Age fort at Old Sarum, Salisbury Cathedral, an Iron Age camp at Clearbury Ring and the Iron Age hill fort of Frankenbury Camp.

Pagan   BURMA
One of the most symbolic of all Buddhist sites, the ancient city of Pagan occupies a small plain near the broad Irrawaddy River, some 90 miles (145km) from Mandalay. It comprises 2217 brick-and-stone edifices, most of which are temples and pagodas, built in the 10th–13th centuries. During this time the city was the centre of a kingdom which was similar in size to modern Burma.

The most impressive structures at Pagan are the whitewashed Ananda Temple with a many-tiered roof and, inside, four magnificent golden statues of the Buddha each some 30ft (9m) high; and the Shwezigon Pagoda, a huge, terraced pyramid with decorative spires, bells, stairways and gates, topped with a dome-shaped stupa and a jewel-encrusted gold 'umbrella'.

Paracas   PERU
This barren peninsula on the coast of Peru is the site of an ancient ceremonial centre that flourished from 600 to 100 BC. It is renowned for the exquisite textiles found on mummified bodies in the underground burial chambers of Cavernas and Necropolis. The textiles are embroidered with motifs of mythical figures, monsters, birds and fish. Vividly coloured paintings of human and feline faces and bold geometrical designs characterise the decoration on the pottery. Some commentators have linked this culture with that of Chavín-de-Huántar *(p419)*.

Persepolis   IRAN
◎ One of three capital cities of the ancient Persian empire, Persepolis was built on a high plateau in the mountains of Iran, a site chosen by Darius I. The construction of the city began *c.*520 BC and it was extensively developed by Darius's successors, Xerxes and Artaxerxes. In the 4th century BC it was sacked by Alexander the Great and then

abandoned. The splendid buildings made from dark grey stone, often polished like marble, included a palace, treasury, throne room and the apadana, Darius's audience chamber. It covers an area of 167 sq ft (15.5m²) and sits on a base 9ft (2.7m) high.

The main hall had a timber roof supported by 36 columns, each 65ft (20m) high. The huge walls, 17ft (5m) thick, were reinforced by large towers at the corners. Outside the city walls were the royal tombs and graveyard. Excavations of the site in 1933 revealed a number of cuneiform inscriptions on stones and on gold and silver plates.

Popovo Polje   BOSNIA-HERZEGOVINA
Strange scenes and figures depicted on unusual funerary monuments give an air of mystery to an area 30 miles (48km) north of Dubrovnik. The stone coffins are carved with images of people, horses, the sun and moon, and a swastika. Although crosses appear on all the burial places, the monuments do not seem to be Christian. The question of who made these burial places and whether their origin lies in a magic cult remains unanswered, but they are often attributed to the Bogomils, members of a religious sect who settled in the region during the Middle Ages.

Qin Shih Huang-di Mausoleum   CHINA
Standing ready to defend their dead master against an unknown foe, the 6000 life-sized soldiers of the 'terracotta army' are often regarded as the eighth wonder of the world. Discovered in 1974 near Xi'an in Shaanxi Province, the site may take generations to yield all its secrets, for it is known that the first Qin emperor, Shih Huang-di, had a 20 sq mile (52km²) compound prepared for his death. Each of the soldiers in the army is different and bears a weapon or artefacts appropriate to his status. They all face east.

Nearby are other sites that have revealed further fascinating finds, among them the largest and earliest bronzes ever discovered in China. All testify to the immense power of a man who could command a workforce

of nearly 750 000 men for almost 40 years on this one funerary complex alone.

Rennes-le-Château   FRANCE
The penniless priest of a small and isolated village, 36 miles (58km) from Carcassonne, found some rolled parchments written in Latin, two of which contained cyphers. In no time at all, the priest acquired a vast fortune, but died in 1917 leaving the source of his wealth unknown. Ever since, speculation has been rife that the priest found in the parchments the key to the location of the treasures of Solomon. The area was once a stronghold of the Visigoths, who sacked Rome in 410 and made off, so legend claims, with the very treasures rumour credits the priest with having discovered.

Rievaulx Abbey   ENGLAND
Nestling among wooded hills in the Rye Valley of North Yorkshire, Rievaulx Abbey has stood since the end of the 12th century. Building commenced in 1132, when the site was donated to a dozen Cistercian monks. The Abbey fared well: its numbers grew to some 140 monks and more than 500 lay brothers under Aelred, its third abbot. By the 15th century, numbers were declining and by the time of the Dissolution of the Monasteries by Henry VIII in 1536, only 22 monks remained. The nave of the abbey, which dates from 1135, is the largest Cistercian example in Britain, and extensive remains of it and other buildings can still be seen.

Rutupiae   ENGLAND
About 1½ miles (2km) north of Sandwich – once one of the leading seaports of England, now 2 miles (3km) from the coast – lies Richborough Castle, the site of Rutupiae. This was one of the most important Roman forts in Britain, built to protect the port and the entrance to an important channel which in Roman times ran inland to the town of Reculver on the north Kent coast. In the 5th century, the fort became part of the defences of the Saxon shore. A Roman amphitheatre and a pre-Norman chapel have also been excavated.

San Agustín COLOMBIA

In the lush green valley of the Magdalena River, which flows from the northern Andes, are the remains of a little-known South American culture. About 370 miles (600km) south-west of Bogotá and near the town of San Agustín, the site contains burial mounds, megalithic structures and large stone sculptures. Crudely hewn figures line the forest paths and streams of the Valley of Statues, the earliest dating from AD 600. Nothing is known of the people who lived there, other than that they were a farming society, nor is it known whether the sculptures were part of a more widespread cult.

Sanchi INDIA

The best-preserved Buddhist monuments in India are to be found at Sanchi about 30 miles (48km) north-east of Bhopal in Madhya Pradesh, central India. Most splendid is the Great Stupa, a domed monument reputedly built by King Asoka in the 3rd century BC to contain the remains of the Buddha. Its four gateways are decorated with fine carvings that depict scenes from the life of the Buddha, and the remains of two of his disciples have been recovered from the site, which was deserted in the 17th century.

Santiago de Compostela SPAIN

⊚ The old city of Santiago de Compostela, in Galicia, has been a place of pilgrimage since the Middle Ages. Roman Catholic pilgrims from all over Europe make their way there, their final destination the 11th–12th century cathedral of Santiago, or St James the Great, whose bones are reputed to lie in a silver casket beneath the High Altar.

The centrepiece of the lavishly decorated altar, made of jasper, silver and alabaster, is a painted wooden statue of the saint.

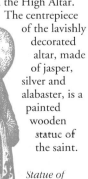

Statue of St James

Talati de Dalt MINORCA

On a tree-covered hill on the main road to Alayor, 2 miles (3km) from Mahón, stand the remains of the most powerful megalithic site on Minorca. It consists of five towers (talayots), circular houses, stone circles and underground chambers. Away from the main tower stands a *taula* (table) and a boat-shaped setting of stones. The site was built around 1000 BC but speculation remains as to who lived here and whether the *taulas* were used as sacrificial tables.

Tarxien MALTA

Some of the oldest and most important Neolithic temples in the world are found at Tarxien, near Valetta. They were built by farmers *c*.3000 BC from gigantic stone slabs covered with capstones.

Mother Earth figure

The temples consisted of open courts, corridors roofed with large stones and sacred chambers with arched roofs in a style unique to the island.

Three temples of this type can be seen today at Tarxien. Their walls are richly decorated with geometric designs, including elaborate spirals, and friezes of animals. Part of a large stone statue of a Mother Earth goddess figure was also found here. Nearby, at Hal Saflieni, is the equally impressive hypogeum (underground chamber), with more than 20 man-made and natural caverns decorated with paintings and carvings.

Tiahuanaco BOLIVIA

The ruins of Tiahuanaco, one of the lesser known pre-Hispanic cities in the Americas, are located 12 600ft (3850m) up, near the southern end of Lake Titicaca, 60 miles (100km) west of La Paz.

Tiahuanaco was occupied from 1500 BC to AD 1200, but the height of its power was from AD 500 to 1000 when it was the centre of an important religious cult, whose influence spread throughout all of Bolivia and southern Peru.

The principal deity of the cult was the staff-carrying doorway god. He is represented in the centre of the monolithic Gateway of the Sun in the enclosure known as Kalasasaya.

The centre of the city covered an area of 125 acres (50ha) and contained ceremonial and religious buildings, most notably the Akapana, a platform mound or temple made of earth faced with cut stone that measures 660ft (200m) square and 50ft (15m) high. Other antiquities include carved stone figures.

Tipasa ALGERIA

Just 42 miles (68km) west of Algiers stand ruins dating from the 5th century BC, when there was a Phoenician outpost there. Later, Tipasa became a Roman colony. According to legend, St Salsa was martyred there, and at the end of the 5th century AD the town was destroyed. Today, visitors can view the remains of four Roman baths, a theatre and a large nine-naved cathedral.

Tombs at Pazyryk KAZAKHSTAN

In the Altai Mountains at Pazyryk, Scythian tombs were preserved by ice shortly after their occupants were interred in the 5th century BC. A fierce tribe of nomads, skilled on horseback and in the art of war, the Scythians are known largely from their burial mounds.

The tombs, excavated in 1929 and the late 1940s, contained a wealth of grave goods. Among them were dismantled wagons, the bodies of slaughtered horses, leather and wooden artefacts, furs, textiles and embroidered silks.

It is possible that the Scythians acted as agents in the trading of silk, and certainly some members of this tribal and hierarchical society of mounted warriors were extremely wealthy.

Trepuco MINORCA

In the fertile southern part of Minorca, on a slight rise on the outskirts of Mahón, stands an evocative megalithic monument. It contains a tower (talayot) and, within a circle of stones, a table (*taula*) that rises to 13ft (4m) with an even higher capstone. Built by the Tower People after 1500 BC, the site included dwellings and fortifications. Ashes of uncertain age and bronze bulls have been found, leading to speculation that the site may possibly have been used for some kind of ritual purpose.

Tustrup DENMARK

In the gentle, rolling wooded country north of Djursland are several megalithic monuments, such as the enclosed structures, including dolmens and capstoned chambers, near the coast and the village of Vivild. In one enclosure, various bowls and ladles were found. The site was occupied 5000 years ago, perhaps by people of the Funnel-Beaker culture, and may have a connection with funeral rites.

Uxmal MEXICO

Abandoned in 1450, the ancient Maya city of Uxmal is the most important example of the Puuc architectural style of the late Classic Period (AD 600–900). The principal buildings that remain are the Nunnery Quadrangle, the Temple of the Magician, four rectangular buildings divided into many small rooms, the Governor's Palace and the House of Turtles, whose name derives from its sculptured frieze. The main part of the city covers more than 160 acres (64ha) with a great deal more land given over to residential dwellings.

Val Camonica ITALY

In a rock-strewn valley 60 miles (100km) north-east of Milan lies Val Camonica, where at least 15 000 carvings have been made on the rocks. They depict a variety of scenes, including religious ceremonies attended by priests, domestic activities and farming techniques. It is thought that they span a period of 6000 years, from the New Stone Age until 16 BC, when the area was overrun by the Romans and the Camuni tribe that lived there was expelled.

Visbek — GERMANY

Among the forest trees, about 20 miles (32km) west of Bremen, lie the sites of Visbeker Braut and Brautigam (bride and bridegroom). Where once there was cleared farmland stand two quadrilateral enclosures ringed by many long dolmens. The enclosures are 260ft (80m) and 350ft (110m) long respectively. Both have varying formations of stones and a large sunken stone chamber. It is thought they were built around 3000 BC, but it is uncertain whether the site was used for special festivals or as a place to gather to watch the sun rise on the summer solstice.

Wéris — BELGIUM

One of Europe's most evocative megalithic sites is situated in the forest of the Ardennes. Near Erezée, 3 miles (5km) from Wéris, a cross-country alignment of monuments has its beginning.

Three menhirs, the tallest 8ft (2.5m) high, create a haunting group. In the chamber of a half-buried dolmen nearby human and animal bones, in addition to pottery fragments, have been found. The monuments date from 3000 to 2500 BC. One theory suggests that their alignment relates to a certain constellation of stars, but who built them remains a mystery.

Camargue horses

egrets and flamingos, which can be seen in the nature reserve on the Etang de Vaccarès. At one time almost entirely wilderness, the region today has about 10 000 inhabitants. Reclaimed land is used to cultivate rice and vines, while the once-wild bulls and horses are now bred for profit.

Citadel — CANADA

◉ The star-shaped Citadel is the largest set of fortifications in North America, located on the cliff known as Cape Diamond in the south-west corner of the old city of Quebec. Cape Diamond rises to a height of 343ft (104m) above the St Lawrence River at its confluence with the St Charles River. The Battle of Quebec, at which British forces under Wolfe defeated those of the French under Montcalm, thereby gaining control of Quebec, took place on the nearby Plains of Abraham in 1759.

Culloden Moor — SCOTLAND

About 5 miles (8km) east of Inverness lies Culloden Moor (also known as Drummossie Moor), the site of the last major battle on British soil, on 16 April 1746. It marked the end of the Jacobite rebellion that sought to restore the Stuarts to the British throne. The Jacobite army of 5000 was led by Charles Edward Stuart (Bonnie Prince Charlie), the Young Pretender; the 9000-strong government force was led by the Duke of Cumberland.

The fighting lasted only 40 minutes, during which time 1000 Highlanders died. In 1881, a cairn was erected on the moor to commemorate the battle.

Ephesus — TURKEY

The ancient city of Ephesus (Efes in Turkish) is situated near the Aegean coast, 4 miles (6km)

from the village of Selçuk. It was established in the 11th century BC by Ionian Greeks and was a centre of worship of the goddess Artemis.

The Temple of Artemis, which housed a magnificent statue of the goddess, was one of the Seven Wonders of the Ancient World. Built in the mid-6th century BC, at the time when the city was dominated by the Lydian king Croesus, it had 96 columns and measured some 370ft by 180ft (113m by 55m).

Ephesus was later governed by Persians, Spartans and Athenians; it became subject to Rome after 133 BC and was destroyed by the Goths in AD 262. St Paul (who died c.AD 61–5) visited the city and later wrote letters to the Christian people there.

Marble figure of Artemis

Fuji-Hakone-Izu National Park — JAPAN

◉ Mount Fuji (p358) is the centrepiece of this 476 sq mile (1232km²) national park, as it is of Japanese religious and cultural life. But it is not the park's only notable feature: hot springs, lava cliffs and cascades are evidence of the geothermal activity in the region and the Izu Peninsula has seven active volcanic islands off-shore. Nature has tempered its volatility with forests of azaleas, cherry, pine and fir trees, and humans have contributed more than 2500 species of cactuses, grown in a special part of the park. It is also home to many species of birds and the Japanese dormouse.

Guilin — CHINA

The hills around the Chinese city of Guilin form a spectacular landscape. Rounded, steep-sided pinnacles of limestone rise

TIMELESS LANDSCAPES

Some places have a quality that, down the centuries, has drawn people to them in search of spiritual fulfilment. Their remoteness, their immense size, or their unusual formation appears to inspire contemplation and nourish mental tranquillity. In such surroundings, people can learn to relate to nature's other creations and to understand their own humanity.

Anuradhapura — SRI LANKA

◉ This is the best known of Sri Lanka's ancient ruined cities. It was founded in the 4th century BC 127 miles (205km) north of Colombo, and was the first Sinhalese capital of Sri Lanka. Anuradhapura, which means 'city of happy people', contained palaces, temples, pools and baths and huge, bell-shaped Buddhist stupas known as dagobas. It is also the site of a peepul tree reputed to have grown from a branch of the bo tree under which Buddha was sitting when he found enlightenment. Abandoned some time in the 11th or 12th centuries, the city was overgrown by jungle. The ruins were found by British travellers in the 19th century.

Bassae — GREECE

◉ The temple at Bassae, on Mount Lykaion in south-west Arcadia, is dedicated to Apollo, the god of musical and poetic inspiration but a god also who

sent disease. It was designed by Ictinus, one of the architects of the Parthenon in Athens (p411) and architect of the temple at Eleusis. The temple was built in the 5th century BC for the people of nearby Phigalia after they had survived an epidemic of plague. The ruins were discovered in 1763, and the temple has since been almost entirely rebuilt.

Benbulbin — IRELAND

Legend honours the huge flat-topped mountain of Benbulbin, which rises 1730ft (527m) above the plain at Sligo Bay in north-west Ireland, as the home of Fionn mac Cumhaill and his 3rd-century warriors; to the Irish poet W.B. Yeats it was a major source of inspiration. The mountain's steep, corrugated walls, made up of layers of soft black shale laid down some 320 million years ago, have been eroded by glaciers and mighty Atlantic storms. Only the upper layers of hard limestone, covered with peaty heathland and some left-over arctic-alpine plants, remain intact.

The Camargue — FRANCE

An area of 300 sq miles (780km²), comprising mainly salt marsh and lagoon, the Camargue is located in the Rhône delta in southern France. It is famous both for its free-roaming herds of horses and bulls and as a resting place for migratory birds, such as abruptly from the flat plains on either side of the Li River, and run for some 30 miles (50km) along the bank. On the river, trained cormorants are still used to dive for fish, which they are prevented from swallowing by collars around their necks.

The area is a prime example of tower karst, a limestone landform riddled with caves and passages. The landscape is carved by rainwater; turned slightly acid by carbon dioxide in the air, it slowly etches away the limestone.

Head-Smashed-In Buffalo Jump   CANADA
The name of this site in southern Alberta graphically describes the event that occurred here for about 6000 years. Situated south of Calgary in the Porcupine Hills near Fort Macleod, Head-Smashed-In is the place where the indigenous plains people drove herds of buffalo (bison) to their death over a 33ft (10m) cliff in a highly efficient form of hunting.

The annual stampeding of buffalo began around 4000 BC and continued until the early 19th century.

Independence National Historical Park   USA
This is one of the most important historical sites in the USA. Independence Hall stands in the Philadelphia park where the Declaration of Independence was proclaimed in 1776. Written by Thomas Jefferson, it announced the secession of the 13 American colonies from Britain. The Liberty Bell, rung on the occasion of the proclamation, is also housed in Independence Park.

Iona   SCOTLAND
The island of Iona, off the Island of Mull, is the site of a monastery established in AD 563 by the Irish missionary St Columba, who wished to convert the inhabitants of northern Britain to Christianity.

The monastery, built of wood and wattle, was destroyed by the Vikings on several occasions and later rebuilt; on three of these raids the abbot and monks were murdered.

By the 12th century, the original monastery had declined and a new one was set up nearby

by the Benedictines. It was deserted in the 16th century but has now been restored.

Ivanovo Churches   BULGARIA
Near the village of Ivanovo, in a deeply eroded gorge of the Rusenski River, a monastery is cut into the rock which contains magnificent biographical and religious wall paintings of the 13th and 14th centuries. Made by monks who went there searching for the ascetic life and the renewal of sacred art, the paintings are masterly. Furthermore, in their portrayal of nudity they are more daring than any earlier works.

Kerkuane   TUNISIA
Archaeologists fight time and tide to reveal the splendours of the Punic town discovered at Kerkuane, Cape Bon, on the north-east coast of Tunisia in 1952. Founded c.570 BC, the town was built to an obvious urban design, with wide streets, and survived until 256 BC when it was sacked by the Romans.

The houses, faced with a coloured clay, are remarkable for their similarity; the status of their inhabitants is revealed only by size and orientation. Layer upon layer of sand has preserved the mosaic-decorated pools of the baths and the drainage system.

Figurines in the sanctuary suggest that it was dedicated to a god of hunting and fishing, reflecting Kerkuane's proximity to the Mediterranean Sea that now threatens to swamp it.

L'Anse-au-Meadow National Historical Park   CANADA
'The creek in the meadow' – L'Anse-au-Meadow – is a Norse settlement situated in an isolated area on Epaves Bay in the north of Newfoundland. Artefacts found at the site have been radio-carbon dated to AD 970–1000, providing indisputable evidence that the Vikings reached North America in pre-Columbian times. The settlement, which includes nine turf-built houses, was discovered in 1961.

Látrabjarg   ICELAND
Geologically ancient basalt cliffs, the highest of which reach 1700ft (520m), tower over the sea at this most westerly point of

Iceland and Europe. It is separated from Greenland by less than 180 miles (290km) of freezing water. The Látrabjarg cliffs are 7 miles (11km) long and are alive with birds, providing a home for guillemots, cormorants, gulls, kittiwakes and puffins. Seals bask off the nearby lighthouse and water spouts reveal the presence of passing whales.

Mesa Verde   USA
Mesa Verde is a region of precipitous canyons and wooded plains 34 miles (55km) west of Durango in south-western Colorado. It is renowned for the pueblos, or cliff dwellings, of the Anasazi people that date mainly from the 11th to the 13th centuries. The largest of these is the Cliff Palace, a four-storey complex of 220 rooms and 23 sacred underground chambers, or kivas, in which ceremonies took place. The palace held some 250-350 people. Mesa Verde was designated a national park in 1906 and is the most popular archaeological site in the USA.

Anasazi cliff dwellings

Mount of Olives   EAST JERUSALEM
A rocky outcrop of limestone, the Mount of Olives lies to the east of Jerusalem, overlooking the Old City across the Kidron Valley. Sacred to Jews and Christians alike, it is the site of the traditional Jewish burial ground and the supposed location of Christ's Ascension; the Garden of Gethsemane is located nearby.

The mountain has been a place of sanctuary since the days of Solomon and David, and the site of many Christian churches and shrines since at least the 4th century AD. It comprises three peaks, the most southerly of which (2652ft/808m) is regarded

as the Mount of Olives proper. At 2684ft (818m) Mount Scopus in the north is the highest.

Mount Olympus   GREECE
The highest point in Greece, at 9570ft (2917m), Mount Olympus is a fitting home for the gods. This practically inaccessible throne of Zeus, on the border of the present-day provinces of Thessaly and Macedonia, was not conquered by mortal man until 1913. Homer, in his *Odyssey*, described the mountain as being

Mt Olympus

free of storms and basking in clear air. This may sometimes be true of the peak, but the lower reaches of the mountain are frequently shrouded in a belt of cloud.

Mount Sinai   EGYPT
Situated in the south-central part of the Sinai Peninsula, Mount Sinai is a granite peak 7497ft (2285m) above sea level. It is also known as the Mountain of Moses and as Mount Hareh, and is sacred to Christians, Jews and Muslims as the place where God gave Moses the tablets incised with the Ten Commandments. The Monastery of St Catherine at the foot of its northern slopes, built in AD 530 and inhabited still by a few monks, members of the Orthodox Church of Mount Sinai, is probably the oldest continuously occupied Christian abbey in the world.

Mount Tai   CHINA
Mount Tai (in Chinese, Taishan) is the most sacred of China's mountains, revered by Taoists and Buddhists. It rises to a height of 5067ft (1544m) above the plain of the Yellow River in the Shandong province of eastern China. The area is rich in fossils, medicinal plants and ancient ruins: evidence of long-standing human settlement on and around the mountain dates back 400 000 years. Every year between February and May

pilgrims go to Mount Tai to take part in the ritual of climbing the 7000 steps that lead to the temple of the Jade Emperor on the summit. During their six to seven-hour climb, they pause at wayside shrines to offer prayers to the gods.

Oberammergau GERMANY

Set in a tranquil valley high in the Bavarian Alps is the village of Oberammergau. The craggy heights of the Alps towering above the scene make the village appear insignificant, but once every ten years Oberammergau becomes the setting for one of the most famous theatrical performances in the world.

Since 1634 the villagers have staged the Passion play in celebration of their deliverance from the plague. Throughout their 350-year history, the performances at Oberammergau have only been stopped twice: in 1870 during the Franco–Prussian war, and during World War II, when religious plays were banned.

Olympia GREECE

Now a village and national sanctuary, Olympia is situated in Ilia, southern Greece. From around 1000 BC, it was the chief sanctuary of Zeus, and from 776 BC the site of the pan-Hellenic religious festival. This was held every four years and became the model for the modern Olympic Games. Archaeological remains include the Temple of Zeus, dating from 460 BC, the Temple of Hera, 600 BC, the Stadium and the workshops of the celebrated sculptor Phidias, whose work included the friezes on the Parthenon (p411).

Runnymede ENGLAND

The peaceful meadows and woodland of this Thames-side site overlook the spot where King John signed Magna Carta in 1215. This great document laid down that there should be no punishment without fair trial and that many ancient rights of England's people should be preserved. On a hill overlooking the river there are two memorials, one commemorating the signing of Magna Carta, the other dedicated to the Commonwealth

airmen who lost their lives in the course of World War II. Close to the river, a memorial has been erected to the former American president, John F. Kennedy.

Sagarmatha National Park NEPAL

⊚ This national park in Nepal, on the border with Tibet, takes its name from the Nepalese for Mount Everest (p352), which means 'whose head touches the sky'. The park covers an area of 480 sq miles (1240km²) and, in addition to Everest, includes seven peaks more than 23 000ft (7000m) high.

The park was founded to protect the flora and fauna of the area and also the way of life of the Sherpas. Wildlife of note includes the blue Himalayan poppy, the calling hare, or pika, the Tibetan mountain shrew and the woolly hare. Also found here are the silver mountain butterfly (one of 30 species of butterflies) and 120 species of birds, among them the Himalayan griffin-vulture. The area is said to be the home of the legendary Yeti.

St Kilda SCOTLAND

⊚ The small group of volcanic islands known as St Kilda is situated in the Outer Hebrides, 110 miles (180km) from the Scottish mainland. It is the most remote archipelago in Britain. The largest islands are St Kilda

Atlantic puffin

(Hirta), Soay and Boreray. These and the smaller islets constitute a wildlife area of international importance, particularly as a breeding site for gannets, fulmars and puffins.

More than 50 000 pairs of gannets alone breed on St Kilda every year, which makes the archipelago the largest gannetry in the world. The islands were inhabited for 2000 years until 1930, when the last 36 people abandoned their homes.

Shansi Loess CHINA

The extraordinary landscape of this region of northern China has earned it the nickname 'Land of the Yellow Earth'. Deposits of a fertile yellow windblown silt known as loess are both deep and widespread, and although other places in the world possess quantities of loess, nowhere is the effect so striking as here. The hills, roads, fields and rivers are yellow, and even the atmosphere is seldom free of a yellowish haze.

Farmers in the Shansi region have traditionally lived in caves beneath their fields: the smoke from their hearth fires escapes through shafts dug in the grainfields overhead, and visitors are often taken aback at the unexpected sight of plumes of smoke apparently rising from the earth.

Silk Road ASIA

The ancient overland trade route from China across central Asia to the West is known as the Silk Road. The best-known route, dating from the 2nd century AD, ran from Xi'an through the Gansu Corridor, which covered 750 miles (1200km) from Gansu province to Xinjiang region, then passed through Tashkent, the oldest city in central Asia, and Samarkand (p146) to the eastern end of the Mediterranean. Later, in the time of the Sui dynasty (581– 618), traders went farther north and finished their journey at Istanbul. By means of the Silk Road, Chinese techniques for paper making, iron smelting, silkworm breeding and irrigation were brought to the West, while China received pomegranates, grapes, lucerne and cotton. Buddhism, too, spread from India to China along the Silk Road.

Sumer IRAQ

In Mesopotamia, the land lying between the Euphrates and Tigris rivers in Iraq, 3000 years before the birth of Christ there were a dozen independent city-states, among them Kish, Ur and Nippur, which made up the region of Sumer.

The people were skilled in weaving, pottery, leatherwork, metalwork, building, sculpture and agriculture.They are also believed to have invented the

earliest form of writing, for some 50 000 clay tablets covered in cuneiform script have been found at Nippur, 60 miles (100km) south of Babylon (p418). Each city had its own guardian god for whom there was a dedicated temple.

Tassili N'Ajjer National Park ALGERIA

⊚ Extraordinary 'rock forests' sculpted by nature from soft sandstone are the most amazing geological feature of this park in the Sahara desert. Equally impressive, and of immense significance, are the ancient paintings and hieroglyphs engraved on the rocks, although no one knows who painted the pictures, and the hieroglyphs elude translation.

Drawings of hippopotamuses indicate that the region was once much less arid than it is today, and buffaloes, rhinos, giraffes and elephants, extinct here for several thousand years, are all depicted.

Vale of Kathmandu NEPAL

⊚ The beautiful Vale of Kathmandu lies at an altitude of 4600ft (1400m) above sea level and is surrounded by massive mountains. It is little more than 15½ miles (25km) long and 9 miles (14km) wide, but for thousands of years it has been at the crossroads between two great Asian cultures – Indian and Tibetan-Chinese – and it shelters three ancient royal cities, Patan (p411), Bhaktapur and Kathmandu itself, as well as religious sites, villages, caves, springs and lakes.

Yu Yuan CHINA

Built in 1577 by Pan Yunduan for, and in honour of, his father's old age, this garden is wonderfully evocative. Hidden by high brick walls is a small lake spanned by a zigzag bridge, goldfish ponds, rockeries, pavilions and tea-houses separated into three distinct areas. The Pavilion of Spring served as the headquarters of the Small Sword Society when it led its uprising against the Qing dynasty and the colonial powers in 1853. Today, the garden is a popular attraction, thronged with people and hung with lanterns during festivals.

INDEX

Acknowledgments

Picture credits *l = left; r = right; t = top; c = centre; b = bottom*

1 Adam Woolfitt/Susan Griggs Agency; 2/3 Michael K. Nichols/Magnum Photos; 5*l* M. Denis-Huot/Hoa-Qui; 5*r* Thomas Hoepker/Magnum Photos; 6*l* A.N.T./NHPA; 6*r* Dr Georg Gerster/The John Hillelson Agency; 7*l* Richard Kalvar/Magnum Photos; 7*r* David Paterson; 8*t* Adam Woolfitt/Susan Griggs Agency; 8*b* Sassoon/Robert Harding Picture Library; 9 James D. Watt/Planet Earth Pictures; 12/13 M. Denis-Huot/Hoa-Qui; 14/15 Loic Jahan/Explorer; 15 Spectrum; 16/17*t* Sygma; 17*b* The Mansell Collection; 18 Archivo Consorzio Frasassi; 19/20 Enzio Quiresi; 21 Archivo Consorzio Frasassi; 22 Kotoh/Zefa Picture Library; 22/23 Si Chi Ko/The Image Bank; 24 M. Huet/Hoa-Qui; 25 Adrian Arbib/Tony Stone Associates; 26 Anthony Bannister/NHPA; 27 Anthony Bannister/Oxford Scientific Films; 28*t* Anthony Bannister/NHPA; 28*b* Peter Johnson/NHPA; 28/29 Anthony Bannister/NHPA; 30 John Cleare/Mountain Camera; 30/31 Richard Packwood/Oxford Scientific Films; 32 John Cleare/Mountain Camera; 33*t* Bruce Coleman; 33*b* M. Denis-Huot/Hoa-Qui; 34/35 Dieter & Mary Plage/Bruce Coleman; 35 The Mansell Collection; 36 Mary Evans Picture Library; 36/37 Dieter & Mary Plage/Survival Anglia; 38/39 Kevon Schafer/Martha Hill/Tom Stack & Associates; 40*t* Aldus Archive/Syndication International; 40*c* Mary Evans Picture Library; 40*b* The Mansell Collection; 41 Julian Fitter/Oxford Scientific Films; 42*t* Georgette Daouwma/Planet Earth Pictures; 42*b* David J. McChesney/Planet Earth Pictures; 43*t* Schafer/Hill/Tom Stack & Associates; 43*b* Tui de Roy/Oxford Scientific Films; 44/45 David Parker/Science Photo Library; 45 Robert Harding Picture Library; 46 Eli Reed/Magnum Photos; 47*t* Dr Georg Gerster/The John Hillelson Agency; 47*b* Mary Evans Picture Library; 48/49 James Fraser/Impact Photos; 50 Stewenmans/Zefa Picture Library; 52 David Muench; 53 John Blaustein/Susan Griggs Agency; 54/5 François Gohier/Ardea; 56*t* The Hulton Picture Company; 56*b* Ray Halin/Tony Stone Associates; 57 Mary Evans Picture Library; 58/61*t* David Muench; 61*b* Jeff Foott/Bruce Coleman; 62 David Lyons/Planet Earth Pictures; 62/63 Layda/Bildagentur Schuster/Robert Harding Picture Library; 64 Zefa Picture Library; 65*t* The Kobal Collection; 65*b* David Muench; 66*tl cl bl* Superstock; 66*br* Walter Rawlings/Robert Harding Picture Library; 67*t* Werner Forman Archive; 67*b* The Image Bank; 68/69 David Muench; 70*t* E. Hummel/Zefa Picture Library; 70*b* Michael Freeman; 72/73 David Muench; 74 J.A.L. Cooke/Oxford Scientific Films; 75*t* Alain Tomas/Explorer; 75*b* Bob McKeever/Tom Stack & Associates; 76/77 Terry Donnelly/Tom Stack & Associates; 78*t* François Gohier/Ardea; 78*b* Badlands National Park Service; 79 Rod Planck/Tom Stack & Associates; 80/81 P. Vautney/Sygma; 82*t* David Curl/Oxford Scientific Films; 82/83 P. Vautney/Sygma; 84/5 Thomas Hoepker/Magnum Photos; 86/88 Adam Woolfitt/Susan Griggs Agency; 89*tl* The Mansell Collection; 89*tr* Adam Woolfitt/Susan Griggs Agency; 89*b* Zefa Picture Library; 90/91 Shostal Associates/Superstock; 92 Giraudon/The Bridgeman Art Library; 93*t* Dr Georg Gerster/The John Hillelson Agency; 93*b* Mary Evans Picture Library; 94 Dennis Stock/Magnum Photos; 95/96*t* Scala; 96*b* Dennis Stock/Magnum Photos; 97 Scala; 98/99 E. Bach-Gräfenhaim/Britstock-IFA; 100*l* Bildarchiv Huber; 100*r* The Mansell Collection; 101*t* Koerner/Britstock-IFA; 101*b* Robert Harding Picture Library; 102/103 Zefa Picture Library; 103 Ancient Art & Architecture; 105*t* British Museum; 105*b* Sonia Halliday Photographs; 106 The Bridgeman Art Library; 106/107 Ekdotike Athenon; 108*t* The Hulton Picture Company; 108*b* National Anthropological Museum, Athens/Robert Harding Picture Library; 110 Reflejo/Susan Griggs Agency; 110/111 B. Regent/The Hutchison Library; 113 Robert Harding Picture Library; 114 Ashmolean Museum; 115*tr* British Museum; 115*tl* Scala; 115*b* Reflejo/Susan Griggs Agency; 116/117 Erich Lessing/Magnum Photos; 117 Shirley Heaney/Horizon; 118*t* Scala; 118*b* Farrell Grehan/Susan Griggs Agency; 120 Ara Guler/Magnum Photos; 120/121 Adrian Woolfitt/Susan Griggs Agency; 122*t* Bildarchiv Preussischer Kulturbesitz; 122*b* Picturepoint; 123*l* The Mansell Collection; 123*c* The Hulton Picture Company; 123*r* Bildarchiv Preussischer Kulturbesitz; 124/125 William McQuitty; 126/128 Harry Brown/Griffiths Institute; 129 Times Newspapers; 130/131 Richard Nowitz/Explorer; 132*t* The Bridgeman Art Library; 132*b* The Mansell Collection; 133*t* Peter Caine/Horizon; 133*b* Ira Block/The Image Bank; 134 The Bridgeman Art Library; 134/135 Fred Mayer/Magnum Photos; 136 K. Goebel/Zefa Picture Library; 137*b* Fred Mayer/Magnum Photos; 138/139 Nabeel Turner/Tony Stone Associates; 139 Michael Holford; 140*t* Marc Riboud/Magnum Photos; 140*b* Edinburgh University Library; 141 Abbas/Magnum Photos; 142 Ronald Sheridan/Ancient Art & Architecture; 142/144*l* Robert Harding Picture Library; 144*r* Roger Wood; 145*l* Jehangir Gazdar/Susan Griggs Agency; 145*r* The Hulton Picture Company; 146 Francesco Venturi/KEA/Susan Griggs Agency; 147 Roland & Sabrina Michaud/The John Hillelson Agency; 148*t* Francesco Venturi/KEA/Susan Griggs Agency; 148*b* Roland & Sabrina Michaud/The John Hillelson Agency; 149*t* British Museum/Robert Harding Picture Library; 149*b* Francesco Venturi/KEA/Susan Griggs Agency; 150 Roland & Sabrina Michaud/The John Hillelson Agency; 150/151 Adam Woolfitt/Susan Griggs Agency; 152*l/c* Roland & Sabrina Michaud/The John Hillelson Agency; 152*r* Picturepoint; 153*t* The Hulton Picture Company; 153*b* Picturepoint; 154/155 Paul Ricketts/Horizon; 155 The Hutchison Library; 156 G. Dambier/Sygma; 157 Michael Holford; 158 Mark Godfrey/Magnum Photos; 158/161*t* Robert Harding Picture Library; 161*b* Piers Cavendish/Impact Photos; 162/163 Marc Riboud/Magnum Photos; 163 Nigel Cameron/Robert Harding Picture Library; 166/167 Robert Harding Picture Library; 167 Steve McCurry/Magnum Photos; 168/169 Marc Riboud/Magnum Photos; 169 Leon Schadeberg/Susan Griggs Agency; 170*t* Paolo Negri/Tony Stone Associates; 170*bl* Thierry Cazabon/Tony Stone Associates; 170*br* The Mansell Collection; 171 Zefa Picture Library; 172 Robert Harding Picture Library; 173*l* Dr Georg Gerster/The John Hillelson Agency; 173*r* Gamma/Frank Spooner Pictures; 174 Adam Woolfitt/Susan Griggs Agency; 175 Robert Harding Picture Library; 176/177 Zefa Picture Library; 177 Charles W. Friend/Susan Griggs Agency; 179*t* Tony Stone Associates; 179*b* O. Luz/Zefa Picture Library; 180 Chris Rennie/Robert Harding Picture Library; 180/181 M.P.L. Fogden/Bruce Coleman; 180*l* Chris Rennie/Robert Harding Picture Library; 181*r* Faria Castro/Frank Spooner Pictures; 183 Images; 184/185 Tony Morrison/South American Pictures; 185 Robert Harding Picture Library; 186 Photograph by E.C. Erdis, Peabody Museum, Yale University & 1913 National Geographical Society; 187*t* Tony Morrison/South American Pictures; 187*b* Walter Rawlings/Robert Harding Picture Library; 188*t* E. Pasquier/Sygma; 188*b*/189 Tony Morrison/South American Pictures; 190/191 A.N.T./NHPA; 192 Spectrum; 192/193 Sonia Halliday Photographs; 194*l* British Museum/Michael Holford; 194*r* Tor Eigeland/Susan Griggs Agency; 195*t* Westermann Schulbuchverlag GmbH; 195*b* Bruno Barbey/Magnum Photos; 196 Ancient Art & Architecture; 196/197 Ernst Haas/Magnum Photos; 197 Kobal Collection; 198 NASA/Science Photo Library; 198/199 A. Papazian/NHPA; 199 Victor Englebert/Susan Griggs Agency; 200*t* B. Jones & M. Shinlock/NHPA; 200*b* Peter Scoones/Planet Earth Pictures; 201*t* Scala; 201*b* Tor Eigeland/Susan Griggs Agency; 202 Adam Woolfitt/Susan Griggs Agency; 202/203 J. L. Nou/Explorer/Robert Harding Picture Library; 203 Raghu Rai/Magnum Photos; 204*t* Colin Jones/Impact Photos; 204*b* Raghubir Singh/The John Hillelson Agency; 205 Ross Greetham/Robert Harding Picture Library; 206 Dick Clarke/Planet Earth Pictures; 206/207 Gamma/Frank Spooner Pictures; 208 Peter Ryan/Science Photo Library; 209 Robert Hessler/Planet Earth Pictures; 210 Kathie Atkinson/Oxford Scientific Films; 210/211 Kelvin Aitken/NHPA; 211 Valerie Taylor/Ardea; 213t Pete Atkinson/Planet Earth Pictures; 213*c* Max Gibbs/Oxford Scientific Films; 213*b* Howard Hall/Oxford Scientific Films; 214*t* Neville Zell/Oxford Scientific Films; 214*c* Peter Parks/Oxford Scientific Films; 214*b* Fred Bavendam/Oxford Scientific Films; 215 Bill Wood/Bruce Coleman; 216 Popperfoto; 216/217 Colin Monteath/Mountain Camera; 218 A.N.T./NHPA; 219*t* The Bridgeman Art Library; 219*bl* Popperfoto; 219*br* Colin Monteath/Mountain Camera; 220 M. Serraillier/Rapho; 220/221 Manfred Gottschalk/Tom Stack & Associates; 222 Robert Harding Picture Library; 224/226 Douglas Botting; 227*t* D & R Sullivan/Bruce Coleman; 227*b* Douglas Botting; 228 Peter David/Planet Earth Pictures; 228/229 Peter Parks/Oxford Scientific Films; 230 Peter David/Planet Earth Pictures; 231*t* James Carmichael/NHPA; 231*c* The Hulton Picture Company; 231*b* John Lythgoe/Planet Earth Pictures; 232 Colin Jones/Impact Photos; 232/233 Michael Nichols/Magnum Photos; 234 W.V. Norbert/Oxford Scientific Films; 235 Michael Freeman; 236*t* W. V. Futtkamer/The Hutchison Library; 236*b* Color-foto Jesco/The Hutchison Library; 237*t* Michael K. Nichols/Magnum Photos; 237*b*/238/239 Shostal Associates/Superstock; 239 Zefa Picture Library; 240 Rosenfeld/Zefa Picture Library; 241*t* Harold Paolo/NHPA; 241*b* Bruce Coleman; 242 Gavin Newman; 242/243 NASA/Science Photo Library; 244 Gavin Newman; 245*t* Peter Scoones/Planet Earth Pictures; 245*b* Timothy O'Keefe/Bruce Coleman; 246 Piers Cavendish/Impact Photos; 246/248 Martyn Chillmaid/Oxford Scientific Films; 249 Horst Munzig/Susan Griggs Agency; 250/251 Dr Georg Gerster/The John Hillelson Agency; 252 Robert Harding Picture Library; 253 Aerofilms; 254 Robert Harding Picture Library; 255*t* Janet & Colin Bord; 255*c* Comstock; 255*b* Brian Shuel/Collections; 256 Anthony Howarth/Susan Griggs Agency; 256/257 Adam Woolfitt/Susan Griggs Agency; 258*t* Aerofilms; 258*b* British Library; 259 Homer Sykes/Network; 260/261 Louis Salou/Explorer; 262 Paul Broadhurst/Janet & Colin Bord; 263*t* Aldus Archive/Syndication International; 263*b* J. Allan Cash; 264/265 Adam Woolfitt/Susan Griggs Agency; 265 John Sims/Impact Photos; 266*l* Sonia Halliday Photographs; 266*r*/267 Adam Woolfitt/Susan Griggs Agency; 268 Archiv für Kunst und Geschichte; 268/269 R. Schmid/Bildarchiv Huber; 270 Klaus Aarsleff/Fortean Picture Library; 270/271 Martzik/Bavaria Verlag Bildagentur; 271 Klauss Aarsleff/Fortean Picture Library; 272/273 Zefa Picture Library; 273 Mike McQueen/Impact Photos; 274 F. Jack Jackson/Robert Harding Picture Library; 276 Robert Harding Picture Library; 277*t* British Museum/Michael Holford; 277*b* Staatlichen Museen Preussischer Kulturbesitz; 278 Robert Aberman/The Hutchison Library; 279 Tom Nebbia/Aspect Picture Library; 281*t* Mick Csaky/The Hutchison Library; 281*bl* Tom Nebbia/Aspect Picture Library; 281*br* Jeremy Walker/Tony Stone Associates; 282/283 Zefa Picture Library; 283 Science Museum/Michael Holford; 284*t* Doug Armand/Tony Stone Associates; 284*b* Sir Norman Foster & Partners; 284/285 Mary Evans Picture Library; 285 Paul van Riel/Robert Harding Picture Library; 286 Eric Crichton/Bruce Coleman; 286/287 Guido Alberto Rossi/The Image Bank; 288*t* Neil Morrison/Impact Photos; 288*b* Peter Hendrie/The Image Bank; 289*t* Robert Harding Picture Library; 289*b* Penny Tweedie/Impact Photos; 290 Penny Tweedie/Colorific!/Telegraph Colour Library; 291*t* Thomas Hoepker/Magnum Photos; 291*b* Penny Tweedie/Panos Pictures; 292 Robert Harding Picture Library; 292/293 Harry Gruyaert/Magnum Photos; 294 Robin Smith/Tony Stone Associates; 295 Yves Gellie/Odyssey/Impact Photos; 296*t* Harry Gruyaert/Magnum Photos; 296*b*/297 Robert Harding Picture Library; 298/299 Tony Linck/Shostal Associates/Superstock; 300*t* The Saint Louis Art Museum, Eliza McMillan Fund; 300b Dr Georg Gerster/The John Hillelson Agency; 301 Ohio Historical Society; 302/303 Dr Georg Gerster/The John Hillelson Agency; 304 Cornell Capa/Magnum Photos; 305t Larry Dale Gordon; 305*b* Dr Georg Gerster/The John Hillelson Agency; 306*t* The Mansell Collection; 306*b* Dr Georg Gerster/The John Hillelson Agency; 306/307 Kunsthistorisches Museum, Wien; 308 Janet & Colin Bord; 310/311 Richard Kalvar/Magnum Photos; 312/313 Robert Harding Picture Library; 314*t* Brother Bertram/Pacific Marianist Archives; 314*b* Wilson North/International Stock Photos; 315*c* The Hulton Picture Company; 315*r* Bruce Coleman; 316 John Lythgoe/Planet Earth Pictures; 316/317 Robert Harding Picture Library; 318*t* J. Allan Cash; 318*b* Heather Angel/Biofotos; 319 Edinburgh Photo Library; 320 David Yates/Susan Griggs Agency; 321 Tony Stone Associates; 322 Antoinette Jaunet/Aspect Picture Library; 322/323 David Beatty/Susan Griggs Agency; 323*t* John Yates/Susan Griggs Agency; 323*b* Rob Cousins/Susan Griggs Agency; 324/325 Robert Harding Picture Library; 326*t* The Mansell Collection; 326*b* The Hulton Picture Company; 327*t* The Mansell Collection; 327*b* The Kobal Collection; 328 Gerold Jung/The Image Bank; 328/329 E. Streichan/Shostal Associates/Superstock; 330*l* Robert Harding Picture Library; 331 Richard Philpott/Zooid Pictures; 332 Nicolas Thibaut/Explorer; 332/333 Etienne Poupinet/Explorer; 334/335 Nicolas Thibaut/Explorer; 335*t* Richard Kalvar/Magnum Photos; 335*b* Peter Carmichael/Aspect Picture Library; 336 Sassoon/Robert Harding Picture Library; 336/337 M.R. Phicton/Bruce Coleman; 339 Victor Englebert/Susan Griggs Agency; 340*t* John Reader/Science Photo Library; 340*c* R.I.M. Campbell/Bruce Coleman; 340*b* Brian Seed/Aspect Picture Library; 341 Jonathan Scott/Planet Earth Pictures; 342 Robert Harding Picture Library; 342/343 Bob Campbell/Survival Anglia; 344/345 Anthony Bannister/Oxford Scientific Films; 345*tl* Chris Knight/Survival Anglia; 345*tr* Peter Davey/Bruce Coleman; 345*b* Damm/Zefa Picture Library; 346*t* Tony Stone Associates; 346*b* John Moss/Colorific!; 347 Mirella Ricardi/Colorific!; 348/349 Pamla Toler/Impact Photos; 350*l* Raghubir Singh/The John Hillelson Agency; 350*r* Robert Harding Picture Library; 351*t* Raghubir Singh/The John Hillelson Agency; 351*bl* The Bridgeman Art Library; 351*br* The Billie Love Collection; 352/353 David Paterson; 354*t* Chad Elders/International Stock Photos; 354*b* The Bridgeman Art Library; 355 Eric Shipton/Royal Geographical Society; 356*t* Picturepoint; 356*b* Aldus Archive/Syndication International; 357 T. Hiebeler/Zefa Picture Library; 358/359 David Paterson; 359 The Bridgeman Art Library; 360 Paolo Koch/Robert Harding Picture Library; 361*t* David Paterson; 361*b* Ernst Hass/Magnum Photos; 362/363 Colorific!; 364*t* Kent & Dana Dannen; 364*bl* Library of Congress; 364*bc* Valentine Museum, Richmond; 365 Virginia State Division of Tourism; 366/367 David Paterson; 368 Michael Jenner/Robert Harding Picture Library; 368/369 Simon McBride/Comstock; 370*t* Picturepoint; 370*b* Robert Harding Picture Library; 371*t* Mary Evans Picture Library; 371*b* Paul Broadhurst/Janet & Colin Bord; 372/373 Simon McBride/Susan Griggs Agency; 374 Mary Caine; 375*t/b* Simon McBride/Susan Griggs Agency; 375*c* City of Manchester Art Galleries/The Bridgeman Art Library; 376/377 Kotoh/Zefa Picture Library; 379*l* Politikens Pressefoto/The Press Association; 379*tr* Theatre Museum, Victoria & Albert Museum; 379*br* Royal Library, Copenhagen; 380 National Museum, Copenhagen; 380/381 Dennis Orchard/Bruce Coleman; 381 Dr Harold Edgerton, MIT; 382 Painting by Sir Gerald Hargreaves, collection of Mrs Sandra Buckner, Nassau/Mary Evans Picture Library; 383*l* Images; 384/385 David Paterson; 386/387 The Kobal Collection; 387*t* The Bridgeman Art Library; 387*b* David Paterson; 388 Bodleian Library; 389 Bildarchiv Preussischer Kulturbesitz; 390*t* Richard Ashworth/Robert Harding Picture Library; 390*b* Timothy Walker/Oxford Botanic Garden; 391*tl* Fitzwilliam Museum, Cambridge; 391*bl* Ashmolean Museum, Oxford; 391*r* Museo del Prado; 392 British Library; 392/393 Adam Woolfitt/Robert Harding Picture Library; 394 Adam Woolfitt/Susan Griggs Agency; 395*t* British Library; 395*c* Victor Englebert/Susan Griggs Agency; 396 The Fotomas Index; 397*t* Robert Harding Picture Library; 397*b* Popperfoto.

Illustration credits

David Atkinson: 93, 105, 121, 133, 136, 145, 156, 171, 187, 258, 301, 304, 308–9
Richard Bonson: 334–5
Stephen Conlin: 104–5, 108–9, 119, 182–3, 267, 274–5
Chris Forsey: 46, 71, 112
Tony Graham: 341
Vana Haggerty: 240
Maxine Hamil: location maps, 302, 303, 304, 305, 309
Trevor Hill: 174–5
Gary Hincks: 21, 338
Steve Holden: 78
Richard Hook/Linden Artists: 17
Stephen Lings/Linden Artists: 41
Mainline Design: 357
Janos Marffy/Kathy Jakeman Illustration: 25, 57, 83, 218, 231, 244, 249, 294–5, 360, 376
Coral Mula: gazetteer
Richard Orr: 226, 234, 235
Paula Soper: location maps
Technical Art Services: 10–11, 141, 396–7
Roger Wade-Walker/Kathy Jakeman Illustration: 24, 112–3, 128–9, 164–5, 178–9, 280, 331, 382–3
Brian Watson/Linden Artists: 37
Steve Weston/Linden Artists: 50–1, 61, 64

We would also like to thank Caroline Boucher, Clive Gregory, Jennet Stott and Roger Few.

40-383-1